Recasting *Persian Poetry*

Recasting

Persian Poetry

Scenarios of Poetic Modernity in Iran

Ahmad Karimi-Hakkak

UNIVERSITY OF UTAH PRESS

SALT LAKE CITY

LIBRARY OF CONGRESS CATALOGING-IN-PUBLICATION DATA

Karimi-Hakkak, Ahmad.
    Recasting Persian poetry : scenarios of poetic modernity in Iran /
Ahmad Karimi-Hakkak.
        p.   cm.
    Includes bibliographical references and index.
    ISBN 0-87480-492-2 (alk. paper)
    1. Persian poetry—20th century—History and criticism.
2. Poetics.   I. Title.
PK6418.K37   1996
891'.551309—dc20   95-42219

For Nasrin

forever

Contents

Acknowledgments

In this book I argue that the process of esthetic change, and the readings and writings designed to bring it about, are ultimately collective and communal. The Iranian poets, critics, and readers who offered their views about poetic modernity by initiating diverse departures from the conventions of classical Persian poetry were constantly inspired and challenged by networks of individual intellects and intellectual currents vaster, more intricate, and more numerous than can be captured adequately in a single work. The writing of this book has been a similar process. In the ten years I have been working on it, many more individuals and institutions have contributed to the process than I can name here. From the theorists and scholars whose works I have appropriated, to the community of colleagues in the humanities who have commented on its various parts, to the friends, acquaintances, and students who responded to the issues I have raised, all have shared the experience with me.

Still, I would like to acknowledge the help I received from a few individuals and institutions, thereby registering my heartfelt gratitude. From the beginning, Walter Andrews, Michael Beard, Jerome Clinton, and Mohamad Tavakoli-Targhi have accompanied me along the path which has led to this book. David Bevington of the University of Chicago, Afsaneh Najmabadi of Barnard College, and Suzanne Stetkevych of Indiana University read the completed manuscript and offered many insightful ideas. Jeffrey Grathwohl and Rodger Reynolds of the University of Utah Press have been most generous in their support and very discerning in their editorial suggestions. Institutionally, a University of Washington Graduate School Summer Research Grant in 1986 first afforded me the opportunity to begin the explorations that have since evolved into this work. More important, a six-month professorship awarded me in 1992 by the University of Chicago's Middle East Center and the Committee on Comparative Studies in Literature provided the respite essential for completing the manuscript. Finally, members of my most intimate community, my family, have given me all that lies outside research and scholarship, but which makes these possible. By their absorbing presence, my sons Kusha and Kia have kept me focused on the future, even as I was busy examining the past. About my wife Nasrin I can only say that if I could imagine a community that did not have her at its very center, I would want no part of it.

Parts of this book were previously published in *Comparative Literature* and *Critique,* whose permission to republish them here is gratefully acknowledged.

A Note on Transliteration

Throughout this book I have tried to make my argument as accessible as I can to readers interested in literature, esthetic theory, and literary history, but not necessarily familiar with the Persian poetic tradition. Accordingly, in transliterating Persian words, I have used a simplified version of the Library of Congress system designed to approximate the sound of Persian words without getting entangled in diacritical or other esoteric marks. Neither have I attempted to distinguish among the variety of the letters in the Persian script which relate to the words' Arabic or Persian origins. Nor have I reproduced the silent letter "v" in such words as "khab" or "khahar." I have also simplified the names of the individuals whose works or views I discuss, using complete names only on their first appearance, referring to them subsequently by the most familiar one-word name by which they are known, thus Iraj, Parvin, or Nima, instead of Iraj Mirza, Parvin E'tesami, or Nima Yushij. Similarly, I have used the original Persian titles of books, poems, and other writings only on their first appearance, relying thereafter on their English translation for purposes of discussion. In all such details, as in the entire project, I have let myself be guided by one overriding desire: to contribute, however little, to the study of literature from a truly universal perspective.

Introduction

A Model of Poetic Change

Recent developments in literary studies have begun to make it possible to explore areas of cultural experience that have been invisible and, therefore, unarticulated. The process of literary change—the breakdown of old and established norms, conventions, and systems of esthetic expression; the loss of once powerful and pervasive paradigms; and the emergence of new poetic codes and modes of signification—is being reconsidered in light of poststructuralist literary theory. Thus, an attempt to apply the insights gained into the phenomenon of poetic change along a diachronic dimension to the study of the process by which the poetry of modern Iran came into existence may well reveal the ways in which esthetic traditions renew themselves at certain historical junctures. Such at least has been my ultimate hope in writing this book.

The nature and significance of poetry in modern Iran cannot be understood without a close reading of the conditions that gave rise to it and the processes that determined its shape. The principal condition was Iran's familiarity with European cultures, and the processes consisted of a series of negotiations and contestations within Iran's literary community. The ideas and arguments presented, the scenarios envisioned, and the textual examples offered were the result of a continuous dialogue with the tradition of classical Persian poetry on the one hand and, on the other, with largely imaginary ideas about "European literature." There has been a tendency in traditional literary scholarship on the subject to speak of modern Persian poetry as the result of a sharp break with the past. This is more a rhetorical posture than an accurate description of modernism in Persian poetry. The classical tradition was not completely abandoned even by those who were rejecting it.

From the very beginning, poets and critics of all stripes have emphatically, at times self-consciously, defined themselves by their relation to the tradition out of which they emerged. Both traditionalists and modernists have expressed their esthetic ideas in terms of the classical tradition—the former as the heirs to it, the latter as rebels against it. Based on these assumptions, I argue for a new way of conceptualizing the way the production and dissemination of poetic meaning came to be different from the analogous practice in the classical culture of the Persian-speaking peoples. This, I contend, is essential to a greater appreciation of the ways in which modern traditions arising out of a common past differ from it.[1]

I begin this study of modernity in Persian poetry in what I imagine to be the last moment when the classical poetic system was still firmly in place. In historical terms this would mean around the middle of the nineteenth century when Iran began to establish more or less regular cultural contact with European countries, whether directly or through British India and the Ottoman empire.[2] I intend to follow the process to the point when the basic shape of a new esthetic system has been realized. At various stages along the way, I illustrate the perceived opposition between the new and the old, an ever-changing relation in itself, through detailed examinations of a series of texts, poetic or otherwise. These texts have been selected for their illustrative power as well as their potential to embody significant implications for poetic change. Thus, I illustrate an early stage from texts which still preserve their links with the classical system. In time, as the process begins to reverse itself, I examine texts which, while preserving elements of the classical system, must be considered ultimately as illustrative of a new system of signification. Eventually, of course, the poetic text and the social context surrounding it conspire to create a new interpretive community with its own keys to reading poetry and writing it. The existence of such a community is itself the clearest indication of cultural transference from one system of poetic signification to another.

THE CURRENT ENVIRONMENT

I begin by reviewing very briefly the various expressions of the phenomenon known in Persian as *she'r-e now* (new poetry), which will allow me to set forth the terms of my own theoretical approach and prepare the ground for a closer examination of several stages in the process. In much of the discourse on the contemporary poetry of Iran, the concept of *she'r-e now*—or as some prefer to call it, *she'r-e emruz* (poetry of today)[3]—is posited cognitively in opposition to a category generally referred to as *she'r-e kelasik* (classical poetry) and *she'r-e sonnati* (traditional poetry).[4] This binary opposition was set up in the 1950s and 1960s, and still remains operative as a basis for the classification of poetry in contemporary Iran. The difference between the new poetry and its opposite is usually related to two characteristics. First, the new poetry is said to differ from the old in that it no longer follows the rigid formal rules and generic divisions of the classical poetry or of the contemporary practice modeled on it. The apparent unevenness of poetic lines on the page and the irregularity of the rhyme and meter that make the new poetry visibly and audibly different from the classical models render it conceptually opposed to them.

Second, it is widely believed that the new poetry relates to its social context in ways significantly different from the way the classical poetic canon does. The latter, or a great majority of works in it, are thought unconcerned with such issues. When a classical poet is seen as having tackled the social issues of the time—as these are understood by modern-day Iranians—it is judged to be an exception to the rule.[5] Clearly then the contemporary practice identified formally or generically with the classical poetry is suspect. Typically, modern poetry is viewed as that which demonstrates its willingness to address important social and political issues, classical poetry is not.

This binary system of differentiation has distorted our view of the process of poetic change in modern Iran. First, it has given rise to an automatic link between the ideals of progress, democracy, and freedom, on the one hand, and the desire to liberate poetry from rhyme and meter, on the other. An alliance of despotic monarchs and obscurantist clergy are seen as having a vested interest in preventing the birth of modern poetry. A "literary revolution," very much comparable to the Constitutional Revolution of 1906–1911, is thought to have ended the rule of the old poetic regime.[6] Second, it has resulted in a number of erroneous assumptions about a large number of poets and their discursive activities. The traditional practice of poetry is thought to have continued until the 1920s—or 1930s, or later—when Nima Yushij began his lonely crusade to modernize Persian poetry in the face of solid opposition from an assortment of social forces opposed to the new poetry. It has also led to other distortions, such as those I discern in the dynamics of poetry in Iran through the twentieth century, which will be discussed as my argument unfolds.

One result of the dichotomy between new and old Persian poetry deserves to be mentioned here: an exaggerated sense of the literary gulf that separates modernist poetry from its opposite, whether practiced by one's next-door neighbor or a relic from olden times. Because poets like Dehkhoda, E'tesami, and Lahuti have produced poems which in form are indistinguishable from classical Persian poetry, their work is seen as essentially the same as the classical poets' and essentially similar to each other's. Nima, however, receives practically all the credit—or blame—for changing Persian poetry's forms and genres, for thematizing sociopolitical issues, and for "fathering" the new poetry.[7]

This situation has relegated at least two categories of poetry to the margins of Iranian literary culture. First, poems which have been written by modernist poets but which accord, formally and generically, with the poetry of former times are viewed at best as insignificant relapses or occasional exercises in frivolity. The situation is seen at its most dramatic through the career of Nima himself. We know that Nima began by writing poetry in the classical style, and continued the practice up to the end of his life, even as he began advocating a new approach to writing poetry. Yet, until recently these compositions had not been collected properly; they have yet to be studied seriously.[8] Second, the varied experimentation which is the center of my attention in this book has remained badly misunderstood and grossly underestimated. In the writings of Nima's immediate followers we find little awareness of the part that poets before Nima played in the historical process of poetic change in Iran.[9]

The constitution of formal, generic, and thematic differences as the main criteria for distinguishing new Persian poetry from the old has furthermore altered our perception of the history of Persian poetry in Iran in the twentieth century. As early as 1914, E. G. Browne took the Western scholars of Persian poetry to task for not acknowledging the significance of a modern poetry in Persia. "Certain European students of Persian," he writes in the opening pages of *The Press and Poetry of Modern Persia,* "constantly assert that there is no modern Persian poetry worth reading." He states that those who believe so "have not taken the trouble to look for it or read it."[10] Browne defines Iranian poetry's capacity to address sociopolitical issues, particularly the theme of patriotism, as the essence of modernity in Persian, as well as Arab and Turkish, poetry.[11] Thus, thematically at least, Iranian poetry of the early twentieth century is seen to have contributed to the emergence of the new kind of Persian poetry, although the exact nature of that contribution has not been made clear.

Yet, the discourse of the new poetry, enunciated in the middle decades of the century, seems to contradict that earlier impression. The need in that discourse to envision the new poetry as the ontological opposite of the old worked in time to conceal the historicity of the process of poetic change. A new generation of literary intellectuals rallied behind Nima essentially because it saw in him a leader capable of initiating a discourse powerful enough to marginalize the opposition to his vision by casting the opponents as perpetuating a defunct world view.[12] Expressing their views with the force of conviction, Nima and his followers articulated the concept of poetic modernity primarily in terms of an oppositional political stance. It is this view, which portrayed Nima as a solitary soul facing a millennium-old literary tradition, that has remained essentially unchanged. In reaction, those whose conception of poetry was being violated began to frame the argument in terms of poetry as a highly cherished symbol of cultural purity being threatened by "foreign" influences and "alien" concepts. To them, the new poetry was a highly visible sign of cultural capitulation because it violated the "spirit" of the Persian language and Iranian culture. They saw the kind of poetry written by Nima and his young followers as evidence of their unfamiliarity with a glorious tradition which they imagined as embodying that spirit.

More recently, the concept and process of modernity in Persian poetry has begun to be expressed in more measured terms. The views expressed by Nima's followers have in time moderated, and studies like Yahya Arianpur's *Az Saba ta Nima* (From Saba to Nima) have begun to change the narrative of Iranian literary modernity in perceptible ways. The imagined opposition between today's poetry and that of the past has begun to give way to historical surveys of the rise of modernity in Persian poetry. Two scholars deserve special mention in this regard. Gholam-Hosayn Yusofi, a notable professor of Persian literature, was the first prominent academic to work tirelessly toward guiding the discourse on the new poetry away from the polemics of the 1960s. I stress Yusofi's academic position because for decades modernist Persian poetry was viewed as an aberration unworthy of serious scholarly attention.[13] Guided by an early acquaintance with the Western tendency toward close textual readings, Yusofi began to concentrate on individual texts in order to arrive at a judgment about them based on artistic merit rather than on formal properties or social stances. His last work *Cheshmeh-ye Rowshan* (The Clear Fountain), published in 1991, must be considered the fruit of his search in that realm.

Simultaneously, Mohammad-Reza Shafi'i-Kadkani, also a university professor of Persian literature and a noted modernist poet himself, began to focus on the changing social contexts that lay behind various views of modernity in Persian poetry. His effort culminated in a brief book entitled *Advar-e She'r-e Farsi az Mashrutiyyat ta Soqut-e Saltanat* (Periods of Persian Poetry from the Constitution to the Fall of the Monarchy). Here, Shafi'i points to many linguistic, rhetorical, and formal aspects which characterize various periods in the seventy-year history he outlines. An essential assumption implicit in his approach is the constant tension between continuity and change in poetic practice not only of different poets but also of the same poet at different times and under differing circumstances.[14]

For my part, I begin my examination of the process of modernity in Persian poetry with a simple assumption: the desire to be modern must be sought in the specific rhetorical posture, the semantic and lexical spheres of the words, and in a plethora of other units and elements that make up the system of poetic communication in a specific culture. It is, after all, the manner in which individual poets juxtapose old and new elements and structures that communicates an impression of the text as old, new, or both at one and the same time. The precise ways in which each text differs from age-old usages developed and sanctioned by an already existing system of poetic signification provide us with indices of innovation at every stage in the process. Only with this in mind can we account for the phenomenon of texts which adhere to traditional meters and rhyme schemes and are yet perceived as ultimately new or at least different from the old.

Conversely, only if the notion of modernity is rigorously separated from the way a poem looks on the page and sounds to the ear can we begin to assess the contribution of its significatory mechanisms to that perception. It is true that Nima eventually succeeded in disconnecting Iranian readers' habitual association of it with certain visual and auditory specifications. It is true further that he did so by disrupting the expected relationship between the appearance of the poem and the poetic devices employed in it. This does not mean, however, that adherence to traditional formal features makes a poem old in any significant sense. I bring this book to an end with a study of Nima's contribution to the process of poetic modernity to emphasize my contention that Nima's efforts mark not the beginning but the culmination and completion of that process and that, in a very real sense, the process had begun a century earlier in a very different culture, socially and esthetically.

It is an underlying assumption of this book that a better understanding of the negotiations, competitions, and contestations that lay behind the emergence of a modernist poetry in Iran constitutes an integral and significant part of the effort to enable this millennium-old poetic culture to express the modern condition. As the various chapters of this book make clear, a succession of Iranian intellectuals, from Akhundzadeh to Nima, began to define and describe the classical system of poetic signification and communication in the Persian-speaking cultures in such a way as to make the drive to change it an imperative. To achieve that, they constructed the idea of a "European poetry" which, they argued, had contributed to palpable advances in European societies. That paradigm, I contend, had little to do with any particular esthetic movement or poetic trend in Europe. It was rather part of a new cultural imaginary, a construct necessary if the age-old poetic culture was to be challenged and changed. An inherent implication of this contention is that beyond formal and thematic distinctions that determine the boundaries of poetic signification and communication for each generation, we can view the search for a modern poetry as a specifically and demonstrably social process. It begins in response to ever-changing social conditions, and continues in various ways until the opposite perception becomes current: that the quest has achieved its purpose, and "the new"—in this case a new kind of Persian poetry—has replaced the old.

THE THEORY

At this point, I think it appropriate to present an outline of the theoretical model on which my argument is based throughout this book. This will allow us, in the first place, to conceptualize poetic change as a social process evolving in stages and increments and involving a variety of visions and approaches. Second, within the specific terms of this project, the approach may make it possible for future scholars to classify various esthetic products within a constantly evolving culture-system. Most specifically, the presentation will, I hope, enable me to present an outline of the emerging poetic system at various stages by examining a few texts. My ultimate hope is that, given the theoretical framework, the close examination and analyses of a handful of texts will allow some generalization.

Within the general framework of semiotics, then, I see my own project as one of examining the process of poetic change in time.[15] An essential assumption here holds that the generative ambience of poetic production affects the manner in which poets present meaningful messages through the creation of text. Adapting some rather elaborate theorizing of the phenomenon of change in semiotic systems to my specific area of investigation, I intend to show the process by concentrating on the interaction of competing social and esthetic perceptions over time. Generally speaking, semiotics relates the process of poetic change to a variety of shifting cultural systems of which language is by far the most significant. As in the natural language of a culture at any given time, in cultural traditions there are moments when the esthetic system opens itself up to external influences. New concepts are introduced into it, and new ways are devised to articulate these concepts. For a while, the old and the new cohabit the cultural spaces of which the poetic text is an example and a simulacrum. Poets begin to use existing words in new senses, or forge new terms or linguistic relations, or otherwise encode their messages in hitherto unprecedented ways. In this way, they restructure the "language of poetry"[16] and create areas of ambiguity in that language. This goes beyond enabling them to communicate their messages in poetic ways to convey the impression that their work is "new." In time, as new relations between the language of poetry and perceptions of the world gain currency, new relevances are discovered, new areas of poetic meaning are appropriated, and new functions are assigned to esthetic entities. Eventually, the new elements find their place in the poetic culture and assume fairly stable relations with other concepts and categories which make up that culture's view of the world. Thus, as a new esthetic system comes into view, both the manner of thematization and the means of expression can be reformulated. Traditional literary criticism describes such periods as times of transition.

Obviously, in the early stages of the process, only those individuals whose system of cultural identification and categorization has been affected by the flow of concepts from outside the culture-system can identify with the new phenomenon. It is their view, say of poetry and its social function, rather than the total culture's, that begins to change. It is possible, therefore, simultaneously to have in a society differing definitions of poetry and of poetry's relationships with its encompassing environment and the uses it may or may not be put to. It is similarly conceivable that individuals separated by their world views may envision, advocate, or implement differing kinds and degrees of change. These differing visions might be seen not only in the society at large but also within an individual, or even within a single text. By the same token, a single vision may be implemented diversely within a single career or at different stages in the process of creativity. The diversity may give rise to the perception of sameness or opposition in poetic texts. Because the system of poetic signification changes gradually, it would be more precise to speak of different stages of recognition of the new phenomenon and adaptation to it. Nevertheless, within the system that articulates the new in contradistinction from the old, at every stage we have one form or another of the old/new dichotomy. In a more general sense, in all esthetic traditions and at all times, old and new are present in a single cultural or textual space and interact with one another. As a feature of artistic communication, ambivalence is a constant feature of poetic texts. It is also true that this quality becomes more and more generally perceptible in "periods of transition."

In time, the new elements and the organizing principles underlying them are assimilated into the culture through sustained practice. As a series of negotiations, contestations, and competitions takes place within the society, these new elements and principles may come to be shared by a significant social group. The balance between old and new elements begins to shift as the old is made new and the new begins to be seen as having existed previously, until a new system begins to emerge. This new system may initially be described in terms that tend to emphasize the difference between the old and the new. In the case of the cultural product we have here, the new esthetic system, including new thematic preoccupations and formal divisions, gains currency as it succeeds in marginalizing the old, now increasingly viewed as an irrelevant survival. However, the culture eventually works toward a new definition of the contested phenomenon—poetry in this case—capable of encompassing both the old and the new.

Since I intend to focus on a few important stages in this complex cultural process, my aim is to describe certain basic characteristics of each stage in a series of poetic texts and the discourses surrounding them. This approach will reveal a variety of means and methods which several generations of Iranian literary intellectuals used in order to communicate their ideas through the medium of Persian poetry.[17] To that effect, I have drawn extensively on the views of two literary theorists who, I believe, have contributed significantly to our understanding of the phenomenon of literary change. Mikhail Bakhtin's dialogical principle and Yuri Lotman's diachronic principle form the twin theoretical foundations on which I have based much of my argument in the following pages. Naturally, in my effort to apply the complex notions they have offered to particular textual structures produced in a single culture I will end up simplifying them considerably. A brief exposition of their ideas at this point will enable me to explain the underlying assumptions which have informed my work.

From Bakhtin I have taken the basic notion of poetry as a form of social discourse: that all utterance, even the most personal, already assumes an interlocutor and that, therefore, in Bakhtin's own words, "every literary work is sociological . . . internally, immanently,"[18] lies at the heart of my project. As a discourse developed within—and submitted to—an ever-changing social context, poetry is in constant dialogue with prior discourses, as well as with discourses yet to come. It responds to their assumptions and limitations and anticipates their reactions. The historical moment when poetic change becomes a matter of cultural concern coincides, in Bakhtin's mind, with a moment of awareness of other cultures and openness toward them. "Verbal and ideological decentering," he says, "occurs only when a national culture sheds its closure and its self-sufficiency, when it becomes conscious of itself as only one among other cultures and languages."[19] As we move from the subversive discourses of nineteenth-century Iranian reformers to the affirming rhetoric of Nima's admirers, a recognition of the inherent sociality of textual entities is crucial to our understanding of the phenomenon of poetic change in Iran. Similarly, the stages I identify and examine along the way are, as we will see, immersed in a variety of discursive activities which define the poetic text and its properties.

Bakhtin begins with the obvious notion that in a given culture, at a given time, the language of literature is used in a variety of ways by different authors. Poetic signs are thus born within a socially determined space which makes linguistic units correspond to diverse meanings and concepts. Syntactic, semantic, and rhetorical conventions, as well as diverse contextual meanings responsible for the perception of poeticity, are developed within this space as well. Indeed, context itself may be understood as a social space that admits into it a bewildering variety of factors. In the textual analyses I present, I attempt to identify those nodal points between the text and its context which have ultimately determined processes that have made contemporary Iranian poetry a meaningful cultural product. The very fact of the social substantiveness of language implies the external and prior existence of the world formed in the poet's consciousness, itself a social entity. My entire project acknowledges from the beginning the fact that a great part of the meaning of such cultural products as poems is of a social nature and delivered into it from outside the text.

My reliance on the notions advanced by Yuri Lotman is more extensive and more complex, requiring a greater exposition of some basic principles. Of all the semioticians who have addressed the problem of literary change, I have found Lotman's approach most applicable to an investigation of the process by which the drive for artistic innovation finds expression in the works of art themselves. In numerous writings, Lotman defines many of the concepts that clarify the process by which systems of artistic signification change. At the most abstract level of conceptualization, Lotman regards poetry as a "secondary" semiotic system based on a "primary" one, namely language. Rather than reflecting an existing condition, the distinction serves the purpose of analysis. As Lotman observes, "the data of ethnography and archeology do not enable us to distinguish any period . . . during which the system of natural language was already available and yet there were still no secondary systems, either social, religious, or esthetic."[20] In the case of a millennium-old poetic system, this distinction simply underscores the appropriateness of the study of change in light of the most subtle transformations, sometimes barely visible, in the lexicon of poetry and in the various nuances discernible in the discursive activities that surround the issue.

I also adopt Lotman's views in my analysis of the process of stereotyping which allowed the Iranian reformers of the nineteenth century to sabotage the Persian poetic tradition which they meant to change. Lotman believes that, by their very nature, acts of describing complex systems of communication like poetry tend to organize and simplify the objects of description by banishing the nondescribed entities within the system into the realm of nonexistence. "The very fact of description," he says, "heightens the degree of organization and diminishes the dynamism of the system."[21] However, such entities, while appearing superfluous and unworthy of description from the synchronic point of view, can be viewed from a diachronic viewpoint as the system's "structural reserve." This is Lotman's phrase for those elements or entities within any system which enable it to change while remaining itself. As seen in chapter 2, the stereotypical image of classical Persian poetry some nineteenth-century Iranians presented made it appear indeed unnatural, incomprehensible, and irrelevant. Such descriptions led to the opinion that poetry had be changed in drastic ways. This perception in turn persuaded the Iranian poets of the early twentieth century to try to alter, expand, or otherwise change the significatory mechanisms of the classical poetic tradition thus "described."

Building on various ideas of earlier theorists, from Saussure to Bakhtin, Lotman has developed a stage-by-stage model of the actual process of change in a complex semiotic system like poetry. I have found this model extremely relevant to my pursuit in this book. In fact, I concur with Ann Shukman who for this very reason has called Lotman "a pioneer in the study of how a semiotic system functions in time, how it alters, renews itself or decays, and of how the new ones come into being."[22] Lotman's varied and numerous theoretical observations make any summary presentation inadequate. I rely here on two of his works on the subject: a 1977 translation entitled *The Structure of the Artistic Text,* and a 1977 translated essay entitled "The Dynamic Model of a Semiotic System." These will provide some key concepts that will, I believe, facilitate our entry into the process as it has unfolded in the Persian tradition.

In the latter work, Lotman addresses the widespread perception that semiotics is not equipped to deal with changes along the diachronic dimension. That perception, he maintains, has been widespread at least since Saussure's notion of the synchronic aspect of language became an operating principle in various linguistic and literary studies. Saussure's primary concern, Lotman reminds us, consisted of describing synchronic states of the language. Accordingly, he did not consider significant those features of the linguistic system which were characterized by instability and irregularity. But this does not mean that he failed to recognize the presence of such features, although it is true that he considered them "of little importance" for his purposes. Lotman cites Saussure's own words on the issue:

An absolute state is defined by the absence of change, and since after all language is always in transformation, however slight, in order to study a state of the language, one must in practice ignore changes of little importance in the same way as mathematicians ignore infinitesimal quantities in certain operations such as the calculus of logarithms.[23]

Lotman argues that Saussure's acknowledgment of the ever-changing nature of language means that, like his initial opposition of the synchronic and the diachronic, his depiction of the synchronic as relatively free of change must be seen as a heuristic device, and not to be confused with an actual mode of existence. The recognition of change as a constant feature of dynamic semiotic systems must therefore be assumed as part of all literary analyses along the diachronic dimension. In point of fact, the failure to do so has given rise to another misconception, namely the identification of the synchronic with the static. Lotman states that as early as the 1930s, Roman Jakobson was trying to prevent this mistake from taking over the scholarship on literary change. He cites Jakobson's warning in *Theses of the Prague Linguistic Circle:*

It would be a serious mistake to treat the static and the synchronic as synonyms. The static section is a fiction: it is no more than an auxiliary scientific technique, not a particular mode of existence. We can consider the perception of a film not only diachronically, but also synchronically: but the synchronic aspect of a film is not identical with a single frame isolated or extracted from the film. The perception of movement is present also in the synchronic aspect of the film. It is exactly the same with language.[24]

Lotman attributes the perception of a static quality in many semiotic descriptions to "certain fundamental features of descriptive methodology," and concludes: "Without a careful analysis of why the very fact of description transforms the dynamic object into a static model, and without the necessary correctives to these methods of scientific analysis attempts to arrive at dynamic models can be no more than good intentions."[25] The distinction between a "system" and its "model" is noteworthy here in light of my implicit distinction throughout this book between the classical tradition and the stereotypical image of it constructed by successive generations of Iranian modernists. It is indeed the latter which gives rise to the "metalanguage" (to use Lotman's term) with which Iranian poets and critics described the tradition they had set out to change.

With those initial premises, Lotman begins to outline a "dynamic model" for describing literary structures, one that would not render its object static. Relying on the works of Tynyanov and Bakhtin, he draws on a trilogy of concepts: system vs. extrasystem, univalence vs. ambivalence, and nucleus vs. periphery. He explains the distinction between systemic and extrasystemic elements in semiotic systems in terms of an unceasing process of interaction between language and its surrounding context:

> One of the chief sources of the dynamism of semiotic structures is the constant process of drawing extrasystemic elements into the realm of the system and of expelling systemic elements into the area of non-system. A refusal to describe the extrasystemic, placing it beyond the confines of science, cuts off the reserve of dynamism and presents us with a system in which any play between evolution and homeostasis is, in principle, excluded.[26]

The manner in which Lotman relates the inherent dynamism of the literary system to the sources which activate that dynamism in socially consequential ways makes the examination of the actual historical process of poetic change in cultures possible. To conduct that examination, one would have to distinguish among the various descriptions, existing simultaneously, of a single object within the culture. Two of these descriptions, standing at decisive cultural junctures in more or less oppositional relations to one another, receive special attention in Lotman's theory. On the one hand we have the way a system views and describes itself and perceives itself as having been described throughout its life. So long as the system's description of itself remains essentially unchallenged, the system continues to consolidate itself, and its basic features remain unchanged. In such a situation, univalence, defined as "an intensification of homeostatic tendencies," prevails, and each individual achievement "is praised as a skillful execution of the canon."[27]

At the other pole, we have the way the system is viewed either from outside itself, or by a subgroup inside the system which may have developed—or be developing—its own separate description of the system. Let me add that in this context extrasystem and extrasystemic do not necessarily mean foreign, external, or nonnative. Nor do they have to have emerged from a nonnative origin or contain a foreign perspective. Rather, they refer to a view of the system which has evolved independently of the system's internal dynamics—its discourse, its self-perception, or its ideology. While a system's internal description of itself constitutes a subclass of the system itself (Lotman calls it "self-description"), its description from the outside forms, in Lotman's words, "a metalanguage," a way of talking about the system which at once complements and contradicts the system's own view of itself.

THE APPLICATION

The specific historical circumstances Lotman envisions as making visible the constant interaction between the system and the extrasystem are worth citing directly:

> At a given moment in the historical existence of a given language, or, more widely, of a given culture in general, a sub-language (and sub-group of texts) isolates itself in the depths of the semiotic system and comes to be regarded as the metalanguage for the description of the system.[28]

Such, it seems to me, was precisely the case in Iran in the second half of the nineteenth century. At that time, the social group I have named the "new intellectuals" used their familiarity with European cultures in order to offer their own "description" of the classical poetic tradition in the Persian language in opposition to the description which had allowed that tradition to evolve through the centuries.

That is the idea I have tried to convey through the title of chapter 1. It examines the emergence of the metalanguage used by certain Iranian intellectuals who had been exposed to what Lotman considered extrasystemic influences. Akhundzadeh, Kermani, and Malkom represent a community of reformists who began to express their views about the contemporary practice of poetry and about the tradition which it claimed to be continuing and enhancing. It is important to realize, in view of Bakhtin's idea of the sociality of literature and literary discourse, that this metalanguage described the actually existing poetry in terms contrary to the social ideals of civilization, progress, and democracy—all nonesthetic concepts. My focus on three different types of discursive activities is designed to highlight some specific aspects of such subversive acts, therefore offering a view of the interface between ideology and discourse.

Lotman also stipulates the specific way this "rhetoric of subversion" begins to produce a "perception of one's own system as incorrect."[29] The perception, he argues, is related to the desire to create a system out of the structurally unorganized material existing inside and outside a specific system of literary communication. Lotman returns to this crucial moment in the closing section of *The Structure of the Artistic Text*, stating the problem in terms of an increasingly evident social debate:

> When a writer, in the heat of literary dispute, condemns the art of the preceding period for its limited possibilities and its conventional language, and proposes a new art with unlimited possibilities, we should realize that

we are dealing either with sheer rhetoric or a mistake, which is more often than not sincere.[30]

The evidence from my study suggests strongly that men like Akhundzadeh, Kermani, and Malkom intended the subversive rhetoric they initiated for specific reasons of a sociopolitical nature. Their rhetoric, in other words, was a purposeful gesture and part of an overall agenda of social change in Iran. Approximately a century later that purpose was fulfilled in the "rhetoric of affirmation" which sought to legitimate Nima's poetry as appropriate, relevant, and beautiful. In studying change in the artistic systems, it is important to take note of counter-descriptions, because they underlie the kind of creative practices which Lotman considers moving away from an "esthetic of identity" and directed toward an "esthetic of opposition."[31]

At the level of the text, Lotman pursues the growing complexity of the process of change through the concepts of univalence and ambivalence. Extending Bakhtin's analysis of the phenomenon of ambivalence, he directs the concept toward a specific view of the interplay between continuity and change at the level of the artistic text. As the metalanguage of the system continues to challenge the tradition and traditional practice, the system responds by incorporating into it a variety of new elements. The result is the textual cohabitation of new and old elements, itself a sign of increasing ambivalence within the system. Just as "an increase in internal univalence can be considered an intensification of homeostatic tendencies," Lotman says, "the growth of internal ambivalence corresponds to the moment of the system's transformation into a dynamic state in the course of which that non-defined is structurally re-disposed." Thus, Lotman concludes, "a growth of ambivalence is an index of an imminent dynamic leap."[32]

My evidence suggests that the first major locus of such a state in Iranian poetic culture must be sought in the host of poems known in traditional literary criticism as the patriotic qasidas and political ghazals of the constitutional era. As we shall see in chapter 2, poets like Dehkhoda and ʿAref, as well as many of their imitators and continuators, turned the desire of the previous generation into a series of affirmative poetic actions. In these works, the idea of an effective, relevant, and comprehensible poetry takes the form of recognizable textual maneuvers, within the formal or generic dictates of the classical system. This enabled them to disseminate their ideas in ways that the culture perceived as new and relevant, at least in some aspects. Yet, the way innovative strategies were implemented allowed these texts to be seen as by and large conforming to the existing system of poetic signification and communication.

In *The Structure of the Artistic Text* Lotman places the specific textual manifestation of growth in ambivalence within the context of the interplay between tradition and innovation: "Every innovative work is constructed of traditional material. If a text does not sustain the memory of traditional construction, its innovativeness will no longer be perceived."[33] Early scenarios of poetic modernity in Iran sought to balance the creative spirit in content against an idea of formal or generic continuity. Even though many features of the patriotic qasidas and political ghazals of the early twentieth century were indeed constructed of the material of the classical qasida and ghazal, their authors typically viewed their work as different from the traditional practice. They justified this difference with reference to the thematic preoccupation of their texts. This tendency seems to suggest that they viewed modernity primarily in terms of thematic, rather than formal or stylistic, concerns. Those textual aspects—expressive devices, meter and the rhyme-scheme, or the system of figures of speech—which were commonly perceived as poetic because they produced esthetic pleasure had yet to be incorporated into the dynamics of poetic change.

As modifications of poetic elements are absorbed by the system, texts with a claim to difference begin to exert a cumulative pressure in the push toward the new system. Thus, under certain conditions, what I call "elemental change" in this book must be seen as part of an overall strategy for the creation and communication of meaning through poetry. At such times, while one group of poets and readers may be satisfied with elemental innovations, others are likely to continue the drive toward greater differences with, and further departures from, the traditional system. The dynamic tension which is thus established—and which I illustrate in chapter 3—is likely to continue so long as the interpretive community surrounding the poetic text has not rallied around one vision of poetic utterance in preference to all others as the final outcome of a movement. Debates similar to what I illustrate through Bahar and Rafʿat's differing visions must be seen as having in fact continued throughout the time period this book encompasses. The dialogic posture with the literary tradition finds its actual manifestation in exchanges between diverging ways contemporary individuals relate to that tradition.

Chapter 3 is designed to demonstrate further the differing notions of relevance in the context of these ongoing dialogues. In that sense, this chapter brings together some of the major concepts developed by the two theorists on whom I have drawn so extensively. While the presence of such dialogues distinguishes periods of relative stability from those of rapid and radical change when the system begins to open itself to systemic influences, their character and content may give us a chance to view the exchanges in relation to the environment which gives rise to them. In my analysis of the Bahar-Raf'at debate, in other words, I have brought to bear Bakhtin's view that the entire verbal aspect of human beings belongs not to the individual but to his social group. In Bakhtin's own words:

> The motivation of our action, the attainment of self-consciousness (and self-consciousness is always verbal; it always leads to the search for a specific verbal complex) is always a way of putting oneself in relation to a given social norm; it is, so to speak, a socialization of the self and its action.[34]

Chapter 4 is meant to illustrate a particular aspect of that exchange, namely borrowings from other culture-systems. This is an exceedingly complex process, and all I have been able to do is address a single aspect of it. In its search for alternative approaches to change, an esthetic system may begin to admit into itself elements and structures which it previously may have felt unnecessary. The purpose, whether stated or implicit, is to facilitate ever greater departures from preconceived notions of meaning and signification. The texts I examine here do play their part in redirecting the poetic discourse away from its systemic links with the native practice, albeit in subtle and complex ways that lie outside my project. The specific textual manifestations of this move may consist of a variety of alternative modeling activities, ranging from wholesale adaptations of formal, generic, or thematic features associated with an alternative esthetic system to perceptive moves away from poeticity toward the prosaic in the native esthetic system. As I hope my examination will reveal, even though such texts encode the desire for a new system of poetic signification and communication in a diversity of ways, they are characterized ultimately by their common drive toward systemic change.

Parodic encounters with the traditional system of signification are a case in point, as are imitations of European verse forms or genres in Persian. Of all the types of systemic departures I have analyzed in this study, Lotman concentrates most extensively on the function of parody. In parody, he argues, a traditional structure is "assumed to exist, but it is expressed by purely negative means." This, according to Lotman, explains why parody, in spite of its often direct and stark opposition to an existing system, cannot play a primary part in bringing about literary change:

> If parody is to be perceived in full as an artistic phenomenon, literary works must exist and be known to the reader which, in destroying the esthetic of cliches, create a truer structure, one opposed to parody and more accurately modeling reality. Only when the reader is aware of such a new

structure can he supplement the destructive parodical text with an extra-textual constructive element; only the presence of this structure conveys the author's point of view on the parodied system. Therefore, being a vivid and, in a certain sense, laboratory genre, parody always plays a secondary role in literary history.[35]

This observation must be borne in mind in reading my analysis of the kind of oppositional posture illustrated through Lahuti's *"Beh Dokhtaran-e Iran"* (To the Daughters of Iran). Similar observations can be made about attempts to introduce the sonnet, thought to be comparable to a variety of Persian lyrical forms, into Persian. Conceived as part of the drive toward poetic modernity, the composition of poems modeled after European poetic genres implies that those genres must have been thought of as the systemic equivalent, in the modern world, of certain forms in the classical Persian tradition. The myriad of efforts illustrated in this book through certain borrowings by Bahar, Iraj, and Parvin are similar in nature.

In discussing the part that ambivalence plays in the process of poetic change, Lotman distinguishes between two kinds. The first, as we saw above, is that which does not violate the culture's sense of itself in any radical way. In fact, even though it may give rise to conflicts that have to do with perceptions of poetry versus prose or with the way certain texts relate to generic rules, in the end they tend to convey an idea of the system's dynamic interaction with its surroundings. In this sense, far from submitting the system to a structural crisis, such texts may even contribute to the system's continued survival. The second type of ambivalence provokes the opposite response. Chapter 5 examines a small sampling of such texts. Distinct from the elemental changes which typify the first type of ambivalence, the textual strategies assumed here are threatening to the system in that they envision a different type of poetic system. As we shall see, poets like Lahuti, Raf'at, and 'Eshqi depart from the existing tradition in systemic ways, and are therefore perceived in opposition to the norms that define the system. In their desire to modify or change the kind of coherence perpetuated by contemporary practices, such poets are seen as revolutionaries participating in a battle against their own culture. Readers see their work as the locus where seemingly harmless innovations gather to sabotage the system's idea of itself, its esthetic worth, or its social function. Whereas ambivalence of the former type may be thought ultimately to enhance the system's capacity to remain viable under changing conditions, this type of ambivalence is seen as detrimental to the system's continued life.

'Eshqi's insistence on an alternative approach to the making of metaphors is of special importance here. The unpredictable multiplicity of utterances, envisioned and implemented subjectively, is particularly threatening to the imagined integrity of a tradition thought to reflect the collective spirit of the ages. Yet, that is precisely what 'Eshqi's approach invites. What I have called a "perceptual" or "experiential" approach to composition aims indeed to submit the notion of convention to profound rethinking. It is on that basis that Nima Yushij introduces his own store of innovative ideas and approaches. Traditional articulations of modernity in Iranian culture assign this part to Nima and his followers. Within the terms of my study, however, this vision of poetic change can be seen in the poetry of a generation of poets situated historically between the Constitutional Revolution (1905–1911) and World War II. I have called the kind of change envisioned here "systemic" because it has initiated the drive toward a new kind of coherence.

A similar conviction motivates me in chapter 6, where I show the emergence, finally, of an interpretive community essential to the transformation of new coherences into an esthetic tradition. If we compare the discourses I examine in chapter 1 with those illustrated in chapter 6 we see the moving spiral of social action having come around full circle from a rhetoric of disavowal and disruption to a rhetoric of affirmation. The nineteenth-century intellectuals' forceful disruption of the processes of poetic signification and communication in Iranian culture, having gone through several stages, did eventually lead to the hermeneutic activity necessary for a perception of stability.

To demonstrate the inherent sociality of the poetic discourse and to illustrate the way an interpretive community is formed is to point to a validation process necessary for the success of all visions, political, religious, or esthetic. Much as in the case of prophets, the vicissitudes of Nima Yushij's life, as well as the poetic vision he espoused, have become bases for attribution of meanings to his poetry. We have indeed come full circle since the time when Akhundzadeh, Kermani, and Malkom insisted on the presence of readers who despised the Persian poetry written by Sorush or Qa'ani. In Iran of the mid-twentieth century, Tabari, Kasra'i, and Akhavan tell us, there are readers who understand Nima's poetry, find it socially relevant and esthetically pleasing.

It must be obvious by now that I conceptualize the attribution of relevance—or lack thereof—to poetry as a collective social act in which poets, critics, and readers partake. Interpretive communities constantly elevate one—or some—from among many valid approaches to reading, relegating all others to the realm of nonexistent. The individuals whose writings I examine in this book are no different. Their approach has practically concealed all the other paths that might have been taken to arrive from Qa'ani to Nima. As a result of their efforts, we may wish to view the modernist poetry of Iran as the only, the "natural," alternative to classical Persian poetry. Our story, however, would not be complete without an account of the visions enunciated and abandoned, alternatives proposed but not practiced, and efforts undertaken to no avail. In that sense, all those whose visions have been discarded are also part of the process of poetic change in Iran.

THE METHODOLOGY

The theoretical observations of Mikhail Bakhtin and Yuri Lotman have begun to make us keenly aware of the complexities of a systematic study of the phenomenon of literary change. Both theorists demonstrate these complexities through their concentration on individual authors or texts, viewed in their full sociality. The study of cultures and poetic traditions outside their purview necessitates constant modifications as well as a reluctant acceptance of the need to reduce their scope.[36] In so doing, I have tried to focus my attention on the most crucial carriers of poetic meaning.[37] I trust this methodology has afforded me the essential analytical tools to examine the locus of change in the poetic texts I analyze.

Naturally, the texts I have selected for examination are those I consider most appropriate for the task at hand. Only after I have analyzed each text's potential to illustrate a significant trend will I attempt to move to a level of generalization capable of demonstrating that trend. In other words, I begin at the level of textual structures that lend themselves to close readings, and then move to that of the social structures that relate to the text's generative ambience. Working outward from the center of individual poetic texts, I try to identify those linguistic structures and semantic relations which, in the way they relate to the reader, convey the emotive and cognitive aspects of the poet's perceptions. More significantly, I try to address those elements or structures likeliest to change the reader, the poet, or the cultural environment that have brought them to mutual interlocution. Thus, much of my effort will be directed toward uncovering the processes by which linguistic signs are employed and made to signify. Still, I hope to make it clear as I go along that in doing so I work ultimately toward the grounding of poetic structures in social ones. Finally, the time span I have carved out of the flowing mass of history is designed to highlight the essential sociality not only of human actions but also of human feelings, motives, and drives. The movement made visible in this book from the near total rejection of one specific cultural practice to the equally embracing affirmation of another will, I trust, corroborate that conviction.

As a governing metaphor for the thrust of my argument, the idea of "recasting" is relevant to my purpose in at least two senses. The process by which cultural products made of the stuff of language are produced and exposed to social air is indeed akin to the act of melting an old object, pouring it into a new and differently shaped container, and allowing it time to harden. The metaphor helps us to see the material of the language, already freighted with conventional and habitual usages which bestow meaning on all utterances, as highly diffuse in its social dispersal. Obviously, the desire to create esthetically pleasing objects depends for its fulfillment on approving glances from others. It is of crucial importance to poets—and to cultures—that their poems be thought of as pleasing and not as repulsive. Whatever the judgment, when it is expressed by a chorus of rising voices speaking in unison, or is perceived as such, social and cultural consequences are sure to result.

In another sense, "recasting" refers to a reassignment of roles. And yet, however different the new roles may be, actors end up dramatizing or presenting something separate from their lives as real human beings. Naturally, they try to perform their part as convincingly and well as they always have. However, to posit the idea that one kind of poetry may be "natural" would be to confuse actors with the personages whose actions they are dramatizing. This metaphor also relates the interplay of continuity and change to socially produced expectations which poets try to fulfill. As configurations of social forces change, so does the "role" poet-actors are expected to play. The manner in which poets and readers conceive of this role and the way they communicate their conception to each other and to their contemporaries ultimately shed light on the conditions governing their existence in society.

Before I end this Introduction, I would like to use the luxury of a moment's respite to reflect on the journey that has brought me to the shore of the ideas expressed in this book. I have a vivid recollection of my own conversion, as a young Iranian nurtured on the poetry of Ferdowsi, Rumi, and Hafez, to an advocate of "The New Poetry." I can still see the face of the teacher who tried to explain the meaning of the phrase *jigh-e banafsh* (purple scream) to the class of youngsters of which I was one. The phrase, first used in a "modernist" poem, had been seized upon by traditionalists and was being flaunted as a nonsensical one typical of the entire emerging corpus. "Can't you see," our teacher said, his face communicating a desperate desire to be understood, "can't you visualize before the eye of your mind the color on the face of the man who is uttering the loudest scream you can imagine?" What a genuinely "new" idea, I remember thinking, to express the loudness of the scream in terms of the color the act of uttering it brings to the face! At that moment, I experienced a new dimension of understanding, and *she'r-e now* had won its newest convert. Thinking back, I see my teacher's explanation, regardless of its correctness or validity, as producing in me the specific pleasure of imagining an idea in a new way. It was only one step from that pleasant feeling to an appreciation of the way modernist Persian poetry can "make" sense in ways that differentiate it from classical Persian poetry.

Increasingly fascinated by the poetry produced around me, I have seen myself grow more and more curious about the story of this poetic tradition in the thirty-some years that separate me as the author of this book from the convert of my little anecdote. Today, when I look back at my previous assessments of the modernist tradition in Persian poetry, I ask myself what in my experience may have informed the evolution of my views. As one exposed at a young age to the celebratory discourse surrounding *she'r-e now,* I have always found that poetic tradition esthetically satisfying and socially significant. Still, my familiarity with theories of human discourse has affected my views considerably. While trying not to lose sight of the enthusiastic advocate I have been, I hope I am no longer captive to that youthful enthusiasm. Having grown up with modernist Persian poetry, having lived with it and loved it, still loving it immensely, I now return to it, I hope, fairly unfettered. I have worked on this book not to make everyone love what I have always loved, but in search of a better understanding of the processes and practices that have made the poetry of contemporary Iran such an impressive cultural achievement.

Chapter One

A Rhetoric of Subversion

On an early spring day in 1849 at the court of young Naser al-Din Shah Qajar (r. 1848–96), prime minister Mirza Taqi Khan Farahani, known as Amir-e Kabir, severely rebuked the Malek al-Sho'ara (King of the poets) Habibollah Qa'ani, perhaps even threatening to have him bastinadoed. The poet had just recited, or was in the midst of reciting, his panegyric qasida in honor of the prime minister, calling him a just and virtuous ruler who had taken the place of one unjust and cruel. Court chroniclers of the period have not provided us with many details about the incident, and successive generations of historians have added their own particular spins to it.[1] No contemporary sources I know of attempts to account for the Amir's unprecedented outburst beyond citing his "natural" dislike of poetry and poets or alluding to this unusual reaction as evidence of the reformist prime minister's firm resolve to bring the financial excesses of an obliviously prodigal court under control.

We do not know whether the Amir chided the poet in public or privately, whether he may have interrupted the recital or allowed the poet to finish the ceremony before reproaching him. Neither the Amir's words nor the poet's reaction are known to us. *Sadr al-Tavarikh,* which seems to have been the original source of all subsequent references to the episode, portrays the patron as angry at the poet and the poet as apologetic and ashamed of himself.[2] By some accounts, the Amir grew angry "because"—or "when"—he "realized" that the court poet was "lying." After all, in a dozen similar qasidas, Qa'ani had previously praised the very man he was now disparaging as cruel and unjust. But for almost all chroniclers and historians, literary or political biographers, the significance of the incident between the poet and his patron seems to reside primarily in the fact that he took the opportunity to cut Qa'ani's handsome stipend and, in the process, to make of him an example for other hangers-on in the court.

Whatever the details, the story is worth contemplating as an incident involving a poet and a reform-minded member of the Iranian elite, a man many consider a precursor of political and cultural modernization in Iran. A prominent courtier of many years, the Amir must have been thoroughly familiar with the function of the court poet as panegyrist. Qa'ani was after all only discharging part of his official duty: celebrating the office by praising the officeholder. Was there perhaps something specific in this particular qasida that may have offended the prime minister? Beyond such specifics, what can we venture about the cultural background or ramifications of the Amir's unprecedented reaction? Most of the historians of the period and biographers of the poet and the patron have cited a particular bayt (line) of Qa'ani's qasida as either the occasion for the Amir's anger or as evidence of the poet's moral depravity. Here's the line in question:

> beja-ye zalemi shaqi neshasteh ʿadeli taqi
> keh mo'menan-e mottaqi konand eftekharha[3]

> (in place of one cruel and vicious is seated one just and virtuous so faithful men of virtue would feel much pride)

Indeed, the line constitutes the emotional center of the panegyric. Weaving the patron's given name, Taqi, into the fabric of the poem, it contrasts the phrase in which it occurs with an exact metric parallel that contains the exact opposite sense. The two phrases ʿadeli taqi (a just one who is also virtuous) and zalemi shaqi (an unjust one who is also cruel) contain the same number of syllables in the same order and combination of long and short syllables, and are complete sajʿs (rhyming phrases), both internally and in their endings. As such, morphologically and syntactically, they form two interchangeable units of speech providing contrasting meanings. One might easily reverse the order of their appearance in the line and communicate the opposite sense, without changing anything about the line's internal structure. Switch the two phrases and you might be saying, in effect, that in the place of one just and virtuous is seated an unjust and cruel one.

The contrast between justice and injustice, cruelty and virtuousness, and other binary oppositions which abound in the poetic tradition of the Persian language are such that in this instance they only communicate a conception of the two rulers as complete opposites.[4] But the idea of a cruel and unjust man being replaced by a man of opposite character traits ignores many of the real complexities that the Amir, the poet, and their audience must all have known well to have marked the occasion of the previous minister's ouster and the present one's accession to the seat of power. One scholar even speculates that the Amir was angry because he considered his predecessor no less honorable than himself, or at least he wished to give this impression.[5] If a deposed prime minister's character can be assailed in terms so antithetical to that of the present patron whose every act is being praised as just and virtuous, wouldn't it be just as easy for this or another poet to praise the next patron by castigating the deeds of this one in similarly categorical terms?

In more technical terms, conventional devices of the Persian qasida, in this case techniques known in traditional poetic criticism as the *tazad* (contrariety) and the *tebaq* (coincidence), virtually eliminate the possibility of any departure from binary oppositions in the discourse of the panegyric. In the line cited above, such a linguistic structure prevents the poet from articulating the character of the two patrons in anything but the most categorical of terms. In the nineteenth-century Iranian practice of poetry, strict and unquestioned adherence to such conventions had effectively eliminated all possibilities of relative distinctions.

I stress the exclusive nature of binary oppositions because in their inability to conceive of any difference in terms other than utter opposition, they illustrate a far larger issue. The "language" of classical Persian poetry, particularly the lyrical tradition in it, had gradually given rise to a relatively closed system of poetic signification and communication which did not allow for the assimilation of new elements. At the same time, the dynamics of contact with linguistic and poetic systems hitherto unfamiliar to speakers of Persian, was fast giving rise to the perception of an immediate need for a more open system of cultural communication. My contention in this chapter is that as Iranian culture began to gain access to nonpoetic discourse or alternative systems of poetic expression in Western societies, a fairly definable social group began to agitate against the old system of poetic expression. This social group constituted an increasingly important segment of the Iranian elite of the second part of the century to whom I refer simply as "the new intellectuals." Fully aware of the power of poetry as a cultural medium of expression, this group found many of the classical poetic conventions too restrictive for the expression of its views and the description of the specific sociopolitical situation at hand. Consequently, it began to work toward changing Iranian society's poetic imaginary, now by criticizing this or that poet, now by setting contemporary poetry against the inherited tradition, at times even by rejecting the entire tradition, offering in its place an alternative poetic system which it described as actually existing in Europe.

Amir-e Kabir's chastisement of Qa'ani may have struck the literary establishment of the time as a solitary, even eccentric exercise of political authority. But throughout the half century that followed, a growing number of voices was heard deriding the existing poetic practice, characterizing it now as incomprehensible, nonsensical, and ineffective, now as positively harmful, a cause (even *the* cause) of Iran's backwardness and misery. Coming from an increasingly influential social group, these voices began to state the case against poetry in equivocal, noncompromising terms: poetry as it was practiced in their native culture was esthetically repulsive, morally decadent, and socially harmful. When an idea of an alternative kind of poetry can be gleaned from their criticism, this is usually envisioned as the precise opposite of the then current practice. In its most radical form, their discourse implicates nearly the entire canon of Persian poetry in what is articulated as the follies or crimes of contemporary poets. Nonetheless, exceptions are always allowed. Whole periods, certain thematic strains, or at least individual poets, are judged as deserving of a positive view on some grounds. But these were usually described as the exceptions that testified to the truth of the decadence which had overtaken the practice of poetry in their time.

In attempting to alter the inherited cultural structures which they had come to view as an obstacle along the path to "progress" and "modernization," the new intellectuals found themselves engaged in an inevitable confrontation with the tradition-bound social institutions and forces of which poetry and the poets were no insignificant part. Intent on making use of what social energies they could mobilize for the task of erecting new structures along the lines of European societies, they began to construct an alternative poetic imaginary, that of European cultures, as the ideal model to emulate.

Thus even as they engaged themselves in destroying the prevalent poetic notions, the new intellectuals, not nearly as versed in the classical art of poetry as the forces they sought to oust, began to produce new definitions for such basic concepts as "literature" and "poetry," chart the course of poetic evolution in the Persian language, and generate new ideas about the proper relationship between poetry and society. Poetry was being redefined in ways that would enable it to take an active part in the process of social realignment which the new intellectuals thought necessary if Iran were to catch up with the countries of Europe. Accordingly, the poetic views of the past had to be changed in such a way as to make that new function possible. The process of simultaneous subversion and empowerment thus initiated must be seen in its full sociality in any attempt for a better understanding of the rise and evolution of poetic modernity in Iranian culture. More specifically, an exposition of the discourse of these early intellectuals constitutes a necessary preamble to any treatment of modern poetry that proposes to move beyond prevalent dichotomies between the old and the new, the traditional and the modern, the classical and the contemporary. In traditional literary criticism, as it pertains to poetic change in Iran, the evolution of poetry through the past century or so is explained essentially either in terms of innovations in rhyme patterns and metric rules (usually attributed to individual efforts of a few "modernist" poets) or alternatively as certain changes in thematic preoccupations of clusters of poetic texts widely seen as resulting from—and keyed to—sociopolitical events.[6] Little account is taken of the social environment in which the idea of poetic change was first enunciated or of the aspirations which inspired that idea, of the various stages through which the process has moved, and of the factors which have played a part in that process. Such an account, in terms both of the poetry and the discourse accompanying it, lies at the core of my project, and an examination of the moment when the idea of poetic change first becomes socially significant is the subject of the present chapter.

THE PARADOX OF LITERARY RETURN

Qa'ani is perhaps as appropriate a figure as any through whom to gain entry into the poetic practice against which the new Iranian intellectuals began to voice their objections as well as share their vision of a new kind of poetry. As the most important poet of nineteenth-century Iran and a central figure in the Literary Return Movement,[7] Qa'ani had begun his poetic career in an environment in which poets were trying to recapture the glory they perceived as having been lost to their immediate predecessors. In time, he had become the most important figure in that movement, a view which remains as valid today as it was a century ago.[8] For this reason, a basic understanding of Qa'ani's poetic career and the Return Movement may provide a relatively stable background against which we can view the rise of a "modern" poetic consciousness. Briefly, the poets of the Return Movement believed that Persian poetry had grown in elaborateness over time so much that it had lost its original simplicity of diction and clarity of expression. Particularly in recent centuries, they thought, this poetry had given way to bombastic wordplay of the so-called Indian School in Persian poetry.[9] Writing early in the twentieth century, Bahar was summing up the opinion of several generations of Iranian poets associated with the Return Movement when he characterized the Indian School as one marked by "weakness of words and poverty of meaning" which sought strength in "an excess of images . . . and fanciful visions lacking in eloquence and true beauty."[10]

However, to be useful as a point of departure, the ideas of the poets associated with the Return Movement must be placed in the larger cultural context within which they were operating. Historically, the generally unsympathetic attitude of the nineteenth-century poets of Iran toward the Indian School can be traced to the often problematic relationship between the poets of Iran proper and the Persian poets outside it during the centuries when "Iran" was becoming increasingly identified as a territorial, rather than a cultural and linguistic, entity. From the sixteenth century on, the absence of court patronage for nonreligious poetry at the courts of Isfahan had pushed the center of the Persian poetic culture to the Ottoman Empire, to Central Asia, and most importantly to India. This in turn gave rise to the particular poetic "language" associated with the Indian School. In time, a quarrel revolving around the relative merits of Iranian and Indian poets had ensued and continued throughout the eighteenth century.[11]

With the resumption of court patronage in the nineteenth century, the poets of Iran were once again seeking to regain the cultural hegemony they saw their predecessors as having lost. Their view of the language of the Indian School as bombastic and elaborate and of its meanings as farfetched and insignificant was part of a national Iranian discourse aimed at reversing a cultural trend which had pushed their poetic tradition toward what they perceived as an inevitable decline and decadence.[12] To remedy the situation, the poets of the Return Movement advocated a return to that part of the classical tradition of Persian poetry which they felt had not yet been tainted by influences from such foreign climes as those of Anatolia or India. One consequence of their position was the emergence of a view of poetic imitation not as a dialogue across time, but as an echo of what was judged to be the most authentic poetic voices in the entire tradition.[13] This notion of imitation gradually altered the dynamics of continuity and change in Persian poetry. In former times, such practices as *tazmin* (thematic imitation), *esteqbal* (welcoming, reception), and *eqtebas* (adaptation)[14] fostered a rapport between poets of various epochs and resulted in a loose meeting of the minds between contemporary and past poets. Now, the Return Movement poets' practice of *taqlid* (imitation) tended to reject the immediate past as alien, employing instead styles associated with the earlier poetic schools, the so-called Khorasani and Eraqi. Through poetic utterances lexically, rhetorically, and stylistically approximating the best representatives of those early schools, poets like Qa'ani endeavored to restore the millennium-long tradition of Persian poetry to what they perceived as its "original" simplicity.

The notion of an "original spirit" having gradually given way to what was commonly viewed as "unnecessary or unwarranted complexities," deserves a momentary reflection. As a quality which distinguishes poetry from ordinary speech, verbal complexity is a feature of poetic communication. In all textual structures the degree of complexity is ultimately related to the nature of the information the text seeks to transmit. Theoretically, however, an important distinction arises here, one which accounts for the growth of complexity in semiotic systems through time. While it is true that the information content transmitted through a poem can neither exist nor be transmitted outside the particular artistic structure of that poem, semioticians view this as a systemic propensity, and not the result of accidental or individual choices. In Lotman's words, "as the nature of the information grows more complicated, the semiotic system used to transmit that information grows more complicated."[15] The great advantage of this manner of envisioning the difference between an early simplicity and a later complexity in a poetic tradition is that it gives a systemic status to complexities of the kind that was originally posited by the poets of the Return Movement. In this way, such concepts as simplicity and complexity find their place in the movement of the poetic praxis through time as well as a function of the nature of the information poets set out to transmit.

In practice, the Return Movement's assignment of a negative status to the "complexities" of the Indian school resulted in the subordination of the individual poetic voice to the authority of a past, an entity thought to contain the opposite tendency. Two distinct voices, attempting to express drastically different concerns, collapsed into one, turning the dialogue of the poetic culture through time into something akin to a mere confirmation of the voice of the distant past. In the words of one contemporary scholar, whereas in former times a "web of intertextual patterns kept the past alive in the present and allowed the tradition to look simultaneously backward and forward at any one time," the poets of the Return Movement tried "to emulate masters of the past and to recreate individual and period styles."[16] Thus, the poets of the Return Movement viewed their effort as restorative. By emulating such poets as Manuchehri, Anvari, and Khaqani, they would ensure a return to the "true" classical tradition of Persian poetry. To the new intellectuals, however, the whole of the poetic tradition seemed to have played little part in the process of "positive" social change. On the contrary, it had actually thwarted all yearnings for progress and reform through literary production. More than any other single polarity this difference lay behind the ensuing cultural confrontation.

The drive to modernize Iranian society through reform had also brought about the idea of poetry as a socially significant discourse, either contributing to social progress or inhibiting it. Persian poetry was increasingly being seen as having changed in time, first to have evolved and been perfected in the hands of poets from Rudaki to Hafez, and then to have declined afterwards. While both the Return Movement poets and the new intellectuals shared this view, they differed considerably about the solution to the problem. Without an exception, the poets and literati of mid–nineteenth-century Iran believed that a return to the fountainheads of poetry would rejuvenate it by returning to the actual practice the potential to express issues of contemporary concern. The new intellectuals, on the other hand, thought it impossible for the tradition that had led to the contemporary practice to be capable of anything substantially different.[17]

As the most significant poet of the Movement, Qa'ani was well endowed to restore Persian poetry to its original state. He is universally remembered by his contemporaries as having a prodigious memory filled with the entire range of tropes and images, myths and metaphors that the tradition had to offer. The well-known anecdote about his having composed an entire qasida of over one hundred lines in minutes along the way to a patron's home testifies to this trait.[18] When he lost his father, Qa'ani tells us in his autobiography, "need forced me to become my own father . . . and I judged the path of my forebears a worthy one to follow."[19] Qa'ani's father was indeed a minor poet, but the metaphor of the path of the forebears has significant implications for the poet's own view of his craft as the continuation of the inherited tradition. From the perspective of those who had been exposed to European poetic cultures, however, poets like Qa'ani appeared as the perpetuators of a poetic tradition incapable of expressing their concerns and preoccupations. Though Qa'ani saw himself as striving to correct the tradition he had inherited by following in the footsteps of the best of his forebears, an increasing number of his contemporaries began attacking all efforts at continuing an unredeemably outdated tradition.

The reason why the poetry of Qa'ani and others of his generation appears to modern critics to stand in such an oblique relationship to its social context is that while the poet's culture was beginning to realign itself with Europe, his poetry, still based on the native paradigm of a past era, seemed to evoke resistance to that process. Qa'ani typified that resistance in many ways. Because he was an excellent craftsman,[20] his qasidas and ghazals struck his contemporaries as indistinguishable from those of the early masters of Persian poetry. His most important prose work, the *Parishan*, presented the latest link in a long chain of proud imitations of Sa'di's *Golestan*, written six centuries before. In his poetry, as in his prose work, he had created a linguistic universe which, like that of the classics of Persian literature, was comprehensive, all-inclusive, and complete in its epistemological certainties. In them, an unchanging nature continued to provide the arena for the poet's lawlike explanation of human behavior. Viewed in terms of the aspirations of the Return Movement, his works signaled, in the simplicity of their diction and clarity of their expressive devices, a strong desire to effect change in the "language" of the Persian literature of the recent past. From the perspective of the new intellectuals, the same works signified not only stagnation but also regression in their growing dependence on the paradigms and patterns of an essentially different world.

Traditional literary criticism in Iran postulates that poets like Qa'ani had no sense of the changes to which their culture was being subjected.[21] This is clearly not true. Some of the figures involved in the Return Movement were among the elite of the Qajar court, directly involved in the affairs of the state. The oblivious detachment that contemporary criticism attributes to them has its origins in a rhetoric aimed at subverting the poetry of the nineteenth century. What is true is that the esthetic structures with which poets like Qa'ani worked tended to transport them to a mode of composition and expression which did not communicate any consciousness of the kind the new intellectuals envisioned. The system through which Persian poetry expressed itself had become almost completely closed over the centuries to the extent that it had left little space for any intrusion from outside. Even the most resolute advocate of literary change would be bound by the forms and genres, tropes and expressive devices which governed the poetic system.

Let us assume for a moment the poetic language of a tradition can be divided into the artistic discourses of various periods and cultures within that tradition and that these discourses may in turn be said to determine the semantic fields of various individual poets. The poetic language of a period can then be said to consist of the semantic universe that contains the totality of means of expression available to a certain generation of poets. For the poets of the Return Movement, the center of that universe was occupied by a set of rules and requirements that governed the system of classical poetry of the Persian language. This poetry, having grown in sophistication over the centuries in philosophical discourse and the discourse of love, seemed to allow little room for the expression of concrete sociopolitical concerns.

The emergence of the power of memory as the seminal quality of a poetic temperament can itself be taken as a sign of the hold that inherited poetic structures can exercise on the individual mind. Values lauded and prescribed in numerous nineteenth-century *tazkereh*s (biographies) or manuals of poetic craft confirm such concepts as authority, convention, and continuity. In these, we find abundant exhortations to the aspiring poet to learn the rules of prosody, to follow in the footsteps of the classical masters, and to carry within memory as much of the best compositions of the past as possible.[22] It seems only natural that poets should see themselves as seeking, through a return to the golden age of Persian poetry, to restore vigor to the poetic culture of their age. In practice, every image they resuscitated, every rhetorical strategy they revived, every poem they composed further grounded contemporary practice in the esthetic system which they had inherited. By simplifying the language of the classical tradition, they preserved the system of poetic signification and communication on which that language was based.

The response to the poetry of the Return Movement was immediate and uncompromising. At a time when literature was thought to play a crucial part in the national culture the practice of Iranian poets provided eloquent testimony to the depravity of the entire literary canon. This impression in turn gave rise to a stereotyping tendency which all but obliterated the distinctions that had given rise to the impressive variety of texts, trends, and discourses within the Persian poetic tradition. The whole of Persian poetry was being seen as rooted in a system of esthetic expression that was unnatural and unrelated to real life experiences. The impression was then used as part of the effort to enlist literary talents in the cause of sociopolitical change. Theoretically, such situations mark the beginning of the drive toward esthetic change. At such times, Lotman observes, movement is possible along two paths, increasingly seen as incompatible: a movement which aims to reconstruct the system from within, and a movement which proposes to discard the whole system. When the latter tendency takes over, he observes, "the existing system is accepted as the initial, negative background, [and] the new system of artistic language is activated in relation to the old as its negation."[23]

This observation reveals the paradox of the Literary Return Movement in Iran. Although the Iranian poets of the mid-nineteenth century by and large considered themselves innovators, the new intellectuals saw them as slavish imitators of a bankrupt esthetic. To them, the entire Iranian culture appeared in need of drastic reform, and poetry was no insignificant part of the deformity they proposed to remedy. Their response to poets like Qa'ani reflects the growing rift in Iranian culture throughout the latter part of the nineteenth century between the traditional literati and the reformists. Starting literally or metaphorically from the margins of Iranian social structure, the individuals who provide our focus in this chapter launched a series of attacks against the center of the esthetic culture occupied by men like Qa'ani. The changes they sought to bring about in the poetic discourse of their culture gradually began to be voiced as actually existing in European cultures, an entity which they forged and posited as the ideal they wanted to emulate. The distinctions they made between the poets of their time and European poets had far less to do with any existing literary trend in Europe than with the direction in which they sought to guide the poetry of their own culture. Similarly, the stereotypes they drew of the native poetic tradition had far more to do with the part they imagined poetry could play in the process of sociopolitical change than with any studied observation of the native poetic tradition.

The alternative paradigm the new intellectuals upheld and advocated is not easy to identify in terms of a cohesive set of specific principles and practices. Although they had obtained some exposure to European literatures through such intermediaries as India, the Ottoman Empire, and Tzarist Russia, their knowledge of European languages, particularly Russian and French, and their acquaintance with the European writers they often cited—Gogol, Pushkin, Chernyshevsky, Rousseau, Molière, and Hugo—remained superficial, sketchy, and indirect. None of this, however, deterred them from constructing the idea of European literature as a model to be emulated. Europe was considered an advanced culture, and European literature was seen as having played a decisive part in that advancement. The qualities this group imagined to exist in European poetry stood in sharp and illuminating contrast to what Lotman calls the "negative background" which characterized the native tradition. It is particularly important, in reading the arguments they presented, to bear in mind the imaginary nature of their model as we come across such designations as "European literature," "the poets of Europe," or "the practice of criticism in European countries."

POESY, CRITIQUE, DIALOGUE: AKHUNDZADEH

For our purposes, the earliest substantive attempt at redefining literature and redirecting the social energy it contains came from Fath-ʿAli Akhundzadeh, (1812–1878) a major advocate of cultural reform.[24] Akhundzadeh, born in the northwestern Iranian province of Azerbaijan, had witnessed the annexation of his birthplace by Russia at age sixteen. Writing on a variety of topics in Russian and Azeri Turkish as well as in Persian, he nonetheless focused his ideas on cultural reform in Iran. As an essayist, he helped shape nineteenth-century debates on the reform of the Arabic alphabet for Persian, on religious reform, and on political modernization throughout the Islamic world. His views on literature and poetry are scattered throughout several of his essays. In an assessment of his part in the debate on the need for modernizing Persian poetry, I find it necessary to point out the context of each observation in order to make his words as meaningful as I can. Only then will I comment on the significance of the passages cited as an early instance of a social discourse articulated by the new intellectuals.

Posing as the translator of three letters supposedly exchanged between two princes, one Iranian and one Indian, Akhundzadeh begins his *Maktubat* (Correspondences), a book published in 1865, with a set of definitions. He transliterates into the Persian script "certain words in the languages of Europe" (*alsaneh-ye farangestan*) together with expanded definitions, so that "readers will be aware of their original meaning."[25] Poesy (he writes the French word *poésie* in the Persian script here) is one such word, defined as follows:

> Poesy consists of such a composition as to include the expression of the conditions and character traits [*ahval va akhlaq*] of a person or a (group of) people [*tayefeh*] as it is in truth [*kama hova haqqoh*], or of the exposition [*sharh*] of a topic, or of the description [*vasf*] of the circumstances of the world of nature in verse in the utmost excellence [*jowdat*] and effectiveness [*ta'sir*].[26]

On the basis of that definition, Akhundzadeh later delivers a scathing criticism of the poetry written in Iran, this time posing as one of the two imaginary correspondents. He says that the use of the word *she'r* (poetry) by Iranians in reference to the kinds of composition he criticizes reveals their pure and profound ignorance. Iran's literature (again he uses the French word *littérature* in the Persian script) consists of writings on how to perform various ablutions and other banal religious rituals, of the narration of certain baseless stories which they call miracles, or of compositions "filled with hyperboles [*eghraqat*] and exaggerations [*mobaleghat*] and rhymestering [*qafieh-pardazi*] and complex phraseologies ['*ebarat-e moghlaqeh*] and boundless flatteries [*tamalloqat-e bi-andazeh*] which they (Iranians) have dubbed history, and they do not know at all what poesy should be like [*keh poezi cheguneh bayad bovad*]." This utter ignorance, the princely persona states, has led Iranians to call all manner of "hollow" (*porpuch*) verses poesy. Furthermore, they "fancy that poesy consists of versifying a few meaningless words [*alfaz-e bima'ni*] in one specific meter [*yek vazn-e mo'ayyan*] and of rhyming their endings, and of descriptions of beloveds with unreal qualities (or adjectives) [*sefat*], and of the praise of Spring and Autumn with unnatural [*ghayr-e tabi'i*] similes, just as the divan of one of the latest poets of Tehran, known as Qa'ani, is filled with such nonsenses [*mozakhrafat*]." The fact of which Iranians are woefully unaware, and to which they have given no thought, is that "in poesy, the subject-matter (or content, or theme) [*mazmun*] ought to be far more effective [*mo'asser tar*] than the subject-matter of prose compositions."27

The only exception to this cultural lack worth mentioning, according to Akhundzadeh, is the work of Ferdowsi, the poet of the heroical verse-stories known as *The Shahnameh*. He is the only Iranian poet who composed anything comparable to the works of Homer and Shakespeare: "In truth it can be said that in 'the nation of Islam' [*mellat-e eslam*] it is only the poems [*ash'ar*] of Ferdowsi that is *poésie*." And if people would only open their eyes to "the truth of *poésie* [*haqiqat-e poezi*], they would probably be able to compose poems [*she'r*] like those of Ferdowsi."28

Homer and Shakespeare in fact become touchstones against which Iranian poets are measured throughout the writings of Akhundzadeh. The reasons he gives for holding these poets up to Iranians as ideals to emulate are important to note. Immediately after excepting Ferdowsi, Akhundzadeh's mouthpiece stresses that poetic eloquence resides not in the extraordinary and the impossible, but rather in the possible:

> In old times, among the Greek nation there was a famous poet by the name of Homer, and he has versified the battles and factual events of the Greek nation in ancient epochs, as well as the struggles and arts of their heroes just as has Ferdowsi, in such a way that thus far no creature has been able to compose poems like his. Also among the English nation several hundred years ago there appeared a poet named Shakespeare who has versified the calamities of English kings in so effective a manner that when hearing them, however hard-hearted the listener might be, he cannot help but weep.29

Capable of affecting audiences of all times and all cultures, men like Homer, Ferdowsi, and Shakespeare are true poets, their works factual and effective. Almost all other Persian poets, particularly those of contemporary Iran, are described as pretenders whose verses consist entirely of false and unnatural exaggerations. That, in a word, is why their compositions are incapable of affecting even their contemporary readers. To the extent that poets speak of real events and factual occurrences they are true to their calling; where they allow wild flights of fancy they lose their right to that august title. That distinction provides an initial yardstick by which Akhundzadeh measures poets and their work.

A second principle, equally central to Akhundzadeh's plan for cultural reform, relates to the belief that exposing faults and flaws gives rise to dialogue and eventually leads to improvements of various kinds. In fact, much of his wide-ranging rejection of religious dogma is rooted in a singular assurance that an awareness of this fault will persuade people to change their beliefs. This basic assumption leads to Akhundzadeh's extensive attempts to expose deformity wherever he sees it. In fact, a simple assumption regarding the natural human proclivity toward betterment lies at the base of Akhundzadeh's conviction about the salutary effects of criticism and persuades him to explain the concept to Iranians.

The idea of criticism is contained in the titles of Akhundzadeh's two epistolary essays in Persian on the art of writing, "Resaleh-ye Irad" (Treatise of Disapprobation) and "Qeritika" (Critique). These essays convey a deeply felt desire to familiarize Iranians with the notion and activity of criticism as it is practiced in Europe. The effort finds its fullest expression toward the close of the first essay, where the author's critique of a contemporary history takes the shape of an imaginary dialogue with its author. Akhundzadeh then addresses the editor to whom he plans to send his essay in these words:

> I dispatch these dialogues to the office of the Tehran newspaper, and declare that this practice [criticism] is common in Europe, and that it contains enormous benefits [*favayed-e 'azimeh*]. For instance, when someone writes a book, another person writes a critique [*iradat*] on it. This, however, includes no words of disparagement and disrespect about the author, and everything that is said is stated tactfully. This action they call criticism [*qeritika*].
>
> The author responds to him (to the critic), and then a third person comes forth, either showing the truth in the author's reply or judging the critic [*irad konandeh*]'s observations superior. The result of this activity is that little by little verse, prose, and other compositions in the language of every people in Europe becomes devoid of all manner of shortcomings as far as possible and attains to perfection.[30]

Akhundzadeh appeals to the editor to pioneer the practice of criticism in Iran, pointing in particular to the beneficial impact of such an activity on the nature and kind of imaginative literature produced in that country:

> If this practice gains currency through the Tehran newspaper, it will doubtless lead to progress in the future (generations of) Iranians. . . . Specifically, they will cease the versification of ghazals and qasidas which at the present time are composed without any content [*bimazmun*] and without any enjoyment [*bilazzat*], and is of no use whatever [*hich fayedeh nadarad*], and they will begin to write poems in the masnavi form after the example of Ferdowsi's *Shahnameh,* Shaykh Sa'di's *Bustan,* and the like, works which enshrine

stories [*hekayat*] and express the conditions and manners of diverse groups. In prose, also, they will turn away completely from the childish rhyming hyperboles and idiotic analogies [*tashbihat-e ablahaneh*], and will seek only pleasing themes [*mazmun-e marghub*], themes which shall appeal to the reader, and which the listener shall find enjoyable. And then authors shall achieve fame. For surely, reacting to the beauty of the theme [*hosn-e mazmun*], readers shall send to him letters of praise and not of criticism [*iradat*].[31]

The same notion of criticism pervades the second essay, entitled simply "Qeritika," also addressed to the Tehran editor. Here Akhundzadeh singles out a contemporary Iranian poet, Sorush, known by the honorific title "Shams al-Sho'ara" (Sun of the Poets) for detailed criticism. He begins by criticizing the editor for allowing the poet's biography and a sampling of his ghazals and qasidas to occupy over two pages of his four-page newspaper. "I ask you in fairness," he writes, "what benefit does the knowledge of the lineage and life of a poet like Sorush . . . contain for the nation?"[32] Turning to the poet himself, he calls Sorush an insincere liar who, like his ancestors before him, composes rhymes only in hopes of receiving reward from his patrons. Most definitely, opines Akhundzadeh, such a man does not deserve the honorific appellation "Sun of the Poets."

Akhundzadeh then sets out to prove his claim that Sorush is not a good poet. He cites two major qualities for good poetry—that is, beauty of subject matter (*hosn-e mazmun*) and beauty of expression (*hosn-e alfaz*). The qasida published in the paper, he argues, is devoid of both qualities. Besides, "in some places, even the meter is not without fault." The composer, therefore, cannot properly be called a poet. The reason why the poem's subject matter is not beautiful has to do with the fact that it refers to some beliefs of the Shaykhiyyeh sect in Shi'ism, a topic fit for debate by clerical leaders and not by poets. In addition, regardless of the truth or falsehood of the theological position espoused in the poem, "such arguments possess no novelty [*torfegi*] and freshness [*tazegi*]". The poem's theme then is "very disgusting [*makruh*] and utterly unacceptable [*mardud*]." Sorush's qasida fares no better in the matter of beauty of expression. The poem's words, Akhundzadeh maintains, belong more appropriately to preachments uttered upon the pulpit; they are certainly unfit for poetry in the eyes of all those who possess "good taste and sound disposition."[33]

Akhundzadeh singles out a few lines of Sorush's qasida for closer examination, zeroing in on the conventional *do'a* (prayer) which closes the poem. He cites the poem's last line which contains the poet's pen name as an occasion to address him directly:

> Sorush, madh-e rasul-e khoda va ʿetrat guy
> keh sayyeʾat-e to ra bestorad chonin hasenat.

> (Sorush, sing the praises of God's prophet and his family,
> for such good deeds will eradicate your sins.)[34]

"The Sun of the poets," mocks Akhundzadeh, "wishes to deceive God's own prophet to earn forgiveness for his sins and reward for such nonsense!" He chides Sorush in these words:

> No, sir! excuse me! God's prophet has more sense than the editor whom you have duped into wasting a whole issue of his newspaper on such absurdities! No, your excellency Sun of Poets! Your sins will not be forgiven. If you wish God's prophet to be satisfied with you, act in accordance with his instructions, and do not inflict harm upon your fellow Muslims![35]

In this way, a conventional poetic trope, typical of the qasida genre in the Persian poetic tradition, is taken as a logical statement and presented as evidence of the poet's moral depravity. Transported to the plane of intellectual discourse, the statement contained in the *doʿa* provides grounds for the condemnation of the poet on charges of attempting to deceive God, the greatest conceivable sacrilege.

Akhundzadeh next protests the cultural harm arising from the acceptance of individuals like Sorush as great poets and of their compositions as poetry. This is particularly obvious to readers removed from the culture of the poet. He relates how he once had tried to justify to an Englishman named Mr. Fisher the convention according to which Iranian poets are given titles like "Sun of the Poets." The Englishman, he recalls, had quickly dismissed his argument that this was only a convention, and it does not really mean that Sorush's position among other Iranian poets must be regarded as analogous to that of the sun among heavenly stars. "Your habits are not binding on others," Mr. Fisher protests, "and foreign nations contemporary with the nation of Iran do attach meaning [*maʿni*] and relevance [*monasebat*] to such appellations." They shall then ask whether Iranians are indeed so unaware of the art of poesy as to consider such unworthy men deserving of such honorifics. Besides, the Englishman goes on, future generations of Iranians who, "in comparison with our age, shall definitely be far more advanced in sciences," will examine the compositions of this age. Wouldn't they feel shamefaced that "their fathers have judged such unworthy men their foremost poets, and have bestowed upon them appellations befitting poets like Ferdowsi, Nezami, and Hafez?"[36]

Pressing the twin issues of poetry's intellectual content and cross-cultural perceptions, Akhundzadeh reserves his severest critique for an idea particularly repulsive to the new, secular intellectuals. At one point in his qasida, Sorush implies that only the Muslims are truly human beings, likening the rest of humanity to "insects" (*hasharat*). This idea, Akhundzadeh says, is both false and extremely offensive. Furthermore, it runs counter to Islam's own view of the followers of other religions. Here, too, he puts the protest in the mouth of the Englishman:

> You yourself be the judge. Is it befitting that such distinguished European philosophers, sages, writers, poets, historians, and inventors as Voltaire, Montesquieu, Rousseau, . . . Shakespeare, Volney and Byron, among others, be counted among insects, but a useless creature named Sorush—and many others like him—be included in the ranks of humanity? This attribution which your nation's poet has given to us detracts nothing from our worth. Rather, its harm returns to you, for we shall everywhere look upon you as inferior and judge your reasoning to be on a par with that of children, and we shall laugh at you.[37]

An old cultural bias expressed through a conventional poetic trope is thus manipulated to produce a highly repulsive, morally indefensible meaning. Akhundzadeh closes his essay by declaring the poem in question factually untrue, esthetically disgusting, and culturally harmful.

Using an esthetic terminology and a set of criteria independent of the Persian poetic tradition, he declares the poetry of his culture defunct. In his criticism, the practice of measuring poetic excellence against the achievements of the classical masters gives way to the logical discourse emanating from Europe. He thus undermines the native understanding of the status of poetic statements by introducing consciousness not nurtured in the native culture. Redefining the criteria by which poetic compositions are judged, Akhundzadeh works toward the conclusion that all poetic meaning ought to be logically sustainable, socially desirable, and culturally sensitive. The refusal to produce the kind of meanings and ideas that Europeans like Mr. Fisher, or Iranians familiar with their sentiments, would consider appropriate, beneficial, or progressive is equated with failure to produce any meaning at all. Worse yet, such refusals will produce positive social harm by not allowing people to distinguish such distasteful statements from poetry. In such statements we can see examples of an emerging discourse with which the new Iranian intellectuals conducted their social debate with the traditional literati.[38]

The rather strong sense of the presence of the subject, a discriminating mind touched positively or negatively by the texts it contemplates, allows

Akhundzadeh to revisit certain fundamental esthetic concepts. His subjectivity serves a strategy aimed at enlisting poets in the cause of cultural reform. If that purpose necessitates a shifting catalogue of acceptable voices in the tradition, he will not shrink from that. Thus, while in one essay, he mentions Ferdowsi as the only poet worthy of emulation, in another he includes Saʿdi, Nezami, and Hafez as well. At one point, in an attempt to discredit Sorush, he is even willing to give Qaʾani a niche in the pantheon of poets, for, even though his poetry lacks the beauty of substance, at least it possesses the beauty of words, and "is after all a kind of poetry and an art."[39]

Such shiftiness is significant in that it underlines the absence of a set of esthetic criteria by which the new intellectuals of nineteenth-century Iran evaluated the poets and poetry of their tradition. The desire to produce a new kind of poet, a like-minded soul who would propagate the project of social reform through the persuasive power of poetry was paramount. Poets of the past served the purpose only insofar as they could present the sharpest contrast to the contemporary poets who bore the brunt of their criticism. In submitting the current practice of poetry to criticism, men like Akhundzadeh set up a polemical rhetoric which aimed at harnessing the energies of poetry in the service of radical cultural change.

It is worth reiterating at this point that essentially all of Akhundzadeh's objections to Persian poetry stem from two core concerns. First, literature as it was practiced in his time reflected little of its surroundings because it was conceived and executed under the weight of a logic and grammar of creativity that was defunct. Second, as a result of the first, Persian poetry had lost its essential function, its potential for leading to actions that would be morally edifying and socially desirable. Following models of former times, poets were seen as failing to produce anything related to contemporary "life." Throughout the process of literary change in Iran, various scenarios for modernizing Persian poetry, while expanding its thematics well beyond Akhundzadeh's concerns, have preserved the twin concepts of social relevance and positive effect. Conversely, charges of irrelevance and moral depravity have been used to marginalize the practice of poetry seen as traditional. All this testifies to the lasting impact of Akhundzadeh's inaugurating enunciation.

Throughout the decades that separate Akhundzadeh's writings from the Constitutional Revolution of 1906, the diverse strands of his criticism were woven into the tapestry of cultural change in Iranian society. His ideas about poetry and criticism were assimilated into the discourse of nearly all the intellectuals that followed him. His methodology of argumentation through dialogue was extended into every other sphere of social life. Such prominent reformists as Kermani, Malkom, Afghani, and Maragheh'i among others reiterated his critique of Iranian affairs with greater coherence and enhanced cogency.[40] The force in their criticism of Iran's literary culture arose in part from the fact that Akhundzadeh's successors were more centrally preoccupied with esthetic concerns and more capable of using rhetorical devices than was Akhundzadeh.

POETRY, HISTORY, AND MORALITY: KERMANI

The issue of poetry's impact on individuals and societies was treated most extensively in the writings of Mirza Aqa Khan Kermani (1854–1896), a polemicist with a rich background in Persian literature and a passion for introducing cultural reforms in Iran. An early convert to Babism, Kermani wrote several important historical works and was once a member of a literary circle in Isfahan where, according to one observer, "new and progressive ideas" were discussed.[41] In the emerging debate on poetry, he asserts that Persian poetry constitutes the cause of a manifest social malaise. He advocates a radical realignment of Iranian literature in accordance with the practice of poetry in European cultures. His Europe, however, is no more a real entity than Akhundzadeh's.

The clearest expression of Kermani's ideas occurs, significantly, at the head of a verse appendix to *Nameh-ye Bastan* (Book of Ancient Times), a historical work written in the early 1890s in the same meter and diction as Ferdowsi's *Shahnameh*.[42] Throughout this work, the theme of cultural decline in Iranian society constitutes a constant presence. Preempting objections to his style of historiography and to the patriotic poems he had affixed to the book, Kermani responds to his detractors in an epilogue. It is here that he formulates a direct causal relationship between ideas disseminated through Persian poetry and the moral, social, and cultural decline in Iranian society:

> Because I have composed this brief history with reference to antique traces, ancient scripts, and the essential discoveries of the historians of the present age, I am also ending the book with an epical [*epopiki*] conclusion in the manner and style of European poets. Some of Iran's masters of perfection [*arbab-e kamal*] and fortune-blessed *littérateurs* [*odaba-ye farkhondeh-fal*] might raise the banner of debate and object to me, saying: "What manner of writing is this, and what style of versification and poetic composition? In contrast to the totality of Iranian poets, you have violated the manner and demeanor which befit tail-wagging flatterers [*kaseh-lisan-e mobasbes*], strayed from the straight path of prudence which requires self-debasement

and flattery, and are speaking thus truthfully and seriously. Tread the path as have previous seekers," they may advise.[43]

On the basis of this initial contrast, Kermani presents his observations concerning the effect of Persian poetry on the course of Iranian history. The direct causal relation he stipulates between poetic ideas and the perception of a historical decline in morality, radical as it was, must be seen both as an instance of a general idea, and as a motive force for social mobilization:

> In response I state humbly that trees ought to be known by their fruits, and [human] undertakings by their results. None can question the effectiveness and creativity of Iran's ancient men of eloquent speech. Nor do I doubt the tenderness and delicacy of their poems. The playfulness and frivolity of poets of recent ages are similarly a matter of common consensus. It ought, however, to be seen what the work of our littérateurs and poets has thus far brought about, what fruit has been produced by the saplings they have planted in the garden of speech [*bagh-e sokhanvari*], and what harvest has cropped up from the seed they have sewn.[44]

The sapling/fruit and seed/harvest imagery enables Kermani to point his finger of blame for Iran's backwardness at Persian poets, both old and new. In what two decades later E. G. Browne calls "a monstrous exaggeration of the real facts,"[45] Kermani lays the blame for everything, from the downfall of old, presumably glorious dynasties to the moral turpitude which nineteenth-century European visitors felt present in Iran, at the doorstep of Persian poets:

> Once we have looked into the history of the Islamic poets and their praised patrons, we will say: it was indeed the poems and panegyrics of Abu Nowwas and the like that threw the Abbasid caliphs into the habit of drinking and snoozing and other kinds of corruption. It was the qasidas of Onsori and Rudaki and Farrokhi and suchlike that brought about the demise of the Samanids and the Ghaznavids. . . . It was the sycophancy of Anvari and Zahir and Rashid and Kamal that gave rise to such wicked and self-conceited kings. It was the love lyrics of Sa'di and Homam and their cohorts that corrupted the morals of Iranian youth. . . . It was the despicable abstruseness of Khaqani and the likes of him that led astray Mirza Mehdi Khan and the author of [*Tarikh-e*] *Vassaf.* It was the long-windedness [*nafas-derazi*] of Saba and overelaborateness of Shehab and fatuousness of Qa'ani that has today eradicated the love of virtues and hatred of vice from the nature of Iranian nobility, availing them of extraordinary viciousness and turpitude.[46]

Kermani next presents a contrasting description of the "true" poetry which he ascribes to Europeans and that which goes by that name in Iran:

The poets of Europe, too, have produced and are producing all kinds of poems, but they have laid poetry and poetics on such firm foundations [*taht-e tartibat-e sahiheh*], and have adopted their poems with logic [*mota-beq-e manteq*], in such a way that no effect arises from their compositions other than the enlightenment of thoughts [*tanvir-e afkar*], the eradication of superstitions [*raf'-e khorafat*] . . . , the encouragement of the populace toward virtue [*tashviq-e nofus beh fazayel*], the turning away of hearts from vice [*rad' va zajr-e qolub az razayel*], the inclination to learn from examples, and the love of one's country and nation [*'ebrat va ghayrat-e vatan va mellat*]. And this indeed is the proper meaning of the prophetic tradition which states: "poetry is indeed of philosophy."

Yes, the true effects of poetry include elevating the heart, moderating the spirit, and the enhancement of the faculty of reasoning in the human mind. Poetry ought to lead the people along the path of perfection, virtue, and moderation, not to that of evil and vicious deeds, etc. The only Persian poet whom the *littérateurs* of Europe admire is Ferdowsi of Tus, whose poems in *The Shahnameh*—even though they are not free from exaggerations in some places—inculcate love of nationality, courage, and bravery to an extent. And in some places he even strives to improve our morality.[47]

Kermani then states that his "humble poems," too, have been composed in order to provide an illustration of the ways in which Iranian poets may "emulate the poets of Europe" *(eqtefa-ye beh sho'ara-ye farangestan).* He ends the passage by urging the poets of his time to realize that the kind of poetry which serves no useful cause and leads to no moral end is bound in the end to produce harm.

Kermani's logic is muddled from the very beginning. Even if we grant him a direct causal relationship between "the qasidas of Onsori and Rudaki and Farrokhi" and "the demise of the Samanids and the Ghaznavids," are we then to accept the implication that these dynasties provided occasions of pride for Iranians? Kermani himself evaluates the Samanids and the Ghaznavids very differently in his historical writings.[48] And wouldn't the same relationship obtain between "the overelaborateness of Shehab and fatuousness of Qa'ani" and the demise of the Qajars, the present ruling dynasty? Why has the "bad" poetry of the contemporary epoch, instead of contributing to the demise of the Qajars, caused them to lose "their love of virtue and hatred of vice?"

That is not the point, though. Kermani is clearly not concerned with providing a logical discourse on the social impact of classical Persian poetry. He simply wishes to see the present and future poets of Iran participate in cultural reform. His assumption about a direct relationship between the moral, ideological, or political messages communicated through poetry and the presence or absence of moral traits within the society do merit attention, of course. The lack he has detected in his society is of poets willing and able to engage themselves in the kind of social restructuring he judges desirable. Behind the historical relationships he assumes between poetry and social conditions lies a radical Iranian nationalist's desperate desire to see contemporary poets begin to articulate his concerns in their compositions. That is why he holds Ferdowsi up as the only poet whose work, *The Shahnameh,* can serve as an example to contemporary poets of Iran. As the work thought to contain the greatest expression of a national "Iranian" sentiment against the Arab overlords ruling Iran in the three centuries after the Arab conquest, *The Shahnameh* is naturally privileged as the native model of poetry worthy of emulation. That is also why Kermani himself imitated Ferdowsi's epic style, first in his verse epilogue and later in a more famous verse history of ancient Iran entitled *A'ineh-ye Sekandari.*[49] Finally, Kermani's upholding of "the poets of Europe" as examples to follow also reveals its true significance when we begin to look to the ideological purpose behind his rhetoric. Here too his objective is not to provide an account of the ways in which the poets of Europe may have contributed to the shaping of events in their cultures. Certainly, he offers no examples of such efforts nor names any individual European poet or historical event. Rather, the "sound foundations" on which the poets of Europe have built their poetic structures, and which allow them to enlighten and educate their readers, is what Kermani is groping for. He leaves it to the poets of Iran to devise and lay those foundations. All he can do is offer his own "humble poems" as one instantiation of the effort.

POETRY, COMPREHENSIBILITY, AND RELEVANCE: MALKOM

At about the same time, a far more elaborate and comprehensive, if somewhat less violent, criticism of Persian poetry came from Mirza Malkom Khan (1833–1908), a controversial advocate of radical social transformation in late nineteenth-century Iran.[50] Malkom's charges have less to do with the social consequences of poetry than with the communicative processes employed in it. The distinction becomes significant because Kermani's rhetoric is ultimately aimed at a thematic opposition between the existing poetry and the ideal one, whereas Malkom concerns himself first and foremost with the notion of an ideal poetic language. In other words, he views the medium of poetry as a significant sign of modernity in Persian poetry. Judging by the way his concern has been echoed by successive generations, Malkom's argument must have contained a more effective formulation of the problem of the poetic change. He specifically targets those literary conventions which, in his view, have rendered Persian prose and poetry incomprehensible to vast numbers of readers.

The most detailed example of this occurs in a narrative essay entitled "Sayyahi Guyad" (A Traveler Relates).[51] Here, Malkom depicts a succession of scenes observed by an educated contemporary Iranian residing abroad, perhaps somewhere in Europe, on a return trip to his homeland. Highly concerned with the state of affairs in his country, the expatriate Iranian describes his encounters with different groups of the country's elite. Having left a gathering where he has witnessed an argument between a high-ranking official and a clergyman, he stumbles into some gatherings which he refers to as strange orders of diversely oriented madmen. The madmen all belong to what he terms the Clan of the Crooked Vision (*tayefeh-ye kaj-binan*). They include arithmomancers, astrologers, and poets, a group whom he picks for particular attention.[52] Describing the members of this group as people who "believed that language has not been invented for the purpose of expressing ideas [*ada-ye matlab*] but for the arrangement of rhyming phrases [*tartib-e saj'*]—and for wasting time [*tazyi'-e vaqt*]," he observes:

> In adherence to their creed, this latter species of madmen, known to the people as nonsense-mongers [*yaveh sara*], never sought meaning, whether in speech or in writing. They considered complexity of speech [*eghlaq-e kalam*] the utmost accomplishment, and spent most of their life studying complicated verbiage [*alfaz-e moghlaqeh*]. When they listened to someone, it was not to see what he was saying. Rather, they would want to see what new word [*lafz-e tazeh*] he would utter. . . . The more incomprehensible an utterance, the more highly they would prize it, and when they wanted to praise an author, they would say: "the rascal is so eloquent nobody can understand his writing."
>
> Because they considered rhymed prose the finest of all compositional arts [*sanaye'-e ensha'*], they set themselves no purpose in writing beyond arranging rhymes, and would often weave several lines of nonsense in order to produce a single rhyme. In their writings, wherever the word *vasel* [arrived, reached] occurred, inevitably the word *hasel* [obtained, achieved] would make an appearance in its wake, every *vojud* [being] would be *zijud* [generous], and every *mezaj* [disposition] was *vahhaj* [radiant].[53]

The goal of complexity and the search for rhyme, the narrative argues, has led to two undesirable characteristics in poetic compositions of Iran. First, it has severed all connections between poetry and whatever reality may exist outside it, what in a generation will become the ultimate object of poetry's attention. Second, it has led to a slavish imitation of old poets regardless of their worth, merit, or relevance to the present age. The authority of the past, operating through the memory of the contemporary poet, has produced not poets but poetasters. The expatriate Iranian continues:

> They had a few pat, inherited words [*chand kalameh-ye moʿayyan-e mowrus*] which the entire community of nonsense-mongers had memorized and would use indiscriminately in all their correspondences. Even in the days of the cholera they would write: "your noble missive arrived in the most auspicious of times." And there was none to ask: "You unfair nonsense prattler! if the time of the cholera is the most auspicious of times, then what is the most inauspicious?"

> . . . .

> They had written books that even after the tenth reading one would still be as confounded in understanding the meaning [*dark-e maʿni*], as at first reading. I read a hundred books by them and I found not a single new idea (i.e., content, subject-matter) [*matlab-e tazeh*]. Every page that my eyes chanced upon featured a Joseph lost in the well of some chin-dimple. There were moths of the heart burning in the fire of love; there were snakes of tresses that coiled around the face of the beloved. In every line the poet would drain the goblet, fit the arrows of eyelashes in the bow of eyebrows, and snatch up the polo ball of the forlorn lover's heart with the polo stick of some beloved's tresses.

Moving closer to the purpose at hand, the narrator goes on:

> I saw a thousand qasidas—all in the same manner, and following the same pattern—in which the composer began with a description of the Spring, raced back and forth many times between the mountain and the plain, between the sea and the river until, having survived a thousand adventures, he would finally reach the person of the patron. Then, breathless he would spin rhymes covering everything from the patron's eyelashes to his horse's tail. And in the end, after countless hyperboles [*eghraqha-ye bihad o andazeh*], when he would be stuck in the bottleneck of rhyme [*tangna-ye qafieh*], he would close by imploring the emerald dome to allow, "So long as time shall hold the spheres so tight / So long will patron's life evoke delight [*ta jahan dar zaman nehan bashad / ʿomr-e mamduh javdan bashad*].[54]

The expatriate Iranian remains a silent bystander as poet after poet recites his compositions to the apparent delight of the other participants, each attempting to upstage the preceding one by uttering an even more abstruse series of conceits, metaphors, and allusions. Through his frequent asides, however, we learn of his inability to appreciate the discourse that rouses almost everybody else to enthusiastic praise, and of his outrage at what he calls the absurdity that binds the assembly together. Eventually the narrator gives vent to his pent-up feelings through a surrogate character, described as "a foulmouthed youth" (*javan-e harzeh-dara*). Suddenly leaping from a corner of the assembly, the latter is said to protest thus:

> O you stupid prattlers! What do you understand from such delirious nonsense, and why do you persist so in squandering your own time only to arouse disgust in other people's minds? Are you the enemies of your own time? How much longer will you keep the human imagination enchained in such senseless prattle? How much should the people of this country toil to comprehend what absurdity you mean to utter?
>
> . . . .
>
> Why don't you express yourselves in such a way as to make sense to each other, and add something to your audience's knowledge? What use is there in this knotting of words [*taʿqid-e alfaz*], in this profusion of rhyme [*kesrat-e saj ʿ*], that makes you so vainly labor in vain? Any half-wit with a degree of aptitude in the lexicon can broach words so as to puzzle everyone. Verbal eloquence [*fesahat-e kalam*] does not arise from abstruse expressions. Good composition resides in the clarity of the figures of speech [*safa-ye khialat*] and ease in the comprehension of ideas [*sohulat-e fahm-e matlab*], not in increased verbal absurdities [*ezdiad-e taʿassor-e ʿebarat*] which your authors have produced, and which you have taken, and continue to take, as your models [*sarmashq*].[55]

When the young man begins to relate the assembled poets to their classical predecessors, scorn gives way to oscillation. First, he accuses them of slavishly following in their footsteps without questioning the efficacy of their imitation: "Have you ever questioned your classical authors," he asks, "saying 'O silly scribe! O personless poetaster! O hypocritical hack! Why do you squander your time on such absurdities and heap upon mankind such platitude?' " A moment later, however, the young man seems to reconsider his view of the tradition inherited by contemporary poets. Says he:

> You who worship the poet-philosophers of the past [*hokama-ye qodama*], why then do you not follow them in the act of composition? In

every problem you cite them as evidence, but in the art of composition
[*fann-e ensha*], wherein they are indeed masters of the latter-day poets
[*mote'akhkherin*], you reverse their rules. As much as they insisted on the
clarity and ease of expression, you strive for obscurity and complexity of
composition.

Turning to an enunciation of the path poets ought to take inevitably
brings in the comparative perspective, as it did in Akhundzadeh and Kermani's discourses. In Malkom's writing this view is mediated through the
concept of translation. The foulmouthed youth continues:

> In all languages, words are subordinated to meanings [*loghat tabe'-e
> ma'ni ast*]. But you subordinate your meaning to wordplay, and in expres-
> sion often transgress your original intention just so you can follow the rules
> of rhyming prose. . . . Ideas must be expressed in such a way as to allow a
> piece of writing to preserve its good compositional attributes [*mohassenat-e
> ensha*], whatever the language into which it is translated. You are unaware
> of the ugliness of your writings because you have, since your childhood,
> grown accustomed to broaching together absurdities. However, if you were
> to read the translation of your own writings in other languages, and would
> contemplate their meanings without regard to the rhyme, then you would
> realize what nonsense you have woven together.[56]

Malkom's episode of "The Assembly of the Poets" gathers together the
diverse strands we have been following throughout this chapter. Before analyzing the position enunciated here, however, I would like to examine the
rhetorical process through which he attempts to subvert the traditional practice of poetry. I conclude this chapter by highlighting the significance of the
statement about translatability as an esthetic criterion. In this way, I hope
first to work toward an appreciation of the relative cohesiveness of the vision
enunciated by the nineteenth-century reformists. Second, by delineating the
relationship between their activity and that of the poets who inhabit the same
social space in the first decades of the twentieth, I hope to justify my contention that the emergence of a modern poetry in Iran constituted a social process to which successive generations contributed.

The episode I have cited in some detail occupies an important position
within a larger text, namely Malkom's "Sayyahi Guyad" (A Traveler Relates).
An analysis of it will have to take into account that larger text as well as the
internal rhetorical, dialogic, and structural features of the episode itself. As
an expatriate Iranian on a visit to his homeland, the narrator of "A Traveler
Relates" assumes from the beginning the posture of an outsider. He is guided

by his friend to the gathering of several "strange orders," all of which are said to belong to the Clan of the Crooked Vision. The assembly of the poets constitutes the third in a chain of social situations viewed from this particular perspective—that is, an outsider's viewpoint. Before entering the assembly of the poets, the traveler and his friend had visited a group of men who would cure physical ailments with the aid of arithmomancy and another group in which members would deduce the fate of the people with reference to the conjunction of the planets.

Juxtaposed to such practices as magic medicine and astromancy, the reference to poetry becomes marked in social terms. Like those practices, poetry as it exists is related to superstition, an association which is reiterated toward the end of the young man's protest. To align the practice of poets with those of the hack doctor and the stargazer, in other words, strongly implicates them in the social ills of which Iranians are becoming increasingly aware. Like those "unscientific" practices, poetry can then be blamed for the country's backwardness. Malkom's strategy in this juxtaposition helps to place the text's ultimate meaning and message in the context not just of the need for esthetic innovation but, more pressingly, of a comprehensive project of social, political, and cultural reform. Poetry, as it is described in the episode, is seen as desperately in need of change.

Similarly, the encounter between the "foulmouthed youth" and the assembled poets can be viewed as epitomizing a larger social confrontation between the forces of cultural rejuvenation and those of the status quo. Just as clinging to medical practice in the fashion of the medieval doctor or continued adherence to the geocentric view of the universe signifies ignorance of the scientific achievements of modern times, thereby testifying to a society's backwardness, so does writing poetry in the manner of the old poets. At the same time, the two notions which the poets of the Literary Return Movement had combined into a single attitude toward their poetic tradition are being separated from one another. Respect for the old masters need not give rise to a feeling that the moderns should adopt them as models for their own practice. It is possible to honor Avicenna while accepting the fact that the theory of the four humors has been superseded. And an affirmation of the Copernican view of the universe does not necessarily mean denying the fact that Ptolemaic cosmology was once valid. By the same token, poetry, as it was practiced in the system of poetic composition used by classical poets, can and must be changed in Iran as it has in Europe. Any practice based on the contrary assumption signals ignorance of a principle as manifest as that of scientific change. The foulmouthed youth's expression of dislike for the compositions he has just heard is based, in short, on a relational assumption of poetry's relevance. What makes possible the extension of that feeling from the world of science to the universe of poetic discourse is Malkom's strategic placement of the text which contains it.

The cause for the stagnation of Persian poetry is revealed by the closed, clublike nature of the assembly. Cultural insularity has not allowed any outside interference in the workings of the poetic tradition. Throughout the exchanges that take place among the poets, the assembly remains unaware of the presence of the young man and the narrator-traveler. In the young man's soliloquy against the assembled poets the brunt of the attack is on exactly the poetic characteristics and tendencies most cherished by men like Qa'ani. When he tells the poets that they would realize the absurdity of their work were they to see their poems translated, he is really suggesting a new criterion, one which would begin to open up the closed circle of poetic production in the Persian language. Thus, the soliloquy reflects the young man's view of the consequences of insularity not just for poetry but for other spheres of cultural activity as well.

Viewing the assembly as a simulacrum of Iranian society adds dimensions to its ultimate meaning which lie beyond my concern here. Suffice it to say that by telling the story of the disruption of the peaceful gathering of a few poets engaged simultaneously in mutual admiration on the surface and professional rivalry underneath, Malkom's traveler relates the account of a multifaceted historical confrontation between the new intellectuals trying to set forth the paradigm called "Europe" and the tradition-bound poets who continued to draw on native esthetic resources for reform. Bent on refashioning every aspect of Iranian social life along European lines, the former adopted a discursive strategy which included assaults on those social institutions and practices which they perceived as obstacles on their path. Typically, the attack included charges of anachronism, ignorance, or corruption. Those involved in such institutions were customarily accused of perpetuating the status quo in order to shore up their sagging social status and power. The foulmouthed youth's litany of charges against the assembled poets must be situated ultimately within that larger discourse.

The speech itself is worth analyzing for its rhetoric. The young man's initial question, "What do you mean by such delirious nonsense?" clearly contains its own answer: nothing. That answer is reinforced, and the accusation further advanced, by a second interrogative: "Why do you persist so in squandering your own time and arousing disgust in other people's minds?" Far from being an inquiry about an observed phenomenon, the question underlines not just the uselessness but the positive harm of the assembly's proceedings by moving from the charge of idleness to that of causing aversion in others. That the predicted reaction of "the others" (*digaran*) is placed in dramatic contrast to the response just observed by the speaker (the audience express their enthusiastic appreciation of each performance loudly) serves to place the assembled poets not just at greater distance from the people outside but in opposition to them. In this way, the participants in the assembly are depicted as opposed to an imaginary "real" poet and a "true" audience for poetry. Thus emerges an "other" audience, present somewhere outside the assembly, yearning for a "different" kind of poetry. The "real" audience of "true" poetry is thus envisioned as desiring the opposite of the incomprehensible nonsense recited and applauded in the assembly of the poets.

The second question—"how much longer are you going to . . . ?"—is even more rhetorically charged. The speaker does not really think that the day will come when the individuals assembled here might be persuaded to write the kind of poetry which he and the people he presumes to speak for would approve of. However, characterizing the activity at hand as inhibiting the human imagination is tantamount to defining the true poetry as that which would enable the human imagination to soar. At the same time, this contains a tacit acknowledgment of the power of poetry, an utterance which can as well lead to liberation as to enchainment. The idea of a new kind of poetry is tied not to a definable set of characteristics, but to a desirable outcome.

As in Akhundzadeh and Kermani, here too, an assumption regarding the presence of a collective entity outside the poet and the critic forms part of the discursive strategy. Malkom's traveler and the young protestor both speak of a "people" who want to understand what poets say, but who are repulsed by a combination of unimportant or frivolous content and abstruse or cumbersome language. When they do take the trouble, they are disappointed to find their poets' utterances to contain nothing meaningful. The rhetorical question, "How long should the people suffer to comprehend what nonsense you may have meant to express?" already assumes that when people read what passes as poetry in their culture their reward does not match their effort. Significantly, both of the examples the young man cites to illustrate this point contain metaphors of creativity. "What mean you," he asks, presumably referring to some images used in the recitations he has just heard, by "the high-soaring falcon of poetic temper?" (*shahbaz-e boland-parvaz-e tab*ʿ?), and what in the world is "the maiden of speech?" (*dushizeh-ye kalam*?). In effect, he is declaring two central images for the creative imagination, well known in the Persian poetic tradition, to be hollow phrases signifying nothing. In doing so, the foulmouthed youth effectively negates classical modes of conceptualization which allow contemporary poets to view their practice as creative.

It is from this negative stance that the youth turns to a more positive aspect of his idea of poetry. In asking the question, "Why don't you express ideas in such a way that you would understand something of your own words and that you would add something to the knowledge of your audience?" he gives the first indication of a move toward what true poetry ought to be and do. Here the function of poetry is keyed directly to its clarity of expression, a feature of the poetic language. Further on, the youth begins to describe eloquence (*fesahat*) as a quality lying beyond verbal complexities. In his view, beauty of composition resides in simplicity rather than in the sophistication which follows from gaining mastery over an established tradition. By giving new meaning to old words, the youth begins to enunciate an idea of poetic excellence which renders poetry needless of traditional expressive mechanisms. In so doing, he sets out to change the very mode of perception according to which poetry is conceptualized and described in the culture.

With the accusation that the poetry of the assembled poets is incomprehensible to the people, the young agitator moves to the heart of his message. Let us examine that claim through a close reading of the account presented by the expatriate narrator. Obviously, communication does take place among those assembled, both poets and participants, with the notable exception of the expatriate narrator and the foulmouthed youth. We know this because every time a poet recites a piece others respond with cries of adulation and joy, accompanied by sonorous expressions of praise regarding the excellence of the piece just recited. The narrative refers to such responses several times. Thus, even though the traveler-narrator's own account of his experience with the assembly lends credence to the foulmouthed youth's objections, his description undermines the young man's views. He can tell us he is not alone in his inability to understand what the poets say, but can we believe his statement that the people do not understand the kind of poetry recited in the assembly? Nevertheless, the young man is not completely alone in his negative reaction; behind him we have the traveler-narrator who, even though he has read a thousand qasidas, still fails to understand the kind of poetry these poets recite. The conclusion is inescapable: while the statement that "the people" do not understand this kind of poetry cannot be taken at its face value, it remains true that there are individuals who find such compositions incomprehensible. Then there are those, like the traveler-narrator, who even though they may be familiar with the Persian poetry of the past, find the poems recited in the assembly repulsive. To them, it is not this poetry's incomprehensibility, but the obvious absence of a social purpose which appears loathsome.

It is significant in this connection that the foulmouthed youth does not offer any poem of the type of poetry he advocates. He can only describe his ideal of poetry in terms of its opposition to that which is presented in the assembly. We know that the poetry he would like to hear arises out of the desire to communicate with masses of people, that it is inspired by a serious social purpose, and that it is expressed in an uncluttered language. We know further that such a poetry contains new ideas, and that it will favor those ideas over verbal sophistication. We know finally that, because of these characteristics, it will automatically be incorporated into the life of the community. All this is contingent on the poet freeing himself—or herself, if the phrase applies—from poetic conventions of the past. Neither the foulmouthed youth nor the traveler nor even Malkom present a more specific idea of the poetry they seek or offer a textual example of it.

The passion vented in the assembly, like that evident in the writings of Akhundzadeh and Kermani, arises ultimately as a consequence of the presence, in a single society, of individuals with irreconcilable views of poetry and of their native poetic culture. The social contestation that the assembly epitomizes points to several common notions that unite the new intellectuals in their contempt for their poetic culture. In the first place, these individuals, unlike the poets they chastise so vehemently, stand in an oppositional relation to the poetic tradition they have inherited. Secondly, wishing to move Iranian society toward a new path,[57] they advance a model of poetic expression which they describe as existing in European societies, but which they do not articulate in any specific way. Finally, they believe that whatever their vision of social change, they will have to enlist the masses of people in their cause if it is to be realized. All this leads them to an inevitable confrontation with those social institutions which look to the tradition itself as a source of cultural renewal. Malkom's episode of the poets' assembly constitutes, in my view, the most comprehensive and coherent formulation of this cultural confrontation in late nineteenth-century Iran as it pertains to poetry.

THE SEARCH FOR AN ALTERNATIVE PERSPECTIVE

Recalling the historical sketch of the Literary Return Movement with which I opened this chapter, we can begin to view the activity of the assembled poets in perspective. As a project for the restoration of originality, simplicity, and greater communicability to the Persian poetic tradition, that movement was premised on the distinction between two periods in the history of Persian literature: a golden age roughly preceding the Mongol and Tartar invasions of the thirteenth and fourteenth centuries, and a period of decline and degeneration following the establishment of the Safavid Dynasty in the sixteenth century when poetry had lapsed into bombast and tinsel. Return Movement poets viewed change in terms of efforts to approximate the compositions of the earlier masters. They did not think it necessary, or even appropriate, to question the tradition's capacity to foster a rejuvenating spirit. The new intellectuals, however, convey a deep-seated ambivalence on the value of the poetic tradition of the Persian language. On the one hand, they seem to express the idea that the classical system of poetic signification and communication is insufficiently expressive of the actual social conditions and, therefore, in need of change. On the other hand, mindful of the glory that various European Orientalists have found in classical Persian poetry, they seek to portray the contemporary practice as a deviation from the norms established by the ancients.

This ambivalence toward the tradition finds its most explicit expression in "A Traveler Relates." At one point, the narrator refers to classical Persian poets as mere "describers" (*vasef*) and "versifiers" (*nazem*), instead of the more culturally respected appellation of "poets," and calls the assembled poets blind imitators of unworthy predecessors. At another, however, he chides them for deviating from the principles the ancients have prescribed through their practice. That, he states, is why they have ended up producing works that, in language as well as in ideas, testify to the very process of decline and degeneration which they wish to reverse.

The desire to recast Persian poetry, motivated by a general agreement about the necessity of poetic change, was accompanied by only the sketchiest idea of the desired end. The emergent notion of Iran as a modern nation-state necessitated the universal approving nod to Ferdowsi since his epic work *The Shahnameh* had been identified as the prime literary text wherein that idea had been deposited. Ferdowsi was judged a poet worthy of emulation not because of any intrinsic difference between his esthetic ideas and those of other classical poets, but because the ideas found in his work fitted the new intellectuals' agenda for cultural reform. But even Ferdowsi's practice was not totally unproblematic. In launching his attack on the poetry of the past, Kermani specifies that Ferdowsi, too, "is not without exaggerations in some places."[58] Naturally, the matter becomes more complicated in the case of the poets less identified with a singular vision or poetic genre. For Akhundzadeh, Sa'di's *Bustan* is a model of the *masnavi* which contemporary practitioners may follow, while Kermani mentions Sa'di as a prime culprit in corrupting the youth of Iran. Akhundzadeh himself seems to have changed his views concerning the merits and faults of certain Iranian poets. Although in his earlier essay he had reluctantly given a niche to Qa'ani, in his later writings he condemns his poetry as being filled with unreal descriptions and unnatural allusions. Clearly, something has changed the new Iranian intellectuals' relationship with the native poetic tradition, submitting their sense of its overall worth and value as well as the relative merit of the individual voices within it to a crisis.

As with Akhundzadeh and Kermani, Malkom's characters attempt to prove the deficiencies of the native modes of poetic expression with reference to contexts outside it. The foulmouthed youth tells the assembled poets that their practice is the reverse of what constitutes a universal norm observed by all the poets in all the languages of the world: the primacy of meaning over the word. He asserts further that the reason why Iranian poets are not revolted by the monstrosities they produce has to do with long-held beliefs and habits inculcated in them since childhood. He concludes that they would surely become aware of the absurdity of their work were they to contemplate the translations of their compositions stripped of all their ornaments.

The reference to translation as a criterion by which a system of poetic signification may measure itself gives a new significance to the above observation. Indeed, it signals the emergence of a new criterion, one developed from outside the system, for evaluating Persian poetry. "The demand for description," Lotman says, "arises at certain moments of the immanent development of a language." That "language," in this case, consists of the emerging discourse aimed at changing the traditional practice of poetry. The "description" taking shape within the esthetic culture of Iran at this time begins to become visible in light of these theoretical observations: the gradual solidification of such formal features as rhyme and meter has given rise to a distorted view of the classics, prevalent among contemporary poets. At the same time, cultural insularity has deprived them of exposure to alternative views of the nature and social function of poetry. The situation does not allow them to see their condition as the intensification of a chronic cultural malady. To remedy it, the new intellectuals propose a heavy dose of exposure to European culture, especially European poetry. Malkom's focus on the issue of comprehensibility also reveals its ultimate significance here. In highly complex semiotic systems, Lotman argues, where there is a constant "tension between understanding and non-understanding, . . . the shift of accent from one pole to another of the opposition corresponds to a particular moment in the dynamic state of the system."[59]

The confrontation between Iranian poets and the new intellectuals was indeed based on divergent "descriptions" of the nature and social function of poetry. While the poets of late nineteenth-century Iranian society conceived of their calling as an artistic craft anchored in an inherited esthetic system, the new intellectuals had come to view poetry as a significant social discourse. Beginning with the assumption that, in Europe, poetry had played a significant part in the Renaissance and the Reformation, the Enlightenment, and the French Revolution, they dreamed of a future poetry in Iran equally capable of instigating passions that could be mobilized to advance the cause of social change. Whereas the poets explored the linguistic resources and structures available to them and set out to prove their worth and their innovative spirit by exploiting the resources of their linguistic and poetic systems even further than had their forebears, the new intellectuals were intent on enlisting the potentialities of poetry in the service of progress. The desire to harness the emotions which only poetry can arouse in the service of their cause appeared to them the first important step along the way to recruiting the masses in their vision of reform and modernization.

Finally, within the episode of the assembly, tension is heightened by the theatricality of the narrative, itself indicative of a strong sense of the audience. The utterances of the assembled poets are incomprehensible not just to the foulmouthed youth but to "the people." They are judged to be irrelevant not simply by the traveler-narrator, but by "the people." Whatever the people may believe about poetry, we know it coincides not with those of the poets but with those of their detractors. In terms of the overall discursive strategy of which this episode is an example, the poets of late nineteenth-century Iran are portrayed as ultimately aligned with the rulers for whose pleasure they would produce all manner of falsehood and absurdity. The implications of such an emerging discourse for the social function of poetry ought to be obvious, and aspiring poets are left with two options. They may side with the rulers, whose power and glory depends on enchaining the masses, or they may side with "the people" and try to give voice to their aspirations and concerns. Malkom has textualized this choice by first elevating the assembly to the status of a sign for the Iranian society, and then by aligning the foulmouthed youth, the traveler-narrator, and himself with the people, an absent presence facing a few poetasters paralyzed in the grip of the tradition.

The assembly, in sum, depicts a complex and layered event, a source of meaning fraught with many implications for literary change. Within it, both the message and the medium communicated by the poets stand in conceptual contrast to that conveyed through the protestations of the expatriate Iranian and his mouthpiece, the foulmouthed youth. Whereas the former recite polished poems in strict adherence to inherited rules and patterned after various classical models, the latter express their meaning in pulsating prose pieces understandable to all who can read and to the many more who may have it read to them. The text conveniently ignores the fact that the poems recited in the assembly drive the participants to applause because the imagery used in them forms part of a heritage shared between poets and their audiences. Instead, the author declares his own ignorance of the shared poetic discourse to be the present social norm, and the assembly's norm to be a survival unfit for his time.

Malkom's discursive strategy of fictionalizing his views on poetry makes his statement far more effective and more expressive than those of all his predecessors and contemporaries, Akhundzadeh and Kermani included. His text contains the reasons why Iranian society ought to rethink its poetry. Yet, by presenting his views in the guise of a travel journal he distances himself from the rhetoric of the youthful protester and the more seasoned traveler-narrator. Acting as buffers, these two personae help to bring the problem of poetry to the fore, each presenting a different layer of it. Like Malkom himself, the narrator takes the view that poetry as it is practiced in his native culture serves no purpose and that readers are beginning to lose their grasp on the system of poetic expression because of their exposure to modern European cultures. For his part, the foulmouthed youth illustrates that concern with an impatience which underlines the urgency of the problem. While both the traveler and the youth advocate a different kind of poetry, their reasons are different. The traveler rejects the contemporary practice of poetry in Iran because he believes it to be old and defunct. The foulmouthed youth, however, simply does not comprehend it. The former believes that no new ideas can be found in it; the latter demands that poetry deal with ideas. In theoretical terms, while to the young man the system of codes on the basis of which classical Persian poetry has traditionally conveyed its message ought to be discontinued because it fails to communicate anything, to the connoisseur of poetry that system ought to change because it cannot communicate any new ideas. Malkom thus distinguishes between the quality of effectiveness, on the one hand, and the prerequisite necessity of comprehensibility, on the other. In this way, Malkom demonstrates the need for change without having to place himself in the position of advocacy or agency, as do Akhundzadeh and Kermani.

As I hope I have demonstrated, from the beginning the poets' assembly assumes the status of a simulacrum for nineteenth-century Iranian society. Like the larger narrative of which it is a part, the vignette of the confrontation between the poets and their detractors presents a likeness of an actual social schism. I believe it also contains a parable of the evolution of the Persian poetic tradition from the beginning to the present. Let us recall that the traveler relates how a succession of poets read their poems to the assembly, each trying to add something to the complexities of the previous speaker. Taken along historical lines, the statement becomes telling indeed as it depicts the unfolding of the dynamics between the poetic tradition and the achievements of individual poets. It is as if each poet, guided by the performances that have preceded his, in the end measures himself and is measured by the distance he has pushed the tradition forward. Against the ever-changing, yet stable background of the tradition, each individual poet both alters and sets the standard for the one that is to follow, at once acting and being acted upon, being a product of the past and a maker of the future. He is, in short, a carrier of social and esthetic forces which we see unfolding in time.

This shrewd treatment of the dynamics of tradition and individual innovation, seen in conjunction with the notion of insularity, leads to one conclusion only: the only way out of the impasse presented by the poetic tradition is to break free from the closed circle of Persian poetic production and circulation and move toward poetic vistas unknown to Persian poets. That position is as much a part of the rhetoric for poetic change in the nineteenth century as it is today. It is implied in Akhundzadeh's insistence that the Persian language has no equivalent for such terms as "*littérature*" and "*poésie.*" It becomes more explicit in Kermani's assertion that the poets of Europe have subordinated poetry to reason. And it finds its fullest expression so far in Malkom's notion of translation as a test of meaning.

The writings of such men as Akhundzadeh, Kermani, and Malkom illustrate the initial stages in an ongoing cultural process by which the desire to reform Iranian culture has submitted the concept of traditional Persian poetry to constant critical revision and reevaluation. As we have seen throughout this chapter, the social reformers of the nineteenth century equated classical Persian poetry with the lyrical tradition in it and stereotyped the latter concept in terms of a pathological obsession with an idealized sense of beauty stylized through analogies based on the beloved's anatomy. On that basis, they described the contemporary practice of poetry as a paralyzing preoccupation with ossified rules of the past. This two-stage process of reduction must be borne in mind throughout the subsequent discussions as I refer to the conventions and expressive mechanisms of classical Persian poetry.

The scenarios I have expounded in this chapter were aimed essentially at the creation of a kind of poetry different from that which could be produced with reference solely to native conventions. Rejecting the position advocated by the poets of the Literary Return Movement, the new intellectuals organized their objections around the way poetry was conceived and the mechanisms and methods by which it was produced. Their various discourses were all predicated on an assumption unprecedented in the millennium-old tradition which formed the poetic heritage of all contemporary Iranian poets: in order to make poetry relevant, useful, and comprehensible, poets had to recognize the insufficiency of the inherited system of poetic codes and move beyond emulating this or that trend or tendency. In terms most often used by the nineteenth-century reformers, life could be breathed into the moribund body of Persian poetry only if the achievements of European poets were incorporated into the native system of poetic signification and communication.[60] The adoption of the poetic practices of Europe would do for Persian poetry what adherence to such European notions as civil and individual liberties, rule of law, and the ideal of democracy would lead to in the Iranian body politic.

The story with which I began this chapter, that of the clash between Qa'ani and Amir-e Kabir, does have something of a happy ending. The prime minister who, we may recall, had threatened to bastinado the poet, is said eventually to have yielded to courtly intercessions on behalf of the poet. Having been told that, in addition to his poetic talents, Qa'ani was proficient in the French language, he reportedly charged him with the task of translating into Persian a French book on botany. Even something of the poet's stipend was paid back to him as compensation for the job.[61] Thus, the weaver of abstruse, offensive, or nonsensical words became the transmitter of practical information and useful knowledge to his compatriots. Meanwhile, the search for a new and different kind of poetry—one that would be judged relevant, useful, and comprehensible—continued unabated, turning from a rhetoric of subversion to the practice of a new generation of poets involved in a real political revolution. That topic will form the focus of my inquiry in the next chapter.

Chapter Two

Poetic Signs and Their Spheres

From the point of view of literary history, the status of much of the poetry written in Iran in the early decades of the twentieth century remains unclear. Terms like *she'r-e mashruteh* (poetry of the constitution) or *she'r-e dowran-e mashruteh* (poetry of the constitutional era)[1] are commonly used to refer in general to the body of poetry written in the early decades of the twentieth century before the predominance of *she'r-e now,* and more specifically to the poetry thematically related to the Constitutional Revolution of 1905–1911. Traditional literary criticism assumes that this poetry is more political, more topical in theme, and more loosely organized in form than the classical lyrical canon. It also notes that this corpus encodes the attitude of the poet toward the sociopolitical events of the time in a way different from what a classical ghazal or qasida would, although it has not elucidated the nature of that difference. Naturally, such descriptions leave aside a whole body of poems which, though produced in that period, may have nothing to do with the events of the Iranian Constitutional Revolution, its causes and consequences. In a more specific sense, "poetry of the constitution" may refer to the ghazals and qasidas composed in the years of that revolution which express support for sociopolitical change in Iran from a democratic, socialistic, or nationalistic stance. As such, the poetry of the constitutional era conforms to traditional formal and generic conventions of classical Persian poetry.

Such designations as the "patriotic qasida" (*qasideh-ye vatani*) or "political ghazal" (*ghazal-e siasi*) also seem to embody similar assumptions.[2] Iranian critics often conceptualize a patriotic qasida as one which harnesses the poetic resources of that classical "poetic type" in the service of new thematic concerns.[3] Instead of expressing praise for the patron, the beloved, or both, the poem is primarily a paean to the motherland. Critics describe the political ghazal as one wherein the poet's sentiments and thoughts about such ideals as liberty, the rule of law, and a constitutional system of government have come to replace his longing for union with the always beautiful, often unyielding beloved.[4] In such conceptualizations, critics have paid little attention to the way in which such substitutions and replacements take place in the text, to the way in which such shifts are received by readers, or to the effects of this redirection of poetic entities on the generic or systemic status of the ghazal or qasida. Naturally, systemic or structural relations between the patriotic qasida and political ghazal of this period and the vast corpus of classical texts which go by the same name, and which are thus altered irreversibly, have remained unexamined, as has the relationship between this poetry and the poetry of later generations. It is my contention that a close analysis of the textual properties, rhetorical strategies, and expressive mechanisms employed in these poems can shed some light on their status within the tradition of Persian poetry and on the formal and generic divisions which they affirm and alter simultaneously. Persian literary history has been so ambiguous that we need to see the precise part these texts have played in the process of poetic change. That task occupies my attention in this chapter, and I intend to approach it through an extensive exploration of the textual properties of two poems—a qasida and a ghazal—written during this period.

A NEW VISION FOR POETRY, A NEW APPROACH TO ANALYSIS

Within the literary culture of early twentieth-century Iran, we witness a number of basic tenets which form the foundation of Iranians' view of their literary past, of the nature of the contemporary poet's task, and on the shape of the poetry to come. First, the literary historical view initiated and advanced through the Literary Return Movement is solidified and inscribed on the cultural space: Persian poetry is seen as having gone through a golden age followed by a period of decline and decadence. Second, this perception is combined with the one initiated and advanced by the new intellectuals, namely, that in Europe literature has played an important part in the steady march of modern civilization. The contrast that thus emerges provides the motive force behind the desire for poetic change. All attempts at giving expression to patriotic, progressive, or democratic aspirations in poetry are interpreted as a welcome departure from an ossified tradition and part of the drive toward a new kind of poetry. In a great many essays on poetry, mostly published in the burgeoning press of the constitutional era, an expression of these sentiments is followed by appeals to poets to inculcate in their readers the ideals of liberty, constitutionalism, and the rule of law.[5] In these exhortations, we begin to see a vision of poetry that at times goes beyond thematic concerns to address features of the poem which have to do with the poet's conception of his craft. This emerging vision commonly relates to the manner in which poems are made, to the poem's diction and tone, and to the set of relations possible between poets and readers. Instances are too many to enumerate. I shall confine myself to two examples recorded by two astute observers, one Iranian, the other Western.

The first occurs in an unsigned article, perhaps written by ʿAli-Akbar Dehkhoda, entitled "*Tajdid-e Hayat-e Adabi*" (Literary Revival), published in the 27th issue of *Sur-e Esrafil,* dated April 29, 1908.[6] The article opens with the statement that poetry is the highest of the literary arts and that the literature of every nation provides the best measure of its past advancement or decline and the best guide to its future prosperity. It then presents a sketch of Persian—which it calls "Iranian"—literary history: despite the general decline that marks the poetry of the recent centuries, the best poets have always met their social responsibility by instilling morality in the populace, by spreading knowledge of the human sciences, and by attempting to moderate the excesses of power. The essay then reiterates the position which by now has become the standard narrative of literary history in Iran:

> Nor is this idea concealed from anyone, that in the past four or five centuries when the Voltaires, the Rousseaus, the Diderots, the Schillers, the Bacons, the Pushkins, the Chateaubriands, the Hugos and thousands of other men of letters and poets have enriched the literary universe of the European nations, raising the standard of prose and poetry to the level of Raphael's paintings and Michaelangelo's sculptures by embodying in them precise human thoughts and expressing through them delicate truths of existence, our literature in general and our poetry in particular have remained stagnant or have declined, and our men of letters have engaged themselves only in slavish imitation of the classics and in juggling the words of the classical poets [*shoʿara-ye kelasik*] back and forth.
>
> And this stagnation or decline, which without any notable exception has continued for five centuries in Iran, has, with the clarity of a mirror, made manifest the literary demise and moral decadence of the nation.[7]

The article next mentions several men, including Malkom, who have prepared the ground for a literary revival, and then points to a new direction deemed appropriate for contemporary poetry in Iran. To illustrate the nature of this direction, it features a qasida by Seyyed Nasrollah, a little-known poet, as evidence that "for the first time our poems have changed their approach to expression [*maslak va tariqeh-ye ada*], thus erecting a new structure [*bena-ye jadid*] on the foundation of fresh principles [*bar bonyan-e osuli tazeh*]." This the article welcomes not just as an excellent political poem but one heralding a new kind of poetic expression. The qasida that follows adheres to all the norms of the classical genre with no innovations in the metric system, in rhyme, nor in other formal and generic specifications. Thematically, too, it deals with a subject matter frequently treated in the classical courtly qasida, namely the poet's advice to the patron. However, this time the advice, rather than being disguised as the praise of any real or desired virtues, is cast in the form of a warning.

Nasrollah begins his qasida by chiding Mohammad-ʿAli Shah, the penultimate Qajar king, for turning his back on the national assembly or parliament. Cataloguing all the aberrations that have marked the king's reign, the speaker recommends that the king should "read again the history of Europe's revolutions." He closes by reminding the king to stand firm against foreign influences, to be truthful to his subjects, and to mobilize them in eradicating all traces of evil. Unlike the classical panegyric where advice is issued in as subtle a way as the poet is capable of, Nasrollah's advice appears direct and dire. By stressing the moral superiority of the poet, the poem seems to reverse the traditional relationship that obtains within the classical qasida between the poet and the patron. Moreover, it focuses on problems of sociopolitical moment, cataloguing actual events, and giving vent to real concerns. The poem thereby creates a textual environment markedly different from that of the classical qasida. It also flaunts its imagery of a society within which the poet, the patron, and the reader are situated, a contrast with the tradition of the occasional panegyric wherein the poet typically envisions a direct relationship between himself and the patron.

The article's enthusiastic endorsement of the poem as evidence of a literary revival can thus be seen as an attempt to inscribe significance to the poem's tone and imagery, and to relate thematic difference to these. The text which has violated the norm in one aspect of the traditional practice is seen as standing in contrast with the whole of that tradition. The tendency to interpret one set of textual properties in terms of another and to transfer the impression across the various systems which comprise a poetic text constitutes a common property of semiotic systems. Lotman attributes the rise of this tendency to heightening ambivalence, a cultural-semiotic phenomenon intimately connected with a semiotic system's state of simultaneous ossification and softening:

> The state of ambivalence arises in two possible ways: as the relationship
> of a text to a system now not operative, but preserved in cultural memory,
> . . . and as the relationship of a text to two mutually unconnected systems,
> when, in the light of one system, the text is permitted, but, in the light of
> the other, forbidden.[8]

Both of the features delineated here can be seen in the rhetoric presented in
the article that introduces the poem. The qasida in question is classical in all
its formal features, and is recognized as such. In its rhetorical posture, however, it alters the norms associated with that genre. In other words, it relates
differently to the system of poet-patron relationship than it does to the system of expressive devices. It therefore qualifies as a qasida, yet it is seen as a
sign of literary revival. The vision presented in the article, in other words,
diagnoses the first set of relations, namely those that exist in the poem's
rhetorical posture, as permitted, and ignores a second set—that is, those that
pertain to the poem's formal and generic status. The difference between this
qasida and a stereotyped notion of the classical Persian qasida thus carries
over to the system of expressive devices as well, and the poem is not seen just
as rhetorically different, but as totally new.

The second text I cite as evidence of a nascent vision of poetry comes
from Edward Granville Browne, still the most influential source of ideas
about the poetry of the period. In "The Translator's Preface" to *The Press
and Poetry of Modern Persia* (1914), Browne criticizes the Western scholars
who "constantly assert that there is no modern Persian poetry worth reading." He attributes this "pernicious error" to a combination of political mal-
ice and sheer ignorance and emphatically asserts that poetry is alive and well
in Persia. "In fact," he observes, contemporary Persians have shown great
poetic vitality in the years of the Constitutional Revolution. Under happier
circumstances, he concludes, this poetry "would, I am convinced, have ultimately effected moral and material regeneration of the country." Browne also
uses the mirror metaphor to explain the relationship between political events
and poetic themes:

> Of this renewed vitality the modern Press and Poetry are a reflection
> and manifestation, and I venture to think that neither the originality nor
> the merit of the literary products of the Persian Revolution, whether in prose
> or verse, will be denied by any competent and unprejudiced observer. True
> literature is the mirror of contemporary thought and sentiment, and the
> alternating phases of hope and despair of the Persians during the last eight
> years (1905–1913) are well reflected in the ephemeral literature of that period.[9]

The degree of correspondence Browne perceives between "true litera-ture" and political developments indicates a new conception of the social status of poetry. First, his juxtaposition of prose and verse, poetry and the press, forces attention on the verisimilitude with which poetry comes to "re-flect" the sociopolitical reality. Then, his use of topicality as the sign of a new mode of poetic production highlights the difference between contemporary poetry and the classical practice. As a result, he seems to recognize the new proclivity to give poetic expression to the emotions that sociopolitical events utilize as the sign of an emerging poetic practice. Thus, engagement with sociopolitical issues of the time is seen as an important source of vitality of contemporary poetry. Some Westerners maintain there is no modern poetry to speak of in contemporary Persia because they expect to see compositions similar to those of the Persian classics they know. Beyond his acknowledg-ment of a difference between contemporary practice and classical composi-tions, Browne anchors his perception of the distinction in the use of an idiomatic diction and the novel images of the contemporary poets.

Lotman's notion of ambivalence in semiotic systems allows us to system-atize such observations. He articulates textual manifestations of the notion of difference or norm-violation in terms of specific lexical, semantic, syntactic, and rhetorical features of a literary text. An ambivalent text, in Lotman's view, is one in which each of these systems may be based on different grounds, use concurrently different elements, and relate to one another in different ways. In other words, a poem can be called ambivalent when the co-*existence* and co-*operation* of various systems, relations, and elements can be demonstrated in it. In terms of literary history, Lotman interprets the presence of ambivalent texts as the sign of an opening up of the literary system in preparation for a dynamic leap. This in turn gives rise to diffuse boundaries, blurred lines, and indeterminate statuses, signaling an intensified desire for innovation. An understanding of the relations that govern an am-bivalent literary structure, therefore, constitutes a crucial part of the apprecia-tion of the process of esthetic change. At the same time, Lotman is explicit about the need to move beyond conceptualization of innovation in terms only of ruptures with the past: "If a text does not sustain the memory of the traditional construction," he states in *The Structure of the Artistic Text,* "its innovativeness will no longer be perceived."[10]

I propose to reduce the scope and range of these theoretical notions in order to apply them to a rather specific set of textual relations. Moreover, rather than pursuing the sources of those innovations in linguistic and cul-tural spaces beyond the texts themselves, I limit myself to a discussion of textual loci of innovation. In doing so, I assume the presence of an expanding discursive universe, forged and fostered through a system of social communication which includes political, journalistic, and other social activities around the texts under analysis. Clearly, whatever figures in a poet's encoding strategies is rooted in this universe and determined by it. Similarly, at the reception end, I assume that the universe of discourse determines how readers decode poetic messages. The specific operations of this discursive environment may in turn be related to reading in European languages or translation from those languages, to the convergence of literary and nonliterary speeches, and to the dictates of a growing audience for poetry, among a variety of other contextual factors.[11]

A second set of my assumptions has to do with certain inherent capacities of ambivalent texts. I maintain that texts in which old and new elements cohabit the same space and cooperate in the production of meaning can open the system of literary signification and communication to greater changes. This is so because, within the text, changes in one system, such as the lexical, begin to affect other systems, allowing them to be experienced slightly differently by readers who absorb the text as a unitary structure. Eventually, differences in one system contribute not just to the perception of a difference in other systems, but also to the way the text as a whole is received. Thus, departures from traditional usages in a single system make it possible for the poem to begin to modify the reader's perception of the other systems operating in the text. Similarly, deviations from existing norms in one text prepare the ground for further, more systematic or substantial revisions in the total system of poetic production, and consequently the greater opening-up of the entire tradition. Obviously, without the kind of analytical tools that would reveal the changes that reside in the text, we cannot understand the total impact of textual innovations.

It follows then that an analysis of the ways in which the functions of a poem's linguistic devices differ from those of the same devices used in more traditional—and therefore less ambivalent—poems may lead stage by stage to fresh insights into the very process of poetic change. In the first place, analysis of individual texts reveals the ways in which poets seek to express their desire to be innovative. Secondly, the study of individual innovations viewed in conjunction with one another points to a fresh understanding of how individual innovations contribute to greater changes in diverse aspects of the system. Finally, considering accumulated change along the diachronic dimension enables us to explain how individual innovations in various elements eventually lead to the change in the system of esthetic interaction. Any attempt at understanding the process of literary change in terms independent of personal proclivities must therefore begin with analyses of single textual entities. For my part, I hope to show the variety of departures from the traditional expressive system of classical Persian poetry through the most illustrative examples of ambivalent texts in the poetry of early twentieth-century Iran. I have selected for that purpose one qasida and one ghazal, which I think best serve that purpose. The analysis of these two poems form the focus of my work in the rest of this chapter.

A "POLITICAL" QASIDA: DEHKHODA'S "REMEMBER . . ."

'Ali-Akbar Dehkhoda's (1880–1955) famous poem best known by its refrain "Yad Ar . . ." (Remember . . .) is the first poem I offer for close consideration. A *mosammat* in form—therefore an esteemed variety of the qasida genre[12]—and an elegy in content, "Remember . . ." has since its composition been felt to be "different" from the traditional practice of the time, both in terms of the qasida genre and of the elegiac mode.[13] However, that difference has never been textually demonstrated. The poet himself seems to have taken pride in his accomplishment; he has called it "on par with the first rank of European poems."[14] Many critics, too, have praised it as an excellent composition with "strong traces of European influence" and as an early "specimen of modernist poetry of Iran" and "an example of the poet's innovative talent and delicacy of taste."[15] The poem commemorates the martyrdom of Mirza Jahangir Khan Shirazi, the principal editor of the constitutionalist newspaper *Sur-e Esrafil,* executed on June 24, 1908, by the order of Mohammad-'Ali Shah. As his close friend and collaborator, Dehkhoda wrote the poem after he fled to Europe, there to establish himself—and his newspaper—in Switzerland. It first appeared in the third and last issue of *Sur-e Esrafil* published in Yverdon, Switzerland, on March 8, 1909.[16] Here is the text of the poem, followed by my literal translation:

Ay morgh-e sahar cho in shab-e tar
bogzasht ze sar siah-kari
vaz nafheh-ye ruhbakhsh-e ashar
raft az sar-e khoftegan khomari
bogshud gereh ze zolf-e zar-tar
mahbubeh-ye nilgun 'emari
yazdan beh kamal shod padidar
v-ahriman-e zeshtkhu hesari
yad ar ze sham '-e mordeh yad ar

Ay munes-e yusof andar in band
ta'bir-e 'ayan cho shod to ra khab

del por ze shaʿaf lab az shekar khand
mahsud-e ʿadu beh kam-e ashab
rafti bar-e yar o khish o payvand
azad-tar az nasim o mahtab
z-an k-u hameh sham ba to yek chand
dar arezu-ye vesal-e ahbab
akhtar beh sahar shemordeh yad ar

chon bagh shavad dobareh khorram
ay bolbol-e mostmand-e meskin
v-az sonbol o suri o separgham
afagh negar-khaneh-ye chin
gol sorkh o beh rokh ʿaraq ze shabnam
to dadeh ze kaf qarar o tamkin
z-an now gol-e pishres keh dar gham
na-dadeh beh nar-e showq taskin
az sardi-ye day fesordeh yad ar

Ay hamrah-e tih-e pur-e ʿemran
bogzasht cho in senin-e maʿdud
v-an shahed-e naghz-e bazm-e ʿerfan
benmud cho vaʿd-e khish mashhud
v-az mazbah-e zar cho shod beh kayvan
har sobh shamim-e ʿanbar o ʿud
z-an k-u beh gonah-e qowm-e nadan
bar badieh jan sepordeh yad ar

chon gasht ze now zamaneh abad
ay kudak-e dowreh-ye talaʾi
v-az taʿat-e bandegan-e khod shad
begreft ze sar khoda khodaʾi
nah rasm-e eram nah esm-e shaddad
gel[17] bast zaban-e jaj-khaʾi
z-an kas keh beh nuk-e tigh-e jallad
maʾkhuz beh jorm-e haq-setaʾi
paymaneh-ye vasl khordeh yad ar[18]

(O bird of the dawn! when this dark night
has put aside its black deeds,
and at the life-giving breath of the dawn
slumber has departed from the heads of the sleepers,
when the beloved of the indigo throne

has loosened knots from her golden tresses,
God in His perfection has become manifest,
and the evil-natured Ahriman has withdrawn to its citadel,
remember the dead candle, remember.

O friend of Joseph in this bondage!
when the truth of your dream has become evident to you,
when, your heart full of joy, your lips full of sweet laughter,
envied by your foes, fulfilled as your friends might desire,
you are gone to the arms of your loved ones and your kinsmen
freer than the breeze and the moonlight,
remember him who for a while through nights
of longing for union with the loved ones
sat with you counting the stars.

When the garden turns green again,
O poor, distraught nightingale!
and the landscape becomes like a Chinese painting gallery,
with hyacinths, oleander, and marjoram,
when the rose has turned red, dewdrops like sweat on its face,
when you have grown restless and unyielding,
remember the budding rose, bloomed before its time,
which, before it could tame the flame of desire,
withered in sorrow at the chill of winter.

O companion of the son of Emran in the desert!
when these numbered years are passed,
and that choice witness of the feast of wisdom
has made manifest His promise,
when every morning, from the golden altar
the scent of ambergris and aloe has risen to the heavens,
remember him who, yearning for a glimpse of the promised land,
has, for the sin of an ignorant people,
yielded up his life in the desert.

When times have turned propitious once again,
O child of the Golden Age!
and God, gladdened by the obedience of His servants
has resumed His divinity,
when there remains not the fashion of Eram nor the name of Shaddad,
when mud has stopped the tongue of spite,
remember him who, for the crime of praising the truth

has drunk the draught of union
from the point of the headsman's sword.)[19]

Exploring some of the poem's major systems—rhetorical, lexicoseman-
tic, structural—in search of specific points of departure from the traditional
methods of making poetic signs will enable us to see how the poet has recast
the various linguistic resources to serve the specific purposes occasioned by
the poem's theme. We may thus observe the choices the poet has made
among the diverse formal, generic, and thematic antecedents potentially
available to him at the time of composition. His manipulation of the linguistic and poetic options at his disposal can then be related to his desire to direct
the poetic tradition toward those usages that best serve his specific purposes.

It is important initially to clarify the immediate context surrounding the
poem's composition and those contexts within which it was presented to its
original audience as well as to subsequent generations of readers. When it
first appeared in *Sur-e Esrafil,* the untitled text of "Remember . . ." was
headed by the following caption: "The testament [*vasiyyat-nameh*] of my
peerless friend [*dust-e yeganeh-ye man*], the offering of an unworthy brother
[*baradari bivafa*] to that most holy and high spirit [*ruh-e aqdas-e aʿla*]."[20]
Years later, Dehkhoda related the circumstances of the poem's composition
in some detail. Then, some decades after the poet's death, this narrative
found its way into his *Divan* as an additional prologue to the poem. In the
1981 edition of Dehkhoda's *Divan,* that narrative, placed next to the original
caption, precedes the text of the poem:

> On the twenty-second day of Jemad-al-ula, 1326 lunar [June 22, 1908],
> the late Mirza Jahangir Khan Shirazi (may God's blessing be upon him),
> one of the two principals of *Sur-e Esrafil,* was arrested by the cossacks of
> Mohammad-ʿAli Shah, and taken to the Bagh-e Shah. There, on the twenty-
> fourth day of the same month, he was strangled with a rope.
>
> Twenty-seven or twenty-eight days later, several of the freedom-seekers,
> myself included, were exiled from Iran. And after a few months, under the
> tutelage of the late blessed Abol-Hasan Khan Moʿazed al-Saltaneh Pirnia,
> grounds were prepared for the newspaper *Sur-e Esrafil* to be published in
> Yverdon, Switzerland.
>
> During this period, one night I saw the late Mirza Jahangir Khan in a
> dream. Dressed in a white attire (which it was his habit to wear in Tehran),
> he said to me: "Why did you not say: 'He fell young' [*chera nagofti u javan
> oftad*]?" From this phrase I understood [*az in ʿebarat chonin fahmidam*] that
> he was saying: why have you not spoken or written of my death anywhere?
> And instantly in my sleep this sentence came to my mind: "Remember the

dead candle, remember" [*yad ar ze shamʿ-e mordeh yad ar*]. In such a state I awoke, lighted the lamp, and wrote three stanzas of the following *mosammat* before the dawn had approached. The next day I corrected the writings of the previous night, and added two other stanzas to it. It was printed in the first issue of *Sur-e Esrafil,* published at Yverdon in Switzerland.[21]

Detailing a dream-dialogue between the poet and his deceased friend, this prologue already renders the meaning of the caption cited before more specific, particularly the poet's designation of the poem as a testament (*vasiy-yat-nameh*). The poem is therefore intended to be seen as Jahangir's posthumous will, its words conceived initially as spoken by the martyr and addressed to his friend and colleague who still lives and can speak. However, critics have from the beginning missed this significant shift in the subject position and its rhetorical implications; the fact that it is the martyred journalist, not the exiled poet, who utters the poem's words has gone totally unnoticed. Browne, for instance, has rendered the Persian word *vasiyyat-nameh* into English as "in memory of," thereby collapsing the double-layered status of the text—first, as the words spoken by the dead journalist to the living poet, and then as those related by the poet to his readers. In his rendition the poem depicts Dehkhoda as the sole speaker and sender of the poem's message.[22] Similarly, Yusofi, who presents a pithy analysis of the poem, takes no notice of it as the utterance of the martyred journalist.[23]

At any rate, it is worth emphasizing that the initial caption and the later prose prologue construct a fiction crucial to our understanding of the rhetorical situation the poem depicts. According to that fiction, the poem consists, on one primary level at least, of words spoken by a person different from the poet, a persona. As a speech by the executed journalist to his friend containing the request to remember the dead candle, the poem becomes self-referential, closed, and retrospective. It is Dehkhoda the poet who, through the act of composition, turns that request into an outward-looking, open, and prospective discourse. Structurally, the phrase that most directly links the dream to the poem is that which comes to the poet's mind as a result of his martyred interlocutor's reproachful question. When Jahangir's apparition asks the dreaming Dehkhoda why he has not spoken of his death, the latter thinks: "Remember the dead candle, remember!" This emphatic imperative gives the poem its central theme and is recorded verbatim at the end of the first stanza. The poet tells us that he interpreted the question "Why did you not say: 'He fell young'?" as his friend's admonition that he had not recorded the death anywhere. Rhetorically then the admonition "Why did you not say: 'He fell young'?" and the imperative "Remember the dead candle!" are both spoken by the martyred journalist. When this same imperative sentence turns into the refrain in a poem written by Dehkhoda and addressed to all readers of all present and coming generations, it assumes a public status absent from Jahangir's utterance. The negative interrogative "Why did you not . . . ?" has now been turned into a positive, emphatic imperative which as the poem unfolds gathers momentum through repetition. The transformation, too, lends power to the poet's focusing on the act of remembrance as a gesture performed on the public, political scene. Not only is it good and proper that those who fall in a popular political cause be remembered by their surviving comrades but also that the memory should be transmitted to others who pursue and cherish similar ideals, especially after the shared ideal has been realized and the "child of the Golden Age" has arrived in "the promised land." In the political culture of modern Iran, this is the first time a fallen hero is celebrated in so public a manner.[24]

Theoretically, then, the poem in its initial conception as a dual utterance attributable at once to Jahangir and to Dehkhoda, offers an explicit illustration of what Bakhtin envisions as the dialogic nature of all acts of verbal communication. "All utterance," he maintains, "always already implies an interlocutor." Bakhtin concludes that all verbal activity belongs not to the unique subject but to the social environment of which the individual is always already a part:

> The motivation of our action, the attainment of self-consciousness (and self-consciousness is always verbal; it always leads to the search for a specific verbal complex), is always a way of putting oneself in relation to a given social norm; it is, so to speak, a socialization of the self and of its action. Becoming conscious of myself, I attempt to see myself through the eye of another person, of another representative of my social group or of my class.[25]

The signifying structures through which this basic sociality is expanded are constructed in such a way as to strengthen the sense of camaraderie between the speaker and the listener. This in turn sharpens the opposition the poet presents between the sociopolitical environment in which the martyred journalist has been deprived of life and a future age when his ideals shall be fulfilled and himself remembered. To achieve the first objective—that is, the underlining of the unity of purpose between the journalist and the poet which is later generalized to the relationship between the poet and his readers—the poem uses in the first four stanzas four pairs of culturally marked signs to illustrate the kind of relationship which binds the two interlocutors together: bird of the dawn and candle, Joseph and his cellmate, the nightingale and the rose, Moses and his companions in exodus. In perfect parallelism, the poem uses four sets of opposing signs that communicate the contrast between the conditions under which the martyr should be remembered and those under which he has lost his life: night and day, exile and homeland, winter and spring, desert and the promised land. These pairs of culturally recognizable binary oppositions serve to emphasize the contrast between the present and the future. The resultant perception is then literalized in the final stanza where, as we shall see, poetic effect is achieved primarily through phrases which, even though they convey essentially the same sets of relations, present explicit syntheses between traditional poetic signs and new ones. In short, we have here a clear instance of the cohabitation of old and new elements in a single textual space.

Within that overall structure, the locus for the development of the theme of remembrance shifts between the two contexts of nature and history and propels the poem along two distinct dimensions, the spatial and the temporal, toward an increasingly public realm. Thus, the figure of Jahangir, having been initially concretized through the image of the dead candle, is subsequently turned into an abstraction and generalized in two different contexts: that of myth (Joseph's cellmate and Moses' desert companion) and that of nature (a dead candle in the sun and an early rose withered in springtime). As the poem unfolds, each of the two contexts expands the situation at hand along some dimension. The singing of the nightingale in springtime, envisioned as the act of remembering the early blooming rose now withered, will last as long as human society can recall the fate of the journalist strangled by a despotic monarch. Similarly, the return of Joseph to Canaan and that of Moses and his people to the promised land exceed, by their sheer mythical force, the dimension of the events which the poem seeks to record. But by linking the event of Jahangir's execution to these natural and mythical occurrences, the poem magnifies the significance of the event beyond all literal domain.

At the same time, the poem's vision is realized through the certainty with which its words are infused. Both in Jahangir's request to Dehkhoda and in the poet's injunction to posterity, the speakers ask their audience to remember something not if but when certain conditions have passed and their opposites have come to prevail. By tying a vision of the ideal future to such natural certainties as morning sunrise and the springtime rejuvenation of the garden, the poem presents the fulfillment of its speaker's desire as the inevitable reality of the future. The same effect is produced along the axis of time, thereby redoubling the force behind the vision. Just as Joseph did return to Canaan and the Jews did arrive in the promised land, the golden age will, most certainly, dawn in the poet's beloved country. United as they are in their vision of the future, however, the poet and his comrade differ in the reality of their present circumstances. While the comrade "has drunk the draught of union"—a phrase signifying salvation and union with God—the poet is left to suffer through the miseries of night, winter, bondage, and desert.

Thus, as readers, we experience the dual relationship: unity of vision and contrast in actual position. This dual relationship is first foreshadowed in the caption where the poet refers to himself as an "unworthy brother" and to his martyred friend as a "most holy and high spirit." Here, martyrdom is seen as an honor; the journalist has attained it, whereas the poet has been deprived of it. This semantic contrast is magnified as Dehkhoda repeats the analogous conditions that have separated the two. The bird of the dawn contemplating the fate of the dead candle and the nightingale brooding over the withered rose transfer their accumulated significance to the image of the child of the golden age. He in turn is reminded of the man executed for the "crime" of praising the truth at a time when the name of the despotic king Shaddad and his fabled garden of Eram have been eradicated from human memory. Along the way, Dehkhoda's use of such traditional images as Joseph and Moses, or the rose and the nightingale, turns private virtues like the love of freedom and truth or faith in God into communal ideals. This process of creating a reservoir of shared values bestows social significance on the act of writing the commemorative poem.[26]

Within each stanza, the theme of remembrance is ordered in the form of a single syntactic pattern: Oh "B," remember "A" when condition "X" has turned into condition "Y." The pattern is repeated in every one of the poem's five stanzas, each time through a series of signs which, in combination with the previous ones, heighten the expressive potential of the utterance. Each of the two pairs of elements in this formula is related to the other by two distinct sets of relations. "A" (Jahangir in the world outside the poem, the speaker in the dream described in the prose preface, the object of the act of remembrance in the poem) is united with "B" (Dehkhoda in the outside world, the dreamer in the dream, the agent of the act of remembrance in the poem) in ideal and purpose, but separated from it by circumstances that prevent him from realizing that ideal. Condition "X," however, stands in opposition to condition "Y," but will inevitably be replaced by it. Each individual stanza uses a repertoire of devices which reiterate these relations while expanding the theme along spatial or temporal dimensions, thereby deepening and broadening its significance. Every time, the process results in a perceptible enhancement of the poem's communicative power.

In the first stanza, the bird of the dawn is asked to remember the dead candle when night has turned to day. The identification of the dead candle as a signifier for the martyred journalist, established extratextually by Jahangir himself and confirmed in the text through the adjective "dead" (deadness is the quality which the candle shares with Jahangir),[27] provides the grounds for another identification, that of the bird of the dawn (in poetic speech the semantic equivalent of the nightingale) as a signifier for the poet. This trope, however, is quite traditional; it is used in numerous classical ghazals written in the Persian language. In one particularly illustrative instance, Hafez elevates it to the central trope of his ghazal by using it in his opening address:

> benal bulbul agar ba manat sar-e yari-st
> Keh ma do ʿasheq-e zarim o kar-e ma zari-st
>
> (Lament, nightingale, if you mean friendship with me,
> for we are two despondent lovers, lamenting our vocation)[28]

Here the speaker invokes the bird to sing if it means to show its camaraderie in love; singing, he says, is all such doleful lovers as the nightingale and the poet were made to do. The node thus established lies behind the conception of poetry and music as "composition," as well as many familiar linkages between poetry as "literature" and poetry as "song." This traditional poetic node gives rise to—and itself undergoes—significant realignments in Dehkhoda's poem. With it as intermediary, the message "O Dehkhoda, remember Jahangir when night has turned to day" is transformed into a more public message, with significant implications for the bonds which may connect poets and poetic personae to the sociopolitical events of their country: "O poet, remember the martyr when the night of oppression has turned into the day of liberty." The request that the dreaming man understood to lie behind his comrade's interrogative—"Why did you not say: 'He fell young'?"—is now discovered to be the exact equivalent, in terms of its semantic content, of the first stanza.

According to the generic conventions of Persian lyrical poetry, the nightingale and the candle remain spatially and temporally separated by their respective surroundings. The poetic locus of the nightingale is the garden, as Dehkhoda depicts in the third stanza; that of the candle is a room, a chamber, or some other enclosed space, where it is lit in order to dispel darkness. The nightingale, as the appellation "*morgh-e sahar*" (bird of the dawn) suggests, is associated with the day, more specifically the dawn, when it professes love for the blooming rose. Yet, the two images fit the situation of the exiled poet and the martyred journalist in ways that no other poetic pair in the classical canon can: the candle that was Jahangir has been extinguished in the dark night of despotic rule in Iran, and the nightingale that is Dehkhoda feels it incumbent on himself to recall the event in his song.

The temporal dimension in Jahangir's question to Dehkhoda is also worth noting. The martyr has fallen young, a fact which, reiterated in his admonition, affects Dehkhoda's understanding of his task as poet. He must perpetuate the memory of his deceased friend. The phrase "when night turns to day" is thus a way of placing the images of the candle and the nightingale in their natural time frames. Night is the time when candles are lit, dawn is the moment when nightingales begin to sing. However, as the request is being poeticized in terms of the dead candle being remembered by the bird of the dawn, the temporal dimension is first introduced as a literal entity connecting the night when the candle was put out and the time when the bird appears on the scene. It is only natural that the bird of the dawn should be told to remember the dead candle when the dark night has ended and the beautiful day has dawned because that is literally the time when birds begin to sing.

The day/night contrast is then given cosmological and cultural significance through the idea that the passage of time from night to day prepares for the appearance of God (Yazdan) and withdrawal of Satan (Ahriman). The poet's strategy here enables readers to interpret the temporal concepts along an axiological line. In their association with Zoroastrian beliefs—and therefore with Iran—the culturally anchored entities of Yazdan and Ahriman mark the ground on which the meaning of the night as a cultural negativity and the day as its opposite comes to rest.[29]

The operations of the stanza augment this initial cultural connection by specifying two social and human conditions. First, this "dark" night has to "put aside" its "black deeds." Second, the "life-giving" breeze of the "dawn" has to dispel sleep from the "heads" of "the sleepers." Each set of statements helps in at least three ways to supply a social context for the negativity of the concept of night in relation to its opposite, day. With each operation, the meanings of night and day are nudged a step closer to assuming a public and social dimension. First, in Persian, as in many languages, the adjectives dark (*tar*) and black (*siah*), do allude to unfortunate and undesirable circumstances associated with human conditions. Words and phrases such as *tireh-bakht* (dark-fortuned), *tireh-ruz* (possessor of dark days), or *ruzegar-e tireh va tar* (dim and dark days) illustrate this association. Conversely, a word like *nafheh* (breeze), in conjunction with *sahar* (dawn), connotes a turning of fortune as much as it denotes the end of a dark night in the passage of time. The binary oppositions of night and dawn, sleep and wakefulness, and the lifelessness of sleepers, juxtaposed to the life-giving quality of the dawn breeze, set the scene for the poem to harness their potential meanings for new purposes.

In the poem the word *siah* (black) is combined with the word *kar* (deed) to form a compound *siah-kari* (black deeds), a concept which, in its very abstractness, transfers the connotations of the word "black" to human deeds and actions. This transference communicates the idea that the condition of absence of fortune is caused by, or at least related to, human actions. The next image, that of the life-giving dawn breeze driving sleep out of the heads of the sleepers, opposes "night," the agent of the previous action, to "dawn," a living force. As the night ceases to fill the air with darkness, dawn dispatches its life-restoring breeze. We are really in the world of human society where an undesirable entity gives way to one fondly anticipated. Moreover, the transitive verb "put aside"—literally "put down from the head" (*bogzasht ze sar*)—assumes the presence of the power of will in the night, thus giving a human quality to the compound *siah-kari* as the action of the night. The same effect is produced through the second image as the dawn is assumed to possess the power to drive sleep away from heads. For the sleepers to wake up, both conditions have to be present: the night's action of ceasing its black deeds and the dawn's dispatch of the life-giving breeze. Only then will the sleepers awake (i.e., regain their senses). In combination, the two images slide the meanings of these temporal agents toward a sphere of signification that favors social action over natural occurrence. Thus "black deeds" come to refer to atrocities, one example of which is the execution of the constitutionalist journalist. And the word—and concept—"night" assumes a new dimension of meaning previously nonexistent in the poetic tradition.

The nightingale's witnessing of the end of the night and the approach of the dawn as the inaugurating condition for the act of remembrance (and of reminding others through singing) begins a second process of concretization. In a move similar to the first—that is, from the phenomenal world to the cultural context and from there to the text at hand—new associations derived from the tradition focus on the poet's view of himself: Dehkhoda equates Jahangir with the dead candle, while depicting himself as the functional equivalent of the moth, an entity inspired by a manifestly inferior feeling. In the classical tradition, the moth and the candle come to stand for two differ-ent kinds of love. The superficial infatuation that causes the moth to ap-proach the candle, yet retreat from its burning flame contrasts with the true love that enables the candle to remain steadfastly in place and burn out. One of the best-known treatments of the motif can be found in Saʿdi's *Bustan*, where the two are placed in dialogue. First, the moth questions the candle's shedding of tears. "I am the lover, burning befits me," it says. "Why then are you shedding tears, burning, and moaning?" The candle answers by say-ing that the wax that forms its body has been separated from the nectar that is its sweet soul. For that reason, says the candle, it feels the pain befitting true lovers. It then contrasts this condition with that of the moth's frivolous infatuation with the light and the heat it emits:

> To bogrizi az pish-e yek sho'leh kham
> man estadeh-am ta besuzam tamam
> to ra atesh-e 'eshq agar par besukht
> ma-ra bin keh az pai ta sar besukht.[30]

> (Raw in love, you flee from a single flame
> Whereas I stand to burn whole.
> Where love's fire only singes your wing,
> Look! It burns me from head to foot.)

Thus, the candle emerges as the true lover burning in silence, while the moth, who had begun the challenging exchange, is portrayed as a superficial lover not even worthy of the name. In another context, this time in his preface to *Golestan*, the same poet bids the nightingale to learn true love by contemplating the moth expired in utter silence at the foot of its beloved, the candle. The moth's lifeless body provides a lasting example to all the novices who long to experience the unique condition known as love:

> Ay morgh-e sahar 'eshq ze parvaneh biamuz
> k-an sukhteh ra jan shod o avaz nayamad.[31]

> (O bird of the dawn, learn love from the moth.
> Life has departed from its burned body, yet it spoke not.)

The hierarchy thus established remains constant in many love lyrics in Persian. The capacity for silent and resolute suffering emerges as the essential attribute that distinguishes true and pure love from emotions commonly so called but not quite achieving that exalted state. Such at least are the criteria by which degrees of sincerity and purity of love are measured.

In "Remember . . ." the chain of associations initiated by the word "candle" first passes through the figure of the bird of the dawn, and is anthropomorphized through the latter's identification with the poet. Jahangir's admonition caused Dehkhoda to see himself as the moth who has fled the flame and his deceased friend as having stood resolutely in place. Aided by his poetic heritage, he begins to turn this feeling into a determination to sing his friend's love in his poem. Since it has not been his lot to be the dead candle, nor even the lifeless moth, he may play the part of the nightingale and perpetuate the memory of his deceased friend through his song, an injunction to posterity to remember the fallen martyr of a common cause. It is precisely this feeling that he communicates through the caption wherein he calls himself an "unworthy brother" and exalts his comrade as a "most holy and high spirit." As Dehkhoda introduces these classical structures into a qasida that commemorates a political martyr, he gives rise to a process whereby their conventional poetic value, hitherto used exclusively in the lyrical discourse, begins to shift to the social sphere. In this connection, Dehkhoda's use of the compound *morgh-e sahar* (which contains an allusion to the dawn) instead of the word *bolbol* assumes an added dimension in that it makes the opposition between the night and the dawn, now understood in their specifically sociopolitical senses, textually visible.

The processes I have outlined here affect the remaining imagery in the poem's first stanza as well. In the phenomenal world, dawn provides a natural prelude to day; in the poem, therefore, the association of night with tyranny and of dawn with the end of that tyranny leads naturally to the dawn of cosmic beauty. This in turn bestows the aura of divine affirmation on the struggle going on between the forces of night and day. This contrast between the two entities as conceptual opposites culminates in the eventual appearance of Yazdan and the withdrawal of the evil-natured Ahriman, corroborating the poet's initial depiction of what precedes their appearance as the dark night of despotic rule in his country. On the one hand, the war imagery surrounding the two cosmic, yet culture-specific, antagonists serves to universalize the opposition between "this dark night" and the divine day described in the stanza. On the other hand, the same imagery concretizes the outcome as a propitious future destined for the country. In this way, the dark night of the poem covers a semantic field which, while appropriating certain conventional connotations of the image, transfers them to the social arena in which the poem is placed. Through such expressive strategies the night comes to assume an added metaphorical dimension totally new to the semantic field of that concept in Persian poetry, and one which has been used by almost all succeeding generations of the so-called politically committed poets.[32]

The use of the interpellative "this" (*in*) in reference to the night highlights two meanings, only one of which I have addressed above. More immediately than the political situation in the poet's country, the phrase "this night" can be taken as a reference to the time when the poem was written. Dehkhoda himself tells us so in his prose preface. Having been awakened from his dream, he says, he lighted the lamp and began writing the poem. In light of that assertion, let us pause a moment longer on the image of the candle. The shift in the meaning of the night has already begun to affect our reading of the candle's function. The candle that illuminates this night is no longer the entity depicted in the tradition, the illuminator of the lover's dark night of separation *(shab-e hejr)*, or the soul mate of the despondent lover shedding tears in commiseration. It is not the light present in the night of the union *(shab-e vasl)* either, depicted as sharing the joy by immersing the lover and the beloved in its beneficent light; nor is it the benign nocturnal presence in the gathering of a few kindred spirits united in their quest after love. None of these conventional images fit the candle, now dead, exhausted by the kind of night the poem has described. This candle has in fact been dislodged from its conventional grounding to serve as the dispeller of the pervasive darkness *this night* emits. It is a figure which, in the context of this particular poem at least, can signify the fighter who has given his life to eradicate the dark night of oppression and despotism. He may have fallen, but his cause will be taken up by none less than his heavenly analogue, the sun which will eventually defeat the night. While preserving aspects of its old poetic connotations, the figure of the candle, like that of the night, has now appropriated onto itself meanings that direct it toward novel usages.

In this the candle is aided not only by the new areas of signification into which its companion concept, the night, has been moved but also by the actual circumstances surrounding the poem. The poem, we recall, was in fact written in the middle of the night in the light of a lamp. The night and the day, the candle, the moth, and the nightingale, having now assumed clear sociopolitical senses, begin to impart new connotations to other entities in the poem. As the poem progresses, a whole network of images, figures of speech, and other elements inhabiting the space of lyrical poetry in Persian is transformed into new images communicating concepts which previously lay outside the tradition. By expanding and extending meanings fixed by conventional usage, Dehkhoda turns them into more fluid signifiers capable of communicating messages which serve his theme.

As we continue reading the poem, at least two structures set up in the first stanza carry their significance over into the four subsequent ones. First, the syntactic pattern remains constant. So, in the second stanza Joseph's companion in bondage is asked to remember his cell mate after he has been reunited with his kinsmen and loved ones; in the third, the nightingale is asked to remember the early-blooming rose withered in spring; then Moses' fellow traveler in the desert is asked to remember the fallen companion; and finally, in the fifth stanza, the child of the Golden Age is asked to remember the man killed for the crime of praising the truth. The other structure, reinforced through the parallel syntax, is the increasingly explicit links between the poem's situations and agents and the political reality that has occasioned the poem. As a result, each pair of actors is identified with Jahangir and

Dehkhoda, each temporal concept equated with the present and future political situation in Iran.

The second stanza casts the theme of remembrance in terms of the speaker's request to the "friend of Joseph in bondage." When he has returned to his kinsmen and loved ones "freer than the breeze and the moonlight," he should remember the person who has accompanied him through nights of longing. Once again, there can be no doubt about the eventuality of Joseph's—and his friend's—return to Canaan. Just as the night *will* turn into dawn, Joseph and his friends, too, *will* return to their homeland and kinsmen. For Muslims this certainty is grounded in the authority of the Koranic narrative. The confirmation of that authority in classical Persian poetry enables the poet to utilize the narrative in accordance with his own purpose. Classical depictions of the emotions associated with the promise, however, allow Dehkhoda to reproduce them with minimal narration. Hafez's best-known treatment of such feelings should suffice for illustration:

> Yusof-e gom-gashteh baz ayad beh kan'an gham makhor
> kolbeh-ye ahzan shavad ruzi golestan gham makhor.[33]

> (The lost Joseph will come back to Canaan, be not sad.
> The cottage of sorrow will one day turn into a rose garden, be not sad.)

The allusion to Joseph's dream relates to another theme as well: that of the exile's dream of return to the homeland. This further prompts the episode toward the public realm. The cultural belief that dreams featuring martyrs will be fulfilled[34] is reinforced through the pattern, initiated in the first stanza, of asking to be remembered when that dream turns into reality. This in turn buttresses the certainty of the exile's return predicated upon his being able to do so freely. By depicting his martyred friend as heralding the fulfillment of his dream of return from exile, Dehkhoda creates a deep-structured parallel between the two stanzas. Just as surely as night will turn to day, the dreamer's dream of return to the homeland will be fulfilled in all its perfection. Similarly, the contrast between the present and the future, initiated in the previous stanza, is seconded here in the image of the poet at present, alone and separated from beloved and kin, and that of his future freedom and union with his loved ones.

The lexical units on which the structure of the stanza's argument rests center around the notion of dream (*khab*) and dream interpretation (*ta'bir*). Each of these words is used in two interrelated senses present in the Persian language. *Khab,* meaning both sleep and dream, not only refers to the thoughts, images, or emotions occurring while we sleep but also connotes the conditions for which we long. *Tàʿbir,* too, means both the act of assigning meaning to the stuff of dreams and to the fulfillment of our wishes. Thus, the literal meaning of dream (in his sleep, Dehkhoda sees the apparition of his martyred comrade) and its meaning as desire (Dehkhoda longs to return to Iran) begin to merge with the belief that his dream will come true. To-gether, the two meanings push the concepts of dream and interpretation, as they are used in the poem, from the personal space of the dreamer's psyche to the public arena of a political exile's return. Because the reader and the poet share the assumption that dreaming of martyrs means that one's own dream (or desire) will be fulfilled (or it will, so to speak, find its "true" interpretation), then Dehkhoda's dream of return to Iran, an event contin-gent on the reversal of the present political situation, will come to pass.

The third and fourth stanzas take the context of the first two, and expand it along a dimension which emphasizes the condition of fulfillment rather than that of deprivation. Through these middle stanzas, the poem gradually concentrates attention on the ideal future—and, therefore, on the act of re-membrance. The third stanza achieves this by organizing essentially the same set of relations as in the first stanza around two central figures in the lyrical tradition. The nightingale is asked to remember the early-blooming rose— withered at the chill of winter—when it finds itself amid the vernal beauty of the garden. The word "nightingale" here is as appropriate to the setting of the garden as the appellation "bird of the dawn" was to that of the transi-tion from night to day. But the shift also functions as a catalyst for the passage from winter to spring, an event which in the phenomenal world occupies a greater time span than the turning of night into day. The setting further affords Dehkhoda a more detailed description of the circumstances of future recollection. Whereas in the first stanza it is the dawning of another day that instigates the act of remembrance, here it is the coming of the season of rejuvenation that revives the memory of the dead rose in the nightingale's mind.

As the temporal dimension expands, it brings into sharper focus the final outcome of the speaker's request: the act of remembrance. The nightingale's song, itself the expression of the mental operation of remembrance, arises as a result of the bird finding itself surrounded by flowers of many colors and scents. Thus, although in the classical tradition the early-blooming rose often functions as an emblem of anachronism,[35] here the same rose is perceived as somehow having caused, or contributed to, the arrival of the season of blos-soming. Since the poem itself has already been established as the equivalent of the nightingale's song, Jahangir is associated in the reader's mind as help-ing to achieve the ideal situation Dehkhoda longs for. In another sense, the union described here stands in agreement with that portrayed in the second stanza in that it is depicted as a state of bliss for the individual agents. In one, it is Joseph's friend who reaches the arms of his beloved and kinsmen, in the other it is the nightingale that attains union with the rose.

But if in the third stanza, expressive devices help to focus the reader's attention on the poem as the evidence of the act of remembrance, in the fourth they act to bring the public realm within its grasp. The strategies employed here help the reader to explore the truth of the martyr's prophecy. The desert companion of Moses is asked to remember his fallen fellow traveler once he has arrived in "the promised land." The mythological core of the last phrase, the Israelites' relationship with God, is further strengthened by the linguistic force of the phrase stating the reason for the fallen man's death: he has fallen "for the sin of an ignorant people." The result is a remarkable widening of the poem's vista. The temporal dimension opens far wider than before, and we are no longer waiting for night to turn into day or winter into spring. Rather, we are asked to wait until "these numbered years are passed." It is on these expanded grounds, the most public domain yet, that the poem builds its signifying edifice: that of the destiny of a whole "people."

This stanza also expands the sphere depicted in the second one, to which it is united through biblical allusion. Clearly, the sight of the promised land by the Jews fleeing their Egyptian captivity possesses greater magnitude than Joseph's return to Canaan. Once again, cultural associations rooted in the Islamic narrative of the Israelites' exodus from Egypt carry the stanza closer to conveying its message in relation to topical sociopolitical events. The story of Moses and the Israelites searching for the promised land is the closer to such ideas as nation and country. Semantically, too, these words find their nearest equivalents in the political language of the constitutional period through some of the poem's most civic words such as *qowm* (people) and *arz* (land). The Koran's narrative of the exodus tells the story of a whole nation's return to the land destined to be theirs by divine decree, not that of an individual's reunion with his family and friends.[36] In the poem, this public event has been concretized through the sighting of the golden altar. Harking back to the initial image of Yazdan appearing "in all His perfection," here Dehkhoda expresses the reference to God in terms of the "choice witness of the feast of wisdom." Thus, while the reader's attention is fixed on the concrete image of "the golden altar" metonymically representing the promised land, the realm of the poem's conceptual operations grows spatially and temporally to embrace the whole of the poem's message, recast in terms at once more literal and more encompassing in the fifth stanza.

Finally, after the climactic expansion of the fourth stanza, Dehkhoda returns to the thoughts the dream has aroused in him. The ideal state, expressed in the previous stanzas as the dawning of the new day, Joseph's return to Canaan, the coming of the spring, and the arrival of the Jews in the promised land, appears here as a future "Golden Age" (*dowreh-ye talaʾi*). Dehkhoda's use of the phrase, a loan translation from European languages with no precedence in Persian poetry,[37] helps to clarify further the condition which has thus far been conveyed only metaphorically. As a translated expression anchored in Greco-Roman mythology, "the Golden Age" was known to Iranians familiar with European cultures. Nineteenth-century historiographers like Kermani used it in reference to the lost glory of pre-Islamic Iran.[38] In the sense of an ideal time lying in the future, however, I have found no precedence for it. Similarly, the phrase "the child of the Golden Age," meaning an Iranian citizen of a happy future, appears without precedence. In fact, the idea of individuals or generations as children—that is, products—of the age they live in seems to have no precedence in the Persian language or its poetic tradition. Through their contextual connection with the familiar mythical narratives of Joseph and Moses, as well as the textual parallelism within the poem, these concepts are naturalized in the poem. In other words, the metaphorical charge of certain familiar images allows hitherto culturally unmarked phrases to become poetic signs. At the same time, their newness allows the poet to guide them freely in any direction he deems appropriate. In the case of "Remember . . . ," linkages with such conventional signs as the nightingale in the vernal garden, Joseph reunited with his father, or Moses in the promised land, have made it possible for Dehkhoda to use the phrase "the Golden Age" in the sense of a future state for his country. Through a similar process, the phrase "child of the Golden Age" has come to mean Iranians living at that happy time.

Nonetheless, the allusions to the mythical despot Shaddad and his fabled garden of Eram anchor the new concepts in conventional references. A legendary king named in the Koran, Shaddad is well known in classical Persian poetry, as is the garden he is believed to have conceived as a paradise on earth. When the speaker asks his audience to remember the executed man after these images of injustice have been erased from human memory, he is employing a series of references familiar in the social discourse of his culture. Allusions to the Pharaohs, Nimrod, and Shaddad abound in the political and journalistic prose of the Constitutional Period, especially in the struggle to oust Mohammad-ʿAli Shah.[39] The poignancy of such references is enhanced markedly when we begin to think that the execution of Jahangir actually took place in a garden-garrison in Tehran known as Bagh-e Shah (literally, the king's garden) and that this was common knowledge at the time. Thus, un-like Joseph and Moses, the allusion to King Shaddad and the Garden of Eram does not function solely on the basis of knowledge derived from the poetic culture of the past. Rather, it serves simultaneously to underline the inauspicious present and, through opposition, the poem's promise about the future. The "propitious times" heralded in the stanza will be different from the continuum that includes the world of Shaddad and Eram as well as that of Mohammad-'Ali Shah and his garden-garrison, because in those happy times all despots and their artifices will have been eradicated from human memory. That when this occurs, God, too, shall resume his rule over the universe, further raises the stakes by portraying the present as a moment of cosmic disorder when God has forsaken his throne under protest. This idea focuses attention once more on the poem's initial stanza where we saw the reappearance of Yazdan and the withdrawal of Ahriman.

The cosmic coup depicted in the final stanza serves a further function as well. If in the natural course of time's progression the dawning day might once more turn into night, if another winter may follow even the most delightful season of vernal growth and blossoming, the Golden Age of the last stanza, linked with the eventual triumph of God Almighty over all the forces of evil, is doubtless an irreversible state. The very idea of a new Golden Age in the poet's country, fortified by the notion of God's restoration, suggests the thought of perfect and permanent bliss. The interplay of forgetting and remembering, perceptible from the beginning, culminates in this final interaction between the new and the old.[40] While Mohammad-'Ali Shah's name will be eradicated from the collective memory, the name of Jahangir—and of all the others who have given their lives to make the future happiness possible—will adorn history and poetry alike. In that sense, the existence of the poem itself guarantees the fulfillment of the vision enshrined in it. If Jahangir's apparition had to appear to Dehkhoda in a dream for us to have the poem, the very existence of the poem gives us reason to believe that the promise it contains will be fulfilled. Both the slain journalist and the surviving poet are necessary for the poem to exist—and for the struggle to achieve its end.

In the service of communicating this assurance, unique to the conditions that occasioned the poem, Dehkhoda has combined the myths and metaphors present in his culture with new elements from which he derives poetic quality and which he turns into new poetic signs. If Akhundzadeh, Kermani, and Malkom contributed to the process of poetic change in Iran by demanding the expulsion of certain elements from the existing system of poetic expression, in this poem Dehkhoda lays the ground for a new, expanded expressive system. He accomplishes this, in the words of Yuri Lotman, by "drawing exrasystemic elements into the realm of the system."[41] The total effect of the approach is the perception of a new way of conceiving and expressing ideas through poetry, one in which poetic quality arises from constant and mutual interaction of marked and unmarked, old and new structures and entities. Most remarkable to our study of poetic change is the manner in which such interactions begin to draw new concepts out of traditional signs. Without changing conventional signifiers, Dehkhoda enables them to operate in spaces wherein they begin to mean something different, however slightly, from what they have in the hands of Sa'di or Hafez. Signifiers like the nightingale and the rose or Joseph and Moses come to signify concepts on a plane distinct from the cultural spaces wherein they have been inscribed traditionally. Instead of openly discarding or violating traditional poetic signifiers in favor of new ones, Dehkhoda makes them signify new concepts.

Thus, even as the poem flaunts its traditional signifiers, it relates these to concepts markedly different from their counterparts in the classical qasida. The dead candle still stands as a paradigm of resoluteness in love, but the love it exemplifies is for the ideal of freedom for the motherland. Its meaning thus altered, the image leads the reader to thoughts of enlightenment and liberty rather than of the beloved's beauty. Through similar operations, the nightingale is keyed to a drastically different concept. In perpetuating the memory of an early-blooming rose now expired, it testifies to the presence of the poet who commemorates the martyr whose life was given over to the cause of freedom for his country. Unlike the lover of the Hafezian ghazal, this poet will sing not to remind his audiences of the sincerity of his love for the beloved. Rather he will remind them of all those whose sacrifices ensure a golden future for an entire people.[42]

Finally, because in classical lyrics the nightingale's song stands for the poet's song, here the change in the function of the song signals a corresponding shift in the social function of poetry within a changed social context. Poetry exists as an instrument to record the trials and tribulations not of individual lovers but of those luminaries whose struggles crystallize the aspirations of countless others for a better future. The poet's function is thus transformed into a demonstrably social one: guiding the collective memory of his community through new patterns of forgetting and remembrance. The complex of associations built around the nightingale/poet and the song/poetry nodes thus leaves a surplus of meaning for the poet as the shaper of communal memory.[43] To sum up, an exploration of "Remember . . ." can serve as an illustration of how a poet can take over the fields of discourse previously thought external to his craft and use them to modify, expand, or otherwise alter the tradition in search of meanings that he or she perceives as relevant. Ultimately, of course, in any discussion of the process of change in a poetic system, the fact of this cohabitation must be related to the degree to which the various elements combine to produce the impression of a unified structure with a discernible artistic purpose.

A "PATRIOTIC" GHAZAL: 'AREF'S "THE MESSAGE OF FREEDOM"

Abolqasem 'Aref (1882–1934), better known as 'Aref-e Qazvini,[44] is the author of the other text I intend to focus on. A far more public figure as a poet, 'Aref is quite representative of the poetic voice searching for ways of breaking through existing poetic borders. Whereas Dehkhoda's choice of a little-known subgenre called the *mosammat* may signal a strategy to change the poetic system from its margins, 'Aref's concentration on the ghazal, the most central genre within the lyrical tradition, indicates an urgent desire to break through systemic constraints. Departures from the norms observed and upheld over a millennium in the genre considered most expressive of the lyrical impulse and the crowning achievement of poets are tantamount to esthetic sacrilege. In terms of consequences, too, modifications of the elements within the significatory system of the Persian ghazal exerted an extensive and immediate influence on the process of change in the system of poetic encoding prevalent in the tradition.

I have selected a most famous ghazal of 'Aref's as a way of illustrating the expansion of the ghazal's expressive system in order to adapt that genre to topical expressions of a sociopolitical nature. The ghazal known as "Payam-e Azadi" (The Message of Freedom)[45] was reportedly first sung to the accompaniment of musical instruments on a festive occasion in the fall of 1911. The celebration, sponsored by the literary circle of the Democratic Party of Iran, had been billed officially as "the national festival in commemoration of the victory of the supporters of the constitution and the defeat of Mohammad-'Ali."[46] It provided an ideal occasion for a popular poet and singer like 'Aref to sing one of his political songs in praise of the constitutional system of government. According to Browne, who attended the celebration, 'Aref "undertook the role of the minstrel and, in a most charming and affecting manner, sang the poem which he had composed for the occasion."[47] Again, I give the text of the original ghazal followed by my literal translation:

> Payam dusham az pir-e may-forush amad
> benush badeh keh yek mellat-i beh hush amad
> hezar pardeh az iran darid estebdad

hezar shokr keh mushruteh pardeh-push amad

ze khak-e pak-e shahidan-e rah-e azadi

bebin keh khun-e siavosh chesan beh jush amad

hakhamanesh cho khoda khast monqarez gardad

sekandar az pay-e takhrib-e dariush amad

bara-ye fath-e javanan-e jang-ju jami

zadim badeh vo faryad-e nush nush amad

vatan-forushi ers ast in ʿajab nabovad

chera keh adam az avval vatan-forush amad

kesi keh ru beh sefarat pay-e omidi raft

dehid mojdeh keh kur o kar o khamush amad

seda-ye naleh-ye ʿaref beh gush-e harkeh resid

cho daf beh sar zad o chon chang dar khorush amad.[48]

(Last night a message came to me from the wine-selling elder:

Drink wine, for a whole nation has come to itself.

Despotism tore a thousand veils from Iran,

a thousand thanks that the constitution has restored the veils.

From the spotless grave of those martyred on the path to freedom

see how the blood of Siavosh has begun to boil.

When God willed the demise of the Achamanians,

Alexander moved to destroy Darius.

Wishing for the victory of the fighting youth,

we drank a cup, and the roar arose: "May it be wholesome!"

Treachery is hereditary: it is no wonder.

Adam was the first to betray his homeland.

He who went to the embassy, pursuing some hope,

came back blind, deaf, and dumb. Spread the good news.

Whoever heard the sound of ʿAref's laments,

he hit his hands upon his head tambourinelike and clamored like a

   harp.)[49]

The public nature of the occasion at which this ghazal was sung "most charmingly" sets it apart from that of Dehkhoda's elegiac poem, written in the middle of the night by a solitary poet in exile. It also sets the text somewhat apart from the traditional locus of the performance or recital of the Persian ghazal, typically envisioned as the assembly of a few kindred minds closed to the uninitiated.[50] These differences are notable in that the participants in the celebration can be said to be connected by a public political cause. Attending a party to celebrate their victory over the king intent on destroying the constitutional system, they must have brought to it a collective joyous mood. That cause and mood enable us to approximate the effects of the ghazal's individual statements as they are received by the audience. I have therefore organized my approach to the poem with a view to the gradual unfolding of its structure as it is internalized by the audience attending the celebration. Browne points to the possibility that the text of the ghazal may have been handed to the audience in advance of the performance.[51] If so, the audience may be assumed to know beforehand that the poem to be sung is a ghazal. At any rate, the poet's reputation as a composer and singer of ghazals and the accompaniment of musical instruments make it likely that even before the poem was sung the audience was prepared to hear a ghazal. We can therefore surmise that 'Aref's poem was received by an audience expecting to hear a ghazal with a political message.

The poem opens with the news of a message from the old wine-seller, a very common motif in the classical Persian ghazal. The entire first hemistich, in fact, establishes a direct link between this ghazal and numerous classical examples of the genre. In Hafez alone, one can point to several ghazals beginning with the motif of a message from the wine-seller, often described as a *pir* (old man, leader, guide). The message is either addressed directly to the poem's speaker or relayed to him through some intermediary.[52] Here, however, the content of the message initiates a difference from that typical of the ghazal tradition. Occupying seven hemistiches, the information-content of the message consists of two parts: first, the command or instruction to drink wine (the first two words of the second hemistich), and then the reasons for it. Through the latter the speaker of the ghazal articulates his political views, presenting them as the reasons that have motivated the wine-seller to bid him to drink. As the fiction of the wine-seller's message recedes to the background, the message assumes another status: the singing poet's advice to the audience to raise their cups in celebration.

Like widening circles, three themes—respectively of a public, historical, and cosmic significance—emerge as the *pir* elaborates on his reasons. First and most specifically, the nation has come to itself. Here, the opposition between despotic rule (*estebdad*) tearing the veil and the constitution (*mashruteh*) restoring it, reflects the complete opposition between the past and the present, thereby fortifying the idea of the nation as an unconscious entity which has now gained consciousness. Second, the continuity implied in the depiction of the blood of Siavosh boiling from the graves of the young martyrs of the constitutionalist cause links the current struggle to an ancient mythic dichotomy about thematizing innocence unjustly punished. Finally, on a cosmic plane, the idea that God's will was at work in the defeat of

Darius and the victory of Alexander bestows divine sanction on a contemporary political event—the ousting of Mohammad-'Ali Shah—which the audience has come to celebrate. In affirmation of all this the wise *pir* issues his instruction to rejoice by drinking wine. His wisdom is not directed here toward some philosophical observation like being and knowing, free will or predetermination—issues which are thought to have preoccupied speakers of classical ghazals. Here, a stock figure of the ghazal tradition brings his knowledge and wisdom to bear on a specific event in the actual political life of the community.[53]

To that end, 'Aref has removed three figures of Persian mythology and history from their traditional function in the classical poetry, assigning a new mission to them. In "The Message of Freedom" images of Siavosh, Alexander, and Darius help to relate the emotions aroused by their presence to events not associated with the genre of the ghazal. By way of illustration, compare the allusion to the blood of Siavosh in 'Aref's ghazal to a similar allusion in Hafez:

> Shah-e torkan sokhan-e modda'iyan mishenavad
> sharmi az mazlameh-ye khun-e siavushash bad.[54]

> (The king of the Turks believes the words of falsifiers,
> May he/she feel shame at the injustice of spilling Siavosh's blood.)

Hafez's use of the phrase "king of the Turks" in place of the proper name Afrasiab, the Turanian king responsible for the blood of Prince Siavosh, triggers a dual referentiality. This is a common occurrence in the Persian ghazal, where an entity like "the Turk" refers both to a mythical personage and the speaker's beloved.[55] The equivocation places the beloved in the position of power stemming from his or her irresistible beauty, and the lover in that of the powerless victim suffering injustice. The message is commensurate with the convention of a discourse on love where the absence of any recourse for the lover is emphasized. Only the beloved can redress the situation if he or she can be made aware of the injustice, hence the speaker's wish that the beloved may feel shame. The allusion is used first and last in the service of the discourse on love in that the injustice applies solely to the lover's view of the consequences of the beloved's beauty. The reference to the myth of Siavosh is there only to impart the emotion relevant to the concerns at hand—here, "shame."

In 'Aref's ghazal, Siavosh's blood is said to be boiling "from the spotless grave of those martyred on the path to freedom." The blood acts as guarantor of immortality for the martyrs of the constitutionalist cause by testifying to their innocence and the injustice they have suffered. The phrase "martyrs on the path to freedom," common in the political discourse of the time, determines the function of Siavosh's blood, a sense absent from the classical reference. The appellation is understood to refer to the young *mojahed* (struggler) fighters who have given their lives in the effort to restore the constitutional government. In this way, the blood of the innocent prince of a mythical past provides proof for the justness of the struggle at hand. Enunciated by the all-knowing *pir,* the linkage legitimates the assertion that the path the strugglers—the martyrs, the poet, and the audience—have taken will indeed lead to freedom.

The line that follows the reference to Siavosh advances the legitimation process on three distinct levels. First, insofar as the events leading to the overthrow of the Achamanian king Darius III are registered as strictly historical—that is, having really happened—they provide proof that the struggle being celebrated in the poem will also be remembered in the future. Second, by incorporating the divine will in the antecedent event 'Aref portrays the outcome of the current political struggle as divinely ordained as well. Third, the mention not only of the ancient Persian king but also of his dynasty, the Achamanians, adds a veiled warning by foreshadowing the downfall not just of Mohammad-'Ali Shah but also of the entire dynasty of Qajar kings. We know from 'Aref's biography that in this period of his life he ranked among those who advocated abolishing the Qajar dynasty and establishing a republic in Iran.[56] In all of this, the fact that comparisons, observations, and prophecies are contained in the old wine-seller's message lends the authority of his wisdom and foresight to the political positions represented in the poem.

Having relayed the wine-seller's message, the speaker tells the audience how he obeyed the command by raising his cup, "wishing for the victory of the fighting youth." Both thematically and structurally, this is the moment when, according to the fiction set up in the ghazal, the speaker decides to respond to the wine-seller's call. In doing so, however, he adds a wish of his own. The words with which the line begins can be interpreted in two different ways. *Bara-ye fath* (for the victory) might mean because of the victory, a reading which relates the act of drinking to what has already been accomplished. In this sense, the speaker is understood to be raising his cup because he feels good about the victory that has been won. Alternatively, *bara-ye fath* might mean "wishing for the victory," a reading which opens up the possibility that the victory that has been achieved is not viewed as final and that the struggle must continue. The reading buttresses the notion that, in the previous reference, too, God had caused the defeat of Darius because He had ordained the demise of the dynasty to which he belonged. This in turn heralds the motif of treachery as hereditary, contained in the next line.

The phrase that ends the line, however, contains a new element. The roar of *nush nush* the speaker reports signals a plural utterance, a collectivity of voices that sanction his drinking. If the speaker's drinking represents one man's adherence to the message, the roar he hears points to popular approval of the act. In recording the response to the speaker, the line articulates acceptance of the wine-seller's command. Hearing the roar in turn persuades the speaker that his feelings are in line with those of the people. The message transmitted from the wise wine-seller to the poem's speaker, and from there to the people, has now reached its final destination. The idea of the poem as "message," begun with the word *payam* (message) in the first line, reaches its culmination in the last line where we see the poet describing the gestures that indicate that the people have adhered to the message.

The concepts found in the next line are unprecedented in the Persian ghazal. Here, the charge of treachery—literally the selling of one's country (*vatan-forushi*)—is leveled not against the deposed king but linked to Adam. In the classical ghazal tradition, Adam's expulsion from the Garden of Eden is typically spoken of as a sin, an instance of transgression, disobedience, or rebellion. In more strictly mystical contexts, it connotes an act of defiance illustrative of man's very nature. It is depicted primarily as an occasion to describe the world as a place of alienation and exile.[57] This marks the figure of Adam, the father of all mankind (*abu al-bashar*) and God's choice messenger (*safi-allah*) according to Islam, with an ambivalence that allows the poet to contemplate human nature. He is often depicted as good, but prone to committing sin. Capable of giving life to both Cain and Abel, he leaves the human race with the proclivity to sin as well as the potential to be restored to union with God.

I turn to Hafez again for a classical rendition of the episode of Adam's expulsion from paradise and its implications for human beings:

> Pedaram rowzeh-ye jannat beh do gandom beforukht
> man chera bagh-e jahan ra be jovi nafrusham.[58]

> (My father sold the Garden of Eden for two grains of wheat;
> why should I not sell the garden of the world for one grain of barley?)

Here, as in 'Aref's ghazal, Adam's loss of paradise following the sin of tasting the forbidden fruit, often depicted as wheat in Islamic texts, is articulated in terms of selling, which implies choice, as if Adam has in fact entered into an exchange with God. In both ghazals, Adam's action has led to consequences for his descendants. However, whereas in the classical ghazal the poet relates the act to his own indifference to the attractions of the material world, the poet of the constitutional era relates it to a specific political crime committed by the deposed Shah when he began to oppose constitutional government. The sin or crime is then related to a more serious crime of high treason, that of placing himself under the protection of foreigners, as the poet refers to the culprit as "he who went to the embassy." We know, as did ʿAref's audience, that Mohammad-ʿAli Shah, having been defeated by the constitutionalist militia forces, took refuge in the Russian Legation in Tehran, hoping in vain that the Cossack forces might help restore him to his throne.[59] ʿAref's description of the historical incident reveals the extent of his analogy's efficacy. If Adam was expelled from paradise for defying the will of God, whose will did the deposed king defy? The answer incorporates the myth of Adam's expulsion into the reality of contemporary political events, subtly inculcating the idea of "the nation" (*mellat*) as the deity of the new political discourse.

The opposition between the Shah and the people is also made explicit in this penultimate line. The someone (*kesi*) of the first hemistich, clearly refer-ring to the Shah, is said to have returned "blind, deaf, and dumb." ʿAref's designation of this as "good news" underlines the unity of the wise wine-seller, the speaker, and the audience against the deposed Shah. The contrast is further concretized as the Shah's despondency gives rise to an anticipation of boundless joy in the people. The poem's closing line contrasts Moham-mad-ʿAli Shah's emotional state to that of the poet, now appearing in his own voice through the pen name (*takhallos*) of "ʿAref," and of the people. ʿAref's voice, in the two senses of his song and his poem, excites the people to the point where they come visually to resemble the musical instruments in performance before them.

Structurally, the movement from the wine-seller of the first line to the "whoever" (*harkeh*) of the last helps to open a swath from the lyrical dis-course of the classical ghazal to the open vistas of contemporary poetry. As it passes through the speaker's contemplation of and compliance with the wine-seller's message, and later through his transmission of the message to the people, the message assumes a public significance tied to specific, definable political events recognizable by ʿAref's audience. In the process, the initial assertion that "a whole nation has come to itself" is underscored through a series of signs that help to transform the exclusionary discourse of the Persian ghazal to the public discourse of a revolution in the making and to transpose the enclosed circle of lyrical utterance onto the public space of political com-munication.

The images which close "The Message of Freedom" reveal a typical characteristic of ambivalent texts. The two gestures of hitting oneself on the head (*beh sar zadan*) and being aroused to clamor (*dar khorush amadan*) are more commonly expressions of mourning than of happy excitement, the mood nurtured through the poem. In bringing the fiction of his poem to an end by reporting the people's reaction to the good news of their enemy's despondency, 'Aref seems to have faced a problem. By convention, ghazals that are sung to an audience make reference to the musical devices which accompany the singing. In the classical ghazal, this is customarily done through depiction of the wailing speaker/lover singing to the accompaniment of musical instruments. The sad, sinuous sounds of the instruments reveal their commiseration with the singer. Thus, the tambourine is said to be hitting itself on the head, and the harp is said to be wailing. 'Aref faces the task of closing a happy-ending ghazal with reference to such images. He may well have found the traditional expressive devices wanting. Within the rather limited repertoire of images relating ways of playing musical instruments to human gestures, he may simply not have found images appropriate to the joyous mood he wished to communicate. The semantic span of the word "clamor" (*khorush*), which can mean private wailing or public outcry, does help to bridge the gap between the conventions of the ghazal genre and 'Aref's political message. Still, the gestures of hitting oneself on the head and clamoring do not fit the happy ending the poem means to convey.

The apparent incongruity indicates textual ambivalence in that it demonstrates how adherence to generic conventions may lead to ambiguous utterances. To the extent that the emotional thrust of 'Aref's poem tends to color our interpretation of the closing images, the poet's depiction of the mood must be seen as affecting the traditional meanings of the two verbs. However, to the extent that the closing images can be perceived as unincorporated into the texture of the poem, generic constraints can be said to have stood in the way of the poem's final effectiveness. In either case, the interaction marks 'Aref's ghazal as the site of the cohabitation of new and old concepts and images.[60]

As a final step in demonstrating the dynamics of tradition and innovation in "The Message of Freedom," let me return briefly to the audience experiencing the poem as the poet sings it. Assuming that they have no prior knowledge of the poem's generic status, members of the audience begin, in absorbing the signs presented by the poet-singer, to construct the model of the poem from among those available in the tradition. The poem is registered as a ghazal only if they recognize such formal features as rhyme and rhythm, the number of the lines, the pen name, etc. Certain linguistic units—message motif, the drinking, mention of musical instruments—may also help to iden-tify the poem as a ghazal. Finally, the performance itself—that is, the pres-ence of musical instruments, the singing—may evoke the memory of the ghazal more strongly than that of any other category or class of poem.

But the audience perceives at the same time that the poem's content is not directed toward concepts traditionally associated with the ghazal: no philosophical observations, no expressions of carnal love or mystical experi-ence. In short, the poem is not preoccupied with the motifs easily traceable to the lyrical strain in Persian poetry. Rather, the poem's theme is directed toward certain identifiable events that relate to the community's public life. The audience might further sense that 'Aref has achieved this by juxtaposing certain conventional ghazal motifs to new ones. Explicit political concepts such as nation, Iran, constitution, despotism, and treachery as well as mythi-cal and historical references to Siavosh, Alexander, and Darius have helped to push the meanings the poem communicates in that direction. So have certain terms whose meanings can be directed toward either a political or a lyrical intent: coming to oneself, tearing (or restoring) the veil, clamoring, wailing, etc. As a result, two thematic spheres, previously considered separate, have merged. In the multiplicity of their implications, such terms begin to make the discourse of the ghazal meaningful with reference to events which may have little in common with their traditional signification. Thus, while some properties of 'Aref's poem—mostly formal and generic—ground it in the tradition of the Persian ghazal, certain others—primarily at the level of diction—register it as a political poem. The cohabitation within a single esthetic space of diverse semiotic units, previously operating in unconnected discursive realms, enable the poem to work as a "patriotic" or "political" ghazal—to use the appellation by which such compositions have become known. In writing such poems, 'Aref and other poets of the period convinced their audiences that the qasida, or the ghazal, genres perceived as irrelevant to contemporary concerns, can be made relevant and effective and useful to the common cause.

More than any other type of text I know in the Persian tradition, the political ghazal of the constitutional era justifies Bakhtin's insistence on the genre as the main vehicle of literary change through time. What he states as he theorizes about the rise of the novel in Europe can be applied with aston-ishing accuracy to the process by which the classical Persian ghazal turns into the vehicle of political expression in early twentieth-century Iran. Distin-guishing the genre from such concepts as "schools" or "currents," Bakhtin calls discursive genres "the transmission belts between social history and lin-guistic history" and compares their relative position as if they were characters in the grand narrative of literary history:

The historians of literature do not see, beyond the surface agitation and splashes of color, the great and essential destinies of literature and language, whose chief, foremost characters are genres, while currents and schools are lesser characters.[61]

In both "Remember . . ." and "The Message of Freedom" we have instances of two poetic genres which, while adhering to generic conventions, extend their reach far enough to occupy a cultural space often dichotomized with the lyrical. Whereas the classical Persian qasida and ghazal are thought to be directed toward the variety of emotions experienced by individual human beings, these poems give esthetic articulation to the political discourse of the constitutional era. They do so by directing signs of lyrical utterances toward collective or "national" ideas and events. In so doing, they envision a space wherein all lyrical utterances, past or present, become capable of assuming meanings outside their traditional habitat. Contemplations of history and myth or topical references to events of the day are no longer keyed solely to the world of the human psyche. Even constitutional era assessments of past lyrical performances are affected by this tendency, although that aspect of the issue lies beyond our concern here. Suffice it to recall that it is at this time that Hafez emerges as the supreme lyrical voice, and his ghazals are seen as deeply relevant to the history, society, and politics of his time.[62] The surplus of meaning invested in the genre of the ghazal helps to give it further potential for signifying concepts hitherto thought outside poetry's proper domain. In appearing to work within generic norms and conventions, poems such as the ones I have analyzed here are seen as compositions in accord with their generic status, yet different in their thematic thrust. In them, the appearance of conventionality becomes a means of preserving the memory of the model, while the realignment of internal relations instills a sense of difference that distinguishes them from a great deal of traditional poetry.

Dehkhoda's observation about "Remember . . . ," whereby he judges that poem equal to the best of European poetry, finds its true significance here. It is seen to be not a hollow boast, but an expression of this difference. Nor is the perception confined to a few poets' view of their own works. The entire poetic culture begins to incorporate such texts as valid ways of turning the lyrical impulse into expressions of common sentiments. And thus it is, in the case of Iranian culture, that the rechanneling of the lyrical impulse toward events of sociopolitical moment comes to constitute a primary index of poetic modernity. Individual poets may choose different genres, and their significatory and communicative strategies may differ from one another. As a condition of modernity, however, they must respond to the need for empowering poetic signs to release their meaning on the public plane. In practice, early twentieth-century Iranian poets achieved this by expanding Persian poetry's system of signification while following formal and generic rules. It is in this sense that Bakhtin's linking of "the great historical destinies of literary discourse" with "the destiny of genres" finds its true meaning in the Iranian context.[63]

Once this is accepted as the model of poetic composition appropriate to the society, all texts produced on that basis are judged as instances of relevant and original poetry. They are seen as poetry because they adhere to generic distinctions—still a feature of the poetic culture. They are thus distinguished from what the culture might call nonpoetry. They are considered relevant because they satisfy the demand for social involvement. They are thus distinguished from much that, even though it may be called poetry, is seen as belonging to another world, a different time in the life of the culture. Finally, they are viewed as original because they are seen to articulate those issues which the culture has come to accept as appropriate to poetry, and do so in a way that the best poets of the past would have done had they been living under the present circumstances. In the social practice of poetry, in other words, the specific scenario of poetic modernity advanced in the constitutional period consisted in the type of poetic text illustrated in this chapter. Such texts formed the center, because in them the manipulation of traditional resources had made possible the treatment of sociopolitical issues. They were thus viewed as reflecting the concerns shared by poets and their immediate audience.[64]

Theoretically speaking, such models retain their force and validity until such time as the culture, perceiving itself in changed circumstances, may begin to demand new departures from the current practice, a practice which it then begins to describe as traditional. In historical perspective, much in the practice of poets like Bahar, Iraj, Parvin, and others that is identifiable as qasidas, ghazals and the like fall into this category. It is with reference to this practice that the culture retains the power to distinguish poetry from nonpoetry. The cultural reserve that is thus accumulated may work at a later stage to position these poets against other innovators advancing other scenarios. In the case of Iran, the opposition of poets like Bahar and Iraj to new practices by Raf'at, 'Eshqi, and Nima, to name a few, typifies this tendency. In their search for modernity, the latter group would discard aspects of the traditional practice—generic distinctions, for example—unacceptable to the former. The successful assimilation of one stage in the process of poetic change into the texture of the culture constitutes a necessary condition for beginning the next.[65]

The entire poetic practice of the Iranian constitutional era needs to be defined, described, and analyzed in terms more systemically anchored than it has been thus far. Assumptions about the political or patriotic nature of the ghazal or qasida of the time leave out important aspects of this poetic practice. The current assessment of this poetry as essentially a politicized version of the classical tradition does not allow us to see the *poetic* aspects of the difference it embodies, especially those that relate to the internal structure of poetic relations. Nor does it address the relationship between this poetry and the millennium-old tradition of Persian poetry, nor the process by which it comes into being and gains acceptance. This is particularly important in the case of the poetry most centrally informed by the events of the constitutional revolution. We will not be able to see, nor articulate, the specific ways in which new poetic texts or modes of signification help simultaneously to sustain and to alter older ones. Similarly, the potential of a specific poetic practice to perpetuate and alter an inherited esthetic system at one and the same time remains invisible. Conceptualizing esthetic change solely as an outcome of certain social preoccupations presents a limited view of literary history forever tied to the vagaries of individual taste and subjective judgment.

That, I suppose, is what Bakhtin means when he chides literary historians for getting entangled in "the petty vicissitudes of stylistic modification, themselves tied to individual artists and particular currents."[66] No amount of attention to changes in poetic style, whether conceived as belonging to an individual poet or to a period, would be sufficient to explain the difference between a qasida called "Remember . . ." and the stereotyped notion of the Persian qasida or that between "The Message of Freedom" and the idea of the Persian ghazal current at the time. Nor can an event like the Iranian constitutional movement in itself account adequately for the complex ways in which poets and readers in early twentieth-century Iran formed and transformed their perception of esthetic statements. Expansions and contractions of signs, modifications in poetic structures and relations, and departures from formal and generic rules ought to be studied if the process of literary change is to be comprehended in all its complexity. Poetic practices of the kind I have examined in this chapter create a series of impressions in individual readers who in turn posit them on the social context surrounding each poetic text. In the end, poets and readers, as well as the culture, shape specific attitudes toward the poetic tradition and its relationship with the culture. Only an understanding of the patterns of this interaction can make the dynamics of esthetic change perceptible.

Chapter Three

An Open Literary Culture

 The Iranian constitutional movement gave rise to a vision of the modern era as an age different from the rest of the national history, now imagined increasingly as a single continuous line. The social discourse of the new century's first two decades was informed by the perception that a millennium-old political system of despotic rule had ended. After the Revolution of 1905–11, it was felt increasingly that comparably radical changes ought to occur in the culture. The search for new esthetic principles must be seen as part of a national effort to facilitate those changes, and the idea of a poetry manifestly different from that of the past formed an important part of that endeavor. Within this framework, the question of the relevance of the poetic heritage of the Persian language gradually formed the basis on which poets, critics, and readers conducted the dialogue on the new poetry.

Awareness of a "European" literature was also becoming couched in broad assumptions about a correspondence between literary history and political history. As a unique event in Iranian history and a giant step toward the future, the Constitutional Revolution was thought capable of creating a climate wherein poets comparable to Europe's best would be nurtured. Broad parallels drawn between the Iranian Revolution and the French Revolution brought about an intense curiosity about nineteenth-century French literature, envisioned as the literary consequence of the French Revolution. European Romanticism was thought to have put an end to the classical period in European literature. Writers and poets like Rousseau, Madame De Stahl, Daudet, Hugo, Lamartine, and Chateaubriand became the object of intense attention in historical and biographical sketches, their works widely and variously translated or imitated.

Still, there was little consensus about the shape of the poetry to come, and its exact relation to European poetry or to the native tradition. The classical tradition was at times likened to the millennium-old despotic rule that had preceded the Constitutional Revolution, the analogy leading to a vision of the new poetry as somehow comparable to constitutional democracy. The new poetry would then be articulated in terms antithetical to the classical canon of ghazals and qasidas. As for the details, however, some believed that Iranian poets would have to school themselves on European poetry, while others would have them look deeper within the native tradition. An exploration of the terms and scope of the ensuing debates forms the focus of my attention in this chapter.

As we saw in chapter 2, Iranian intellectuals had already distinguished between the simplicity and clarity of early Persian poetry and the ornate, complicated character of poetry in later centuries. The devastating Mongol and Tartar invasions of the thirteenth and fourteenth centuries provided a convenient divide between the two, and were at times seen as the causes of the cultural demise characteristic of the later period.[1] In the wake of the Constitutional Revolution, the division began to be extended to the relations that connect poetry to its social context. The classical age was imagined not just as a glorious era of esthetic creativity but also as one of concern with the life of the community on the part of poets and other cultural figures. The later centuries, by contrast, were thought to be marked not only by decline in the creative spirit but also, more significantly, by the absence of any discernible connections between poetry and social life. In fact, the derivative nature of poetry in this period was believed to testify to its exclusionary nature, poetry having become an utterance thought to belong only to closed circles of like-minded elites concerned solely with lyrical or mystical expression and skilled in farfetched conceits and other verbal acrobatics.

Thus, in advancing a vision of poetic change, the literary intellectuals of the postconstitution decades were already operating within fairly well defined historical constructs. Whatever their vision, it would have to conform to an already present version of history. It would further have to be seen to stand in contrast to that of the recent past, more or less in the same way that nineteenth-century European poetry was thought to have parted company with that which preceded it. In a sense, these constraints can be said to form the outer boundaries of all the emergent scenarios of poetic change.[2] Internally, the increasingly patriotic and political milieu of postconstitution decades imposed its own constraints on the idea and practice of poetry as an acceptable social activity. On the one hand, the social institution called poetry could not be imagined without regard to the demands of the age, defined fairly clearly as engagement with topical issues of social and political significance. On the other, its practice would have to relate in more or less perceptible ways at least to parts of the tradition. No vision of poetry, not even a single poem, thought to be a sign of alien intrusion into the native culture would have a chance for acceptance; it would simply be dismissed as a sign of Western influence.

Although we can point to advocates of a wholesale break with traditional poetry, as well as to those arguing for unquestioning adherence to it, the debate on poetry became quickly focused on the nature of a new poetry and the scope and pace of poetic change. Naturally, the greater the exposure to European poetry and poetic traditions, the greater the inclination to utilize extrasystemic material to build the modern poetry of Iran. Contrarily, the more immersed a poet or critic was in the classical tradition, the more he or she would be inclined to rely on the means of expression associated with the Persian poetry of the early classical times.

The emerging notion of the present as an age different from, and often contrasted to, the past had implications for the pace of literary change as well. Two basic tendencies can be detected here. Some viewed the age in terms of a gradual movement of events increasingly looking to a historical future for its ultimate fruition. They saw the present as having to await the future for its ultimate significance and value; they envisioned the future as totally different from the past. Almost all the literary figures of early twentieth-century Iran who were associated with a traditionalist outlook on contemporary poetry conceived of their time as a preamble (*dibacheh*) to the future.[3] Others, without denying the validity of the past in relation to itself, conceived of the present as itself a cleavage with the past. This group advocated more radical changes in poetry and tended to dismiss the past as a source of enrichment for the present culture. In fact, they viewed readiness to reject the past as the necessary condition for focusing on the present. Their view of current poetry was not constrained by a notion of it as a mere stage along an uncharted road; it had its own sense of poetic coherence. In my judgment, the inner tension resulting from this dual awareness of the age, both as a locus of actual difference and as a source of development for the future, determined and guided the dialogue between the groups known in traditional literary criticism as the radicals and moderates in the generation following the Constitutional Revolution.

A DEBATE ON POETIC MODERNITY

The combination of assumptions and aspirations inherent in these two tendencies gave rise to a plethora of views on the nature of the relationship between classical and modern literary cultures. The fluidity of the terms of discourse allowed various poets and critics to justify certain specific practices dictated by their ideological positions as the demands of the age. Numerous literary figures can be quoted to illustrate each argument. Because they are so clearly central in the postconstitution literary discourse, I pursue the debate on the problematics of poetic modernization through two literary figures—Mohammad-Taqi Bahar (1880–1951) and Taqi Raf'at (1889–1920)—editors respectively of *Daneshkadeh* and *Tajaddod,* two of the most influential journals of the period.

As two principal voices of the time, these two literary figures provide the most comprehensive articulations of poetic modernity. More important, they reflect the tension I described above and its underlying concerns and considerations. Bahar, firmly convinced that every political revolution must be followed by a literary one, still ends up on the traditional side of the argument, in part because of his classical poetic upbringing. For him, the preservation of what he views as the inalienable spirit of Persian poetry is paramount. For his part, Raf'at, perhaps the most original and articulate advocate of radical literary modernism, espouses a vision which he believes would alter the bases of poetic practice. Beyond the linguistic resources of the Persian language, he places almost no reliance on the traditional practice of poetry. I use the phrase "linguistic resources" here in contradistinction from the wealth of properties, provisions, and ways and means which may be termed more specifically "poetic." I will have occasion to clarify this distinction further in chapter 5 where I examine Raf'at's own poetic compositions. We will see there that this particular Iranian modernist refuses rather self-consciously to rely in any substantive way on the significatory devices of classical Persian poetry.

It is important to reiterate that the Bahar-Raf'at debate, occurring over a decade after the Constitutional Revolution, reflects many of the semantic complexities of an evolving social discourse at its most fluid stage. Throughout the postconstitution debate on literature, such terms as "literary change" (*tahavvol-e adabi*), "literary modernization" (*tajaddod-e adabi*), and "literary revolution" (*enqelab-e adabi*) held a variety of connotations often conveyed through an analogical logic. This logic was itself the vestige of a mode of thinking that had remained substantially unchanged, the desire to overcome its limitations notwithstanding. In the bipolar discourse thus created, "old poetry and prose" (*she'r va nasr-e qadim*) was understood in terms at once contiguous and antithetical to an as yet largely undefined "new poetry and prose" (*she'r va nasr-e jadid*) or "new verse and prose" (*nazm va nasr-e jadid*). The latter concept was generally seen as akin to what was most often termed "European poetry and prose" (*she'r va nasr-e orupa'i*), even though the exact nature of the affinity was hardly a matter of agreement. In short, the language of the debate on modernity in the Persian poetry of the early twentieth century is intricate and opaque, subject to a variety of interpretations that come ultimately to depend on the interpreter's own ideology and vision of modernity. As a result, the poetic discourse that emerges begins to throw all cultural products into two antithetical poles: the old and the new. The idea of relevance, understood as willingness to tackle socially significant topics in an ideologically correct way, appears to be the ultimate arbiter. I shall take the dialogue at its culmination as Bahar's journal *Daneshkadeh* tries to define its place among Iran's literary journals.

The first issue of *Daneshkadeh* appeared on April 21, 1918. Two years before, Bahar had gathered around himself a small literary clique, calling it *Jargeh-ye Daneshvari* (Daneshvari Circle), soon renamed *Jargeh-ye Adabi* (Literary Circle). The word *daneshvari* was a recent coinage taken from the word *danesh* (knowledge or science) and a suffix connoting a disposition toward, a preoccupation with, or an engagement in something. The name change must therefore be seen as a more specific definition of the area of "knowledge" in which the circle was beginning to ground its intellectual activity. Over the following two years, this group grew larger and more influential as it published various literary works in *Now-Bahar, Zaban-e Azad,* and other newspapers of the time. Early in 1918, the group changed its name once more to Daneshkadeh Literary Society (*Anjoman-e Adabi-ye Daneshka-deh*) and appointed Bahar, its best-known figure, as its director *(modir)*. It also began to publish the monthly journal *Daneshkadeh* (the word connotes a place for disseminating knowledge) as a strictly literary periodical. The journal lasted a year with regular monthly issues, except for the final one, advertised as such and numbered as the journal's eleventh and twelfth issues.[4]

Daneshkadeh's contents are varied indeed. Besides Bahar's lead articles, conceived essentially as establishing the group's stance on questions about literary change in Iran, there were two series of fairly extensive prose essays, one written by 'Abbas Eqbal-Ashtiani entitled "Literary History" (Tarikh-e Adabi), the other by Rashid Yasemi on French literary history and entitled, rather pointedly, "Literary Revolution" (Enqelab-e Adabi).[5] A third series, simply entitled "The Great" (Bozorgan), presented brief biographic sketches of various European literary figures, mostly of the French Romantic movement. Through these, Iranian readers became acquainted with Boileau, Rousseau, Daudet, Lamartine, Hugo, and Zola, among others. To further familiarize its readers with European literatures, *Daneshkadeh* also published samples and fragments of writings by European authors translated into Persian.

In addition to the essays on the history of Persian literature, examples of Persian poetry, both of classical and contemporary poets, were given almost equal attention in the pages of *Daneshkadeh,* although in contemporary poetry, the journal featured only a handful of poets. Finally, a remarkable section of many issues contained a contest common in the literary culture of the time. Members of the Daneshkadeh Literary Society were encouraged to versify stories, fables, or aphorisms of various European authors, based on a Persian prose translation of the text. In a section titled "Eqterah" or "Eqterah-e Adabi" (The Test of Literary Talent), the prose translation appeared along with various verse renditions by different hands. Because of its significance as a novel literary practice and its implications for poetic change in Iran, I examine this practice separately in the next chapter.

Through its specific sections and individual items, as in its overall structure, *Daneshkadeh* fostered a climate of great curiosity about the relevance of two broad categories: the classical tradition in Persian literature and postrenaissance Western, primarily French, literary culture. The essay series on the history of Persian literature, for example, opens with a definition of literature according to Persian classics juxtaposed to a definition according to Europeans.[6] Similarly, the essays entitled "Literary Revolution" start off with a sweeping statement concerning the relevance of sixteenth-century French literature for "the present state of [literature in] our country."[7] In its *Eqterah* sections mentioned above, the journal features texts that can be called verse translations of European aphorisms, fables, and stories as well as novel additions to the Persian tradition of moralia literature. Perhaps most visibly, in introducing European poets and critics through brief biographical accounts, it emphasizes their part in changing their literature. While clearly aimed at broadening Iran's literary culture perceptibly, this preoccupation with Western literatures seems to have met from the beginning with some resistance among the journal's readers. In its second issue, *Daneshkadeh* found it necessary to defend its policy of opening up to the West. "Perhaps," says a note bearing the signature of the Daneshkadeh Literary Society, "our readers would ask why *Daneshkadeh* has given priority to the great literary figures of the West and does not introduce the Eastern—our own—great men." It then defended the policy in these words:

Yes! our great men are more dear to us on all counts. However, a knowledge of other nations' poets and literati will be just as suitable to us. We know our own great men. Let us [have a chance to] know the great men of other nations as well, just as the Europeans have gained knowledge of our great men.[8]

Such statements highlight the determination to make the literatures of Western nations meaningful to Iranians. They also underline the desire to harness the literary traditions of Europe as a source of enrichment for an emerging canon of Persian literature expressive of the social concerns most pressing to modern-day Iranians. The soul-searching visible in the pages of *Daneshkadeh* is ultimately indicative of the will to modernize the native literary tradition in such a way that it would serve the needs of Iranian society. In practice this determination is manifested in the tacit requirement that anything published in the journal must in some way contribute to the conception and creation of a modern Iranian literature. In terms of literary history, a canon had to be established that would include the best examples, whether foreign or native, that contemporary poets or prose writers could emulate. In translation, new texts had to be assimilated into the tradition in ways that would allow the translated text to be perceived both as novel and as not too different from traditional poetic texts. Most important, in articulating the task of the contemporary poet, the literary debates initiated by *Daneshkadeh* delineated the boundaries of an emerging vision of change essential to the practice of poetry in the decades to follow.

From the beginning, *Daneshkadeh* acknowledged the presence of diverse literary tendencies and attempted to reason with their advocates and practitioners. In setting out its principles, it sought to steer a steady course between two obstacles: traditionalist isolationism arising from anxieties about foreign elements penetrating into the literary body, and a kind of romantic modernism premised on the near total rejection of the esthetic tradition. The journal rejected—and at times ridiculed—as unreasonable and futile, all insistence on Persian poetry's self-sufficiency as well as all iconoclastic gestures. It recounted the merits of European prose and poetry, offered specimens of it in translation, and weighed the possibility of assimilating it into the native tradition. At the same time, it insisted on the inalienable spirit of Persian poetry which, it said, must be taken into account in all visions of esthetic change.

In doing so, *Daneshkadeh* expanded a basic tenet of nineteenth-century literary reformists by advancing the idea that literary change flows from sociopolitical changes. Focusing on postconstitution Iranian society as the appropriate historical context for such a change, Eqbal-Ashtiani observes:

Thus you see first of all that literature in general is a function [*tabeʿ*] of political revolutions—that is, literary movements occur only in the wake of political movements—and secondly that the literature of every period has its own specific characteristics.[9]

Let us try to visualize this statement between two imaginary poles, one of a modern poetry identical with the classical tradition, the other of a poetry totally unrelated to it. The attempt may enable us to conceptualize the ways in which the practice of poetry, in its systemic links with the classical tradition and in absorbing new extrasystemic elements, actually related to the ensuing dialogue. The idea of literature as a function of political revolutions and of the literature of each period possessing its own specific characteristics would seem to place the vision described here closer to the pole where the new poetry would be independent of the tradition. Theoretically, however, the production of such a poetry is impossible, the endeavor to create it comparable, in Lotman's words, to wishing to play "a game without rules." Lotman views all such seemingly revolutionary gestures as advocating a game "whose rules must be established in the process of play."[10] On that basis, Lotman concludes that the construction of models for works that reflect the esthetics of identity is a far less complicated task than that of constructing models for works that reflect the esthetics of opposition. The latter's complexity, he argues, is due to the heightening of the conflict between the text and the reader's consciousness, itself a social entity:

> In working with phenomena classed under the esthetics of opposition we must distinguish cases when the destroyed cliche-structure exists in the reader's consciousness due to his habits and a certain amount of inertia. . . . Things become simpler when an author uses certain elements in the construction of the work to evoke in the reader's consciousness a structure which will then be destroyed.[11]

In chronicling the course of poetic change in Iran, it is extremely important, I think, to bear in mind the constant interaction between the structure of the poetic system and the elements which seem to negate that structure. Each text, of course, strikes its own balance between systemic structures present in the tradition and elements dictated by the demands of the age (a term almost synonymous with the context) and embodies a different mix of elements which render the total system different from all stereotypical articulations of it. Typically as well as in the case at hand, the more the concept of change moves in time, the more poets and critics accept and advocate—and readers begin to absorb—even greater (meaning more systemic) departures from the tradition. The movement lasts until the culture comes to rest in the perception that the practice of the period does indeed respond to the dictates of the age and does possess "its own specific characteristics."

In *Daneshkadeh*, the advocacy of such a literature is evident in the manner in which the story of the rise and changes of literature in France and other European cultures was presented. As a title, the phrase "Literary Revolution," given to a chronicle of French literature in the seventeenth through nineteenth centuries, seems designed to emphasize the constant metamorphosis of genres and trends. The journal's emphasis on the potential of European literatures for fertilizing the soil of contemporary Iranian literature can be interpreted as a logical part of its mission, based on the perception of an obvious lack in the literature of the time. In the journal's view, this mission would have to be pursued within the framework of a larger imperative, namely the preservation of continuity with the tradition. Only that consideration would render the differences between old and new poetries acceptable to those who saw the essence of the culture itself in the poetry of the past. The fear that Iranian culture might be diminished if Persian poetry is totally Westernized acted as the ultimate check on the postconstitution drive toward poetic modernity. *Daneshkadeh*, in short, saw its mission as one of mediating between the absolute necessity to retain a specifically Iranian spirit in contemporary poetic practice and the determination, where possible, to modernize poetry on the basis of Western models.

The effort to publish the journal had obviously been undertaken with this specific purpose in mind, and *Daneshkadeh* ceased publication a year later when Bahar's group thought its mission fulfilled.[12] What makes *Daneshkadeh* unique in the annals of Iranian literary journals is the fact that in it a multiplicity of views and approaches presented a more or less coherent vision of poetic change. This will become all the more obvious as we compare the voice of that journal with other more traditional or more radically modernist visions present in Iran in the two decades that followed the Revolution of 1905–11. For all these reasons, I approach the task of analyzing the meaning and significance of the literary dialogue it initiated with the contention that *Daneshkadeh* communicated a central and more or less cohesive scenario of poetic modernity. In addition, I intend to demonstrate the centrality of the journal's ideas to the poetic practice of the period.

By far the most coherent series of literary pronouncements made through *Daneshkadeh* are the initial articles written by the journal's editor, Mohammad-Taqi Bahar. In its first issue, under the title of "Maram-e Ma" (Our Ideology), Bahar attempts to place the journal's mission in the context of the Society's initial view of poetry and its subsequent and growing desire to forge what he calls a forward-looking, yet sound and solid, vision. When the Daneshkadeh Literary Society first got together, he writes, its members "only composed ghazals on the models of the old lyricists [*moteghazzelin-e qadim*]." Gradually, as the Society expanded, it thought itself capable of "continuing its endeavor on the basis of newer principles [*osul-e tazeh-tar*]." These newer principles, according to Bahar, include "inquiries in prose and in verse" (*tadqiqat-e nazmiyyeh va nasriyyeh*) and "translations of foreign literature (*tarjomeh-ye adabiyyat-e khareji*)." Bahar sums up the first article of his group's "practical ideology" (*maram-e 'amali*)[13] as "revisions in the manner and method of Iran's literature, with due respect for the old masters' lexical method [*oslub-e loghavi*] and mode and manner of verbal expression [*tarz va raviyyeh-ye ada-ye 'ebarat*], observance of the new style [*mora'at-e sabk-e jadid*],[14] and general requirements of the present age [*ehtiyajat-e 'omumi-ye hal-e hazer*]."

The pattern of shifting emphases, widening intentions, and rising aspirations which Bahar implies in this statement, merits a few observations because it indicates a gradual realization of the inadequacy of the traditional tendencies that had brought the members together in the first place. First, it is clear that as the Daneshvari Circle has evolved: it has come to see the need for producing a type of poetry that would emulate both foreign and native models. The growing conviction that sources other than those in the native tradition must be tapped if Persian poetry is to be made relevant to the present time is quite unprecedented. At no previous period in the history of Persian literature had a poet, literary historian, or literary group articulated the challenge before it in quite this manner.[15] This in itself constitutes a significant departure from the practice of the past millennium. Second, the emphasis on literary translation is noteworthy as a component of the vision described here. The very survival of Persian poetry, Bahar seems to be saying, depends on externally directed modeling activities. At the same time, Bahar's emphasis on pragmatism can be viewed as a balancing principle which would ensure the new poetry sufficient grounding in the tradition of the past. It is this principle, more than anything else, that separates him—and *Daneshkadeh*—from those who would seek modernity even at the price of open ruptures with the tradition.

Finally, by the time the journal *Daneshkadeh* began to appear the need for a new kind of poetry was not an issue. The evolutionary vision Bahar presents here must be seen as essential to his pragmatic approach to the question:

> The world is subject to revolutions. In this changeable and changing environment, from the oceans to mountains and deserts, from great countries to small families, from dress to words and idioms, everything is subject

to mutation and change. It is therefore not surprising if changes occur in our literature, in our language, and in the way we express our intentions. At the same time, however, we do not wish to commit ourselves to a course of action before the evolutionary process commands us to do so.[16]

From the beginning, *Daneshkadeh* tried to steer a course which, while opening the poetic system to greater changes, would not be seen as doing violence to a poetic tradition to which the culture of modern Iran, steeped in the ideology of patriotic nationalism, can point with pride. In Bahar's words, modernism should not be turned into "the pickax against the historical structures built by the poets and literary figures who are our fathers and forebears." Rather, "while repairing the structures erected by them, we begin to lay the foundation for newer structures next to theirs."[17]

That hesitancy, bespeaking a desire to occupy two different spaces at the same time, could not be overlooked from the perspective of radical modernists. The rather clumsy analogy of building one's abode while repairing an older one signaled to them an untenable position. Poets like Bahar were seen, on the one hand, as aware that change is inevitable and, on the other, bent on safeguarding obsolete structures of unproven worth and validity. The most cogently argued refutation I have come across appeared in *Tajaddod* (Modernism), a literary journal which had just begun to be published in Tabriz, the capital of Iran's northwestern province of Azerbaijan. The journal's editor, Taqi Raf'at, a young admirer of European literatures had begun the publication of the journal shortly after *Daneshkadeh* had made its appearance. *Tajaddod's* pages soon became the space where the desire to bring about drastic, revolutionary changes in Iranian literature and culture was expressed. In fact, insofar as an overall critique of the traditional culture of Iran is concerned, *Tajaddod* remains a unique document in the annals of Iranian journalism. Using such terms as "literary despotism," "forces of cultural reaction," and "the dam of conservatism" Raf'at created a mode of discourse on literature wherein advocates of gradual change were aligned with undesirable political elements. More than anyone, Raf'at is responsible for the interlocking of literary and political discourses of modern Iran, still a feature of the literary culture. In his time, the rhetoric worked to push the issue of literary change through a decisive phase. As we shall see in chapter 6, the linguistic node thus created took another turn when it was reformulated by Nima, and eventually found its manifestation in the contemporary poetry of Iran. For his part, Raf'at argued that Bahar's position was illogical and untenable. He began his response by focusing on the metaphor of ancestral structures as the modern poet's abode:

In the above lines you admit a few things. First, that you are afraid [to venture out], preferring to continue to live in your ancestral home. Second, that that structure is in need of repair and that you shall undertake such repair. Third, that next to the above-mentioned structure, you shall erect newer structures. No mason or architect devises a plan of this sort. Such a thought will condemn you to failure.[18]

Raf'at then forges his own metaphor of the modern poet's task. With the determination of a warrior ordering his troops forward, he issues a call to Bahar's younger colleagues to take to the field in the cause of literary revolution:

Literary youth of Daneshkadeh! With the most radical sense of modern-ism [*mofrat-tarin hess-e Tajaddod-parvari*] and the most interminable of lit-erary ideals [*tulani-tarin amal-e adabiyyeh*], call upon all your friends for help and without fear enter the field of battle. Do not be afraid! Fight self-assuredly and incessantly! You shall not reach your goal so easily. . . . How-ever, your unchanneled literary energies will give you a true notion of mo-dernity. Having toiled long and hard, you may find on the blank draft pages before you a few awkward (inaccurate) words [*chand lafz-e ghalat*], a few disharmonious (unrhythmical) phases [*chand 'ebarat-e namowzun*], a few uneven (rough) poems [*chand she'r-e nahamvar*]. But rest assured! Moder-nity will still be far away from you. . . . Modernity is tantamount to a revolution. It cannot be poured into people's eyes with a dropper.[19]

Turning Bahar's words on their heads, he counters the argument which stated that moves toward literary modernity must be synchronized with the general movement of the entire society so that the audience for literature might be kept in view:

Nor should you, friends of Daneshkadeh, anticipate any assistance from popular sentiments [*ehsasat-e 'omumiyyeh*], the national character [*akhlaq-e melliyyeh*], or the thoughts of the social body [*afkar-e hay'at-e ejtema'iyyeh*]. All such generalities are meaningless. Those very popular sentiments and national habits demonstrated a woeful indifference toward such events as the constitutional movement and the civil liberties as well. If you fasten such heavy balls around the ankles of your poetic talents [*tab'-e she'r*] and literary tastes [*qariheh-ye adabi*], you will end up making advancement impossible for yourselves. If you are poets and literary figures, realize that poets and literary figures must be leaders not followers.[20]

Already we can see two dichotomous visions in the positions summarized here. Whereas Bahar would have poets move in step with the larger society,

Raf'at would have them lead the society in the march toward a modern literature. To him, poets are guided by none other than their own personal instinct for a literature that would express individual feelings, sensations, and impressions. Consider Raf'at's choice of words for the product of the most radical sense of modernism. The "awkward words," "disharmonious phrases," and "uneven poems" which modern poets might have to offer as the fruit of their long and hard labor may well appear to their readers as inaccurate, rough, and devoid of rhythm. But that is due precisely to the poet's personal instinct for modernism.[21] In undertaking to create the standards and criteria by which to measure literary products, one risks, by definition, appearing inaccurate or awkward, unrhythmical or disharmonious, rough or uneven. Poets must accept such risks as part of their effort to develop not just the modern poem but also the esthetic criteria for evaluating it.

Bahar responded immediately to Raf'at's refutation of his position in an essay entitled "Enteqadat dar Atraf-e Maram-e Ma" (Criticisms Concerning Our Ideology), published in the third issue of *Daneshkadeh*. In particular, he attempted to elaborate on his analogy of the modern poet's obligations toward ancestral poetic structures. In so doing, he restates the position of *Daneshkadeh* and defends gradualism in matters of literary change. Making a distinction between natural change, where individuals respond to a general demand for new ways and means of expression and artificial experimentation, where changes in literature are initiated "for their own sake," he observes:

> Contrary to those who, not knowing the meaning of advancement, believe that jumping up and falling back down on the ground constitutes progress, we regard natural evolution [*takamol-e tabi'i*] and gradual perfection [*takmil-e tadriji*] to be the only way for a nation to achieve real advancement. We believe a real revolution to be too slow and too imperceptible [a process] to allow our revolutionary authors to exemplify it in their first perfunctory motions, their first harmonious or disharmonious [rhythmic or unrhythmic] [*mowzun ya namowzun*], imitative or innovative [derivative or original] [*taqlidi ya ekhtera'i*] dance.[22]

Using another building analogy, Bahar set out to demonstrate the efficacy of reliance on the materials of the inherited tradition. He writes: "We are dealing here with the question of modes of articulation of meaning [*tarz-e ada-ye ma'ani*]. And the structures of our fathers ['*emarat-e pedaraneman*] mean the philological foundations and the general outline [of that structure]: that is what we dare not demolish." He then issues a challenge to his adversaries:

If you modernists regard the lexicon, phraseology, and literary composi- tions of Iran as similar to the ruins of Tcyphon, say so frankly and fearlessly. We will not attack you; rather we will simply ask you whence, from which kiln or quarry you will provide bricks and rocks so solid, so unique and so ready-made, that we too may find and use them.[23]

The Bahar-Raf'at debate was highly metaphorical, a quality which may well obscure each side's positions on the question of poetic change. They both did clearly desire to conceptualize and articulate the problem despite their many analogies and equivocations. Any attempt to disentangle the strands of the argument outlined here must work its way through the meta- phors presented, challenged, or negated in each discourse. In undertaking such an attempt, I focus on three principal loci of shifting perceptions wherein two distinct sets of attitudes and tendencies can be seen to compete for attention and approval.

First, for both Bahar and Raf'at the notion of the poet's relationship to his social context seems to have been affected by the emergence of a cultural entity named Iran. The cultural and literary heritage of the past is beginning to be described here in terms of an "Iranian" entity. It is "Iranian culture" and "Iranian literature" that forms the subject of ongoing debates, and it is to Iran, rather than to cultural concepts such as "the Persian language" or "the literary heritage of the Persian-speaking peoples," that the participants pledge their allegiance. This shift, from a language-based construct to one in which the sociopolitical ramifications of esthetic changes are fostered, is itself a product of a set of relations recently restructured, namely those that connect the poetic craft with the poet's sense of the society to which he or she belongs. Initiated through the subversive discourses of an earlier generation, poets are now counted among the intelligentsia. As such, they are conceived as social leaders trying to determine the limits and possibilities of social change. Ba- har's emphasis on such ideas as natural evolution and the evolutionary pro- cess, on the one hand, and on the social body, on the other, indicates his determination to relate his understanding of the theory of the evolution to social processes. The idea of culture going through stages analogous to those that may govern the world of nature leads him to a notion of poetic change constrained by forces outside individual reach. Raf'at's characterization of ideas like the national character, the social body, and popular feelings as a series of fictitious abstractions, on the contrary, reveals his reliance on the romantic notion of the visionary poet often at odds with the forces that control the society and constrain his ability to remake it in the image of human ideals. What Bahar points to as determining the possibilities for po- etic change appears to Raf'at as obstacles to overcome. Ultimately, both visions can be said to be based on Western notions of the social function of poetry, one closer to the image of the poet as a social leader, the other to that of the poet as the cultural rebel.[24]

The second place where our two interlocutors diverge significantly is closely related to the first. The acquaintance, however rudimentary, with nineteenth-century European cultures has instilled an impression of the expressive function of poetry in the mind of early twentieth-century Iranian intellectuals. This impression, although detectable through Bahar's position as well, finds a more explicit resonance with Raf'at. For both men the notion of poetic expression seems to be shifting from the act of providing a contemporary voice for universally valid ideas to that of the possibility of expressing one's own specific feelings, emotions, and social condition. The "philological foundations" and "general outline of the literary structures" Bahar alludes to stand in a teasingly oblique relation to the "awkward words," "disharmonious phrases," and "uneven poems" which Raf'at would welcome as signs of modernism. Moreover, the question Bahar poses toward the end—where are Iranian poets supposed to fetch the "bricks" and "rocks" as solid as those found in their linguistic tradition?—appears at once present to Iranian poets and distant from them. The apparent absence of traditional notions of esthetic beauty which repels Bahar if Iranian poets adopt alien images and expressive devices constitutes a legitimate part of the search for a new esthetic for Raf'at. He would see such a pursuit as the very essence of poetic modernity. This incidentally is precisely what Raf'at attempts to illustrate in his own practice as a poet, a topic I return to later in this book.

Finally, while both Bahar and Raf'at anchor their arguments concerning poetry's social function in a notion nonexistent in previous modes of intellectual discourse, they differ in their view of the poet's ultimate responsibility. In their culture, assumptions about the logocentric nature of the classical culture have given rise to conflicting views concerning the contemporary poet's ultimate obligations and responsibilities. Each view in turn has certain ramifications for a poetic practice appropriate to the period. On one side, the idea of poetry as an index of cultural continuity tends to obligate the contemporary poet to preserve the spirit of the culture. On the other, the notion of poetry as an essentially social phenomenon tends to encourage the poet to act as a citizen, with a sense of social responsibility ultimately directed toward the social situation in hand. The conflict between the poet as an agent of preservation versus an instrument of recording the present is phrased in the debate in terms primarily of scenarios for poetic change. The resultant tension, as we will see, turns into an important source of systemic dynamism throughout the twentieth century in the poetry of Iranian culture. In time, the idea that poets somehow "reflect" their social condition in their work contributes to an argument that they ought to do so, eventually raising the notion of commitment in the poetry of the 1950s and later. Any archaeology of the discourse about the primacy of social content in modern poetry, as we shall see in chapter 6, takes us back to social dialogues of the type we are examining here.

It should be clear that the tendencies which emerge in the debate between Bahar and Raf'at point to a far more complex phenomenon in the literary culture of early twentieth-century Iran. The distinction between an evolutionary and a revolutionary view of poetic change illustrates an atmosphere of cultural and esthetic polyvalence where not only relations between poetry and society but also the very basis of poetic signification begins to be a matter of open contestation. Varying degrees of tolerance for rupture, the search for innovation beyond established thematic and generic boundaries, and particularly the linkage between esthetic value and the presentation of sociopolitical issues signal the leap from elemental to structural changes. Of the two tendencies illustrated here, the gradualist position would not initiate formal and generic violations of the traditional poetic system, whereas the more radical position might do so to redress what it sees as a lack in the native tradition.

Having acknowledged that, however, we must look first for the conceptual grounding of such enunciations, and then for still more precise implications of them. Let me take one central concept from each interlocutor and show the principle behind its social operation. Bahar's notion of the ancestral structures, which he articulates in terms of the philological foundations of Persian poetry, must, I think, be understood as a way of relying on the expressive mechanisms present in the system of Perisan poetry to suffice for the expression of contemporary impulses. To him, as to the generations of poets, readers, and critics who have maintained that position through similar arguments, the system of signification and communication forged and fostered through the practice of centuries appears, on the one hand, to be an adequate means of poetic expression and, on the other, to constitute an inviolable entity. This, in effect, is what he means when he speaks of the spirit of Persian poetry. His position implies that Persian poetry can be made to express topical sociopolitical issues. He maintains further that this can be achieved without any need to revamp the classical genres, or poetic devices, or meter and rhyme. In short, with minimal modifications, the native system of poetic signification and communication can be made to serve the purposes of modernity. All that needs to be done is a redirection of traditional means and devices toward sociopolitical thematics. One is therefore justified in deviating from the existing system only insofar as such an act is not expressed, nor interpreted, as indicative of a lack in the classical tradition.

Raf'at's argument about the unsuitability of the ancestral structures, on the contrary, appears directed at the very materials used to produce poetic meaning, as Bahar perceptively points out in his rejoinder. And that, I think, includes such systemic entities as the lexicon and generic characteristics as well as classes and categories of poetry in the inherited tradition. In his view, the very notion of poeticity in Iranian culture must be reconsidered in light of newly discovered esthetic meanings and social functions. The idea of the poet as leader motivated not by any extrinsic force, but by "new thoughts" (*afkar-e now*), "new impressions" (*enteba'at-e now*), and "new sensations" (*tahassosat-e now*) communicates the perception of a void in the native tradition. The radical modernists, in other words, fired by notions of the poet as inspired genius or social rebel, judged the individual mind capable of imagining the collective good. Aware of the historical inevitability of poetic change, they would like to see this genius involved in the act of pushing history forward. The history of the past, too, is beginning to be seen as having moved forward at times because certain individuals refused to conform to inherited norms.[25]

The ever-greater divergence of the two tendencies can be pursued further in subsequent issues of *Daneshkadeh*. Bahar continues his argument in favor of a moderate approach to poetic change in ever-more explicit terms. In issues four and five he publishes two articles entitled, "Ta'sir-e Mohit dar Adabiyyat" (The Influence of the Environment in Literature). Here, he seems to be working within a general framework which can be termed geographic and historical determinism. Relying heavily on the relationships he has already established between the pace of cultural change and the dictates of the social body (*hay'at-e ejtema'iyyeh*) or the environment (*mohit*), he views poetry as a social product whose nature and function are fairly fixed.[26] Taking the concept of the environment in the most general sense of climate and material culture; religious, political, and moral beliefs; and patterns of ethnic assimilation and social interaction, he constructs a direct link between the environment and literature. Countries with a favorable climate, he states, stir the heart and move poets to joyful expression of the natural phenomena, whereas countries with harsh climatic conditions and austere environments direct the mind toward inventions as a way of compensating for the absence of beauty in the physical environment. Similarly, historical phenomena such as imperial expansion and military victories tend to nurture an epic mode of literary expression, while a sense of defeat and general contraction may give rise to feelings of despondency and expressions of submission. He concludes the first essay by urging his colleagues to direct their attention to the social environment: "In order to reform the literature of a nation, one must first bring about reform in the environment." Throughout this series, Bahar portrays poets as constrained by their environment and history, forced to leave in their work traces of the conditions under which they operate. To the extent that their writings can be said to reveal a progression, they communicate a limited view of the part that poets can play in effecting change.

In the tenth issue of *Daneshkadeh*, Bahar publishes an article entitled "Alfaz va Ma'ani: She'r-e Qadim va She'r-e Jadid" (Words and Meanings: Old Poetry and New Poetry). Perhaps the most historically anchored writing in the journal, this essay posits a direct link between gradual sophistication in the literary idiom and the presence of the perception of artfulness or artificiality. It is a natural progression that every nation, in the dawn of the primal plainness of its situation and the simplicity of its condition, has spoken and acted starkly through its words and deeds. In speech as in action, its intentions and emotions can be seen most obviously and simply. Gradually, as civilization takes over, simplicity, honesty, and appeal to the truth fall by the wayside, giving way to formality, hypocrisy, and verbal or nonverbal embellishments. Eventually, the society reaches the point where truth disappears totally, and masses of superstition, layers of nonsense, and piles of verbosity rise in the name of the literary arts and crafts, covering the nation's letters and spirit.[27]

Disingenuous as this grand narrative of cultural history may appear, it does point out certain basic conceptual dichotomies at work in the structures, historical or esthetic, imagined in early modern Iran. Simplicity, honesty, and appeal to the truth form a node of characteristics which distinguish "the literature of Iran" at its originary moment. A particular manifestation of certain romantic notions, this node highlights a feeling of despair rather than issuing a call for cultural change. It grounds the standard narrative of Persian literary history in a sense of history that appears inevitable and beyond reach. In doing so, Bahar voices the sense of frustration many cultural conservatives felt at the time. Unable to articulate a vision of poetic modernity, they sought refuge in grand narratives which in their simplicity seemed to imply that no change was possible at all. To say that the original simplicity of poets like Ferdowsi, Rudaki, and Khayyam has in time given way to the verbal acrobatics of Saba, Sorush, and Qa'ani,[28] is only one step away from negating the possibility of literary change.

But if Bahar, the poet deeply steeped in the traditional practice of Persian poetry, had come to this conclusion, other members of the Daneshkadeh

Literary Society advanced other views. *Daneshkadeh's* overall agenda reflected the desire to influence the course of literary change in Iran. Almost all of the journal's other sections were obviously designed to argue for the possibility of change; they all offered examples of, or guidelines for, the process through which change could be instituted. The articulation of the battle of ancients and moderns (*jedal-e moteqaddemin va mote'akhkherin*) in seventeenth-century France, published in the fifth issue of the journal, is a case in point. Its author, Rashid Yasemi, clearly conceives the event as relevant to the ongoing debate in Iran.[29] He opens the essay by characterizing the writings of the Peliades poets as "sheer imitation of the classics." Even though they lived at a time when "such famous writers as Racine, Molière, Boileau, and others had changed the manner of composition and the taste," these classicists could not grasp the nature and extent of the required change. He closes by relating the account of the "eventual and inevitable triumph" of the moderns:

> Eventually, the supporters of the moderns gained the upper hand. Blind imitation of the Greek ancients faded away in the eighteenth century, the freshness and grandeur of the poetic fancy became the focus of attention, and poets no longer followed the example of the Greeks and the Latins. The classical style continued to exist for a while afterwards, but no longer did anyone follow that style, and its spirit and strength deserted the French literature.[30]

Such narratives point to a central concern of the literary intellectuals about the possibility of innovation within a literary tradition and its nature and extent. It is important, in light of the Iranian debate, that in the above formulation, on the one hand, the French modernists are characterized as having a fresh and grand poetic fancy and are said to be involved in an effort to oppose blind imitation; on the other hand, something called the spirit and strength of French literature is said to have deserted that tradition as a consequence of their efforts.

Perhaps with an eye to such consequences, *Daneshkadeh* seems to pursue a two-pronged course in its advocacy of poetic change: it sets out to effectively illustrate the capacity of Persian verse forms while it demonstrates amply the part that thematic expansions can play in the process. On the latter point, *Daneshkadeh's* attempts also exemplify the journal's view of the dynamics of esthetic innovation within traditional systemic boundaries. The European poems translated into Persian seem designed to illustrate the capacity of expressing a far wider range of themes and topics than has hitherto been recognized.[31] Similarly, by proceeding on the basis of concepts existing both in classical Persian literature and in contemporary French literature, the journal's two essay series—one on the evolution of Persian literature, the other on the French literature of the seventeenth through nineteenth centuries—appear primarily designed to draw broad parallels between the two traditions. The opening sentence in the essay series on French literature is most illustrative in this regard: "of all the periods in French literary history, the sixteenth century is most suitable for the present situation in our country."[32]

Daneshkadeh's desire to bring about literary change without undermining the Persian tradition in turn leads to frequent attempts to contextualize past poetry, to show that the best "Iranian" poets of the past have always provided a voice for their own specific conditions. This aspect of the postconstitution literary culture can best be seen in the contemporary readings of classical texts and perceptions of their relevance to sociopolitical concerns. In *Daneshkadeh,* this effort was conducted predominantly through adding titles, prefatory observations, or different types of commentaries to classical poetic texts published in the journal. It was designed to underscore the engagement of the poets—at least the best of them—in the affairs of their society. Thus a passage from a qasida by the tenth-century poet Daqiqi was given the title of "*Siasat-e Modon*" (Civic Polity), and another by Mas'ud Sa'd (1059–1099) that of "*Enteqad va Siasat*" (Criticism and Politics). A prose preface to the latter poem muses on the perils of a poet's profession and on the part poetry can play in the political life of the community:

> Mas'ud Sa'd-e Salman has composed a qasida about the ruinous condition and the weakness of the Ghaznavid rule, with all the despotism and pharaonic behavior of its kings and ministers. There, he takes the chief minister of the time severely to task. And it can be said that this qasida is the first in the literature of Iran which has been written in direct and plain language about the terrible condition of the people and the corruption [of the state]. It was such qasidas, testifying to the poet's patriotism and mental alertness, which caused him to be arrested and incarcerated for a long time.[33]

The connections forged here illustrate the need to make poetry respond to a growing need, namely to tackle the pressing political issues of the day. The ruinous condition and weakness might well be an allusion to the situation at hand in modern Iran, and the attack on the chief minister might as well have come from Bahar as from Mas'ud. But the connections made between these issues are clearly designed to show the capacity of classical genres like the qasida to shed their image of abstruseness and unintelligibility and be made once again to appeal to the masses. Most significantly, the depiction of this classical qasida as the cause of the poet's fall from some patron's favor can be taken as evidence of a new connection between poetry and politics in the literary culture of contemporary Iran. Such contextualizations of past poetic performances allow us penetrating glimpses into aspects of the creative activity undertaken by Iran's intellectuals in the guise of literary historical scholarship.

The general notion of poetic change advanced and advocated by *Danesh-kadeh,* while undergoing important changes, as we have seen, failed in the end to satisfy those exposed more profoundly to Western cultures. The Circle had originally sought "to give currency to new meanings clad in the garb of old poetry and prose, to acquaint the people with the criteria of eloquence and with the limits of a literary revolution, and to underline the necessity of respect for works of the classical eloquence and simultaneously that of emulating the salient features of European prose."[34] In its structure, this rather cumbersome formulation clearly points to a balancing act, indicating a desire to bring together entities that the culture may have begun to view as problematic or incompatible. Through the metaphor of the old garb it depicts formal elements and generic categories as inviolable. Such features as rhyme and meter, as well as the generic divisions of classical Persian poetry, are thus viewed as essential to poeticity. Similarly, notions like "the criteria of eloquence" (*mavazin-e fesahat*) and respect for the classical masters appear not only as fixed entities but also as timeless qualities worthy of preservation. What modifications may be deemed appropriate in the existing tradition must therefore seek their validity through acceptance by those who have mastered the forms, genres, and criteria of the classics.

The tasks that remain to be accomplished consist of determining "the limits of a literary revolution" and identifying "the salient features of European prose." In short, the authority of the classical tradition severely constrains the vision of an alternative system of literary expression; it does so by making innovation contingent on the approval of the "authorities," presumably those with unquestionable mastery over the tradition. Moreover, the emphasis on "the limits of a literary revolution" clearly suggests a project aimed more at curbing innovation than fostering it. Finally, while acknowledging change as inevitable, the Circle counsels respect for the authority of the classics; and, while mentioning the emulation of European models, it makes any movement in that direction contingent on the recognition of the native tradition's virtues. Where the Circle sanctions innovation, in short, it does so within a definite demand for continuity. Such an attitude was in fact indicative of a determination to sabotage any change rather than to foster it. To the very end, in sum, *Daneshkadeh* continued to advocate a very limited view of literary change.

In their practice, the colleagues of *Daneshkadeh* began to find themselves faced with a dual task. On the one hand, they felt obligated to produce or propagate the kind of poetry that would reflect their vision. On the other, in the face of more radical pronouncements and practices, they felt a mounting pressure to expand their vision of poetic change or risk losing their central position in this important cultural contestation. Already, as we have seen, the first issue of *Daneshkadeh* presented a vision considerably more expanded and more radical than the original formulation, declaring it the group's goal "to revise the style [*sabk*] and the manner [*raviyyeh*] of Iranian literature."[35] Through their dialogues with Raf'at and others, the *Daneshkadeh* group began to broaden its view of poetic change even more than before. Still, Raf'at was far more radical in his insistence to place the question of literature within a national quest after the place of the tradition in contemporary life.

A DEBATE ON SA'DI

No issue made this difference as visible as the debate on Sa'di, the thirteenth-century Persian poet most famous for his beautiful compositions and his commitment to morality. As in the case of the more general one, placing this debate within a broader context will afford us glimpses into the points of contact and friction which marked the contours of the literary culture in early twentieth-century Iran. To men like Raf'at, we recall, *Daneshkadeh's* notion of poetic modernization seemed designed to guarantee the continuation of traditional poetic practice. The scenario of a gradual, measured and ultimately limited expansion of the classical system of poetic expression, in other words, sanctioned the expansion of the existing codes only insofar as attempts in this direction would not violate the classical system of poetic codification. Whatever the perceived need for innovation, it remained tied to a series of inherited criteria ensuring the predominance of a poetic system of expression established long ago. Authorities like Bahar would then undertake to demonstrate the political nature of classical Persian poetry, or at least a political dimension in many of its noteworthy examples.

Naturally, such a tendency would ill serve the purposes of a man who constantly invited his compatriots to reexamine the form and content of their culture. For Raf'at, the fate of poetry was linked to a determination of a larger question: what part of the inherited culture is relevant to contemporary life? He recognized readily the authority of the past as a valid and important vehicle in relation to its own generative ambience. Iranian culture, he acknowledged, had produced a superb literature crafted by brilliant literary figures. That very fact, however, was now acting to stifle the creative energies which could contribute to the emergence of a new literature, comparably relevant to contemporary concerns. The task before twentieth-century Iranians consisted of finding ways to unshackle the present from the fetters of the past. Formulated in this way, the issue became one of a present and clear need to respond to the challenges of an era different from all that had gone before.

The differences between the two formulations eventually found its point of focus in the debate on Sa'di. Both Raf'at and Bahar took part in this debate, as did many others. Many of the issues raised through it bore directly on the question of the nature and extent of acceptable cultural change. Through the debate on Sa'di, then, we might come face to face with the background, context, and terms of a great national debate on Iranian culture, of which the question of poetic modernity is a part. We will see, for example, how the heritage of the past is pitted against the claims of the present as having given rise to a different kind of social existence which ought legitimately to seek its own distinct articulation in and through a new kind of literature.[36] Most specifically, I think an analysis of the debate on Sa'di may provide us with important insights into the question of the form and content of the poetry to come.

A seminal literary figure perceived for centuries not just as an esthetic example, but as a moral guidepost as well, Sa'di is appropriate to my purpose on that account too. In all the intellectual modes preceding that of Iranian modernity he had been canonized as the quintessential moral guide. While his pragmatic approach to ethical questions had continued to make him relevant to a myriad of sociopolitical contexts in all ages and circumstances, his specifically literary achievements had raised him throughout the Persian-speaking world above all other poets and literary figures, bestowing upon him the unique honorific of *ostad-e sokhan* (master of the word/speech). In him the twin powers of moral insight and literary excellence were thought to have come together in a union which gave his works, particularly the *Golestan* and the *Bustan,* the status of a comprehensive compendium in the annals of the Iranian pedagogical system in premodern times. In terms both of eloquence and of morality, these two books were considered second only to the Glorious Koran, and had been taught to youngsters alongside that Holy Book. That perception had been reinforced through the centuries by a succession of imitations, particularly of the *Golestan,* all taking immense pride in deriving their power from Sa'di's authority, each conceding the superiority and continued validity of his instructions. The last of these imitators was none less than Qa'ani, the greatest practitioner of the Literary Return Movement and arguably the best Persian poet of the nineteenth century.[37]

Saʿdi's reputation has waned considerably throughout the twentieth century. Still, his aphorisms, sententiae, and fables and anecdotes appear with remarkable frequency in school textbooks in Iran and other Persian-speaking countries.[38] That Saʿdi should become the subject of a debate on poetic change in early twentieth-century Iran is in itself an indication of the degree to which the literary culture seemed prone to problematizing the classical heritage. The debate on Saʿdi began with an article written by ʿAli-Asghar Taleqani, a young Iranian educated in Europe. Published in 1917 in *Zaban-e Azad* (Liberated Language), it burst on the Iranian literary scene. It caused quite a political stir, resulted in the suppression of *Zaban-e Azad,* and eventually contributed to the fall of the government in power at the time.[39] The article and the responses to it also gave rise to extensive discussions about various functions of Persian literature in contemporary Iran.[40] It will serve our purposes in focusing the Bahar-Rafʿat argument on poetic modernity.

Following in the footsteps of Aqa Khan Kermani of a generation earlier, Taleqani links the country's backwardness to what he describes as the confusing contradictions within the classical culture, of which Saʿdi is both the most typical representative and the clearest example:

> The origin of all our national and social misfortunes [*badbakhtiha-ye melli va ejtemaʿi*] lies only in the inconsistencies [*namowzuni*] inherent in our national educational principles and the ruinous condition [*kharabi*] of our social upbringing which, like termites, have been gnawing the innards of our [sense of] nationality to hollowness for the past eight hundred years. . . . The foundation of our national education rests on the compendium of a few books within our classical and modern literature which, having assumed a status loftier than our Divine Book (i.e., the Koran), have influenced the thought and mind of all classes of our countrymen. The most precious of these is the Collected Works of Mosleh al-Din Saʿdi, which I prefer, in all boldness, to call "the Collected Works of Demise" [*kolliyyat-e tanazzol-bakhsh*].[41]

The author closes by expressing outrage at the fact that, despite all the obvious contradictions in the moral positions Saʿdi seems to have held, all the objectionable views he seems to have endorsed, and all the atrocities he seems to have sanctioned in such works as the *Golestan* and the *Bustan,* he continues to be idolized by contemporary Iranians.

In his response to this article, Bahar wrote an essay entitled "Saʿdi Kist?" (Who Is Saʿdi?). Here, he first places Saʿdi within the many historical and social contexts which have judged him important, always underscoring the effects of social and political circumstance on individual character. He also stresses the continued significance of Persian literature as a defining emblem of cultural existence amid the flux and uncertainty of life in past ages. In a real sense, then, even though Sa'di may have experienced tremendous upheavals, his mind was shaped by the teachings of Ferdowsi and Sana'i, as well as by Greek, Arab, Indian, and Persian philosophy. It would not be appropriate, Bahar concludes, to blame Sa'di for projecting a certain passivity in his description of the human condition and in depicting an acceptance of, and a retiring attitude toward, the injustices exercised by the tyrants of his time. "No less than us," he says, "Sa'di and Rumi have been subjected to those teachings, the times having taught us all in the same school."[42]

Bahar then cites several passages from Sa'di's work in praise of such virtues as faith, conviction, and perseverance and in vilification of vices like indolence, gluttony, and greed. Those passages, he argues, are evidence of the poet's determination to guide human society toward the good. Finally, he expresses outrage at the contemporary critics who would negate the values propagated by Sa'di and other classical masters, but who would offer no alternative moral system, not even a pedagogical plan of their own:

> Those young people who have not benefited from the literature and arts of their own country, who are yet to comprehend European works, sciences, and arts, and who resort to four or five seemingly mystical and ascetic [*sufi-maneshaneh va tarek-e donya'i*] statements [in the works of the classical masters] as reason for the eradication of their excellent teachings must tell me what new guidance or fresh principles they would establish in their place, and what words they would substitute for their counsel. Would they set aside the books of Sa'di and Rumi to open up instead the books and essays of their contemporaries, which contain nothing but nonsense, insults, mistakes, and bad teachings? Those who denigrate and insult Sa'di, Rumi, and Hafez without feeling shame before their spirits, what art [*honar*] and virtue [*fazilat*] have they brought forth? Which books on what more modern and more useful pedagogical principles have they authored or compiled that they already declare the books of Iranian literati [*odaba-ye iran*] defunct?[43]

As in the case of poetic change, Bahar's position here is both simple and forbidding. He counters all challenges to the authority of the past by asking the challenger to produce works that might fill the void which he sees arising as the tradition is rejected. Beyond this rhetorical question, he does not envision any critical attitude as itself capable of creating the impulse toward literary and cultural modernity. For that reason, Bahar's interlocutors often think him too rigid to allow any critical interpretations of the tradition, either esthetic or moral. In fact, the difference between his attitude and theirs has less to do with the need to change poetry or the pace of change than it does with the appropriate posture of the moderns toward the poetic tradition. While men like Taleqani start by faulting the tradition, Bahar appears as its unabashed apologist, willing to reinterpret the tradition for the present age, but not inclined to discard or negate it. While they seem to grope for ways to express a universal contemporary condition, he focuses on adapting what he sees as the past to present conditions. Deeply suspicious of all postures that might result in cultural ruptures with the native tradition, he interprets the criticism of Saʿdi not as signaling a desire for cultural renewal, but as the beginning of cultural capitulation.

The more Bahar elaborates on this issue, the more he seems to revert back to a position markedly more conservative than the one he had taken in the earlier and more general debate. "I undertake to show you," he says to all those who would question the tradition's relevance, "every principle [*asl*] and rule [*qaʿedeh*] which you would consider most modern and most useful to public life [*maʿishat-e ʿomumi*] and social ethics [*akhlaq-e ejtemaʿi*] in [Rumi's] *Spiritual Couplets,* in Saʿdi's *Bustan,* and in the Ghazals of Hafez."[44] Such categorical statements clearly go beyond the issue of the relevance of the classics to the moderns, to shed light on the speaker's view of the nature of the age he lives in. To see in the culture of the past a comprehensive ethical system of timeless and universal validity totally applicable to the modern age is tantamount to denying the very premise of the present being different.

Rafʿat's response to Taleqani's assault on Saʿdi, and to the larger issue of the relevance of the classics to the modern age, was framed differently. He begins his discourse by acknowledging the fact of human sociality and underlines the importance of social context in discussing literature. Contrasting the pace and rhythm of contemporary life, which he sees as determined by the sounds of cannon balls and rifle shots, with what he calls the "slow, frigid, and antique language of Saʿdi and his contemporaries,"[45] he speaks of a gulf in perception that makes it logically impossible for old poets to have expressed the modern condition. At the same time, he acknowledges the emotional appeal of Taleqani's attack on Saʿdi as well as the persuasive power of Bahar's rhetorical defence. Rafʿat then attempts to strip both arguments down to their discursive essentials. Taleqani's indictment of Saʿdi's teachings, he says, is "a sincere outburst springing from the bottom of a heart pained by our social sufferings." At the same time, he counts the excesses to which the author's emotional state has led him. Referring to the charge that those teachings lie at the base of Iran's cultural decline, for example, he states: "every time you abstract and separate one cause from among the many causes of a single effect, you will end up committing this error of excess or inade-quacy" in logic. However that may be, he applauds Taleqani's attempt to open to national debate what had hitherto been a cultural taboo among Iranian intellectuals. Concerning the presence of all the principles of modern life in the works of Sa'di, Raf'at seizes on Bahar's categorical stance. "Had it been true," he observes, "this statement would have been the worst kind of praise [*badtarin-e madayeh*]" for the classical poet. If Sa'di has composed "all the principles and rules of public life and social ethics as warnings [*tezkar*], he has labored in vain, and if he has adopted them [for himself] and has taken pen in his hand to promulgate them, then he has broached together certain discordant principles only to signify his own lack of belief in any of them."[46] Raf'at's dismay at discovering what he perceives as the absence of a discernible moral stance in Sa'di provides support for his contention that the cultural past was essentially different. The world of classical Persian poets appears to him comprehensible in only one of two ways: either it was a world in which a set of principles, lost to the modern consciousness, permitted one to reconcile seemingly disparate moral positions, or it was one so immersed in pragmatic considerations that, to the modern mind, it appears devoid of an overall ethos. In either case, cultural traditions of the past appear inacces-sible to the moderns. Classical Persian poetry would then come to resemble a text written in a different language.

Raf'at uses the concept of translation to emphasize the breakdown of communication between classical poets like Sa'di and Hafez and their readers in modern Iranian society. Unwillingness or inability to admit that the classi-cal tradition is essentially unintelligible to the moderns bespeaks either a rejection of the modern approach or a nostalgic desire to withdraw from the necessities of the modern world into the cocoon of a vanished past. He acknowledges the presence of a moral purpose in Sa'di's works, but thinks it would be foolish to think of it as translatable, let alone relevant, to the terms that govern the modern age:

> A momentary pause on some stories in the *Golestan* would spare us having to belabor the point about our perception of the lessons which we can learn from the works of Sa'di. The first story teaches us that "a well-meaning lie is better than a truth which might lead to injurious conse-quences"; the fourth story suggests that "hereditary tendencies toward crime cannot be corrected through education"; the eighth story communicates [the idea] that "kings must eliminate ruthlessly those whom they fear . . ."; the ninth story implies that "a person's heirs are the greatest of his enemies"; the fourteenth story claims that "a soldier whose ration is delayed has the right to desert the field of battle;" etc.; etc.[47]

Raf'at concludes that such stories, even though manifestly irrelevant to "the world that is constantly being changed and transformed," must nonetheless have been "relevant to their own times." We would therefore be justified in feeling fortunate to have such men in our cultural past. To go beyond that, however, to say that these men had "primal and eternal knowledge in their breasts," indicates an inner servitude "unbecoming of the contemporary youth of Iran." Today, he concludes, we need "other Sa'dis," and in order to become "other," we must inevitably be "modern and modernistic (*jadid va motejadded*). In the meantime, nobody has the right to turn Sa'di into a demigod, envisioning him as perfect. Raf'at ends one such article with the following plea:

> speak to us, the anxious, care-ridden youth of this age, of awareness, not of Sa'di, Hafez, and Ferdowsi. Explain to us the meaning of life [*ma'ni-ye hayat*]. Show us the path to deliverance and salvation [*jaddeh-ye fowz o falah*]. Grant wings to our souls, luster and radiance to our thoughts. . . . Lift the nightmare of decline and demise [*kabus-e enhetat o ezmehlal*] from before our eyes.[48]

And returning to Bahar's defence of Sa'di, he assumes in a subsequent article the same analytical approach to the substance of the current rethinking of the classical poet and the issue of his relevance to contemporary Iranian culture:

> At its core, our challenge is to find out whether the thoughts [*afkar*] and teachings [*ta'limat*] of the poets, literary figures, and philosophers of old times can provide adequate answers to contemporary problems of a modern and innovative nation. In other words, do the poems and prose compositions of our classics produce in us new thoughts [*afkar-e now*], new impressions [*enteba'at-e now*], new awareness [*ettela'at-e now*], new sensations [*tahassosat-e now*], new whatever, or no?[49]

He then focuses on contemporary readers' part in interpreting old texts—parables, aphorisms, and sententiae—in relation to their actual surroundings. Here Raf'at concludes that modern readers bestow on old texts a kind of validity that cannot logically be said to be present in their verbal and linguistic structures. In themselves, "the compositions of the classical masters do nothing other than make us aware of our inherited riches [*ne'matha-ye mowrusi*]." They add nothing to "our present existence, unless we assume that our present existence in itself amounts to nothing." As such, if the debate on Sa'di is designed "to prove that Sa'di's thoughts have been excellent and broad in relation to his own time and environment, we agree." However, if it is meant to lead to the conclusion that "today we can follow these as redeeming instructions, we reject that argument." Does it require proof, he asks, to say that "our classical poets, even with their . . . extraordinary acumen [*zoka'*] and talent [*este'dad*], have inevitably and naturally been unable to see that which we witness today—and which must and does affect and impress us, making us happy or unhappy?" Modern Iranians, Raf'at adds, see beyond their borders "a superb civilization" *(madaniyyat-e 'ali)* and "an evolving humanity" *(bashariyyat-e motakamel).*

Recognizing the fact of their backwardness, they then feel a specific pain at the bottom of their hearts. Raf'at asks:

> Well, which poem, which one of your poets, translates that pain for you adequately [*in dard ra baraye shoma beh khubi tarjomeh mikonad*]? Is Sa'di's exhortation, "O you who have wasted fifty years and are still asleep / Beware for you have only five more days left" [*ay keh panjah raft o dar khabi / magar in chand-ruzeh daryabi*], sufficient to the purpose? And does it relate to this thought [*fekr*] and this feeling [*ehsas*]?
>
> Or, take this verse by Hafez's: "The green field of the firmament I saw, and the sickle of the new moon / I remembered my own tillage and the season of harvest" [*mazra'-e sabz-e falak didam o das-e mah-e now / yadam az keshteh-ye khish amad o hengam-e derow*]. Is this, or any other oft-repeated ghazal or qasida, in any way capable of communicating or ameliorating that pain?[50]

As a rebuttal to Bahar's claim to be able to show all principles and rules of modern public life and social ethics in Sa'di's *Bustan* and Hafez's ghazals, Raf'at's questions merit closer attention. When placed in relation to the "specific pain" he describes, the classical examples he mentions provide a wonderful illustration of the limits of relevance. The two verse lines encode a feeling identical to that which, according to him, "modern Iranians" experience when they contemplate their country's backwardness: a sense of belatedness, of loss of time or opportunity. He is further careful to cite examples that encode that feeling from two different vantage points. In the case of Sa'di's line, an external voice addresses the subject, whereas in the example from Hafez, the feeling is expressed by the agent who has experienced the loss. In the former the structure of the address, "O you who . . ." (*ay keh . . .*) places the speaker in the position of obvious moral superiority. The address comes presumably from one who is himself aware that at age fifty not much is left of one's life; he then communicates that awareness to another. At the same time, while the address may be applicable to countless individual human beings in all times and situations, its metaphorical implications are not designed to extend beyond individual human experience. The concept of fifty (*panjah*) years releases its meaning in contrast to the five (*panj*) remaining days; they both relate to individual life spans. They cannot be perceived as metaphorically alluding to the condition of a society becoming aware of a historical sleep (*khab*) having robbed them of the opportunity to advance. The specific pain which, according to Rafʿat, "modern Iranians" feel when they contemplate their country's backwardness in contrast to the "superb civilization" and the "evolving humanity" beyond its borders falls outside the limits of Saʿdi's line. Through its literal codification of terms of age—fifty and five—Saʿdi's line precludes attempts at transpersonal decoding. Similarly, in Hafez's line the personal nature of the experience expressed through the two verbs "I saw" (*didam*) and "I remembered" (*yadam . . . amad*), alludes to individual human endeavor. So does the reference to what has been planted as "my own tillage" (*keshteh-ye khish*). By their referential nature, such poetic statements exclude the possibility of decodings designed to extend their meanings into the social realm. Rafʿat perceptively senses this shortcoming as he seeks to "translate" the terms of these references into a poetic language which would embody the entity he calls "modern Iranians." He concludes therefore that classical Persian poetry does not communicate the collective—yet specific—feelings which he thinks the poetry of modern Iran ought to articulate.

In theoretical terms, such utterances illustrate the outer limits of what Lotman calls "the multiplanar character of the artistic text." The semantic correlation necessary for transposing poetic signs from the classical context to the contemporary situation has been severed because the system of codes on which Saʿdi's allusion to age and Hafez's allusion to "the sickle of the moon" are based is geared to the evocation of personal reflection. As a result, the classical texts Rafʿat cites cannot be used as a means of recognizing the social situations he believes need to be expressed through Persian poetry. In an attempt to clarify the limits of an artistic text's capacity to traverse between the abstract encoding and concrete instances of decoding, Lotman uses a metaphor which I think helps us understand the distance that separates the abstract situations classical references contemplate from the practical one in which men like Rafʿat find themselves. The absence of common concerns constrains processes of esthetic communication:

> Suppose that a man engaging in an activity has to resort to a model of that activity in order to make sense of it. In laying out an itinerary, for example, a tourist stops his progress while he traces his movements on a map; then he resumes his actual journey. Without defining the essence of these two forms of behavior, let us simply note their clear-cut delimitations.

In one instance practical behavior is realized, in the other abstract behavior. The purpose of the one is to achieve practical results; that of the second is to acquire the knowledge necessary in order to achieve those results. In the first case a man finds himself in a practical situation, in the second in a theoretical one.[51]

Raf'at might well have seen in Bahar's insistence on Sa'di's relevance a position akin to tracing one's route on a map instead of setting out on the actual journey.

In his discussion of "the multiplanar character of the artistic text," Lotman uses a second metaphor to show how individuals sense the difference between actual situations and their abstract formulations in artistic texts. As an analogy conveying the difference between an abstract model and an actual situation, this metaphor applies to my pursuit here insofar as it directs attention to the limits of emotive communication between texts which reflect reality and readers who experience it: "No one would shudder in terror as he examined a battle plan plotted on a map, though he would undoubtedly be aware that the map he was looking at corresponded in reality to a field strewn with corpses."[52]

In other words, even though literary texts derive their unique status as analogues of reality from their inherent capacity to enter into a variety of contexts, their uniqueness among analogues of reality also point to their limitation in communicating feelings across centuries and cultures. The fact that two contemporaries, Bahar and Raf'at, begin to differ on whether articulations of the type Raf'at cites do or do not convey the feelings which he specifies signals a growing divergence concerning the limit of a classical tradition's communicability, and therefore relevance, to contemporary concerns. Ultimately, the answer depends on each observer's perception of the difference between modern times and the classical age. That perception in turn determines the observer's view of the need for instituting change in the system of esthetic signification and communication in a certain cultural milieu. Clearly, Raf'at believes that, in the case of twentieth-century Iran, the limit of the classical poetic tradition's efficacy has been reached, whereas Bahar would argue that it has not. In this sense, Raf'at's conceptualizing esthetic communication as "translation" finds its ultimate meaning. Sa'di and Hafez, he believes, spoke an artistic language foreign to modern Iranians.

A SEPARATE REALITY

The Bahar-Raf'at debates on poetry and on Sa'di constitute the culmination of a serious and sustained dialogue in postconstitution Iranian society. The polemical rhetoric of Akhundzadeh, Kermani, and Malkom have now given way to a reasoned, if still somewhat heated, discourse on issues of moment and import to the cultural situation in which men like Bahar and Raf'at find themselves. Through such exchanges, Iranian culture seeks answers crucial to its continued existence. It seems reasonable in bringing this chapter to a close to examine the significance of the postures discarded and assumed in this historical dialogue. To begin, the willingness to enter into a dialogue on the problem of intelligibility of old texts and the question of their relevance indicates a readiness to move away from the monoglossia that is thought to have governed Persian poetry through the centuries. Beyond that, the fact of the dialogue acknowledges a separate social reality, one which necessitates and nurtures the perception of many meanings, many contexts, and many systems of poetic expression. In *The Dialogical Imagination* Bakhtin notes that, in the course of the historical movement toward cultural polyglossia, "language is transformed from the absolute dogma it had been within the narrow framework of a sealed-off and impermeable monoglossia into a working hypothesis for comprehending and expressing reality."[53] Raf'at's argument about the unintelligibility of past poetry may not have satisfied Bahar, but it suggests a posture markedly different from Kermani's or Malkom's exasperated condemnation of so many ghazals and qasidas. Similarly, Bahar's argument about the spirit of Persian poetry may not have responded to Raf'at's desire to express the present condition in its own terms, but it does suggest not only the presence of a willing listener but also the possibility of active understanding. Concerning the effects attendant on this state of affairs, Bakhtin observes:

> Active understanding . . . by bringing what is being understood within the new horizon of the understander, establishes a number of complex interrelations, consonances and dissonances with what is being understood, enriches it with new moments. It is precisely this kind of understanding that the speaker takes account of. Therefore his orientation towards the listener is an orientation towards the particular horizon, the particular world of the listener; it introduces completely new moments into his discourse: what takes place here is an interaction of different contexts, different points of view, different horizons, different expressively accentuated systems, different social "languages."[54]

Indeed, during the first two decades of the twentieth century, the quest for a Persian poetry for modern Iran gave rise to a series of serious and wide-ranging exchanges which introduced the participants to new contexts, new viewpoints, new horizons. Through such exchanges, Iranian poets, critics, and readers gained an opportunity to explore the nature of their historical situation and to gauge their distance from their classical culture and from other contemporary cultures. In itself, that makes this exchange far more satisfying than the continued silence of nineteenth-century Iranian poets in the face of the kind of assaults on their practice as chronicled in chapter 1.

But there is more to the dialogues I have explored in this chapter. Earlier assessments of Persian poetry, we recall, posited an internal "other," namely the past, and a contemporary culture-cluster known as Europe or the West. In this period, the debate on poetry made it possible to transcend the dichotomies the earlier generations had imagined existed between modern Iran and its classical culture and between Iran and the West; rather, Iranian literary intellectuals seemed to be groping toward an ideal of poetic practice that lay between openness and closure, between rupture and continuity, between innovation and tradition. The fact that a questioner like Raf'at is no longer cast in the mold of a cultural outcast in the act of raving and ranting against real or imagined social adversaries means that awareness of alternative universes of poetic discourse has now legitimized a variety of modeling activities across linguistic and cultural boundaries. Challenges to the moral authority of the native tradition are beginning to make it possible for poets to move beyond the dichotomy of total negation or blind imitation of the classical masters. The emerging notion of the boundedness of all visions has now sanctioned excursions beyond the imaginary borders of the native practice, both in terms of the esthetic operations a poem enacts and of the social action or moral vision it may propagate. As we shall see in the next chapter, even the place of poetry in the total cultural system is subject to reevaluation. Sa'di is no longer automatically charged with corrupting Iranian youth; in time he may even regain his place in the literary culture, not so much as a supreme moral authority but as a poet, the relevance of his moral pronouncements increasingly keyed to his own specific circumstances.

As for the problem of a new poetry, these early debates facilitate the production of a poetry that would not derive its relevance solely from the moral vision enshrined in it. Moral preachment is envisioned, in spite of its historical interpenetration with poetry, as an activity essentially independent of esthetic expression and not as a condition of literary creativity. Just as in the preceding generation Akhundzadeh had advocated separating history from poetry, now Raf'at and Taleqani were leading their culture toward separating poetry from the moral purpose or practical philosophy which it may enshrine. Increasingly, their position is understood without themselves being perceived as rejecting concepts of morality enshrined in classical poetry. Modern Iranians will feel free to roam the field of their past literature and select what moral or poetic principles they deem appropriate for their situation. Beyond glimpses into various intellectual positions on the question of poetic change, the Bahar-Raf'at debate provides us with a point of entry into the consciousness behind the dominant strain in the poetry of twentieth-century Iranian culture. They both define innovation in terms of departures from a collectively and historically determined set of norms and conventions motivated by social considerations. This means that poetic change is conceived in terms of the dialectics of the individual creativity and "the social language" which Bakhtin stipulates, rather than in those of an inherited set of norms and conventions. Innovation is no longer viewed as a vague desire to be of one's own time or to reject the tradition. Its specific contours are now understood to be determined by poets themselves as they contemplate their relations with their culture.

We may even argue that the very concept of the poet has begun to undergo a change as a result of the kind of exchanges I have examined in this chapter. Poets are no longer conceived generically as the wise men of the tribe dispensing moral advice and pointing to the path of worldly happiness and salvation. Rather, they are beginning to be viewed as social beings trying to define their very existence as social beings. Driven by forces, desires, and visions no different from those of the general citizenry, they have the ability to give expression to them through esthetic constructs of a particular kind. Though not quite eradicated from cultural memory, the image of the poet as a sensitive soul who, blessed or burdened by keener perceptions and sensations, is tuned to the nuances of life through mysterious channels begins to lose its color. In its frame, the culture will place the portrait of a citizen, willing and able to validate or vilify the culture by filtering his or her impressions of it through personal perceptions. To see the events that preoccupy the society registered in poetic works signifies a growing harmony between the poet's role as an individual human being and as a citizen. Topicality—defined as a willingness to address contentious social issues through poetic discourse—becomes a sign of modernity, while the opposite tendency will come to mark a poet as traditional.

In time, the culture's perception that poets "reflect" their age is transformed into an expectation and an insistence that they do so. Still a nascent view of the poet's "responsibility," this expectation finds its full fruition in the works of Nima and his followers and in the notion of commitment as enunciated in the 1960s.[55] Moreover, it comes to mean that the ideology of the intellectual elite would dominate the poetic discourse at every stage of its future evolution. In short, what began as the notion of relevance in the latter part of the nineteenth century would in actual historical fact evolve in time into the idea of poetry as a social phenomenon capable of charting the course to a better future, with the power perhaps even to bring about the ideal state.[56] To be taken seriously, poets would at least have to persuade their readers that they adhere to the sociality of poetry.

Finally, I would like to relate the emergence of this notion of poetry and the poet's function to the hesitant appearance of individualism, secularism, and historicism in Iranian culture. To early twentieth-century Iranians, these modern ideologies seemed to preach that all experience begins with the human individual, that the modern society defines the individual differently in relation to the larger entities in which he or she participates, and that sanction is ultimately placed in history rather than in an eternal scheme outside it. Within the historical process, too, each human being, each moment in time, even each incident, was thought to display a character and a significance all its own. The individual human being, in short, was seen to lie at the root of all events and all standards of value. The construct of individual human beings as the center of all perception and vision can be traced in the discourses presented on both sides of the Bahar-Raf'at debates. While the traditionalists urged contemporary poets to "present" their individuality in the "garb" of existing verse forms and genres, advocates of change bade them experiment with new forms and genres. Both sides agreed, however, that Iranian poets ought to place themselves at the center of their world. More than any other structure, esthetic or social, the resulting tension between self and society, between expressive and visionary functions of poetry, determined the course of modernity in Persian poetry.

In that final sense, I see in the vicissitudes of Bahar's and Raf'at's careers a metaphor for the manner in which the culture receives and rewards individual ambitions and convictions. After *Daneshkadeh* ceased publication in April 1919, Bahar, a radical constitutionalist in his youth, went on to live the life of a successful poet, now writing poems against war and social injustice, now celebrating the rule of Reza Shah and Iran's achievements under him. His *Divan* features numerous qasidas, ghazals, masnavis, and ruba'is in praise of human virtues like hard work and perseverance and numerous poetic admonishments against vices like indolence, gluttony, and lechery. He has written eulogies on the brotherhood of mankind and exhortations against weakness, violence, and poverty. In him, we can find traces of the nationalist discourse of the Iranian state in the 1930s as well as predictions about the triumphant approach of socialism. He has sung the praises of pro-Fascist Reza Shah as well as of liberty, democracy, and parliamentary rule. In the mid-1940s, he even served as Iran's minister of education. Today, almost half a century after his death in 1950, he is viewed widely as a major literary figure, although not a modernizer by any account, and retains much of his once tremendous fame and prestige.

Raf'at's newspaper *Tajaddod* ceased publication in April 1920 when the Iranian army launched vehement attacks against Azerbaijan, designed to eliminate the local autonomy movement with which he was associated.[57] Raf'at briefly published another journal, called *Azadistan,* in the besieged city of Tabriz, but only four issues of it were published irregularly over a three-month period. Here he apparently continued his arguments in favor of literary change and published some poems written by himself as well as by various other advocates of modernism in poetry.[58] When the movement was crushed in the summer of 1920, Raf'at fled to a nearby village, there to commit suicide sometime on September 6, 1920. He was only thirty-one years old at the time of his death. In spite of their unique importance as cultural documents, *Tajaddod* and *Azadistan* remain among the rarest periodicals ever published in Persian. Raf'at's own name owes its survival to the efforts of a few disciples and followers who, in writing about him in an admiring way, have preserved not only his memory but also fragments of his writings as well.[59] Beyond personal fortunes, Bahar and Raf'at remain watershed figures in the quest for a modern poetic tradition in twentieth-century Iran. For that reason, we shall have occasion to refer to their work in the coming chapters.

Chapter Four

From Translation to Appropriation

As readers separated from the literary culture of early twentieth-century Iran by the gulf in perception presented and upheld by the discourse of *shĕ'r-e now,* we tend to underestimate the part that various literary borrowings current at the time played in the process of poetic change. That is in large measure because traditional literary criticism has led us to believe that poets like Bahar, Iraj, and Parvin are situated within an existing literary tradition rather than positioned against it. We still imagine these poets as writing in essential accord with inherited norms and conventions, and fail to see clearly all the ways in which they manipulated that tradition in order to make it relevant to their own concerns. Traditional literary criticism in Iran tends to highlight visible breaks with the tradition of classical Persian poetry as the distinguishing feature of new poetry from the old, and this has dulled our perception of those texts in which innovation may have taken other forms. All this has in turn distorted our view of the processes by which poetic innovation was conceived and implemented by pre-Nimaic Iranian poets. Many readers have therefore come to associate openness to experimentation with Nima and his followers. Because a poem can still be seen to be a qasida, a ghazal, a qet'eh or a masnavi, it is judged no different in its internal operations from the canon of such genres in the classical tradition. In other words, formal and generic conformity with the tradition has been taken as the sign of total adherence to the classical system of signification and communication. Conversely, difference in formal features has been raised to the status of the supreme sign of modernness.

As a result of all this, poetic innovations that preceded Nima have remained largely unexplored, buried under appearances of continuity and impressions of sameness. It is true that in Nima's later compositions, his innovative use of rhyme and meter make the difference between the modern and the traditional discernible. In those poems, in other words, departures from the traditional practice of poetry move to the apparent surface of the text. However, Iranian poets before Nima made significant contributions to a new construct of poetic themes, a distinctly "modern" mode of esthetic signification, and even a new and more flexible attitude toward rhyme and meter which find their final expression in Nima's later compositions. For example, the matrix of characteristics and relationships which we associate with the modernist trend in Persian poetry emerged and evolved in the increasingly open literary culture of the 1920s and 1930s. Consequently, we must turn to the generation of poets that preceded Nima in search of the beginnings of a process that culminated in his work. In this chapter, I intend to illustrate a central preoccupation of that generation, namely the way poets like Bahar, Iraj, and Parvin enriched and expanded the system of Persian poetry through their literary borrowings.

A THEORY OF LITERARY BORROWING

It is not so much that literary borrowings have gone unnoticed in the traditional articulations of the process of poetic modernization in Iran. In fact, the influence of translation from European languages is often acknowledged as a matter of course. Translation has been recognized as having played an important part in the process of literary change in Iran since the latter part of the nineteenth century, and that part has been seen to have grown in importance with the passage of time. Historians of Persian literature in the twentieth century have acknowledged the significance of translation as a component of modernity. It has become a cliché of the current narrative of literary modernization that translation from European languages resulted in the "progress" and "advancement" of Persian literature. In this, as in so much else, Rypka has served as a model for Iranian critics, and can be called upon to illustrate their views. He observes that, in Iran, translation transformed the literary language in the latter half of the nineteenth century because "all the antiquated conventions, melismas and pomposities had to be done away with and an attempt made to accommodate the language to the demands of the original texts." And again, that "without these translations Persian belle-lettres and the prose of the 20th century as a whole is difficult to imagine."[1]

Arianpur adds his admiring astonishment to this assessment, speaking of a "strange passion and enthusiasm" (*shur o showq-e ʿajib*) for literary translation that took over the literary intellectuals of the nineteenth century. On the part that translation played in the emergence and evolution of literature in the twentieth century, he stipulates that translators had to follow "the manner of composition" (*shiveh-ye negaresh*) of their original texts, and write in simple and natural prose insofar as they were able to, shunning the use of "rhyming and artificial phraseology" (*ebarat-e mosajjaʿ va mosannaʿ*). This, he asserts, resulted in greater simplification of Persian poetry and prose. "If it had not been for these translations," he concludes, "today's literary composition, which has approached the common parlance even as it has benefitted from the beauty of European literary prose, would never have come into existence."[2]

However, neither Rypka nor Arianpur, nor any other critic or historian known to me, has made any attempt to show the impact of translation in specific ways. I am not aware of any attempt to come to terms with the bewildering variety of literary activities in twentieth-century Iran aimed at naturalizing literary texts of other cultures. Nor has any textual analysis been undertaken to illustrate the impact of such borrowings beyond general observations on personal choices and the dictates of the process of translation itself. Certainly, no critic known to me has examined the impact of translations on Persian poetry, its codes, or its traditional expressive strategies.[3] Moreover, critics seem to have taken the concept of translation in the narrowest and most literal sense of the word, leaving out a tremendous variety of translation-based textual activities. Naturally, implications of such activities for poetic change in twentieth-century Iran have gone unnoticed.

The reasons for this shortcoming are not far to seek. Acts of modeling based on foreign texts tend to complicate the categories through which traditional literary history attempts to articulate change. For one thing, processes of transformation involved in cross-cultural reproduction cannot be conveniently demonstrated through the methodologies of descriptive historiography. For another, the nature of the textual activity involved in such modeling activities often requires detailed analyses of individual texts, therefore precluding sweeping generalizations. Also, critics working in certain specific cultural milieus tend to underestimate the impact of all translation-based literary activities. Where original creative efforts are contrasted with literary borrowing, often viewed as a reflection of a cultural lack, tracing texts to their foreign origin may appear a little like an act of espionage. There may be other complicating factors which need not detain us here. Whatever the reasons, the part that literary borrowing has played in the process of poetic change in twentieth-century Iran has remained unexplored.

In a real sense, to say that in certain cultural circumstances literary translation plays a part in the process of esthetic change is to state the obvious. As Rypka and Arianpur have stated, since the late nineteenth century, translation from European languages, particularly French, has been a central preoccupation of Iranian literary intellectuals.[4] In order to assess the impact of more creative kinds of literary borrowing—adaptation, indigenization, or improvisation—we need to begin at the level of the text, and that would be possible, I believe, only if our analytical tools allow us to see the changes that texts undergo in the process of translation. As poets work to naturalize a foreign text, the specific textual manifestations of difference between what is poetic in the foreign text as compared with their general impression of the same concept in their native tradition becomes clear to them. This awareness, I contend, is fraught with possibilities for esthetic change. As critics, we can only attempt to reconstruct the process with reference to the texts involved. To do that, I need to introduce a few theoretical concepts that will enable me first to carry on with my textual analyses and then to integrate the potential of the process into an understanding of literature as a dynamic system. I suppose that when chroniclers of modernity in Persian poetry make reference to the impact of literary translation, they conceptualize the activity as a source of enrichment for the native literary tradition and as a facilitator of subsequent text-producing activities. In that sense, translation can be discussed as an agent of systemic change, accelerating and facilitating it by making available to writers and readers alike models hitherto nonexistent in the native tradition. The tacit assumption here is that in the exercise of judgment on text selection, on the specific activity of turning unintelligible sounds and symbols into signs and texts intelligible to native readers, and on the framing of the texts (including various acts of footnoting, captioning, or otherwise marking or identifying translated texts and the textual operations they contain) more is involved than free individual choices.[5] Indeed that judgment itself, I believe, is culturally determined and may be correlated with such things as assumptions about the original text's context, speculations concerning the need for the translated text, and expectations of the text's impact on the native literary or cultural system.[6]

In my Introduction, I discussed Lotman's system-versus-extrasystem binary. In the literary system of a given culture at a given time, systemic elements appear as stable, ordered, and organized; by contrast, elements not belonging to the system appear as random, unstable, or irregular. This is so because the system may not be able to envision a relationship between these elements and those within it. The entire corpus of translated literature present in a culture and available to it for modeling purposes may provide an example of this. In other words, once severed from their original system through translation, texts are more or less neutralized from the point of view of their position in that system. Synergistically and paradigmatically, they lose their systemic connections, contemporary or historical, and enter the new system as single entities rather than as parts of a system of literary expression culturally and historically anchored. Thus, detached from their own position in the system of the original language, translated literary texts appear as entities free from the nucleus-periphery tensions within the system into which they have entered. Their place in the new system is determined ultimately by a series of factors related to the native system rather than to their original one.

The system into which a translated text enters responds to it primarily in ways that relate to the system's view of itself rather than to the text's historical position or current status in the original system. If it perceives itself as relatively complete and in no need to change, it may undermine or even discard the text's differences as irrelevant or as signs of inferiority and assign the new entrant a marginal status. In this case the text's affinities with similarly classified texts tend to be accentuated. If, however, the system views itself as deficient and in need of change, it may give the text a central position, and thus allow it to play a significant part in the process of change. What are foremost here, perhaps interpreted as signs of the foreign system's superiority, are the differences between this text and similarly designated native ones.

A corollary question arises at this point: can the body of translated texts existing in any literary culture at any given time constitute a system in its own right?[7] Clearly, as extrasystemic entities imported into the literary system of a given culture, translated texts correlate with that system in at least two ways. First, the principles of text selection are never quite random; they are often correlated with the native system's view of itself. Second, in the act of translation, the specific choices made and norms adopted are in themselves indicative of specific impressions of the native system. As a result, whether the corpus of translated texts can be viewed as a system, the assumption can be made that at certain junctures in the history of a literary system the corpus of translated literature amounts to more than the sum of its parts, that the body of literature translated from foreign languages comes close to constituting an internally structured entity with its own coherence, and that it interacts in some more or less meaningful way with the native literary system.[8]

Let us place this assumption next to another notion which Lotman has set forth and which I described in my Introduction. The space of a semiotic system, he contends, is unevenly structured, with central formations and peripheral elements. The process of systemic change, he argues, is accompanied by a considerable increase in the movement of elements from the periphery to the center and the resultant marginalization of certain central formations. While synchronic descriptions of the system necessarily tend to underestimate or ignore peripheral formations as insignificant, the process of change tends to affirm their presence, thereby pushing them inward in the direction of the center. In its dynamic state, the system facilitates this movement by introducing and highlighting extrasystemic elements or entities. This tendency is accentuated when texts of foreign origin are seen to be similar to certain elements present in the system, however peripheral. Their significance as models to be emulated increases if they are described as central in the system from whence they are imported. In this way extrasystemic elements tend to accelerate the movement of elements within the system, eventually bringing about new arrangements within it.

Theoretically, then, translated literature may affect a living literary tradition in diverse ways, now exposing its deficiency, now confirming its completeness. It may speed up or inhibit change, play an innovatory or a conservatory part. When it does contribute to systemic change, it may do so by expanding the literary system at the level of generic classification, thematic preoccupation, or expressive devices. It may offer new relationships between literary structures and social ones or among alternative thematic alignments; it may expand the thematic range or the expressive mechanisms of the native tradition. In all these cases, it makes a variety of new textual activities possible by providing examples which may have little or no precedence in the system. In sum, translated literature eventually contributes to change in the native tradition by displacing its center of gravity, disrupting the existing center-periphery formations, and changing the system's view of itself.

The implications of these theoretical assumptions for the process of poetic change ought to be obvious. The poetic system of Iranian culture at the beginning of the twentieth century was widely perceived as deficient in certain aspects and therefore in need of change. The introduction of alternative textual models through prose and verse translation was often undertaken with the purpose of remedying the perceived deficiency, and the texts thus generated were viewed widely as models to emulate. Selected from among texts considered central in the culture where they originated, such texts were manifestly different from certain central formations of Persian literature as stereotyped in the literary culture of the time. These works did in fact, as we shall see, give rise to a variety of textual activities based on nonnative sources.

Modeling activities occasioned by translation have yet to be studied in relation to esthetic change in the entire Persian poetic tradition. Consequently, the kinds of correlations that may have existed historically between translated works and the various literary systems of the Persian language have remained unknown. The general impression is that through much of its history, Persian literature penetrated the neighboring literatures, most notably those of the Indian subcontinent and the Ottoman Empire. Influences in the opposite direction have not been examined as much, in part because of the nationalist culture within which twentieth-century literary scholarship has been conducted in Iran. At any rate, the impact of literary translation has remained unincorporated into the diachronic dimension of the Persian literary system. In this chapter we examine the manner in which certain European literary texts were incorporated into the poetic system of Iranian culture early in the twentieth century. As elsewhere in this book, I examine a limited number of texts and certain specific aspects of the activity. The poems I examine have all been conceived directly or indirectly as a result of their authors' contact with certain texts of foreign origin, yet they are remembered today not as translations but primarily as original compositions in the Persian language. Examining such works, on the one hand, in relation to the texts which may have given rise to them and, on the other, in relation to their generative ambience may well reveal the contexts and conditions in which literary traditions begin assimilating elements from other traditions; it may also shed some light on the ways in which literary cultures respond to such assimilations. A better understanding of both tendencies may then elucidate the process of change in an esthetic tradition.

Post-World War I Iran witnessed a bewildering variety of literary borrowings from Western literary traditions.[9] There were formal and generic imitations, blank-verse renditions, and a good deal of prose and verse translations of European poetic works. Regardless of generic type and formal features of the original texts, their Persian renditions were often made to accord more or less with the formal and generic classifications present in the Persian literature of the time. The kind of borrowing I examine in this chapter was no different. It was conceived as a sort of poetic improvisation on a topic thematized by some foreign text. Most commonly, the poet would take the narrative and moral purpose of the original text and compose a Persian poem on it, the product often taking the shape of a Persian *qet'eh* (fragment) or *masnavi* (rhyming couplets).[10] The best-known example of this kind of borrowing remains Iraj's unfinished verse romance, entitled *Zohreh va Manuchehr* (Zohreh and Manuchehr), which is a masnavi in form. In all likelihood, this poem is indirectly based on Shakespeare's *Venus and Adonis,* or some prose version of the Greek myth in French.[11] The literary journal *Daneshka-deh* features scores of similar poems based on works by Boileau, La Fontaine, Rousseau, Platon, Goethe, Schiller, and others.[12]

IMPROVISATION: BAHAR'S "TOIL AND TREASURE"

Mohammad-Taqi Bahar's poem, "Ranj o Ganj," (Toil and Treasure), is known to a great number of Iranians because it has been published in many generations of elementary textbooks in the last fifty years or so. It first appeared in January 1919 in the ninth issue of *Daneshkadeh,* and provides an illuminating example of the sort of borrowing whose nature and significance need to be examined. Here is the poem's text as well as my literal translation of it:

> Boro kar mikon magu chist kar
> keh sarmayeh-ye javdani-st kar
> negar ta keh dehqan-e dana cheh goft
> beh farzandegan chun hami khast khoft
> keh miras-e khod ra bedarid dust
> keh ganji ze pishinian andar ust
> man an ra nadanestam andar koja-st
> pajuhidan o yaftan ba shoma-st
> cho shod mehregan keshtgah bar kanid
> hameh ja-ye an zir o bala konid
> namanid nakandeh ja'i ze bagh
> begirid az an ganj har ja soragh
> pedar mord o puran beh ommid-e ganj
> beh kavidan-e dasht bordand ranj
> beh gav-ahan o bil kandand zud
> ham inja ham anja va har ja keh bud
> qaza ra dar an sal az an khub shokhm
> ze har tokhm bar khast haftad tokhm
> nashod ganj payda vali ranjeshan
> chonan chon pedar goft shod ganjeshan.[13]

(Go work, say not: "What is work!"
for work is an eternal capital.
Watch what the knowing farmer said
to his sons at the time of his rest.
Said he: "Love your heritage well,
for in it is a treasure, hid by our ancestors.

I never knew where it was buried.
To search and to find it is up to you.
Come autumn, plow the entire field,
turn it upside down everywhere,
and in the orchard too leave no spot untilled,
seek out that treasure wherever it may be."
The father died, and the sons, hoping for treasure,
toiled much in turning up the field;
losing no time, with the plow and shovel, they dug
here, and there, and whichever way they could
As fate would, that year, for that good tillage
from each seed sprang seventy seeds.
No treasure was found, yet their toil
did turn out indeed to be their treasure.)

The poem is based on La Fontaine's "Le Laboureur et ses Enfants," the ninth fable in Book Five of *Les Fables,* and was printed together with a Persian prose translation of it with appropriate attribution. Here is La Fontaine's verse fable:

Travaillez, prenez de la peine:
C'est le fonds qui manque le moins.
Un riche Laboureur sentant sa mort prochaine
Fit venir ses enfants, leur parla sans témoins.
Gardez-vous, leur dit-il, de vendre l'héritage
Que nous ont laissé nos parents.
Un trésor est caché dedans.
Je ne sais pas l'endroit; mais un peu de courage
Vous le fera trouver, vous en viendrez à bout.
Remuez votre champ dès qu'on aura fait l'août.
Creusez, fouillez, bêchez, ne laissez nulle place
Où la main ne passe et repasse.
Le Père mort, les fils vous retournent le champ
Deçà, delà, partout; si bien qu'au bout de l'an
Il en rapporta davantage.
D'argent, point de caché. Mais le Père fut sage
De leur montrer avant sa mort
Que le travail est un trésor.[14]

The textual context in which "Toil and Treasure" was first published is significant both internally and in terms of its links with the other sections of the journal. The section which included the anonymous prose translation of the French fable as well as Bahar's poem bore the heading *Eqterah* (literally, meaning "improvisation," perhaps envisioned more precisely as an impromptu test, presumably of poetic *qariheh* "talent"). Its use, in reference to a section in a literary journal which includes the Persian prose translation of a foreign text and one—or a few—Persian poems based on it, seems to have been initiated by *Daneshkadeh.* Where there were multiple Persian poems composed by different individuals, they all versified the basic idea of the foreign text, yet the participants were apparently free to choose the form, meter, or rhyme scheme of their compositions.[15] Both the word "improvisation" and the multiplicity of contributions suggest a sort of poetic competition among the participants, designed in all likelihood to foster the search for the most appropriate and effective ways of naturalizing European literary texts in the Persian language. The competitive aspect of the practice seems to have become more predominant, since the practice soon became known as *mosabeqeh-ye adabi* (literary competition).[16] It found wide currency in the 1930s and 1940s, although one may still come across instances of it in Iranian literary journals.

In *Daneshkadeh,* this section seems to have grown out of a smaller segment, a filler of sorts, usually placed at the bottom of the pages left partially blank by more extensive essays in the journal. In such spaces, aphorisms from many European literary figures were printed in translation. Aphorisms published in the first issue, for example, bear the names of Schiller, Flammarion, Armant, Bordello, and Victor Hugo.[17] The first time the term *Eqterah* appears in the journal, it is accompanied by the subhead *Dar Qateʿ at-e Adabi-ye Faranseh* [in—or on—French literary fragments]. The section following the heading contains a prose translation of a fragment from Boileau's "Pyrrhus," followed in turn by a composition by Bahar billed as a "versified translation of Boileau's fragment" (*tarjomeh-ye nazmi-ye qetʿeh-ye buʾalo*).[18] Such designations are absent from *Daneshkadeh*'s later *Eqterah*s.

Within the section containing La Fontaine's "Le Laboureur . . . ," Bahar's poem is published after the fable's Persian prose translation, a fact that marks the latter as a preliminary, and necessary, step toward the Persian poet's "improvisation." Because we have no evidence that Bahar had direct access to La Fontaine's fable (we know he did not know much French), we may assume that the stylistic features of the Persian prose translation were significant in informing and constraining his composition. So, let me explore that ground a little. Entitled *"Zareʿ va Pesaran-e U"* (The Farmer and His Sons), the Persian prose translation is unpretentious, even by the standards of literary translation current at the time. It is printed in regular prose fashion, filling every line, as if it were a story out of a prose collection in Persian; it does not strive for any rhetorical or lexical embellishments or poetic effect in its syntax or diction. It highlights the moral of La Fontaine's fable by setting the Persian translation of the first two lines in bold letters. Thus, "Travaillez, prenez de la peine: / C'est le fonds qui manque le moins," appears in Persian in a way comparable to: **"kar konid va ranj barid in yek sarmayeh-i-st keh hargez gom nakhahid kard."**

Its prosaic diction and style notwithstanding, the prose translation supplies some of Bahar's key terms, such as *ranj* (la peine/toil), *ganj* (trésor/treasure), *sarmayeh* (le fonds/capital) and *miras* (l'héritage/heritage). It also provides the lexical basis for some of the poetic phrases, clauses, and patterns Bahar uses. For instance, in Bahar's poetic phrase *man an ra nadanestam andar koja-st,* one can easily see traces of the prose sentence *man ja-ye an ra nemidanam* (I do not know its place); or a syntactic pattern like *ham inja ham anja va har ja keh bud* (both here and there and wherever there was) is easily traceable to the sentence *inja va anja va hameh ja* (here, there, and all over). Finally, although the two rhyming words of *ranj* and *ganj* occur in the prose translation, the text does not attempt to harness the poetic potential of the two rhyming words, nor does it even show an awareness of it. Bahar, however, uses each word several times, and rhymes them twice, once in the seventh line and once in the final line. In this way, he highlights the ultimate relationship between the concepts those words express. The culture has exploited this potential even more. In successive editions of Bahar's *Divan*—as well as in the textbooks where the poem is published—the two rhyming words have been elevated to the poem's title.[19]

Bahar's additions and omissions of textual entities are no less significant. He gives an affirmative character to the opening moral *sententiae* by changing the clause describing the capital that is work—*keh hargez gom nakhahid kard* (which you will never lose—into the adjective "eternal" (*javdani*). In doing so, he turns a characterization of work that is negatively phrased into a positive modifier for it. In the episode itself, he omits the reference to the absence of a witness, present in the prose translation as in the French original. In the prose translation, La Fontaine's *leur parla sans témoins* (he told them without [the presence of] a witness) had been translated literally as *bedun-e shahedi beh anha goft* (without a witness he said). However, a subtle shift has occurred in the process. In the original, the word *témoins* rhymes with the "le moins" of the opening rhyme, while the concept behind it conveys the privacy of the husbandman's meeting with his sons. The French phrase then contains a poetic allusion. As is common in the case of family secrets and natural to the circumstances of the episode, the husbandman reveals the secret to his sons in private. That link is absent from the prose translation. In Persian, the idea would be phrased more commonly as *dar khelvat* (in private), *mahramaneh* (secretly), or *dur az cheshm-e digaran* (away from the eyes of others). With its legal and jurisprudential undertones, the phrase *bedun-e shahed* (without a witness) communicates a secretiveness more appropriate to a plot being hatched than to a family secret being shared. This is probably due to the emergence of a legal jargon in the discourse of Iran's modernizing and secularizing culture. The Persian phrase would be more likely to take our attention away from the idea of the lesson that the husbandman wishes to impart to his sons and guide it in unpredictable directions. In other words, even though *shahed* is a proper Persian equivalent for the French *témoins*, La Fontaine's concept has undergone a change in the process of translation from French verse into Persian prose, giving the translation of character on that point which may have appeared odd, out of place, or even misleading to Bahar. He deletes all explicit reference to the privacy of the meeting, relying on the word *beh farzandegan* (to the sons) to convey the idea.

Examples of culturally significant changes are too many to enumerate. Bahar recodes the reference to the sale of the inherited property, expressing the idea instead in terms of the father's advice to his sons: "love your heritage" (*miras-e khod ra bedarid dust*). He thus guides the concept of the heritage toward greater abstraction, metonymically aligning it with such concepts as "the land," and from there to "the country," or perhaps "culture" of Iran; this concept is more closely aligned with the notion of Iran as the "heritage of Iranians," and accords more intimately with the patriotic discourse of the time.[20] In a conceptually contrary move, he concretizes the image of the activity expected of the sons by turning the prose version's rather abstract and awkward formula *qadri esteqamat az taraf-e shoma an ra kashf khahad kard* (some perseverance on your part will unearth it) into *pajuhidan o yaftan ba shoma-st* (to search and to find is up to you). There are other words, too, which he adds in order to make the poem more culturally anchored. Substitutions like *mehregan* for *pa'iz* (the prose version's rendition of the French word *l'août* [August]), and additions like *dasht* (field), *keshtgah* (plantation), *bagh* (orchard), *gav-ahan* (plow) realign the poem's cultural axis, make it more specific, or enhance its power to plant an image in the mind of the Persian-speaking reader.

Most significantly, Bahar successfully turns the dictates of rhyme and meter into a source of palpable poetic effects which most visibly distinguish verse from prose in the esthetic culture of his age. Thus, in the first line the repetition of the word *kar* (work) reinforces the message of the fable that work is an important human activity central to the fable's moral. In the second, the *goft/khoft* rhyme helps to express the father's death in terms of sleep, a metaphor for death. And in the third line, the use of the pronoun *u* (he, she) for the land wherein the metaphorical treasure is buried serves to personify its referent and classicize the poem. The process culminates in the last two lines where the word *shokhm* (plow), used in the prose translation, is paired with the word *tokhm* (seed) and placed within the proverbial phrase in Persian that metonymically refers to a good harvest. Thus, the hemistich *ze har tokhm bar khast haftad tokhm* (from each seed sprang seventy seeds), while covering the distance between the single seed of the sowing time and the seventy seeds of the harvest, at the same time alludes to the far greater space that separates the surface operations of the prose text to the deep-seated poetic allusions embedded in the Persian language.

As for the French fable's moral, Bahar's manipulation of the Persian prose text seems designed to buttress the lesson he detects in it, while emphasizing the work ethic which he, as a leading member of the Iranian intellectual community, appears determined to instill in the minds of his compatriots. His effort is most clearly visible in the poem's closure where the French fable's identification of work and treasure comes to reiterate the everlasting quality of the capital that is work. Whereas a treasure would be an accidental gain, work is an inexhaustible source of wealth, one that the sons can use to good effect every revolving season. Moreover, whereas no source of knowledge can instruct people in the art of hunting for real treasures buried in the ground, the sons can in turn instruct their offspring in the potential of work to be turned into wealth. All of this, while present in the French fable and its Persian prose translation, is accentuated and buttressed through Bahar's poetic rendition, making La Fontaine's moral far more accessible to the Persian poem's readers. Let us recall, for instance, that the original French fable—and the prose translation—ends with a simple equation: "work is treasure" (le travail est un trésor/*kar kardan ganj ast*). Bahar's poem, in contrast, articulates toil as "becoming" or "turning into" treasure, thus wedding the moral and the fable by highlighting the process rather than the outcome: "their toil . . . became their treasure."

One last point merits attention in regard to the moral purport of Bahar's poem. The penultimate line reads thus: *qaza ra dar an sal az an khub shokhm / ze har tokhm bar khast haftad tokhm* (as fate would, that year, for that good tillage / from each seed sprang seventy seeds). In this formulation two forces—fate and human endeavor—are present, both credited equally with the happy outcome of a good harvest. The first, fate, is totally absent from the French fable and, naturally, from the Persian prose version. The translation is very clear on the question of cause and effect here: *pesaran . . . be towri khub shokhm kardand keh . . .* (the sons . . . plowed so well that . . .). How do we account for Bahar's addition of "fate"? I can think of two possibilities. First, the term *qaza ra* (as fate would have it) can be seen as a staple of classical Persian verse, used randomly at times as a filler to meet the demands of meter. In this case, Bahar's use of the term would be seen as a stylistic choice thematically unmarked or unsemanticized. The second possibility is that of treating the term as a meaningful lexical entity—that is, one containing some sense. In that case, a problematic relationship arises between the concept communicated through this term and the one conveyed through another semantic unit *az an khub shokhm* (from—meaning because of, or as a result of—that good plowing). What was it that led to the happy outcome, fate or the good plowing? The text is ultimately ambiguous, seeming to want to embrace both readings at the same time. Are we then to take this as a sign of ambivalence in the poetry of a culture in the process of transition from a fate-based notion of life's vicissitudes to one relying more on human endeavor? I have no answer.

Thus, through a complex process of recodification, which includes lexical, rhetorical, and structural additions, omissions, and revisions, the Iranian poet produces a text which, while exhibiting the basic idea of a foreign fable inaccessible to him in all its aspects, changes it formally, generically, and stylistically in ways that consort with his own specific cultural circumstances. The notion of the heritage, it is worth noting, fits Bahar's relatively conservative agenda for literary change and reflects his anxiety about the course of poetic change in Iran, as we have seen in his debates with Raf'at. This concordance between the meaning of La Fontaine's fable and Bahar's efforts to protect the "spirit" of classical Persian poetry from the ravages of excessive modernism would be fully visible when we once again place the poem "Toil and Treasure" in its original context, the literary journal *Daneshkadeh*. There, let us recall, Bahar's poem appeared next to the warnings he issued against undue departures from traditional poetic practice, some of which we saw in the last chapter. Viewed in relation to the criticisms leveled at his pleas for placing poetic change within general considerations of the tradition's continuity,[21] the poem becomes one more statement on the richness of the ancestral field, a case for the necessity of tending the inherited garden and an effective brief against the losses that might result from venturing out.

The relations between Bahar's poem, the prose translation at his disposal, and the French fable on which that translation is based, exemplify certain complex operations at work in the appropriation of already existing textual entities. In all this, "Toil and Treasure" typifies a major type of literary borrowing current in Iranian culture of the early twentieth century. In it, stylistic and rhetorical choices signify the poet's intention to transport as much of the source text's content into his or her own culture by recoding its constituent and structural elements.

Naturally, such a task involves an initial assessment of the foreign text's poetic potential and projections concerning its place in the native literary tradition. Knowing perhaps that he is ultimately dealing with a text which the French culture has classified as "classical," as "verse," and as a "fable," Bahar sets out to produce a text that would fit within the tradition of classical Persian verse fable. Without direct access to all the aspects of the original text, he finds it necessary to rely on the resources of his own language and esthetic tradition as he attempts to poeticize and classicize the Persian prose translation to the extent possible.

Now, Bahar is well known as an excellent versifier capable of vesting a variety of poetic effects in any prose piece. This capability makes it easy not only to see the point on which his versified renditions may differ from their models but also to assign esthetic, cultural, and ideological significance to them. They can be seen, in effect, as manifestations of the poet's intentions rather than as dictates of verse translation. In the case of "Toil and Treasure," at the same time that Bahar's treatment of the theme places the text well within the tradition of verse fables in classical Persian poetry, the poem's didacticism emits a breath of fresh air because the fable itself is new to the system. It therefore introduces a new way of treating a fable, and suggests a novel set of relations between the moral and the anecdote which upholds, exemplifies, and propagates it. Most of the other Iranian versifiers of La Fontaine were forced either to affirm and reinforce his value system or to risk sounding like pale shadows of classical Persian fabulists like Sa'di, 'Attar, or Rumi. In the first instance, their work tends to exhibit signs of rupture with the Persian tradition of verse fable; in the second, they risk losing contact with the foreign text.

Let me turn finally to the reception accorded Bahar's "Toil and Treasure." The manner in which successive generations of Iranian readers have viewed the poem testifies to the presence of an important tendency in that culture. Virtually all traces of the poem's lineage have been eradicated. Certainly, the poet's own heirs seem to have left their patrimony unplowed. Through the five editions of the poet's *Divan,* published since his death under the supervision of his heirs, there is no mention either of the poem's original context in the journal *Daneshkadeh* or of its relationship with La

Fontaine's fable.[22] The many biographic accounts and commemorative volumes of the poet's life and works contain practically no reference to those poetic compositions that are modeled on texts of foreign origin.[23] Finally, in the elementary and secondary textbooks where "Toil and Treasure" has been published regularly for the past fifty years or so no mention is made of its origin. This omission has been accomplished so successfully that it has led, at least in one instance known to me, to erroneous attribution. Writing in *Ketab-e Jom'eh,* a journal published in 1979–80, a contemporary scholar of Persian literature has speculated that it may have been a translation from an Arabic poem.[24] The cultural assumption that is working through attempts to conceal the nonnative origins of cherished cultural artifacts ought to be obvious: a poet's stature is diminished if a most celebrated composition of his is found out to have been based on an already existing work. The work could then be called not an original, but a "borrowing." At the cultural level, too, acknowledging literary borrowing is tantamount to undermining the integrity of the national culture. The native zeal for constructing and propagating an imaginary of cultural autonomy works at times through the enforcement of a premeditated—or perhaps not so premeditated—scholarly amnesia.

INDIGENIZATION: IRAJ'S "A MOTHER'S HEART"

Similar attitudes seem to have guided the fate of the next text I examine here. "Qalb-e Madar," (A Mother's Heart), composed a few years after "Toil and Treasure" by Bahar's contemporary and friend, Iraj Mirza (1874–1926), has also found its way through schoolbooks to the hearts and minds of generations of Iranians. Even though the poem is somewhat different in its internal textual dynamics as well as in its extratextual relations, it too has been showered with acclaim. It may not have undergone as radical, and as successful, a process of severance from the texts to which it owes its existence, but the cultural dynamics involved in the process are not dissimilar. At any rate, in the most significant cultural fora for its dissemination—that is, Iranian school textbooks—the poem has always appeared as an original composition by an Iranian poet. Here is the poem in its entirety, followed by my literal translation:

> Dad ma'shuqeh beh 'asheq paigham
> keh konad madar-e to ba man jang
> har koja binadam az dur konad
> chehreh por chin o jabin por ajang
> ba negah-e ghazab-alud zanad

bar del-e nazok-e man tir-e khadang
az dar-e khaneh mara tard konad
hamcho sang az dahan-e qalmasang
madar-e sang-delat ta zendeh-ast
shahd dar kam-e man o to-st sharang
nashavam yek-del o yek-rang to ra
ta nasazi del-e u az khun rang
gar to khahi beh vesalam beresi
bayad in saʿat bi khowf o derang
ravi o sineh-ye u ra bedari
del borun ari az an sineh-ye tang
garm o khunin beh manash baz ari
ta barad z-ayeneh-ye qalbam zang
ʿasheq-e bi-kherad-e nahenjar
nah bal an faseq-e bi-ʿesmat o nang
hormat-e madari az yad bebord
khireh az badeh va divaneh ze bang
raft o madar ra afkand beh khak
sineh bedrid o del avard beh chang
qasd-e sarmanzel-e maʿshuq nemud
del-e madar beh kafash chun narang
az qaza khord dam-e dar beh zamin
v-andaki sudeh shod u ra arang
v-an del-e garm keh jan dasht hanuz
uftad az kaf-e an bi-farhang
az zamin baz cho bar khast nemud
pay-e bardashtan-e an ahang
did k-az an del-e agheshteh beh khun
ayad ahesteh borun in ahang
ah dast-e pesaram yaft kharash
akh pa-ye pesaram khord beh sang.[25]

(The beloved sent a message to the lover:
"Your mother fights with me," she said,
"wherever she sees me from afar
she wears a morose face, frowning her brows,
and with her angry glances she casts
sharp arrows at my delicate heart.
She turns me away from her house
like a rock from the mouth of a slingshot.

So long as your stone-hearted mother is alive
nectar will be poison in my mouth, and yours.
I shall not be of one heart and one mind with you
so long as you have not turned her heart bloody.
If you desire union with me
fearless and firm this very hour
you go tear up her pent chest,
take the heart out of that narrow chamber,
and bring it to me warm and full of blood.
That will rub the dust off my heart."
The unwise, iniquitous lover
nay, that shameless, vicious fornicator
forgot the honor of motherhood,
and, senseless from wine and bhang,
rushed forth, threw his mother down,
tore open her chest, grabbed the heart in his claws,
and set out for the beloved's abode, holding
in his palm, like an orange, his mother's heart.
At the threshold, as fate would have it, he stumbled
and his elbow was scratched a bit.
Then that warm heart, still possessing some life,
fell from that uncouth man's hand,
and when he, hasting up, made for it
and moved to pick up the heart,
he heard, coming from that bloodied heart,
in a diminished voice, this utterance:
"Ah, my son's hand was scratched!
Woe, my son's foot hit a rock!")

Like Bahar's "Toil and Treasure," Iraj Mirza's "A Mother's Heart" has been so totally absorbed in the culture of twentieth-century Iran that virtually all its foreign traces have been eradicated, its roots judged a matter solely of scholarly interest. In his notes to the successive editions of Iraj's *Divan*, Mohammad-Ja'far Mahjub mentions two possible origins for the poem. First, the poem is known to have been composed in response to a "literary competition" (*mosabeqeh-ye adabi*) proposed in 1923 by the Iranian expatriate journal *Iranshahr*, published in Berlin. As was common at the time, the journal had offered for versification by Iranian poets three literary passages or fragments (*qet'eh-ye adabi*). The passages had been translated into Persian prose with no specific reference to their origins or the names of their European authors.

The first of these, a vignette containing the theme of Iraj's "A Mother's Heart," was identified only as based on a German text. According to Mahjub, Iraj composed his poem in response to the journal's request to Iranian poets to versify "the theme" (*mazmun*) of the three literary pieces.[26] Mahjub adds his own assessment of Iraj's performance, stating categorically that "in this competition, too, Iraj composed the best poem."[27] In a note to a subsequent edition of the *Divan,* he mentions another possible source, offering a partial translation of it. Again he emphasizes the superiority of the Persian poem over the original:

> At the same time, a French poet named Jean Richepin, a contemporary of Iraj, had versified and published a piece entitled "La Chanson de la Glu. . . ." However, his poem pales and grows dim before Iraj's piece.[28]

As Mahjub seems to suggest, we may well assume that Iraj was familiar with Richepin's poem, especially in light of his relatively advanced knowledge of French and unparalleled acquaintance with French literature. It seems reasonable then to examine Iraj's poem both with reference to the Persian prose passage offered for versification by *Iranshahr* as well as to Richepin's poem. As in the previous case, I draw on the Persian translation in the course of my analysis. Here is Richepin's "La Chanson de la Glu":

> Y avait un' fois un pauv' gas,
> Et lon lan laire,
> Et lon lan la,
> Y avait un' fois un pauv' gas
> Qu'aimait cell' qui n'l'aimait pas.
>
> Ell' lui dit: Apport' moi d'main
> Et lon lan laire,
> Et lon lan la,
> Ell' lui dit: Apport moi d' main,
> L'coeur de ta mèr' pour mon chien.
>
> Va chez sa mère et la tue
> Et lon lan laire,
> Et lon lan la,
> Va chez sa mère et la tue
> Lui prit l'coeur et s'en courut
>
> Comme il courait, il tomba,
> Et lon lan laire,
> Et lon lan la,

Comme il courait, il tomba,
Et par terre l'coeur roula.

Et pendant que l'coeur roulait,
Et lon lan laire,
Et lon lan la,
Et pendant que l' coeur roulait
Entendit l' coeur qui parlait.

Et l' coeur disait en pleurant,
Et lon lan laire,
Et lon lan la,
Et l' coeur disait en pleurant:
T'est-tu fait mal, mon enfant?[29]

Judging by the number of poems in which Iraj has celebrated mothers and motherhood, we may imagine the theme of motherly love to have held a particular appeal to him.[30] That might also explain the striking gravity and seriousness of his composition in contrast with the lighthearted treatment of the subject in Richepin's hand. The colloquiality of the French in Richepin's poem, the lightness with which the poem handles its theme, and the nonchalance with which the murder of the mother is related must have appeared unacceptable to Iraj and inappropriate to the literary culture of his time, even though he himself is famous for his black humor. However, the idea of explicit expression of the moral tacked on to the narrative was itself being rejected by Iranian modernists as a sign of what was often described as "the backwardness of the literature of Iran" in comparison with that of "European literature." As we have seen in the debate on Saʿdi, all explicit expressions of morality were increasingly posited as a relic from the medieval Persian tradition inappropriate to modern times.

The Persian prose text is doubtless closer to him in its depiction of an overwhelming passion as the reason for the crime. Stylistically, too, it features an amorous dialogue between a lover and his beloved placed in a sentimental scene. It focuses on the overriding power of love as the motive force for the crime the young man commits. And in juxtaposing a serene natural scene to the internal passions that drive human actions it exemplifies the melodramatic pathos associated in early twentieth-century Iranian literature with European Romanticism.[31] All this gives the narrative a romantic quality and a tumultuous tenor which seem to suit the terms of poetic expression in Iraj's time. Iraj may well have thought the prose narrative closer to his own heart and more appropriate to his culture.

The romantic opening of the German passage translated anonymously into Persian prose typifies its tone throughout: "It was a moonlit night," the narrative goes. The lover and the beloved, sitting by a stream, are engaged in "intimate conversation" (*raz o niaz*). "The girl" (*dokhtar*) is "drunk with beauty's pride" (*az ghorur-e hosn mast*), and "the young man" (*javan*) is "burning in the fire of love" (*az atesh-e 'eshq dar suz o godaz*). The passage then reports the dialogue between the lover and the beloved. The lover asks his beloved, given that he has bestowed upon her his most precious possession, his heart, whether she still has any doubts about the purity of his love. The beloved responds that the youth still possesses a priceless jewel which she longs to possess: his mother's heart. "If you extract your mother's heart and bring it to me," she adds, "I will feel certain about the truth of your love, and will bind myself to love for you." The passage then relates the momentary storm (*tufan*) which the request stirs up in the young lover's heart, the quick triumph of "the power of love" (*qovvat-e 'eshq*) over "affection for the mother" (*mehr-e madar*), and his unthinking fulfillment of the heinous mission thrust upon him. As he is running back to his beloved, his mother's heart in his hand, he stumbles, the heart rolls upon the ground, and it speaks the narrative's closing sentence: "Were you hurt, my dear boy?" (*pesar jan aya sadameh-i barayat resid?*).

And yet, even this version must still have appeared insufficient to Iraj, especially in its failure to explicitly reiterate its moral lesson, either as a preamble to the narrative or as a closing reflection on it. The terms of Iraj's dilemma begin to be apparent here. He must have thought the theme to which he was drawn deserved a set of lexical and stylistic parameters unavailable in either of his sources. None of his texts provided a sufficient point of reference for the expression of the story's moral import. In fact, the story aside, the dramatic quality of Richepin's poem must have seemed the only characteristic of the French text of any use to him. As for the Persian prose text, the romantic texture of its narrative typical of an important strain in the prose style of the period, introduced into Iran through translations of European, especially French, romantics was considered largely appropriate to prose translations of foreign literature, but not to Persian poetry.[32] Finally, he had to find a way to inject his moral position into the text without appearing backward.

An examination of Iraj's maneuvers between the two texts reveals the specific individual choices he made and clarifies the common concerns of the community of meaning of which he is a member. All poets, of course, approach the task of indigenizing foreign texts with a view toward naturalizing them stylistically, generically, and thematically. In doing so, they may initially use an impression of their poetic culture as the touchstone against which they assess the relevance and utility of foreign acquisitions, and later as a guide to their method of appropriation. If we assume Iraj's acquaintance with both texts, his choices must be judged significant. His account of the beloved's message to the lover, while diverging from both texts in important details of description and narration, enhances certain aspects of each one's style and rhetoric, and amplifies the moral lesson in both. To begin, he departs from both foreign texts in envisioning not a dialogue but a "message" (*paigham*). In both Western texts the lover and the beloved are portrayed in the presence of one another: in one text the woman's request to the lover is reported briefly and directly—"*Apport' moi d'main / L' coeur de ta mèr'*." In the other, the request is made in the course of an intimate scene, and is articulated as the beloved's desire to have further evidence of the lover's professed feeling. Are we to venture the guess that communication in absentia is more natural and more appropriate to a culture where sex segregation is a social norm?

In reporting the content of the beloved's request, too, Iraj steers between the black-humor buffoonery of the French text and the proof-gathering thrust of the Persian prose translation. In "A Mother's Heart," the beloved neither wishes to feed the heart to her dog (in all likelihood, she does not have a dog at all) nor demands further proof of the lover's absolute devotion to her. She hates the lover's mother because of the way she treats her, a deep-seated grudge whose specific instances it takes about a dozen lines to report. She probably already imagines her as her mother-in-law (given the poet's culture, is there any way of consummating the love other than marriage?), and cannot face the prospect of having to cope with that kind of behavior forever. On a more metaphorical plane, the beloved does not wish to share the love of the young man with anyone. The whole idea of the beloved as the taker or stealer of the lover's heart, registered in such classical poetic terms as *del-bar* (heart-taker), *del-roba* (heart-stealer), and *rahzan-e del* (highway bandit of the heart), constitutes a central node in the traditional discourse of the lyrical tradition in Persian poetry. In Iraj's poem, a whole tradition of demand and supplication can be seen through the beloved's desire for the lover's absolute, exclusive, and undivided devotion. The metaphor of the beloved as the stealer of the lover's heart, literalized in both narratives of foreign origin, may have made the theme seem appropriate for versification by Iranian poets in the first place. The thought of an old native idea present in another tradition and expressed in teasingly different ways, is particularly appealing to a culture that finds itself in need of greater interaction with other esthetic systems; naturalizing such a thought may validate the native tradition even as it legitimizes its opening up to nonnative elements and entities.

Closer textual analysis reveals even greater details about Iraj's strategy of indigenization. As the poem opens, we see the poet quickly descending into the narrative without the languid torpor of the Persian prose text. There is no mention of beauty's pride and love's consuming flames. The words 'asheq (lover) and *ma'shuqeh* (beloved) are too well known from the canon of classical lyric poetry to require contextualization. Instead, beginning with line two, we see an exposition of the ways in which the beloved sees the lover's mother as "waging war" (*jang-kardan*) against her. Three specific actions are mentioned. The mother frowns on her, she casts sharp arrows of angry glance at her, and she casts her out like stones from a sling, much as one would repel the advances of an enemy from atop a fortress. The last image fits the situation perfectly in portraying the mother as the defender of a fortress the beloved is intent on capturing, namely the lover's heart. The image series also fits well within the Persian poetic culture in allowing the poet to arrive at the stone/heart node, culminating in the line where the beloved's argument seeks its summation. There, the mother is called *sang-del* (literally, stone-hearted, meaning hard-hearted, inflexible, unyielding). The image is significant in that in classical lyric poetry it is a stock description for the beloved. The mother seems figuratively her own son's beloved and a rival to the new beloved. She therefore will have to be eliminated if the young man is to surrender the fortress of his heart to the beloved.

In lines six through nine the beloved spells out the conditions for her consent. In Richepin's poem the only allusion to the reason why the girl commands the boy to bring his mother's heart to her is that he is *un pauv' gas* who loves someone *qui n'l'aimait pas*. The inference is that she may have made the odious demand not in earnest but as a way to repel an unwanted lover. In the Persian prose text, however, the order is issued in response to the lover's claim that he has already given his own heart to the girl. It is envisioned as a clear challenge from the girl to the young man and as the final evidence of true love:

> The girl answered: "On the path of loving, giving one's own heart is the first step. You possess a precious gem more valuable than your heart, and only that gem can be a sign of the truth of your love. I want that gem from you, that is your mother's heart.[33]

Iraj dispenses with both the dark humor of Richepin's poem and the Persian prose text's metaphorical gems. Commensurate with the verisimilar tone of his story, he makes the beloved admit that she will not be able to be *yek-del* (literally of one heart) with the lover until the sight of his mother's heart "will rub the dust off the mirror of my heart." Besides sealing the beloved's argument, the image serves a purpose more relevant to the poem's moral. The mirror that is the beloved's own heart is covered with dust, and therefore cannot reflect an accurate image of the world outside. The image of the impure heart as a dust-laden mirror harks back to the mystical articulation of human frailties and vices, thus linking this story with an illustrious ancestry in the classical tradition of Persian poetry.[34]

It is in light of this initial hint that the string of negative attributes by which the lover is described and the addition of the account of the lover's use of drugs begin to release their meaning. The young man, by nature unwise (*bi-kherad*) and iniquitous (*nahenjar*), has to make himself senseless on wine and bhang to be able to kill his mother. As one scholar has pointed out, it is a widespread belief in Iraj's culture that only the most errant of natures, aided by the wicked influence of two drugs known for their paralyzing effect on the faculty of reason, can summon up enough evil for so heinous an act as matricide.[35] Thus, the wine and bhang motif, Iraj's most substantive addition to his source texts, becomes the most emblematic also. Indeed, culture-specific treatments of the theme of matricide may be just the lens through which all of Iraj's other relevant devices can be brought into focus. Through the poet's handling of that theme we can watch two contemporary cultures deal with a fundamental taboo. Pushed by their themes to the edges of the culturally permissible, Richepin and Iraj devise different ways of distancing themselves from it, the French poet by the device of the burlesque, the Iranian by adding layers of moral commentary. Modernism may entail more daring departures, but the path to the center will always have to remain open.

As a device to explain the young lover's criminal conduct, Iraj's wine and bhang motif is particularly significant in terms of the opportunity it presents for confirming an important part of the religious ethos of his culture. And if that entails changing the structure, the narrative technique, or the cultural register of his sources it still will have to be done. He alters not just the tone and style but also the structure and logic of his source texts, and he produces a poem that accords as far as possible with the moral and religious convictions of his own culture. In short, the Iranian poet's modifications fortify the moral purpose behind the ideas found in both the foreign texts to which he may have had access. By incorporating the poet's clear, emphatic, and unequivocal judgment about the young man's evil deed, in terms of both his character and the circumstances that prompt him to commit his crime, Iraj has ensured the loving acceptance of his poem, then and ever since. That, I suspect, is the primary function of the string of negative attributes by which he describes the lover and his addition of the account of the lover's use of drugs. The young man was unwise, iniquitous, even undeserving of being called a lover (Iraj corrects himself midway by taking back the appellation "lover," calling him instead a shameless, vicious fornicator). In addition, in order to be intoxicated, he drank wine and used bhang before killing his mother. In thus demonizing the matricide, Iraj produces a poem in total harmony with the moral and ethical bearings of Iranian culture.

For its part, the culture has rewarded him by appropriating the poem as if it were its own. Making reference to the impressive popularity of Iraj's compositions in praise of mothers and motherly love, the editor of his *Divan* describes them all as "so touching as to bring uncontrollable tears to the reader's eyes." He calls "A Mother's Heart" one of those poems that "you would be hard-pressed to find a Persian-speaking school-age child who has not heard many times over." He then states: "So far as I know in every school where a cultural celebration takes place, one of the poems which is almost always recited in the form of a 'declamation' is this very poem, Iraj's 'A Mother's Heart'."[36] Similarly, Gholam-Hosayn Yusofi, characterizing the poem as "a very effective allegory" possessing "the utmost spiritual power," calls it "stronger and more beautiful" than whatever source the Persian prose translation may have been based on. He concludes his discussion of it with this tender evaluation:

> "A Mother's Heart" . . . is doubtless among Iraj's valuable [*geran-qadr*] and "lasting" [*mandegar*] works, and Persian-speakers will always read and repeat it, and its life will be eternal so long as mothers and their love shall be.[37]

Such loving assessments, echoed by at least two generations of Iranian scholars and critics, are often accompanied by assertions about the superiority of this and similarly conceived Persian poems over their sources. This tendency, I believe, points to anxieties concerning the imagined purity of the literary tradition. However, the belief that literary borrowing may, under certain conditions, enrich the native esthetic tradition has remained an abiding feature of poetic evolution in Iran. Beyond that, claims of the superiority of native literary artifacts over what foreign texts their authors may have had as their model abound throughout the life of literature in twentieth-century Iran.

APPROPRIATION: PARVIN'S ''GOD'S WEAVER''

The last text I examine in this chapter, though similar in the way it uses its source, is unique in one important respect. The poet, a woman, turns the poem into an expression of her own condition as a woman poet in a highly patriarchal society. Parvin E'tesami (1907–1941), the first important twentieth-century woman poet of Iran, has traditionally been regarded as an author whose compositions confirm and perpetuate the tradition of poetic advice through versified fables, parables, and anecdotes.[38] In some of her best known and most widely read compositions, the occasion for commentary or advice arises out of a debate between two emblematic entities opposed to one another in an important character trait. "Jula-ye Khoda" (God's Weaver), the poem under consideration here, features one such situation, and the fact that it is based on a text of foreign origin seems to have facilitated her task in that regard. However, as we shall see presently, this has not prevented her from turning the poem into an expression of a deeply personal nature about an intellectual woman in a patriarchal society.

Since this poem is considerably longer than the previous texts I have cited, I find it necessary to depart from my practice of presenting the poem whole; instead, I offer the Persian text in four different segments, separated by the nature of the utterance in each section. My literal translation follows the Persian text in each case. In the first section Parvin sets the scene where a lazy person (*kahel*) contemplates a spider at work:

> Kaheli dar gusheh-i oftad sost
> khasteh vo ranjur amma tandorost
> 'ankabuti did bar dar garm-e kar
> gusheh-gir az sard o garm-e ruzegar
> duk-e hemmat ra beh kar endakhteh
> joz rah-e sa'y o 'amal nashnakhteh
> posht-e dar oftadeh ammma pish-bin
> az baray-e sayd da'em dar kamin
> reshtehha reshti ze mu bariktar
> zir o bala durtar nazdiktar
> pardeh miavikht paida vo nehan
> risman mitaft az ab-e dahan
> darsha midad bi notq o kalam
> fekrha mipokht ba nakhha-ye kham
> kardanan kar zin san mikonand
> ta keh gu'i hast chowgan mizanand
> gah tabah kardi gahi arasti
> gah dar oftadi gahi bar khasti
> kar amadeh vali afzar nah
> dayereh sad ja vali pargar nah

zavieh bi-had mosallas bi-shomar
in mohandes ra keh bud amuzegar
kar kardeh saheb-e kari shodeh
andar an maʿmureh meʿmari shodeh
in chonin sowdagar-i ra sudha-st
v-andar in yek tar tar o pudha-st
pay-kuban dar nashib o dar faraz
saʿati jula zamani bandbaz
past o bi-meqdar amma sar-boland
sadeh vo yek-del vali moshkel-pasand
ustad andar hesab-e rasm o khat
tarh o naqsh-i khali az sahv o ghalat.[39]

(A lazy person fell into a corner languid,
weary, and feeble, yet able-bodied.
He saw a spider above the door, warmly at work,
sheltered from the ups and downs of the age,
having put the spindle of effort to work,
not knowing any path other than action and endeavor,
placed behind the door, yet forward-looking
constantly in ambush for prey.
She wove strands thinner than hair
below, above, farther, closer by
she hung drapes now visible now not.
She made ropes from her saliva,
gave lessons without speech and words,
and wrought thoughts with untreated strings.
Those who know work thus
so long as there is a ball, they strike at the stick.
She would wipe one strand off to make another,
she would fall now to rise a moment later,
her work ready, yet no tools,
circles in a hundred places, yet no compass,
angles beyond counting, triangles innumerable.
Who was teacher to this architect?
She has worked, has mastered the craft,
has become quite a builder in that structure.
Such a merchant will have a profit;
in this one web, there are many warps and woofs.
The spider, dancing below and above

now a weaver, now a rope-walker—
lowly and unworthy, yet proud,
simple, and sincere, yet hard to please—
is a master of the art of drafting and design
her patterns and forms free from error.)

"God's Weaver," formally a poem in rhyming couplets (*masnavi*), is based, as we will see, on an essay by the American journalist Arthur Brisbane. However, the sets of relations Parvin establishes between the two interlocutors, as well as those between the dialogue and the moral, enable the Iranian poet to exploit the potential of the original text so as to make her poem expressive of her own specific condition. In doing so, she produces a work in which the mixture of public and private concerns marks the transition from the classical to a modern universe of poetic discourse.

As in many of Parvin's debate poems, the structure of "God's Weaver" is relatively simple and straightforward. The first section sets the scene. The first two couplets set up the contrast between an indolent man and a spider busily at work. Through the rest of the section, the spider is described in ways that lay the foundation for a series of parallels between the craft of the poet and that of the weaving animal. To accomplish that, a linguistic node connecting the two crafts is utilized to the fullest extent. Beginning with the idea of the spider as weaver, an image well anchored both in linguistic usage and in practical observation, the poem relates the activity of the spider to that of the poet. The verb "to weave" (*baftan*) itself covers a semantic field which the poet manipulates skillfully. In Persian, *baftan* can refer to speech much as its equivalent in English does. Usages such as *sokhan baftan* (to weave words), *she'r baftan* (to weave poetry), *ratb o yabes baftan* (to weave the wet and the dry, meaning to speak all manner of nonsense), *dorugh baftan* (to weave, meaning to tell, lies), *tamat baftan* (to boast, to talk idly) all link the material act of interlacing strands of thread or yarn with the activity of speaking, of uttering words and sentences. Writing poetry, almost from the beginnings of Persian poetry in the ninth century c.e., has been linked with weaving, as numerous usages demonstrate.[40]

In "God's Weaver," this verb provides the central locus for an expanding network of lexical and semantic units whose cumulative force irresistibly coalesces the activities of the spider and the poet—that is, weaving on the literal level and in the sense of weaving words together. Contiguous concepts such as *reshtan* (spinning) and *tanidan* (synonymous with *baftan,* used more specifically for the activity of the spider), nouns such as *tar* and *reshteh* (cord, strand), and agentive nouns such as *bafandeh, nassaj,* and *jula* (variants *juleh, julaheh, julahak*) are all used to underline the centrality of the activity around which the metaphor takes shape. The materials with which the spider works and the product of her labor, too, are named in such a way as to further strengthen this metaphorical dimension.[41] The spider's strands are said to be thinner than hair (line 5), a locution which recalls the idiomatic expression *nokteh-ye bariktar az mu* (a fine point, epigram, or witticism finer than a strand of hair).

Later in the poem, the web is referred to as *atlas* (satin) and *diba* (silk), two fabrics known for their fineness and elaborate patterning. Most important, the product of the spider's labor is called a *pardeh* (curtain, drape, or veil), a word which, while mediating many concepts in the poem, remains firmly centered in the activity of weaving both the material that covers the female body and the poem that hides meaning. The strategy culminates in the lines which sum up the spider's defence of herself:

> Ma tamam az ebteda bafandeh-im
> herfat-e ma in bovad ta zendeh-im
> sa'y kardim ancheh forsat yaftim
> baftim o baftim o baftim.[42]
>
> (We have been the weaver from the beginning;
> and so long as we live this is our profession.
> We have seized every opportunity we have had
> to weave, and weave, and weave.)

Meanwhile, in this initial section the spider's image is, on the one hand, generalized to convey the message of the nobility of work and, on the other, particularized to create a metaphor for the poet as a woman. The animal is portrayed as "sheltered from the ups and downs of the age," "placed behind the door, yet forward-looking," and finally, in a line that can be applied with far greater expressive power to a human being than to an animal, as "lowly and unworthy, yet proud, / simple and sincere, yet hard to please." All this lays the ground for the verbal exchange which, in light of the spider/poet node, is designed to give a particular sense to the image of "the lazy person," situating him in the society in which Parvin is struggling for recognition.

In the second section, lines 17–30, where the descriptive scene gives way to verbal exchange, we hear the lazy person's criticism of the spider's work:

> Goft kahel k-in cheh kar-e sarsari-st
> aseman z-in kar kardanha bari-st
> kuhha kar ast dar in kargah
> kas nemibinad to ra ay parr-e kah

mitani tari keh jarubash konand
mikeshi tarhi keh ma'yubash konand
hichgah 'aqel nasazad khaneh-i
keh shavad az 'atseh-i viraneh-i
payeh misazi vali sost o kharab
naqsh niku mizani amma bar ab
rownaqi mijuy gar arzandeh-i
dibeh-i mibaf agar bafandeh-i
kas ze kholqan-e to pirahan nakard
v-in nakh-e pusideh dar suzan nakard
kas nakhahad didanat dar posht-e dar
kas nakhahad khandanat z-ahl-e honar
bi sar o samani az dud o dam-i
gharq dar tufani az ah o nam-i
kas nakhahad dadanat pashm o kalaf
kas nakhahad goft kashmiri bebaf
bas zebardast-ast charkh-e kineh-tuz
panbeh-ye khod ra dar in atesh masuz
chon to nassaji nakhahad dasht mozd
dozd shod giti to niz az vay bedozd
khasteh kardi z-in tanidan pa vo dast
ro bekhab emruz farda niz hast
ta nakhordi posht-e pai az jahan
khish ra z-in gusheh-giri varehan.[43]

(The lazy person said: "What frivolous labor this is!
The heavens despise such works.
In the world's workshop mountains can be called work,
none will see your work, or you, blade of straw!
You weave a web that they sweep off,
you make a design that they demolish,
no wise person will build a home
that will crumble down from a sneeze.
You build a foundation—but it is flimsy, flaccid
you make fine patterns—but as if on water.
Seek expansion if you are worth it.
Weave a silk fabric if you are a weaver.
None shall make a shirt from your rag,
none shall put in needle your worn-out thread,
none shall see you behind this door,

none shall call you any kind of artist.
The rising smoke can demolish your home, or even a breath;
you get caught in a storm from a sigh, a dampness.
None shall give you woolen yarn,
none shall ask you to make a cashmere.
The vengeful firmament is all powerful;
do not burn your cotton in this fire.
A weaver like you is worth no wage.
The universe is thievish, you too steal from it;
you have exhausted your hands and feet from weaving.
Go rest today, there is tomorrow too.
Before you are tripped over by the world
rescue yourself from this seclusion.")

In relating the lazy person's questioning of the value of the spider's labor, I think the narrator has deliberately designed a muddled argument which would in the end expose the speaker's own jumbled words. The lazy person's criticism, in other words, amounts to no argument at all. His mind is made up even before he speaks, for his first words contain his judgment: "What frivolous labor this is!" He then talks about the heavens' opinion of the work, and begins to express his opinion about the vengeful skies, the thievish universe, and the world which he sees as determined to deal the spider a blow. Watching the spider work in silence, he assumes the posture of the all-knowing man dispensing knowledge, wisdom, and advice. What he ends up producing is a body of words which, unlike the spider's web, has no shape, pattern, or structure.

At the same time, the lazy person's "languid, / weary, and feeble" body, an image depicted at the poem's opening, contrasts visibly with the jumble of incoherent ideas he conveys in his attempt to justify his idleness. These ideas are essential to our understanding of the moral position that will be countered by the spider—and the poet. The man's first point is that the spider's work is insignificant and ephemeral, the work of a creature who itself can be thought of as no more than a "blade of straw" in a world where mountains are worthy of being called work. Furthermore, he charges, the web can be destroyed by a stroke of a broomstick or a sneeze because it lacks a firm foundation. To weave it is no better than making patterns on the surface of water. In his initial reproach, it is worth noting, the word the lazy person uses in reference to the foundation of the spider's web (*sost*= feeble), is precisely the word with which he himself has been described in the first line of the poem. In calling the web a structure of feeble foundation, he may be said in effect to be speaking of his own constitution.

But of course he continues his condemnation, blind to the subtle irony he has created. In a more positive tone, he advises the spider to improve herself and her work (*rownaqi mijuy*), become visible and therefore gainfully employable in terms of human needs and values, and to weave a more marketable fabric. In the same breath, he advises her not to tire herself out, to learn from the world to steal, and, finally, to rest until another day. The lazy person's convoluted logic becomes apparent at this point. He advises the spider to take a rest even as he encourages her to get herself out of her secluded corner. He encourages her to expand her trade even as he bids her, in the language of metaphors: "do not burn your cotton in this fire." The man is literally caught in the shapeless web of his own feebly founded argument, one based entirely on his desire to justify his own inaction. The weakness he attributes to the spider's web is in fact a description of his own words, the only means by which he has made his existence felt in the poem. The lazy man's basic assumption, throughout his speech, is that the spider's activity is aimed at producing a product for a real marketplace, one that would have customers and bring her material profit. That is why he warns the spider that nobody will order fabric from her loom, nobody will make a shirt from her material, and nobody shall compensate her for her labor.

It is this fundamental misconception that the working animal attempts to unravel through her response, lines 31–63. Gradually, of course, an extended catalogue of what makes her so fundamentally different from her detractor emerges from her defense of her own life and work:

> Goft agah nisti z-asrar-e man
> chand khandi bar dar o divar-e man
> ʿelm-e rah benmudan az haq pa ze ma
> qodrat o yari az u yara ze ma
> to beh fekr-e khoftani dar in rebat
> fareghi z-in kargah o z-in besat
> dar takapu-im ma dar rah-e dust
> kar-farma u vo karagah u-st
> gar cheh andar konj-e ozlat sakenam
> shur o ghowgha-ist andar batenam
> dast-e man bar dastgah-e mohkami-st
> har nakh andar cheshm-e man abrishami-st
> kar-e ma gar sahl o gar doshvar bud
> kargar mikhast zira kar bud
> sanʿat-e ma pardehha-ye ma bas ast
> tar-e ma ham dibeh vo ham atlas ast

ma nemibafim az bahr-e forush
ma nemigu'im in diba bepush
ʿayb-e ma z-in pardehha pushideh shod
pardeh-ye pendar-e to pusideh shod
gar darad in pardeh charkh-e pardeh-dar
rakht bar bandam ravam ja-ye degar
gar sahar viran konand in saqf o bam
khaneh-ye digar besazam vaqt-e sham
gar ze yek konjam beranad ruzegar
gusheh-ye digar nemayam ekhtiar
ma keh ʿomri pardeh-dari kardeh-im
dar havades bordbari kardeh-im
gah jarub ast o gah gard o nasim
kohneh natvan kard in ʿahd-e qadim
ma nemitarsim az taqdir o bakht
agahim az ʿomq-e in gerdab-e sakht
an keh dad in duk ma ra rayegan
panbeh khahad dad bahr-e risman
hast bazari degar ay khajeh-tash
k-andar anja mishenasand in qomash
sad kharidar o hezaran ganj-e zar
nist chon yek dideh-ye saheb-nazar
to nadidi pardeh-ye divar ra
chon bebini pardeh-ye asrar ra
khordeh migiri hami bar ʿankabut
khod nadari hich joz bad-e borut
ma tamam az ebteda bafandeh-im
herfat-e ma in bovad ta zendeh-im
saʿy kardim ancheh forsat yaftim
baftim o baftim o baftim
pisheh-am in ast gar kam ya ziad
man shodam shagerd o ayyam ustad
kar-e ma inguneh shod kar-e to chist
bar-e ma khali-st dar bar-e to chist
mineham dami shekari mizanam
juleh-am har lahzeh tar-i mitanam
khaneh-ye man az ghobari chon haba-st
an sara'i keh to misazi koja-st
khaneh-ye man rikht az bad-e hava
kherman-e to sukht az barq-e hava

ma zadim in khaimeh-ye saʿy o ʿamal
ta bedani qadr-e vaqt-e bi-badal
gar keh mohkam bud gar sost in bena
az baray-e ma-st n-az bahr-e shoma
gar beh kar-e khish mipardakhti
khaneh-i z-in ab o gel misakhti
migerefti gar beh hemmat reshteh-i
dashti dar dast-e khod sar reshteh-i.[44]

(She said: "You are not aware of my secrets.
Why do you mock my doors and walls?
To show the path is God's, ours the feet
giving power and assistance His, determination ours.
You think of sleep in this abode
for you know not this workshop, this industry.
We move along the path He has set us.
He is our Master, aware of our work.
Although placed in this corner of seclusion
I hold a passion and a commotion inside me,
my hands are upon a firm loom,
every thread appears silken in my eyes.
Our labor, whether easy or hard
requires a worker, for it is a task.
We do not weave to sell,
we do not ask you to wear our fabric.
These veils you see conceal our defects—
but the veil of your illusion, it's wearing out!
If the veil-tearing firmament tears this veil
I shall set out for somewhere else;
if they destroy this roof and ceiling at dawn
by dusk I will build another home;
should the world drive me out of one corner
I shall set up shop at another.
We who have spent a lifetime inside the veil
have learned patience in the face of adversity:
one moment it is the broom, another it is dust and the wind,
this ancient struggle never gets old.
We are not afraid of fate and fortune,
we are aware of the depth of this tough vortex.
He who gave us this spindle for free

will also provide cotton for the thread.
There is, noble sir, another marketplace
where this commodity is appreciated.
A hundred buyers, thousands of gold treasures
do not equal a single glance from an expert's eye.
You cannot see the drape upon the wall.
How would you wish to see the veil of mysteries?
You who criticize the spider
yourself have nothing but an air of conceit.
We have been a weaver from the beginning,
this is our calling so long as we live.
We have seized every opportunity we've had
to weave, and weave, and weave.
My calling is this, great or small,
I am the disciple, time the master.
Our work is thus, how is yours?
Our bag looks empty? What is in yours?
I set a trap and catch a prey,
I weave and make strands minute by minute.
A speck of dust can ruin my abode?
Where is the abode that you have set up?
My home can crumble from the wind blowing?
Your harvest is burned from lust's lightning.
I despise inaction and indolence,
but you fill your head with the air of pride.
We set up this tent by action, endeavor
so you may seize irretrievable time.
This structure, firm or flimsy
was meant for us, not for you.
Had you engaged yourself in a profession of your own
and made a home from this brick, this mud,
had you put in an effort, picked up some strands
you too could have had a thread in your idle hands.)

As she begins to speak here, the spider makes essentially two points, each of which add to the initial contrast between the two images of the lazy person and the busy animal. First, she says that she does not question her allotted share even though she may not have access to the reasons she was assigned such a task; God is her employer and the one who knows the secrets of her craft. Second, she contrasts at some length her own life and work with the hollow existence of her detractor. Alas, the lazy person has squandered the opportunity afforded him. All the spider can do at this point is to reflect on the loss. Through her, the poet begins to make of the lazy person an example for her readers to behold.

At the same time, the spider's argument, building on the basis of the universal perception of poetry as inspired by vague prompting of the human heart, deepens the analogy that links the spider's activity with the poet's craft. To buttress that impression the poet uses an additional stratagem in the third section, lines 31–63. She alternates between the personal, individual, and singular pronoun "I" (*man*) and the loftier, more universal and plural pronoun "we" (*ma*) to move the poet/spider node closer to the surface of the poem. The spider is indeed both the embodiment of labor (an exemplar of the work ethic when we include the moral in the fable) and a metaphor for the human being who, even though unaware of what motivates her in her work, willingly submits to it because of some internal prompting.

Finally, "God's Weaver" closes with a brief passage that seems rhetorically indistinguishable from the spider's response.[45] This closing passage (lines 64–69), in other words, may be read as the summation of the spider's defense of herself or as the poet's final observations on the story she has just related. Within the context of the debate between the lazy person and the spider, the latter's argument culminates here in the image of the silent spider as a weaver of words. That argument, it is worth recalling, began by portraying the spider as labor incarnate and evolved by accruing a great deal of the poem's metaphorical significance to the spider as weaver. Appropriately, therefore, the terms of dual referentiality used throughout the poem realize their full meaning here. Words like pattern, color, structure, and texture cement the bonding between the two activities of text and textile production. In thus linking the two fields the poet raises the final statement from the level of the spider's defense making a potentially fitting and final response to the real or imagined critics of her own life and work:

> ʿArefan az jahl rokh bar taftand
> tar o pudi chand dar ham baftand
> dukhtand in rismanha ra beh ham
> az deraz o kutah o besyar o kam
> rangraz show ta keh dar khom hast rang
> barq shod forsat nemidanad derang
> gar bena-i hast bayad bar farasht
> ay basa emruz k-an farda nadasht
> naqd-e emruz ar ze kaf birun konim

gar keh farda-i nabashad chun konim
'ankabut ay dust jula-ye khoda-st
charkheh-ash migardad amma bi seda-st.[46]

(Those who know have shunned ignorance
and have woven some threads together.

They have put these strands together:
now long, now short, now many, now few.
Become a color-master while there is dye in the vat.
Opportunities fly away at lightning speed.
If a structure is to be built, you ought to build it.
Many are the days that have no morrow.
If we let go the cash capital that is today
what shall we do when there's no tomorrow?
The spider, my friend, is God's weaver;
her spindle turns, but noiselessly.)

"God's Weaver" is known to be based on an essay entitled "'*Azm va Neshat-e 'Ankabut*' (The Spider's Determination and Vivacity), a translation into Persian of an article by the American journalist Arthur Brisbane. The poet's father Yusof E'tesam al-Molk, a noteworthy early translator, had translated Brisbane's essay, and published it in *Bahar,* a journal he himself edited.[47] The Persian essay begins with a statement relating the fate of a spider to its will, an insight that only close observation can communicate to the viewer:

> The woman who endeavors to keep her house clean knows better than others how much patience and endurance [*sabr o tahammol*] a spider possesses, and how busy the animal appears, as it weaves [its web] in every corner and on every ceiling. As much as one may persist in putting an end to its activity by destroying its abode, the structure of its effort [*bena-ye hemmat*] remains secure from the defects of laxity and indolence.[48]

The essay next describes the spider's "engineering designs" (*tartib-e mohandesi*) and "architectural subtleties" (*zerafat-e me'mari*) as superior to those used in the construction of "the famous Brooklyn Bridge," and praises the animal's "astonishing determination and industry" ('*azm va eqdam-e hayrat-angiz*). It then reports the animal's wordless reaction to the destruction of its web. Shaking off the sadness that has overtaken it momentarily, the spider immediately gets out of one corner and goes to work in another "without losing a moment of its opportunity" (*bedun-e fowt-e forsat*). So long as it has "the fabric" (*maddeh-ye nassaji*) it needs, the spider does not rest from striving and activity (*kushesh va ē adeh-ye ʿamal*). The essay proceeds to liken the worth of the spider's abode in the animal's eye to that of the carpenter's tools, the hunter's trap, the merchant's shop, the inventor's invention, and other "means of subsistence" (*asbab-e ertezaq*). However, the spider wastes no time in mourning the loss of so dear a tool and a possession. Once its dwelling is destroyed, it neither curses its enemy, nor complains about its fate, nor cowers at the thought of similar onslaughts in the future. It simply transports itself to another, perhaps safer, spot, and resumes its "profession or trade" (*herfat ya tejarat*), namely hunting flies (*shekar-e magas*).

The essay's tone changes somewhat at this point as it addresses the reader directly: "Watch the spider's condition carefully as it engages itself in the act of building its dwelling. You will see that it is stout [*farbeh*], strong [*qavi*], and agile [*chalak*]." These qualities are evidence of the spider's will and determination. "Among humans, too," the essay observes, "he who possesses these attributes is happy." However, the essay goes on, a majority of people lack will and alacrity, and even the most enterprising of human souls tend to bend suddenly under the weight of adversity. This is because human beings sometimes suppose that "fate and destiny" (*qaza va qadar*) are at work against them, and that "the times" (*ruzegar*) wreak vengeance upon them. This belief is all too common, for it allows humans to "shun great undertakings," wasting their opportunity in thoughts which they might call "wisdom and philosophy." The essay closes with this observation about two types of attitudes toward success:

> Will and determination are qualities which . . . protect you against the shortcoming that is "absence of self-confidence" [*ʿadam-e ē temad-e beh nafs*].
>
> Some people have a solid will and a strong determination; they advance constantly. Others imagine that nature and natural disposition [*tinat va jebellat*] have created them in such a way that they have to succeed at all times and under all circumstances, and none should ever counter them.
>
> The truth is this: everybody can promote the virtues of determination and vivacity in himself, work hard, and thus approach success as much as possible.[49]

The manner in which Parvin incorporates the Persian essay's arguments, structure, and style in the texture of her poem provides us with an illuminating example of poetic appropriation. She creates a single character, whom she calls "a lazy person" (*kahel*), and places him in dialogue with a hardworking spider. She then portrays the two tendencies described in the essay's close as the two incompatible aspects of the lazy person. The strategy allows her to depict the spider as the concrete manifestation of the ideals of will and determination and the lazy man as inherently illogical. This in turn affects the structure of the poem's argument, making it less an arena of debate between equally arguable, logical positions, and more a forum for developing a new set of relations: those between the activity of the spider and her own activity as a poet. As an ultimate tour de force, the poem structures the contrast in terms of the lazy person's initial "criticism" of the busy spider's work. Consequently, beyond what the lazy person represents in general human traits or attitudes, he comes specifically to signify the real or imagined critics of Parvin's poetry.

As is the case in many of Parvin's debate poems, here, too, the lazy person's reasoning begins to unravel the moment he speaks. In fact, the poem's first word *kahel* (lazy person), has already marked him as the loser of the argument, even before he is given a chance to make his case. This leaves the poet free to direct the spider's response beyond the immediate debate with the poem's lazy man. Through the animal's response, the reader becomes increasingly aware of an external voice merging with the spider's, and that merger leads the poem to its ultimate meaning on the metaphorical plane. Whether because of his own laziness or the force of the spider's logic, we never hear from the lazy person again and, as far as the poem is concerned, the point is made through the spider's soliloquy, which dominates the poem's narrative.

As a working, weaving creature, the image of the spider in the Persian prose essay must have struck Parvin as a particularly apt analogue for her own condition as a woman and her activity as a poet. The animal is the embodiment of silent labor, a combination of qualities which traditional patriarchal societies often regard as appropriate to women.[50] It is oral without being verbal, using her mouth not as an instrument of speech, but as a tool for labor. It is guided in its activity by vague internal promptings rather than by a conscious desire for immortality. With the spider at its center, the narrative would be a silent, gestural one. At the same time, the attributes with which the animal is marked in the Persian poetic tradition have the potential to transmit the message of resolve in enforcing God's will. By giving it the power of speech, the poet makes the spider a verbal creature, speaking and weaving at one and the same time. Once that feat has been accomplished, the attributes by which the spider is marked in the culture can be directed in new ways, hitherto unrealized in the tradition. And thus it is that, merged into a single activity, the spider's simultaneous weaving and speaking comes to signify the activity of composition as the poet's craft. With the words and the voice supplied by the poet, the spider is Parvin in the act of weaving that which is her work.

Of course, all talking animals, in all animal fables, allegorize humans. In "God's Weaver," however, the constant interlacing of narration and weaving—words articulating what hands and feet do, mouth talking and producing the raw material for weaving, and eyes cast now upon the emerging web, the product of the work of hands and feet, now on the lazy person's motionless body—initiates a process of identification between the poet and the animal. This in turn assumes a crucial significance in shaping our view of Parvin's codification strategy. Conceived and enforced through a series of linguistic nodes present in the Persian language, the strategy ultimately produces a particularly expressive image of the spider's—and the poet's—specific work. By building the concept of weaving through a series of words, idioms, and expressions which also refers to the activity of speech, Parvin turns the two fields of discourse into a firm fabric. As the spider makes the gestures, the poet supplies the words that give meaning to them. As the spider makes the moral visible, the poet articulates it in her poem. The poet in effect becomes the voice that the spider lacks. That is why, in the end, when the poet has to exit from the body of the poem (and of the spider), she describes the spider as someone whose "spindle turns, but noiselessly." The words are as applicable to the woman who makes sturdy strands without disturbing those around her as to the poet who makes lasting poems without creating a stir.

In contrast to the spider who, through the poet, becomes a speaking body, the lazy person bursts on the scene as a body of speech, but loses his voice quickly. Whereas the spider's is a silently working body, his is the essence of idleness. This idleness, however, is the manifestation of an internal condition, namely his ignorance. As she begins to speak, the spider declares him unaware of her secrets. First, he does not know that the spider's movements are not performed at her whim, that someone else has decreed them. That someone else is referred to in the poem as the beloved or friend (*dust*), a well-known allusion in Persian mystical poetry to God.[51] It is He who has placed the prompting in her heart, and He who sustains her in her task; it is also He ultimately who is aware of the reasons for the spider's labor. Second, the spider is determined to rise up to the challenge of her destiny because, even though she does not know the secret of her heart's promptings, she knows full well that she ought to fulfill her destiny. Being unaware of the larger scheme of things, in other words, is no excuse for refusing to listen to one's heartfelt prompting or to perform the task at hand, for otherwise one's destiny remains unfulfilled. Third, in calling the man conceited, the spider observes a connection between the man's indolence and an inner tendency: pride. The lazy man's false pride has rendered him incapable of learning the lesson the spider's activity teaches. On another plane, the connection between pride and indolence is significant for the culture which, in spite of its glorious past, finds itself incapable of remedying its backwardness. Together, the three points communicate an image of the lazy man seen through the eyes of the spider as uninformed, unaware, and incapable of learning, the attributes which cover the entire semantic field of the word *jahl* (ignorance). In reference to the lazy man, the concept behind this word plays a key role in the poem's last section, as we will see presently.

Through its discourse, the spider also undoes the materiality of the lazy man's view of work, worth, and value. This culminates in the spider's allusion to another employer, another product, and another marketplace. Whereas the man believes that nobody will commission the spider to make a shirt, the spider refers to her employer (*kar farma*) as the *dust* (friend) and as the "knower of the work" (*kar-agah*). While the lazy person tries to point out the uselessness of her endeavor by stating that nobody will make a shirt out of the material she is weaving, the spider speaks of her fabric as the veil or drape (*pardeh*) that covers her defects. Most important, where the lazy person speaks of wages, expansion, and marketability, the spider responds by referring to another marketplace where the relationship that obtains between work and reward is esthetic rather than material:

> sad kharidar o hezaran ganj-e zar
> nist chon yek dideh-ye saheb nazar

> (a hundred buyers, thousands of gold treasures
> do not equal a single glance from an expert's eye)

The set of relations that emerges from the shifts the spider initiates in her discourse on worth and value is parallel to the material relations the lazy man has enumerated, yet ontologically distinct from them. Here the passion and commotion (*shur o ghowgha*) that motivates the spider's work comes from within her. It most definitely is not a function of material need and does not operate within a system of material compensation or financial reward. In fact, the spider's emphasis is not so much on the product as on the process that leads to it, not so much on what the worker gains, as on the acceptance of her labor communicated through the approving glance of discriminating experts. The word *saheb-nazar,* it is worth noting, literally means "the owner of a view," and has a potent spiritual dimension. An appreciative glance from such an expert is very different indeed from the money exchanged for the possession of any material goods. That is the secret of which the lazy man is so totally unaware.

The final passage opens with this statement: "Those who know ['*arefan*] have shunned ignorance [*jahl*]." The passage that follows may be classed, as I mentioned above, both as the summation of the spider's response to the lazy person and as the poet's observations on the debate. Through it, identification between the labor of the spider and that of the poet becomes complete, and every assertion assumes meaning in two fields of activity. Thus, when we read that the wise have woven *these* strands one into the other, we may take the interpellative word *in* (these) as a reference to the lines we are reading as well as one to the web we contemplate. Similarly, when we read the spider's description of her threads as "now long, now short, now many, now few" (*az deraz o kutah o besyar o kam*), we can't help but think that the two pairs of contrasting adjectives may refer with as much efficacy to a poet's compositions as to a spider's web.

As a Persian poem based on an essay originally written by an American essayist, "God's Weaver" exhibits important connections with, and departures from, both the translated text which inspired it and the poetic tradition of which it has become a part. The general concepts and qualities which the translated essay promotes find full expression in the Persian poem. Work is good and laziness is bad, will and determination are positive human virtues, and limitations of the human condition ought not to give rise to feelings of the futility of life. Moreover, the essay's initial device of the housewife observing the spider at work must have given Parvin the idea of directing her poem toward an expression of her own condition, both as a woman and as a weaver of words. The essay's contrast between the two types of human misconceptions provides an opportunity for the poet to portray the lazy person as the spider's detractor and the concrete manifestation of her brief against inaction and indolence. In all this, she can be seen in the act of interacting creatively with a text which she judges as relevant to her personal condition, her ethical concerns, and her esthetic culture.

At the level of poetic conception, while exploiting and expanding all of the essay's human analogues for the spider's activity, Parvin goes beyond the essay to a poetic analogy relevant to her own personal situation. Weaving her web, the spider resembles at once a craftsman making the tool of her trade, a hunter setting her trap, and an engineer designing a lofty structure. Significantly, the Iranian poet deletes the culture-specific reference to Brooklyn Bridge. Beyond these, however, an aspect of Iranian social life that is totally absent from the essay is all-important to the poet's purpose in that it goes to the heart of the poem as an expression of Parvin's personal condition. In other words, the story of the debate between the spider and the lazy individual provides the literal basis on which Parvin constructs a whole new structure of signification and mode of expression. Thus, by likening the spider's activity to a variety of human professions, she initially links the spider's meaning with a generalized notion of work. The spider is called an architect and builder (*mohandes, meʿmar*), a rope walker (*bandbaz*), a hunter—more accurately a trap-setter—and a master (*ostad*) in every one of these undertakings. We get the distinct impression here that the poet is driving toward the notion of work in the most universal sense and of the spider as worker par excellence. At this stage, she severs the translated essay from all its "American" connections to prepare it for grafting onto a new tradition.

The second stage—that of anchoring the theme in the tradition—begins when we see the weaving of strands and the making of elaborately patterned fabrics emerge as the spider's central activity, that in which she is best. This activity, most perennially associated in Parvin's linguistic culture with the making of poetry, affords her full and thorough appropriation. Ultimately, then, the poem's connections with the Persian literary tradition determine the place of this particular poem in the poetic culture of early twentieth-century Iran. Let us take a moment to explore those connections. In classical Persian poetry, we see the spider primarily as the weaver of intricate webs (and by extension a busy and sly animal) and secondarily as the hunter of insects, most often of flies. Its attributes are anchored in the words with which the animal is referred to in the language. In addition to *jula* and its variants, it is called *karton* (variants *kartoneh* and *kartonak*), *tartanak,* and *tandu.* Its first characteristic then is that of a weaver, reinforced by the scope and variety of words derived from the verb *tanidan* (to weave) that describe it. The animal's second set of characteristics have to do with its being a hunter. It is expressed through such words as *magasgir* and *shir-e magas,* and finds its poetic treatment in many classical texts. The spider's unattractive shape has also provided the basis for moralizing on the insignificance of worldly beauty or the relative merits of beauty in comparison with other human faculties like power, acumen, or perseverance.[52] Finally, the *hadith* about the prophet Mohammad's flight from Mecca to Medina in the company of Abubakr has provided the basis for the reputation of the animal as an instrument of God's will. According to the legend, a spider was commissioned by God to weave an intricate web at the entrance of the cave where the refugees had taken shelter at night. Their pursuers, contemplating the web, concluded that the entrance has not been trespassed in a long time, and did not enter it. God's messenger was thus saved by the natural activity of a spider executing God's will.[53]

Parvin does not tackle the issue of the spider's shape at all, and makes only passing references to the animal as a hunter in lines 4 and 56. In contrast, she uses the idea of the spider enforcing the will of God through her work, an idea centrally relevant to the affinities she seeks between the spider's work and her own as the encompassing frame for her poem. The idea not only informs and inspires the poem's argument, but also reinforces it in both the title and the concluding line. The last line of the poem repeats the title *jula-ye khoda,* and, in a syntactic construct exactly parallel to that of the first line's second hemistich, it reiterates the contrast between the spider and the lazy person. Whereas the latter was characterized as *khasteh va ranjur amma tand-orost* (weary and feeble, yet able-bodied), the former's activity is conveyed in the end through the image of a spindle that rotates noiselessly. Throughout the poem, too, affinities between the spider and the poet inform and guide the poem's mode of signification. From the beginning of the spider's discourse, the animal's articulation of its place (and the place of its work) in the scheme of creation gradually converges with the poet's voice and views to make the closing passage completely equivocal, a classical instance of a double signification. The strands the spider weaves together, as we have seen, comes to coalesce with Parvin's words, lines, and poems. Using a double entendre—that of the web as the spider's dwelling (*khaneh*) and drape (*pardeh*)—Parvin gives the spider's web the status now of an intricate structure, now of a woven product. Let us remember that in Persian the word *bayt* means both a line in a poem and a dwelling place and that the word *pardeh* refers not only to a spider's web but also to a drape and a woman's veil as well. In both cases, the final product's worth is known only to those who have developed an eye for the intricacies and subtleties involved in its production.

Conversely, where in the classical usage the spider's web most frequently exemplifies the ephemerality of human work, in Parvin's poem this aspect of its meaning has been altered to highlight the notion of effort and action (*sa'y o 'amal*). A comparison between "God's Weaver" and 'Attar's parable of the spider in *Manteq al-Tayr* will make my point here. In his introduction, the editor of Parvin's *Divan* refers to "God's Weaver" as "perhaps the most effective poem in the Persian language in praise of effort and action."[54] In a footnote, he cites a few lines from 'Attar's parable in *Manteq al-Tayr,* an allegory of the birds' search for their mythical leader which features numerous animal stories. The parable of the spider's web occurs in the hoopoe's response to a bird's excuse that it cannot leave its home to wander about the world in search of the mythical Simorgh. Following the Persian version, I give the Darbandi/Davis translation:

Dideh-i to 'ankabut-e biqarar
dar khiali migozarad ruzegar
bol-'ajab dami besazad az havas
ta magar dar damash oftad yek magas
pish girad vahm-e dur-andish ra
khaneh-i sazad beh konji khish ra
chun magas dar damash oftad sar-negun
bar mekad az 'erq-e an sar-gashteh khun
nagahi bashad keh an saheb-saray
chub andar dast bar khizad ze pay
khaneh-ye an 'ankabut o in magas
jomleh na-paida konad dar yek nafas
hast donya v-an keh dar vai sakht qut
chun magas dar khandeh-ye an 'ankabut.[55]

(You've seen an active spider work—he seems
To spend his life in self-communing dreams;
In fact the web he spins is evidence
That he's endowed with some far-sighted sense.
He drapes a corner with his cunning snare
And waits until a fly's entangled there,
Then dashes out and sucks the meagre blood
Of his bewildered, buzzing, dying food.
He'll dry the carcass then, and live off it
For days, consuming bit by tasty bit—
Until the owner of the house one day
Will reach up casually to knock away
The cunning spider's home—and with her broom
She clears both fly and spider from the room.
Such is the world, and one who feeds there is
A fly trapped by that spider's subtleties.[56]

The translation conveys many of the intricacies in 'Attar's analogy which I mean to examine here. In the last line, however, the Persian clause *pardeh-bazi mikoni* (literally, you play with the screen/drape/veil/web) establishes a more explicit parallel between the possessive person's love for material things and that of the spider's preoccupation with its web than can be seen in the English translation. Still, it is clear that the thrust of 'Attar's analogy is directed toward the ephemerality of the web rather than the spider's industry. There certainly is no allusion to the spider as enacting the will of God. Structurally, too, the externality of the moral to the story and the generality of its message make this a very different kind of text. In an expressive mode typical of classical Persian poets, ʿAttar has linked the moral and the story through the twin equations of the world with the house (meaning the web) of the spider and human beings. The idea of the intricate web, the spider, and the fly all being destroyed in the blink of an eye would not seem commensurate with the purpose Parvin seeks through her portrayal of the spider. In her determination to make hers a lesson in praise of effort and action, she appears closer to the contemporary American essayist than to the medieval Persian poet.

Parvin's ability to remake the spider in her own image, vesting in it the power to communicate something of her condition in addition to the message of work and resolution, remains at the core of her achievement as an innovator. That innovative power enables her to portray the animal as spinning her webs in every nook and cranny, or hanging her drapes from every wall or ceiling, while trying at the same time to protect the product of her labor from all kinds of ravages. In all that, the spider comes to present a picture not of the human condition in all ages and conditions, but of a little-noticed yet sophisticated, secluded yet forward-looking, humble yet proud poet that Parvin Eʿtesami would like her readers to judge her to be. In the same way, the lazy person provides a concrete, perceptible image of Parvin's real or imagined critics. Thus "God's Weaver" ultimately becomes the locus for articulating the possibilities open to an intellectual woman of Parvin's culture. To the extent that that message can be related to a social situation where women are forced into corners of seclusion by a strongly patriarchal society, their work often branded as insignificant, their existence as precarious as that of the spider, "God's Weaver" can be said to communicate a genuinely original vision. In that fundamental sense, the poem, while owing its existence to the interaction between the Iranian poet and a text of foreign origin, nevertheless finds its ultimate significance in terms germane to the condition of an early twentieth-century woman poet living in Iran.

TRADITION AND THE BORROWED TEXT

By complicating a culture's categories, successful acts of poetic borrowing such as the ones I have examined in this chapter eventually bring about systemic literary change. Ordinarily, cultures tend to perpetuate the perception of clear lines of demarcation between various categories and subsystems within the system of literary production and of solid boundaries between what they claim as theirs and what they see as foreign. Lotman relates this situation to the "grammar" of a literary "language." He views all such interactions as capable of giving rise to two opposing tendencies within a semiotic system. One tendency, motivated by the desire to keep the native tradition pure, strives to transform all extrasystemic elements into "an automatized grammar," that is, change it in light of the native system's own principles of evolutionary change. The other, tending "to destroy this automatization," gives rise to the feeling that certain aspects of the native tradition ought to be discarded. "In an artistic text," he observes, "the mechanism for violating the systemic arrangement acquires a special form."[57]

That special form, assuming different shapes and operating at different levels in different texts, may appear at first as random, irregular, or accidental. Gradually, however, since its operations are related to one another at different levels of the text and at the text/system intersections, it affects the system in two distinct ways. First, within the text, it is semanticized as a result of the "the recoding of the elements of one structural level by means of another."[58] Thus, an extrasystemic presence in the theme may ultimately become meaningful in terms of a poem's style, form, or rhythm. Second, sustained through time and repeated in a significant succession of texts, borrowing it begins to give rise to "external recoding," a process by which readers move from an understanding of individual texts to a perception of the system. The recognition of these two processes is crucial to understanding the dynamics of change in literary systems. Lotman views the first as occurring along a syntagmatic axis, and the second along a paradigmatic one:

> The first instance, like all instances of structuring on the syntagmatic axis, is from the point of view of the addressee, subject to a temporal sequence. The initial elements of the text perceived by the addressee, besides having their own intrinsic meaning, are signals of certain codes or groups of codes (schools, genres, plot types, categorization as verse or prose, and so on) which already exist in the consciousness of the receiver.

> But as soon as the recipient of information is confirmed in his choice of decoding systems, he immediately begins to receive structural signs which clearly cannot be decoded in the chosen key. He may want to brush them aside as nonessential, but their repetition and obvious internal systemic arrangements do not allow him to do so. And so he constructs a second system which from that moment on is superimposed on the first.[59]

The construction in the readers' minds of paradigms of poetic signification and communication that are different, however slightly, from the native tradition is precisely what I think borrowed texts like "Toil and Treasure," "A Mother's Heart," and "God's Weaver" have given rise to in the Iranian literature of the twentieth century. By challenging the existing relations within textual constructs—for instance, between the fable and the moral, between distinct generic models, and between general concepts and individual conditions—such texts alter perceptions of the place of each category within the system. At the level of the system itself, they alter the position of each systemic category and the relations that govern individual categories. In both cases, they ultimately effect change in the esthetic system. In the case of borrowed texts, this occurs, on the one hand, because of the inherent potential of such texts for systemic change and, on the other, because of the culture's capacity, in specific historical circumstances, to classify them as similar to—yet different from—those present in the system's memory of itself.

I use the concept "memory" to explain an important feature of Bakhtin's notion of genres: that genres provide specific complexes of values, definitions of situations, and meanings of possible actions. They are what he calls "congealed events" which provide a relatively stable locus for the manifestation of a culture's specific tendencies without exhaustively defining those tendencies. Each literary work, Bakhtin argues, uses the resources of the genre in a specific way in response to a specific individual situation. While the genre is changed slightly by each usage, it "remembers" its uses.[60] We need the concept of genre to understand specific acts and situations, but in understanding that concept we have not understood everything that is important about those acts and those situations. Through his definition of the concept of the genre, Bakhtin emphasizes the dialogic nature of intercultural textual borrowing. Borrowing from outside one's own culture tends to heighten the culture's internal dialogue, eventually speeding up the system's own dynamics.

Expressed in Bakhtinian terms, Lotman's notion of the impact of intersystemic borrowing may be rephrased as a system's questioning of its own premises as a system. The process often leads to greater and more significant appeals to other systems, and may result eventually in greater systemic alignments with the culture or cultures of reference. This is precisely what happened in the Persian poetry of Iran in the early decades of the twentieth century as extrasystemic literary borrowings began to loosen its formal properties, expand its generic categories, and complement the system of poetic production within it.

Viewed in this light, the role that literary improvisations, indigenizations, and appropriations play in literary history—often intuitively assumed to enrich the native tradition—is seen to be complex and multifaceted. The impact of literary activities based on extrasystemic models is determined by the specific circumstances of the system into which the resulting texts enter. If the literary system is relatively closed and stable, such texts continue to remain on its margins, confirming the system's view of itself as superior, with change unnecessary. Naturally, in this case literary borrowing fails to effect systemic change. If, however, the literary system perceives itself in need of reform, texts of foreign origin may be seen as reservoirs of literary devices, forms, and genres worthy of emulation. They thus begin to participate in the process of change by providing concrete examples of systemic difference manifested in form or in content, in thematic concerns or in expressive devices, in meter or in structure.

The relations between the Persian poems I have examined in this chapter and their direct or indirect sources testify to the perception of a need in early twentieth-century Iran for poetic borrowing. At the same time, the way in which such poems are produced demonstrates the complex operations at work in the process of borrowing from foreign sources. In other words, while highlighting several intertwined notions at work in the process of poetic borrowing, the three poems exemplify a certain strand of that activity particular to a specific literary culture. Thus, whereas the mere existence of the activity may be taken as the sign of a general desire for poetic reform embodied in the shared perception of many poets concerning the potential of foreign texts for enriching the native tradition, the specific choices and particular strategies each poet adopts indicate that poet's vision of the way in which that goal can be achieved. In general, the process involves varying degrees of improvisation, indigenization, and appropriation, and results in a culturally meaningful recodification of constituent elements of the original texts. In all three cases examined here, the Iranian poets have produced poems which can be called classical in their form and genre, but contemporary in terms of their content and message. They have recast the most essential elements of the original texts in the molds offered by their own specific culture. Guided by their individual vision of poeticity, of the interplay of tradition and modernity, and of the moral or ethical forces at work in the foreign texts and in their cultures, they have tried to make their poems as appropriate as possible to their esthetic culture. In all this, they seem to have been concerned, primarily and ultimately, with the effects they produce in their own esthetic environment.

Chapter Five

Dismantling a Poetic System

 To fully understand the intercultural dialogue through which I have
advanced my examination of poetic change in Iranian culture the
reader needs to relate it to the poetic practice of the time. In the last
three chapters I argued that the desire to bring about a new kind of poetry
was part of the intellectual milieu of Iran in postconstitution decades, particularly the one just after World War I.[1] The question of poetry and poets, and
of their social status and function, was a staple of many types of intellectual
discourse, and poetic compositions often featured prefatory material where
poets would expound on their vision of the craft and its future shape. Poetry
was being articulated in terms that allowed more diversity than previously
possible. In some instances, poets found it necessary to purchase space in a
newspaper to publish their poems, which, they were convinced, would reveal
the path to poetic modernity to all open-minded readers.[2] At the same time,
tradition-bound scholars continued to poke fun at the appearance of what
was being billed as *new* poetry.[3]

In this chapter, too, I limit myself to studying the actual practice inspired
by the desire to make poetry new. I do so by examining a limited number of
poetic texts, each communicating a distinct vision of poetic modernity. The
three poems I analyze for this purpose must then be viewed as typifying
various foci of concentrated social and artistic energy aimed at pointing out
the path to poetic modernity. In their diversity—structural, thematic, or formal—they exemplify the most significant among the many scenarios proposed once the perception of a need for poetic change became a matter of
consensus in the culture. At the same time, the response to each, then and

since, can bring into focus the visions adopted or abandoned, values sought or shunned, and paths taken or not. Ultimately the plurality of the poets' approaches will, I hope, reveal something of the intensity of the desire for change, while the response to the poetry will disclose the kinds of artistic constraints in Iranian society after World War I. The three poets whose work I examine—Lahuti, Raf'at, and 'Eshqi—were recognized at the time as major poets leading the movement toward poetic modernity. In the intervening decades, their contribution to the process has been submitted to a series of revisions, but my analyses will help to identify the loci of newness as perceived by their immediate readers.

A PARODIC QASIDA: LAHUTI'S "TO THE DAUGHTERS OF IRAN"

Perhaps the most obvious expression of the desire for poetic innovation can be seen in various frontal attacks on the conventions of the lyrical tradition in Persian literature. Starting in the late nineteenth century, when Akhundzadeh, Kermani, and Malkom led the assault on the Persian poetic tradition, such attacks signaled the desire to free the poetic practice from the constraints imposed on it by the practice of the classical masters. Through their rhetoric, a stereotypical view of the classical poetic system had emerged which equated one mode of poetic expression within the lyrical tradition with the whole of the poetic system. In the decade under consideration here, the poems that debunked that expressive mode came to contain the poet's view concerning the nature of poetic change. In them, formal adherence to traditional conventions ensured the perception of the poet's mastery over the tradition which he would ridicule. At the same time, the poem's own discourse would express the poet's intention to move the system of expression beyond the inherited conventions of the past. As is the case in the first example I have selected, the discursive practice of didactic instruction was often perpetuated, now inspired by novel ideals. Ultimately, this practice undermined that of traditional poetry without committing the poet to a vision of poetic change outside the very system it derided. The final gesture signified deep frustration with the existing tradition as well as the intent to break free from it without offering an alternative.

The text I have selected as typical of this trend is by Abolqasem Lahuti (1887–1957), a revolutionary poet who left Iran in 1922 to live in the Soviet Union.[4] In a particularly illustrative parody of a practice widespread in the lyrical tradition, where the poet likens the beloved's body parts to a variety of weapons of war or other dangerous objects, Lahuti mocks the notion of feminine beauty that informs the significatory and communicative processes of the lyrical genres of the ghazal and the qasida. Yet, his poem does not offer any new suggestions for the poetic articulation of the ideal of beauty. Thus, the poet's desire to incorporate women into the social fabric remains part of a political agenda in need of a poetic mode of expression. Conceived as a qasida and entitled "Beh Dokhtaran-e Iran" (To the Daughters of Iran), the poem builds on the poet's opposition to a codification mode which I call "the anatomy of the beloved" imagery. Here's the poem in its entirety, first in the original Persian, followed by my literal translation:

> Man az emruz ze hosn-e to boridam sar o kar
> gu beh divanegiam khalq nemayand eqrar
> ay mah-e molk-e 'ajam ay sanam-e 'alam-e sharq
> hush gerd avar o bar gofteh-ye man del begomar
> ta konun pish-e to chun bandeh beh dargah-e khoda
> labehha kardam o bar khak besudam rokhsar
> likan emruz mojeddaneh vo rasmaneh to ra
> ashkara sokhani chand beguyam hosh dar
> ba'd az in az khat o khalat naharasad del-e man
> z-an keh ba hosn-e to karam nabovad digar bar
> ta kay az zolf-e to zanjir neham bar gardan
> ta kay az mojjeh-ye to tir zanam bar del-e zar
> ta beh kay bi lab-e la'l-e to delam gardad khun
> chand bi mar-e sar-e zolf-e to basham bimar
> beh sar-angosht-e to ta chand zanam tohmat-e qatl
> ya beh mojgan-e to ta chand deham nesbat-e khar
> chand guyam keh rokhat mah bovad dar khubi
> chand guyam keh qadat sarv bovad dar raftar
> mahru'i to vo lazem nabovad bar goftan
> sarv qaddi to vo hajat nabovad bar ezhar
> madh-e to bishtar az harkeh tavanam guyam
> likan inha hameh harf ast o nadarad meqdar
> z-in cheh hasel keh ze mojgan-e to khanjar sazand
> ya beh abru-ye to guyand helali-st nezar
> man beh ziba'i-ye bi 'elm kharidar niam
> hosn mafrush degar ba man o kerdar biar
> 'asheqan-e khat o khal-e to bad-amuzanand
> digar in tayefeh ra rah madeh bar darbar
> andar in dowr-e tamaddon sanama layeq nist
> delbari chun to ze arayesh-e danesh beh kenar

nang bashad keh to dar pardeh vo khalqi azad
sharm bashad keh to dar khab o jahani bidar
hayf nabvad qamari mesl-e to mahrum az nur
ʿayb nabvad shajari chun to tohi dast az bar
tark-e chador kon o maktab boro vo dars bekhan
shakheh-ye jahl nadarad samari joz edbar
danesh amuz o az ahval-e jahan agah show
v-in neqab-e siah az ru-ye mobarak bardar
ʿelm agar nist ze hayvan cheh bovad farq-e bashar
buy agar nist tafavot cheh konad gol az khar
kherad amuz o pay-e tarbiat-e mellat-e khish
jedd o jahdi benema chun degaran madar-var
to gozari beh dahan-e hameh kas avval harf
hameh kas az to sokhan mishenavad avval bar
pas az avval to beh gush-e hameh in nokteh begu
keh natarsand ze kushesh nagorizand az kar
pesar o dokhtar-e khod ra sharaf-e kar amuz
ta bedanand bovad moft-khori zellat o ʿar
sokhan az danesh o azadi o zahmat miguy
ta keh farzand-e to ba in sokhanan ayad bar
beh yaqin gar to chonin madar-e khubi bashi
mes-e eqbal-e vatan az to shavad zarr-e ʿayar.[5]

(From this day on, I have severed my relation with your beauty.
Let people declare me insane.
O moon of Persia, o idol of the eastern world!
Gather your wits and set your heart on my words
thus far, like a slave before God, I have made
lamentations, supplicated myself before you.
But today, seriously and formally
I address a few words to you openly, harken!
From now on, my heart fears not your visage and mole,
for no longer shall I have anything to do with your beauty.
How long shall I place on my neck the chain of your tresses?
How long shall I shoot arrows of your eyelashes at my tattered heart?
How long should my heart bleed for the absence of your ruby lips?
Till when shall I be ill without the serpent of your braids?
Till when shall I charge your fingertips with murder,
or attribute to your eyelashes the quality of thorns?
How long shall I say that your face is moonlike in beauty?

How long shall I say that in height you resemble the cypress?
You are moon-faced, and it is not necessary to state that.
You are cypresslike in height, and there's no need to say that.
Your praises I can sing better than everyone else,
but these are words, devoid of value.
What good is there in making a dagger out of your eyelashes,
or in saying that your eyebrow is a slender crescent?
I am no buyer of beauty without knowledge:
sell not your beauty to me, bring forth deeds.
The lovers of your face and mole are corruptors.
Do not admit such people to your presence anymore.
In this age of civilization, my idol, it does not behoove
a heart-taker like you to be deprived of the adornment of knowledge.
It is a disgrace that you remain in veil when the world is free.
It is a shame that you stay asleep as the world wakes.
Is it not a pity that a moon like you shall have no light?
Is it not a blemish that a tree like you should bear no fruit?
Abandon your veil, go to school, get educated;
the branch of ignorance bears no fruit but adversity.
Attain to knowledge, become aware of the affairs of the world,
and remove this black veil from your beauteous face.
Except for knowledge, what is the difference between human and beast?
But for the scent, what distinguishes the rose from the thorn?
Seek wisdom and, for the cultivation of your own people,
launch a motherly effort just as others have.
It is you who puts the first words into everybody's mouth,
before all else everybody hears your words.
Therefore, tell everyone from the beginning
not to fear work, nor turn away from toil.
Teach your sons and daughters the nobility of work
so they would know that freeloading is a shame, a disgrace.
Speak to them of knowledge, freedom, and toil
so your children may grow up with these words.
Surely if you become such a good mother, because of you
the copper of the motherland's fortune shall turn into pure gold.)

Lahuti's poem is part of a trend in twentieth-century Persian poetry which negates the time-honored codes of the classical tradition. At times, explicitly mocking "the anatomy of the beloved" imagery constitutes an important part of that effort.[6] Typically, in these poems, first the conventional

imagery of the classical ghazal is deconstructed at length with as many variations on "not" as the poet can command. Next, the speaker assumes the
posture of an instructor admonishing the beloved, tradition-bound poets, or
readers. They are asked to take into account the fact that they live in different
times and under different social circumstances which necessitate a change in
all spheres of life. Such poems often close, as Lahuti's does, with reflections
on the nature of the times and its dictates.[7]

"To the Daughters of Iran" opens with the stock posture of negation
typical of this trend, adding the assertion that the speaker is aware that the
"people" may think him insane. Gradually, however, Lahuti engages the
tradition in more creative ways, simultaneously acknowledging and reaf-
firming the beloved's beauty while mocking, in increasingly playful ways, the
poetic conventions for describing that beauty. In the process the discourse
that depicts love as an uncontrollable condition often leading to irrational
behavior begins to take on a caricaturelike aspect depicting the relationship
between the addresser and addressee in classical lyrical genres as unreal, insincere, and even pathological. In fact, by parodying classical lyrics, Lahuti's
qasida seems to underline the seemingly illogical aspects of the discourse on
which the poem's classical counterparts stand.

Lahuti's technique of parody centers around his omission of the terms
which make the relations between the signifiers and their signifieds meaningful. The poem describes the power exercised by the beloved in a series of
synecdochic images without the links that connect these images to their underlying system of signification. In so doing, the poem complicates the reader's understanding of the classical lyrical discourse as the textual manifestation of the beloved's idealized beauty. The conventions that anatomize the
beloved's facial features and stature are thus presented with no reference to
the ways in which each single signifier—the chain, the arrow, the thorn, the
ruby, the moon, the serpent, or the cypress—relates to the system of codification within which it operates. As a result, the relationship between the
maddening beauty of the beloved's long, curled braids that resemble the
chain and the lover's condition of love-crazed behavior, that necessitates his
being chained remains concealed from all those not well versed in the classical
system of poetic expression. Similarly, the reference to the color red, which
provides a link between the beloved's ruby lips and the bleeding heart of the
lover, is omitted, as is the connection between the arrows or thorns that relate
the beloved's long and penetrating eyelashes to the ever-present feelings of
the wounded lover. In the absence of those systemic structures that mediate
between signifiers and what they signify, poetic signs appear arbitrary and
devoid of logic. The technique helps to reverse the poet's initial acceptance

of the people's view of him as insane: in fact, it is not him but the makers and readers of such nonsense who are truly insane!

Within the terms of that parodic twist, the poem holds up to ridicule the entire imagery of the classical lyrical poetry. The figure of speech linking the serpent (*mar*) of the beloved's hair with the condition of the lover—that is, he is dis-eased (*bimar*) because of her absence—is a case in point. In the absence of the references that govern relations between the signifier serpent (*mar*) and the signified diseased (*bimar*) the image is reduced to hollow word-play, as if the entire point in using the image were to create a pair of meaning-less homonyms. What could it mean, Lahuti seems to be asking, to say: "I am diseased because I am away from the serpent!"? Lahuti's clever manipula-tion of the discourse of love in classical Persian lyrics has created a text wherein a double-voiced utterance serves ultimately to show the unnatural and illogical nature of that poetry. Phrased in terms of the Bakhtinian model of the double-voiced utterance, Lahuti's poem encodes the vision of a poetry that would be seen as the ontological opposite of the one he has mastered so well, but is mocking vehemently.[8]

When the poem begins to take a positive turn (line 11), we hear the speaker describing the beloved's total person, body and mind, as well as her social place and potential role in the growth of the society in which she is a member. No longer merely an individual's beloved, she is literally "a daugh-ter of Iran." The poetic description of an "Iranian" woman is transformed from that of an individual reduced to the parts of her body to that of a citizen and a part of the social body. In inscribing the change on the public space of the poetic tradition, Lahuti guides his oppositional rhetoric toward an openly social discourse, taking care to keep his view of the beloved's beauty constant throughout. His "daughter of Iran" is indeed as beautiful as the beloved of the classical poet. However, her beauty is no longer confined to, nor even particularly focused on, those attributes which have given the crazed lover of yore painful pleasure. Instead, it goes far beyond the physical domain to serve the cause of the nation's march toward civilization and a golden future.

Lahuti's depiction of the process of transformation thus initiated extends even further in the poem's final image. There, the beloved, now a citizen, herself turns out to be a potential transformer. As a metaphor par excellence of the miraculous change for the better, the image of the daughter of Iran as a kind of social elixir is powerful indeed. Set against all the ways in which classical poets have articulated the value of the beloved, this image serves to highlight all the opportunities past poets have missed for perceiving—and describing—the real value inherent in their object of desire. Lahuti's device, simple and perfectly appropriate to the pattern he has established throughout the poem, serves doubly to highlight his notion of the inexpressiveness—and therefore inadequacy—of classical poetic devices. The metaphor of the elixir acts not only as a final signifier for the beloved now turned into the daughter of Iran but it also empowers her to rise above even the dehumanizing hyperboles concocted by so many generations of what he wishes us to see as pathological sycophants.

Discursively, Lahuti's strategy of acknowledging and reiterating the true beauty of the beloved allows him to express his point of view in a conventional poetic genre without subjecting himself to the charge of propagating a defunct poetic discourse. The basic perception of the poem's difference from the old canon lies in its thematic distinction, directed not at an individual emotive statement nor at observations of a metaphysical or philosophical nature, but at a specific social position. Beyond advocating knowledge and enlightenment for women, beyond establishing a link between these ideals and the necessity of unveiling, the poem points to a political eventuality expressed through the image of the transformation of a country's fortune. Once again, the metaphor of the elixir serves to express the poet's desire for social change, and is therefore crucial to understanding the expressive operations of the poem as a whole.

But these are not the only ways in which Lahuti's poem lays a demonstrable claim to newness. The manner in which such abstract qualities as the attainment of knowledge, awareness of world affairs, and efforts aimed at educating the nation conspire to produce the idea of "a good mother" inscribed in the last line is markedly different from the way in which chainlike tresses or arrowlike eyelashes or blood-red ruby lips add up to make the beautiful beloved of the old poet. While the idea of the beloved's destructive, yet irresistible physical beauty is seen as based on a self-serving poetic practice with no social purpose, the potential to transform the condition of one's homeland appears as a logical proposition grounded in the social discourse of the time. To the reader of Lahuti's poem, the proposition that an educated woman will be a better mother seems inherently reasonable, whereas an appreciation of the way in which such physical attributes as serpentine tresses and long, dagger-sharp eyelashes signify superior physical beauty depends on an a priori knowledge of a seemingly arbitrary poetic code. In fact, for those with no access to the system of poetic signification in which these allusions are anchored, this manner of describing feminine beauty is more likely to produce disgust than pleasure. As they argued that the traditional poetry was indeed defunct, poets like Lahuti exploited that perception skillfully. Within their poems, they presented the poetic codes of the classical tradition in such a way as to draw attention to their illogicality, ineffectiveness, and plain meaninglessness.

No discussion of this trend in the course of poetic modernity in Iran would be complete without an analysis of the ideology its significatory strategies advance. Clearly, "To the Daughters of Iran" attempts to reintegrate Iranian women into the social sphere and demonstrate the conservatism of traditional poetic practice, increasingly understood as incongruous with the modern age. In the process, the very being and identity of the object of love is transformed, turned from a source of the lover's pain and pleasure to a national resource capable of miraculously changing the fortune of a whole country.[9] By recoding the notion of the beloved, formerly the elixir of the lover's emotions, as a source of public good, the poet goes beyond responding to the classical poet's conventional appeals to the beloved to transform his mental state through a favorable glance. He actually teaches him—as well as his own readers—a new lesson in the social responsibility of poets.

The textual activity through which this shift in the poet's responsibility occurs includes a questioning attitude toward the poetic image of the classical lover's (and, given the nature of lyric utterance, the poet's own) preoccupation with describing the beloved's body. The initial contrast between two distinct temporal spheres—*ta konum* (until now, thus far) and *az emruz* (from today, starting today)—as well as the incessant repetition of *ta kay, ta beh kay, chand* (until when, for how long, how much longer) convey the speaker's desire to liberate himself from a past which he portrays as antithetical to the present. Thus, the poet depicts the moment of the poem's composition as a historical turning point characterized by—or, in a different sense, an opportunity for—a clean break with the past. In an apparently paradoxical move, he relies on the same old appellations for his own purpose. Such words as *mah* (moon), *sanam* (idol), *mahru* (moon-faced), *sarv-qad* (cypresslike in height), *delbar* (heart-taker) all signify continued reliance on conventionalized signifiers of beauty to communicate the poem's parody of the convention. In closer analysis, however, it becomes clear that, in this instance, such terms relate only to the most general descriptive phrases present in the language rather than to specific attributes such as those that relate to the beloved's lips, eyes, or hair. It is as if the poet accepts the terms which underline the general notion of the beloved's beauty, but resists those which break this general notion into its various components—that is, body parts or facial features.

Rhetorically, the poem depicts an address, an instance of direct speech uttered by the speaker to someone exhorted to become one of "the daughters of Iran." In a sense this is an expanded form of a poetic posture popular at the time, an exhortation addressed often by an older person to members of the younger generation. We may recall Dehkhoda's address to the child of the golden age, or Bahar's admonition in favor of labor as the most immediate precursors of this posture. Lahuti depicts an openly pedagogical situation, placing the speaker in the position of a male educator dispensing knowledge and advice to his female pupil, and ending the session by charging the pupil with an extraordinarily momentous mission. This specific rhetorical situation, itself indicative of a cultural preoccupation with the notion of education, throws a particular light on Lahuti's initial debunking of the activity of past poets. Implicit within the poem's discourse as the speaker's own past preoccupation is an activity immediately generalizable to all Persian poets in all past ages: the conventional practice of poetry. This stratagem begins to function as a device that enables the protagonist to speak as an individual who has just undergone a conversion. The strategy is significant in establishing the poem as an utterance aimed at presenting a total break between now and then, between this "age of civilization" and an "other" time when a poet's mission was seen as limited to describing the physical beauty of the beloved in strictly personal terms.

The collective entity to whom the poem is addressed also moves the poem's sphere of action toward the public domain. The phrase "the daughters of . . ." already marks the intended recipients of the poem as siblings related to each other through common parentage. Family ties as emblematic of social relations prevailing in a society constitute quite a traditional trope. In Lahuti's time, this antique metaphor had gained a new sense that served the cause of Iranian identity in demonstrable ways.[10] In this poem, the speaker uses the singular pronoun *to* ("thou" or "you" in the singular and familiar mode) for his intended addressee, as if all the "daughters of Iran" had been rolled into one figure and as if this figure is the same as that which had for a millennium been addressed or described in a certain way in the Persian ghazal tradition. The speaker of this poem has now rebelled against that poetic custom. Thus, addressing a social group, marked by age and gender (*dokhtar* refers literally to one's daughter as well as to a young, usually unmarried woman), helps to generate a consciousness in contemporary Iranian women about the way in which their past counterparts have been seen by poets. The poem in effect asks the "daughters of Iran" to reject that description of themselves. This in turn prepares the ground for the speaker initially to pose as the opposite of the old poet before revealing his own identity as a contemporary poet with a lesson to teach to his young female pupil. The scheme facilitates the simultaneous posturing of the poet as a lover who has undergone a change of heart and as a teacher disseminating important knowledge. Similarly, the addressee attains at once a dual status: a beloved learning what makes her attractive to her lover in this new age, as well as a citizen being educated in the qualities that enable her to play her part in the progress of her country.

What passes from the addresser to the addressee contains first and foremost the poet's view concerning conventional descriptions of feminine beauty in classical Persian poetry. Beyond that, it includes his advice about what she is expected to do to transform her country's fortune. Now only a young pupil, she can become potentially the educator of generations to come if she listens to the advice offered in the poem. Initially, the speaker assumes the posture of a lover who has had a change of heart. The first hemistich, informing the beloved that the lover will no longer love her for her physical beauty, recalls many similar outbursts by despondent lovers determined to change the relationship that has brought them nothing but pain and suffering. The change thus depicted assumes its first layer of added significance when the lover asks the beloved to listen to him attentively as he relates the reasons why he has decided to end the present relationship. As the addresser and the addressee begin to be transformed from the traditional lover-poet and the object of his love, the mood of the poem changes from lyrical to one of purposive didacticism more typical of the qasida than the ghazal and used primarily to transmit important ideas.

A succession of markers signal this thematic move from the lyrical to the didactic. In the first four verses, the lover asks his beloved to hear the account of the change that has come upon him. In the rest of the poem, he explains the change and offers his views about the way the relationship can survive the present crisis. He has thus far supplicated himself before the beauty of the beloved as if she were God and he a slave. Today, however, the lover seeks not a moon-faced beloved, but a "moon" from which the light of knowledge shines forth. He has decided to leave his "cypress" in favor of a tree which bears fruit. The presentation of the lover's condition then begins with an acknowledgment of her beauty and a catalogue of what is lacking in her. It culminates in the clues he gives her on how to be a good mother and the "elixir" of her country's fortune. The content of the speech, the few words (*sokhani chand*) which the lover asks his beloved to hearken can be divided into three distinct parts, each with its own argument and its own mode of discourse. In the first section, lines 5 through 11, the lover tries to distance himself from his behavior in the past. As a repentant lover, he has found that even though his beloved is as beautiful as ever, his praise of that beauty has been hollow and worthless. Furthermore, it has not adequately expressed her real beauty or even complimented her personality. The effect of this realization is a statement of fact predicated upon this portrayal: all this is hollow verbiage (*harf*) devoid of worth (*meqdar*). It is on that basis that the lover's declaration of intent rests. The change that has come over him arises not from his fickleness, but from being awakened to the realization that in the past his words have been hollow and worthless, his behavior pathologically irrational. True, the beloved is beautiful, but that fact in itself underscores the unworthiness of the words which he has used to describe her beauty. At this time, such conventional descriptions are woefully inadequate in that they fail to describe an aspect of the beloved's beauty more important by far than the physical. The addresser then sets himself the task of describing that aspect.

A similar logic inspires the poet's view of his predecessor's articulation of beauty and love. Rather than dealing with the figure of the beloved as a human being, the speaker says, his forebears have portrayed certain parts of the beloved's body as the means of expressing their own emotional states. Thus, to liken the beloved's tresses to chains or snakes constitutes a convoluted way of saying that they feel enchained or poisoned by love. To compare the beloved's eyelashes to arrows or daggers is their way of registering feelings of vulnerability or wounded pride. The female body has thus been turned into a signifier of the male lover's emotions, a sounding board on which poet-lovers of classical lyrics have sought the echo of their own condition. In line 12 the speaker separates himself from such poets and their practice by signaling a shift in the poem's rhetorical situation. Whereas up to that point he was framing the poem's argument in the form of a series of seemingly self-referential reflections—"How long should I . . . ?"—he now begins to decry the uselessness of the activity in terms of an anonymous "they." It is they who, unlike himself, express love for the beloved's body with no regard for her character, knowledge, or actions. He accuses them of being corruptors—literally, *bad-amuzan* (teachers of bad things)—and asks the beloved to send them away so he will be able to impart his lesson to her. In this way, the speaker lays the ground for a shift in his own status from the lover to the teacher, thus preparing for the pedagogical situation that ensues. With no one else having been allowed to intervene, the teacher's authority turns absolute.

We have already seen Kermani's indictment of the corrupting influence of past poets. Lahuti's charges also include perversion of the educational process itself, which the speaker attempts to rectify through his own lesson. Lahuti, I think, has a specific purpose in establishing a link between the traditional discourse of love and the perversion of a pedagogical relationship, a purpose which a close examination of the poem will reveal. The lesson builds on a contrast between the "daughter of Iran" and an entity mentioned first as "a people" (*khalqi*) and a little later as "the whole world" (*jahani*). It is a shame, the teacher tells his pupil, that you are veiled (*dar pardeh*) and a whole people are free (*azad*), a disgrace that you are asleep (*dar khab*) and a whole world awake (*bidar*). The opposition between sleep and wakefulness governs the pupil's—and the reader's—perception of the relationship between the two conditions of "being veiled" and "being free." It is as impossible to remain veiled and attain freedom as it is to be asleep and awake at the same time. Immediately following this, the teacher bids his pupil, now in a more positive vein, to adorn her beauty with knowledge "in this age of civilization." The correlation between the character of the age, a general condition existing in the world outside, and the adornment of knowledge (*arayesh-e danesh*) in the pupil is important in comprehending the strategy involved in the discourse. Civilization itself has been the result of knowledge, something that all "daughters of Iran" lack. In order to be a part of the age, the pupil is instructed to adorn herself with knowledge.

In Persian, the word *arayesh* (adornment) refers to makeup as well; it thus contains a sense in which it refers to a person, particularly a woman's effort to enhance her beauty. Like makeup, knowledge enhances one's beauty, now an inner, yet apparent, attribute. However, it does so in novel ways hitherto inaccessible to women in the traditional culture. Because of their obsession with the beloved's physical beauty, poets of the past have failed to instruct their audiences in attaining inner beauty. This redefinition of beauty culminates in line 17 where the poet returns to two traditional images, the moon and the cypress tree, and recasts these traditional tropes into the mold of his own discourse:

> Is it not a pity that a moon like you shall have no light?
> Is it not a blemish that a tree like you should bear no fruit?

The return to the two conventional images of the beloved as moonlike in visage and cypresslike in stature begins to assume a surplus of meaning here in light of the words of the preceding line. To speak of a lusterless moon and a fruitless tree after such concepts as "knowledge" (*'elm*) and "action" (*kerdar*), without which physical beauty holds no appeal to the speaker, gives them an unmistakable connotation that recalls the trope of knowledge as the guiding light of humanity, a staple of the discourse of modernity in Middle Eastern cultures.[11] The analogy of the relationship between knowledge and action as analogous to that between the tree and its fruit has of course been a perennial image in the didactic discourse of classical Persian poetry.[12]

Thus, the ground is prepared for a lesson delivered directly from the poet who now, having cast off the mask of the lover rather unceremoniously, assumes the role of the social commentator pointing out the path to the golden future. The verb patterns that pervade this final section of the poem signal this shift on the rhetorical plane. Beginning with line 18, we have a succession of imperatives: "Abandon your veil, go to school, get educated" (*tark-e chador kon o maktab boro vo dars bekhan*). This trio reinforces the earlier connection between education and unveiling. The pattern is repeated in the next line where one injunction, to seek knowledge (*danesh amuz*), leads to another, to undertake an endeavor (*jed o jahdi benema*). Gradually, as the imperatives pile up, the image of the daughter begins to grow into that of a mother. Having followed the poet's instructions, the pupil is literally transformed into the educator of a whole nation. At the same time, the teacher who issues these instructions is beginning to imagine his pupil as performing the same function for the next generation of Iranians as he is now performing for her. The degree of consciousness which arises from this teacher's emphasis on the role of his pupil as the educator of the future generation is rhetorically significant. He expects his pupil to teach to posterity what he is teaching her now: the triad of knowledge (*danesh*), liberty (*azadi*), and toil (*zahmat*). Communicated by the mother, the first teacher every child listens to, these lessons will, he states, bring about a transformation in the fortune of the country comparable to the miraculous way in which copper turns into pure gold.

Through the workings of the poem as address, then, the speaker shifts steadily from a private plane to the public realm on two separate levels. As lover, he himself is transformed from a lone repentant lover to an admirer not of this beloved's physical beauty, but of the beauty that the acquisition of knowledge can bestow on all women of Iran. As teacher, he is transformed from the tutor of a single pupil seen in one teaching session to the educator of the future generation's first and foremost educators. The addressee, too, undergoes a comparable change, first from a reified collection of physical attributes—indeed the lifeless object of the lover's gaze—to a beloved worthy of a modern lover's respectful love, and later from an empty signifier measuring the mental and emotional states of classical poets to the supreme educator of a nation on its way to modernity. For both the poet and his audience—the imaginary "daughters of Iran"—these transformations generate a series of subsequent relations hitherto unexplored—and therefore unmarked—in the classical tradition. As poetic personae, both the poet and the "daughters of Iran" turn into teachers engaged in educating themselves as well as countless future Iranians.

The desire, on the ideological plane, to transform the passive object of the medieval poet's gaze into the omnipotent transformer of the country's fortune obviously necessitates a series of rhetorical maneuvers based on reversing the traditional male/female relationship in the culture. It is noteworthy, in this regard, that the moment the "daughter of Iran" enters into the social realm is also the moment she is transformed to the good mother of the poem's last line. Through the poem, in other words, the woman has become an agent of change and a catalyst for cultural transformation. She ought to aspire to knowledge not necessarily for her own sake, but as a patriotic duty. The advice transmitted throughout the poem clearly heralds motherhood as the supreme achievement for all women. The modern poetic discourse ultimately remains as paternalistic and as patriarchal as the classical discourse it parodies. No longer the empty signifier of a concept of beauty completely detached from social reality, the female body is still viewed as the means through which other members of the society become compatible with the age in which they live.

Finally, a word must be said about the importance of the genre through which Lahuti, and a great many other practitioners of this particular trend in Persian poetry, chose to communicate their vision of poetic modernity. Even though "To the Daughters of Iran" is a bona fide qasida with all the formal trappings of that genre, it is one linked to a content that, as we have seen, parodies that genre. Such works often disturb the tradition, moving it in unpredictable directions. Seen as traditional verse forms bent on subverting previous messages conveyed through their past formal and generic counterparts, they stand in an oblique relation to the drive toward poetic change. On the one hand, their transgressive and oppositional messages mark them as attempts to arrive at new systems of poetic expression, presumably privileging greater artistic allegiance to sociopolitical causes. On the other hand, their formal and generic features place them well within the traditional poetic categories. Lahuti's poem is ultimately a qasida, and one through which the capacity of the genre to address social issues is confirmed.[13] In the last analysis, the significance of such texts lies in the fact that, by presenting structures which simultaneously confront and confirm traditional ones, they complicate existing perceptions of the relations that obtain between form and content, ultimately disconnecting one from the other. By mocking the stylized conventions of the traditional ghazal or qasida as contrary to natural or logical articulations, they push the system of poetic signification further toward new conventions, which they view as natural, realistic, or logical. They thus make that system work against itself. In Lahuti's poem the desire to establish a new set of social relations between men and women eventually contributes to the drive toward new processes of poetic communication, both in the act of

composition and in that of reading. In this sense, frontal assaults on an existing esthetic system are related to the rise of new poetic systems in ways
different from attempts on elemental changes in the system. Whereas the
changes initiated by poets like Dehkhoda and 'Aref, which we examined in
chapter 2, tend to convey the message that the existing system can be expanded to serve new purposes, here the perception of a previously existing
idealogy shared between the poet and the reader gives rise to the perception
of a common need to alter, rather than expand, the system of poetic signification and communication. That the desire to synthesize tradition and modernity has already begun to give way to the will to reverse traditional modes
of expression in order to bring about poetic modernity is the final message
conveyed by texts like Lahuti's "To the Daughters of Iran."

THE EUROPEAN SONNET IN PERSIAN:
RAF'AT'S "NOWRUZ AND THE FARMER"

The second trend I illustrate expresses the desire to forge an entirely
new system of esthetic signification and communication in a distinctly different poetic practice. Although neither as prominent nor as widespread as the
practice illustrated by Lahuti's "To the Daughters of Iran," this trend is
noteworthy for its bold ambition to alter the entire formal system of classification in the Persian poetic tradition. In that sense, it demonstrates a tendency contrary to the one illustrated above in that it seeks to break rather
than reproduce the formal divisions of the classical system. In its most radical
form, it aims, as we will see, at realigning the most lyrical Persian genre,
namely the ghazal, with such European forms as the ode or the sonnet. At a
later stage, those Persian poems which express the lyrical impulse through
compositions that do not conform to the metric system of classical Persian
poetry may be considered an extension of this tendency. Unrhymed or
sparsely rhymed, such compositions often visually resemble modernist French
poetry of the turn of the century. With the advent of Nima's innovations in
meter and rhyme, this tendency was gradually abandoned as a fruitful approach to modernizing Persian poetry.

To illustrate this trend, I focus on a poem by Mohammad-Taqi Raf'at.
We have already discussed his views on poetic modernization in chapter 3.
Raf'at's poetic compositions clearly constitute an extension of his emphasis
on the need to revolutionize the literature of Iran. Having witnessed his
penchant for engaging the intellectuals of his time in debates on the nature
of poetic change, on the path to poetic modernization, or on the relevance
of classical poets like Sa'di, we can now examine his practical contribution to

the process by analyzing one of his own poetic compositions. These were predicated on the complete abandonment of traditional Persian verse forms in favor of European ones, particularly the sonnet.

As early as 1918, Raf'at's poems began to appear in the weekly newspaper *Tajaddod* which he edited and published in the provincial capital of Tabriz. Two years later in another essay he would point to these compositions as possible models for younger poets to adopt. Like the essays he had written in response to the moderate approach taken by *Daneshkadeh,* this essay had been written in response to a critical essay published in *Kaveh,* a monthly Persian journal published in Berlin from 1916 to 1922. The journal had from the beginning revealed a literary position more conservative even than that of *Daneshkadeh,* repeatedly poking fun at the poetic compositions that claimed to be innovative, whether in form or in content. In March 1920, as part of its attacks on linguistic and literary innovations, *Kaveh* began publishing a series of articles under the general rubric of "Taraqqi-ye Zaban-e Farsi dar Yek Qarn" (The Progress of the Persian Language in a Century), an obviously ironic title. Here, samples of what the journal considered "good and bad" writings were placed in opposite columns, and *Kaveh* advanced its view about the degeneration of the Persian language and literature through tacit comparisons, ironic or sarcastic notes or asides, and a variety of cryptic comments. The second article, published in the May 21 issue of the journal, contrasted what it called "the beauty and eloquence of Persian poetry" with "the ugliness" of the compositions which it classed as "the Khanvaledeh literature." The reference was to the hostel where many modernist Iranian intellectuals—among them Lahuti, 'Eshqi, and Raf'at—lived during extended stays in Istanbul.[14] *Kaveh*'s examples of good poems, all composed in strict accordance with classical formal and generic rules, consisted of a *mokhammas* entitled "*Nowruz, 1336* [1918]" by a poet named Mahmud Ghanizadeh and a fragment from a *masnavi,* also on the subject of the Iranian New Year, by another poet named Ahmad Khan-Malek Sasani.[15] They were set next to three supposedly "ugly" compositions, the first of which, entitled "Ay Javan-e Irani" (O Iranian Youth), was a Petrarchan sonnet by Raf'at.[16] As evidence of good will, *Kaveh*'s editor said, the journal withheld the names of the poems' authors because "we do not mean to find fault with individuals." At the same time, he expressed the following hope: "When these very persons see the face of their youthful works in the mirror of this journal, they will doubtless come to recognize the ugliness and poor composition (even absence of composition) [*zeshti va bad-tarkibi (balkeh bi-tarkibi)*] of the children of their talent."[17]

Raf'at's response to this essay reflects the same spirit which we saw in his debates with *Daneshkadeh.* He tried once again to rise above the rhetoric of the criticism and to impress on literate Iranians the need for rational debates on poetic change.[18] He opened his argument by stressing the need which drives the modernist impulse. He also criticized *Kaveh's* presentation of the matter at hand, questioning the basis on which the journal selected certain poetic compositions for comparison. To be comparable, poetic compositions must partake of either a common form (*surat*) or a similar subject matter (*mowzu*). *Kaveh* had not taken that point into account. As the title indicates, the subject-matter of Raf'at's own poem is an address to the youth of Iran to renew the glory of their culture through willpower and endeavor. That theme, he observes, has nothing in common with the topic of the Iranian New Year's Day, the Nowruz, which is the subject matter of the poems held up as examples of good composition. He goes on to say:

> The texts that have been made to face each other have no commonalities to provide an appropriate basis for comparison, either in terms of their subject matter or in terms of their meaning. To compare them is like placing a qasida of Manuchehri and a ghazal of Hafez face to face, and asking: "Which one is better?"
>
> Either we must consider apparent forms [*sovar-e zaheri*] and compare qasidas with qasidas and ghazals with ghazals, or we must base our judgment on similar subject matters and compare two different manners of conveying similar messages [*do tarz-e efadeh-ye motafavet*].[19]

The last point is significant in its conception of genre in relation to formal properties of poems. In the first place, here, as in his earlier debates, Raf'at is seeking to undermine the connection between genres and their thematic concerns. More significantly, he attributes a distinguishing status to the manner of communicating meaning. The notion of form—which I prefer to refer to as genre—is subordinated both to the poem's subject matter and its expressive strategies. Within the Persian poetic tradition, the border between genres in general, and particularly between the qasida and the ghazal, had been made increasingly more visible through the classification of these genres in poetic divans and the virtual linking of individual poets with one or another genre rather than through intrinsic thematic or structural differences.[20] Raf'at's line of division, using subject matter and expressive strategies as bases for classification is an important departure from traditional practice in its own right. As we will see in chapter 6, this position, expanded into a principle of poetic modernism, played a crucial part in undermining the idea of verse forms altogether as a basis for classifying poetic texts. It led eventually to the new poetry's typology of poems along the lines solely of thematic and expressive features, much like that common in contemporary Western literatures.[21]

For the moment, Rafʿat presents the argument in order to offer a composition of his own which he thought would provide a good example of a new kind of poetry to be compared with the traditional treatments of the theme of Nowruz, such as the poems which *Kaveh* had praised. Nonetheless, the effort to open the traditional typology of poetic genres to revision has wider implications in the context of the present study for three reasons. First, in the entire process of poetic change, his remain by far the most significant examples of Persian poetry composed, formally at least, in strict accordance with a classical European verse form, namely the sonnet. Second, his poems exemplify efforts to forge a new system of signification. Third, they serve as an important early prototype, albeit through the intermediacy of better-known and more productive poets, of the nature of sociality in *sheʿr-e Now*, as I attempt to demonstrate presently.

Rafʿat's statement that, in order to be comparable, poems ought to share a single subject matter was, as we have seen, placed in the context of his response to *Kaveh*'s cursory condemnation of his composition. He now offered another poem, a Petrarchan sonnet in form, which he thought could legitimately be compared to the traditional compositions on Nowruz. For my purposes, I have selected this poem, in many ways typical of Rafʿat's limited yet important poetic output, as exemplifying his vision of poetic modernity in Iran.[22] Again, my literal translation follows the text of the poem in Persian, entitled "Nowruz va Dehqan" (Nowruz and the Farmer):[23]

> Nowruz ruzegar tokan midehad hami
> banuj-e bakht ra shab o ruz andar aseman
> yek shab beh mah miresad eqbal-e javedan
> ruzi dar aftab hovayda-st khorrami
>
> emsal gofteh bud nadaram degar ghami
> dehqan-e nikbin beh hafidan-e khod nehan
> rahi gerefteh pish beh delkhah-e ma zaman
> jobran-e majara shavad az bish ya kami
>
> nowruz amadi to ze aʿmaq-e mavara
> ommid zendeh shod sar-e afkandeh shod fara
> dehqan-e rad zad beh kamar daman-e qiam
> nowruz chun shod andar orumi banat-e jam
> ba hokm-e naynavaʾ-ye shurideh qatl-e ʿam
> dehqan-e azari ze now alofteh shod beh gham.[24]

(Nowruz, times swing fortune's cradle
night and day in the sky;
one night eternal prosperity reaches the moon,
one day sweet well-being is visible in the sun.

"I have sorrow no more," the hopeful farmer
had said to his heirs privately this year,
"times have taken a turn after our heart's desire
the past will be redressed, for less or more."

Nowruz, you arrived from the depths of beyond,
hope was revived, downcast heads were lifted up,
the upright farmer prepared for an uprising.

Yet, Nowruz, when in Urmieh the daughters of Jam
were massacred on orders from rebellious Ninus
once more the Azeri farmer sank into sorrow.)

"Nowruz and the Farmer" consists of an octet composed of two qua-
trains and a sestet composed of two tercets. As can be seen from the transliterated Persian version of the poem, the rhyme scheme—*abba abba ccd ede*—
corresponds to a most common French variation on the Petrarchan prototype
used by poets like Baudelaire and Mallarmé, among others. In this usage, the
rhyme pattern in the sestet is distinguished by an internal couplet (lines 11
and 13) rather than the terminal one, which is more common in the English
variations of the Italian sonnet.[25] Metrically, however, the poem conforms
with a frequently used traditional pattern in classical Persian poetry.[26]

Structurally, "Nowruz and the Farmer" presents a four-part argument
with a clear progression from the general to the specific and lines of demarcation at the end of lines 4, 8, 11, and 14. The initial idea communicated
through the first four lines states an assumption about fortune and the way
it oscillates between the two poles, concretized here in terms of the sun and
the moon, two celestial objects prominent in classical Persian poetry. This
general statement is then related in the second quatrain to the life of an Azeri
farmer with his optimistic prediction that times of pain and sorrow may well
be at an end. The first tercet describes how the farmer's hopes lead him to
participate in an uprising which he thinks will bring a better future. In the
second tercet, the account of an actual historical event, the government's
crushing of the uprising in the northwestern Iranian city of Urmieh which
dashed those hopes, is given.[27] This account returns the reader back to the
poem's original motif of the pendulumlike movement of fortune through
time.

Emotion, of course, lies at the heart of all lyricism, whether in the Persian ghazal or in the Western verse form known as the sonnet. In trying to trace Raf'at's articulation of sorrow to some model in the Persian tradition, we are driven back to the most general notions of linguistic units acting as poetic signs rather than to any specific function each sign may have performed within the expressive system of the ghazal or the qasida. The articulation begins with two of the most capacious tropes of classical lyrical compositions: the concept of *ruzegar* (times or days, connoting the passage of time), and of *bakht* (fortune, in a general, neutral sense as well as in a specific sense of good fortune). Appearing within the unmarked space of Raf'at's verse form and reverberating in the sphere of the Persian-speaking reader's poetic associations, the two terms begin to alter perceptions of predictable poetic meanings attached to them in more traditional poetic spaces. The result is a process which I refer to as "semantic evacuation," whereby familiar words are emptied of their traditional poetic associations. This prepares the ground for emotional charges other than those already sanctioned by the practice of past poets to make the word a poetic sign.

Next, the two terms begin to take on meanings in progressively new ways and to spread them around, first in the space governing their relations, and eventually in the poem's total environment. Although as tropes, *ruzegar* and *bakht* occur often in the classical lyric, nowhere are they related to each other as they are in Raf'at's poem. The notion of days or times swinging the cradle (*banuj*) of fortune between the two high points of the sun and the moon is, to my knowledge, totally unprecedented in Persian lyrical poetry. In collusion, the two terms help to create the image of a domestic scene where a mother may be seen rocking the cradle of her child. The motherly act of time rocking fortune's cradle in the sky (*dar aseman*), described as happening incessantly (*shab o ruz* [night and day] means all the time), reaches its high points of good fortune in ascendance both to the moon of eternal prosperity and the sun of sweet well-being. This broad, abstract trope finds its concrete application to the case of the Azeri farmer as the latter confides to his heirs his hopeful opinion that "time" has indeed begun to pursue a course that will favor them. Time emerges indeed as the mother of fortune, and the cradle's swing will continue until bad days turn into good ones. As it winds through the sonnet's octet, this image complex conveys a store of associations far beyond, and therefore much broader than, those often repeated in the literary tradition of the past. Rather, evolving on the basis of a scene familiar in many homes, it creates the air of a general view of the human condition. In short, Raf'at's image of the rocking cradle works mimetically rather than through reference to poetic convention. Dislodged from codes of meaning anchored in past practice, the image is then connected with an observable and widespread conception of life outside conventional systems of poetic signification.

A similar operation governs the concrete case of the farmer in conversation with his heirs. The time is "this year," the family that of an "Azeri farmer," described as *nikbin* (literally, good-seeing, meaning hopeful, optimistic, or visionary). The fiction of the poem conveys the notion that, looking into the movement of "fortune's cradle," the farmer observes that their bad days have lasted long enough, perhaps too long; he concludes therefore that the cradle must be starting to move in the opposite direction. "I have sorrow no more," he tells his sons, "for times have taken a turn after our heart's desire." He then clarifies and concretizes his past sorrow: it is related to some nameless atrocity which the poem calls *majara* (literally, that which has passed, often referring to an undesirable event which one hopes to leave behind) and for which the farmer sees redress (*jobran*) in the future. The emotion around which the poem has centered its theme is thus made specific and social at the same time. It is made to relate to the collective fortune, not that of the family alone—which comes to the reader as "we" in the farmer's utterance—but bound by the specific circumstances that have determined the common condition of his time and place—that is, this year in Azerbaijan. Rather than being linked with any specific act or incident, the atrocity is also kept at a vague and generic level. Once again, Raf'at's depiction of the farmer's little drama draws its uniqueness from the fact that it refers to a situation larger than the farmer's family, but not larger than the specific social conditions surrounding it.

A similar effect is achieved through the rhetorical posture the poem's speaker assumes. The address to *Nowruz,* the supreme occasion in the culture for rejuvenation and renewal, places the speaker in dialogue with a millennia-old concept, creating a space wherein contemporaneity meets a perennial cultural value. Occurring three times in the poem, the address informs and invokes a sense of persistent appeal. This in turn gives rise to the image of an individual appealing to a whole culture by recalling one of its most abiding tenets. It does so through the shared cultural assumption of a relationship between natural rejuvenation at Nowruz, which coincides with the beginning of the spring, and Nowruz as the supreme occasion for human resolutions for new beginnings. At the poem's close, the speaker describes the event that neutralizes the rejuvenating power of Nowruz and immerses the farmer back into his sorrow: a massacre (*qatl-e 'am*). The fact that this refers to an actual historical incident in the city of Urmieh, where a group of local women were raped and murdered right at the time of the Iranian new year, further anchors the appeal in social reality.

The notion of the massacre dashing the farmer's hopes for a better future once again emphasizes the communal nature of the poem's articulation of good and bad fortune. Coming from the depth of the culture, Nowruz has failed once again to live up to the life-giving power the culture has assigned to it. Worse yet, it has even proved helpless in protecting "the daughters of Jam." In its references to King Jamshid, the legendary monarch who is said to have initiated the celebration of Nowruz at the beginning of the spring, the word *Jam* opens a cultural dimension which places the appeal in its widest context yet. Even the mythical founder of the celebration is unable to prevent the rape and murder of his own daughters at the very time when the feast he initiated many millennia ago is observed with much ceremony.[28] Here, too, the poem's rhetorical posture and expressive devices have combined to elevate the real and the actual over the mythical and the ceremonial.

As indices of esthetic innovation, the specific features of Raf'at's sonnet become even more visible when we consider it next to other poetic compositions of the period which celebrated Nowruz and the beginning of the Iranian new year.[29] The poems *Kaveh* had selected as examples of "good composition" provide a case in point. Ghanizadeh's qasida, for example, echoes a well-known pattern in the tradition of *nowruziyyehs*[30]—poems composed on the occasion of the new year. It depicts the arrival of Nowruz as a sign of the victory of the army of the just and beautiful spring over that of the horde of a destructive and unjust usurper called winter. The news of the victory occasions an outing into the field and the meadow, where the speaker contemplates nature's beauty. The qasida ends as he raises his goblet to the health of the patron, and wishes the downfall of his enemies.[31] The second composition chosen, a masnavi in form,[32] also begins and proceeds rather uneventfully along well-known traditional lines, although in its conclusion it directs its praise toward Iranians in general instead of an individual patron.

Beyond all thematic or structural connections, in "Nowruz and the Farmer" the borrowed verse form itself forms something of a separate semantic plane possessing its own significance as a sign of departure from the native system of esthetic classification. Naturally, the poem's rhyme scheme flaunts the poem's "foreignness" to those readers unfamiliar with Western verse forms. To readers familiar with the European sonnet, it points to a specific locus of poeticity which Raf'at offers as potentially suitable for the modernization of Persian poetry. From this perspective, Raf'at's criticism of *Kaveh*'s advocacy of the traditional verse forms finds a new significance. "Like all the poems on Nowruz [*nowruzieh-ha*]," he observes in reference to one of the poems set in opposition to his, "that one has employed the clichés [*kelisheh-ha*] and defunct [*az kar oftadeh*] analogies wherein one can find no trace of modernization and advance."[33]

Clearly, Iranian readers would need to make many adjustments in order to accept poems like "Nowruz and the Farmer" as authentic poetic compositions. In compositions where poets explore possibilities of new sources of enrichment for their practice, the more deeply imbedded the loci of innovation, the more difficult it would be for the innovation to be accepted. To change something as fundamental as the rule of monorhyme in the Persian ghazal runs the obvious risk of being seen as unjustifiable tampering, an unacceptable deviation from a long-standing rule. This is the case when the innovation takes the shape of borrowed systems of figures of speech, meter, or rhyme. Because it is visible, a "foreign" rhyme scheme constitutes a more egregious departure from the imaginary "spirit" of Persian poetry, even though it may not be the most substantial one. As the most significant example of Persian poetry composed in accordance with classical European genres, Raf'at's sonnets were initially seen as new poems primarily in that they departed from the formal schemes present in the native system. But they were at the same time examples of socially directed lyrical expressions: they opened themselves to readers' experiences only after testing their willingness to experiment with novel variations on the existing expressive devices in such a way as to minimize systemic dependence on Persian lyric poetry's universe of discourse. These insights must have remained hidden from the casual reader of Raf'at's time.[34]

MIMETIC DESCRIPTIONS: 'ESHQI'S TABLEAUX

To the Iranian readers of the period, a new kind of poetry first became visible in the works of Mohammad-Reza Mirzadeh-'Eshqi (1894–1924), an ardent nationalist and poet of immense talent, though of limited classical education. His contemporaries associated him most with *enqelab-e adabi* (literary revolution), an idea whose gestation, as we have seen, was almost simultaneous with the Constitutional Revolution. In the political atmosphere of his time, 'Eshqi's poetry attracted attention primarily for its ardent nationalist discourse. Yet his solitary attempts to break through the constraints of poetic diction and to liberalize the concepts of rhyme and meter were recognized as well. There was also some consciousness of the fact that 'Eshqi experimented with variations on generic forms and alternative systems of rhythmic expression such as syllabic verse, and that he used a variety of strophic forms of the classical genre known as the *mosammat*.[35]

In a long poem written in the masnavi form entitled "Enqelab-e Adabi" (The Literary Revolution), the contemporary poet Iraj Mirza is believed to have made a satiric reference to 'Eshqi's experimentations with the rhyme schemes of Persian poetry. He ridiculed all contemporary innovations in formal features, particularly experimentations with rhyme, when these were conceived as parts of an overall project of poetic modernity. He put these words in his speaker's mouth:

> Mikonam qafiehha ra pas o pish
> ta shavam nabegheh-ye dowreh-ye khish.[36]

> (Back and forth I juggle the rhymes,
> that I may be the genius of my time.)

In more general terms, too, Iranian poets and readers alike seem to have detected something genuinely fresh in 'Eshqi's poetry. When the young poet was assassinated for his political opposition to the man who would be Reza Shah Pahlavi, many of his contemporaries praised him as an innovative poet and the possessor of a distinctly new style (*tarz-e jadid*).[37] Bahar, for instance, wrote a three-line elegy on his death which ends in this emphatic, if somewhat exaggerated, assessment:

> Sha'eri now bud o she'rash niz now
> Sha'er-e now raft o she'r-e now bemord.[38]

> (He was a new poet and his poetry was new,
> the new poet is gone and new poetry is dead.)

Bahar's judgment of course reflects his own conservative agenda for poetic change, one which, as we have already seen, would not permit any experimentation of the kind that 'Eshqi espoused. Nevertheless, the point remains that 'Eshqi's compositions were viewed as containing something different from all the previous projects for poetic modernity, even though that thing has never been satisfactorily defined.

For the past seventy years or so, critics have frequently reproduced these judgments as evidence of 'Eshqi's contribution to the process of poetic modernity in Iran.[39] However, the precise locus of his innovations remains as obscure as it appears in Iraj's and Bahar's judgments. It is my contention here that 'Eshqi was concerned, first and foremost, with making Persian poetry a site for the expression of individual, existential experience with mimetic, verisimilar images, as opposed to the stylized and conventional imagery characteristic of the lyrical trend in classical Persian poetry. It is my contention further that that aspect of 'Eshqi's contribution remained hidden from his contemporaries, with one crucial exception. The person who recognized the essential element of 'Eshqi's view of a modern Persian poetry was none other than Nima Yushij, the poet who has since been associated most closely with the modernist movement in the poetry of Iran. Nima, who was only one year younger than 'Eshqi, registered his recognition by calling him the only notable force for poetic modernization in his generation.[40] As we will see in chapter 6, Nima's statement stems from his recognition of 'Eshqi as the predecessor whose work he aspired to complete. That recognition, I think, is missing from all assessments of 'Eshqi as the author of "new poetry" and from judgments, in agreement or disagreement, that locate the core of his innovative approach to poetry in formal features or generic classifications.

It is important, of course, to remember that by the time 'Eshqi began to write poetry, the thematic expansion of Persian poetry had been well anchored in current practice. Still, it is in his work that we must seek the first immediately visible signs of the next phase in the movement of Persian poetry toward a new system of signification and communication. An examination of the nature and locus of that unmistakable sign of newness and an analysis of its textual manifestations and systemic implications may therefore prepare the ground for a final look at the shape of the new poetic system. Accordingly, I devote the rest of this chapter to a close analysis of the expressive devices and discursive strategies in the opening passage of one of 'Eshqi's best-known poems. I end by generalizing on the significance of these innovations to the emergence of the new poetry.

The poem known variously as Seh Tablow (The Three Tableaux), Seh Tablow-e Maryam (The Three Tableaux of Maryam), and Ide'al-e Pir Mard-e Dehqani (The Ancient Farmer's Ideal) is a narrative and dramatic composition in 139 stanzas, each containing five hemistichs. Written in 1924, the poem comes in a form known as the *mokhammas*—a poem consisting of segments divisible by five. It consists of three sections, entitled respectively "Shab-e Mahtab" (The Moonlight Night), "Ruz-e Marg-e Maryam" (The Day of Maryam's Death), and "Sargozasht-e Pedar-e Maryam va Ide'al-e U" (The Story of Maryam's Father and His Ideal). The narrative tells the story of an old *dehqan* (farmer, tiller of land) whose life becomes entwined with political events before and after the Constitutional Revolution. In the first section—or tableau—the poet depicts himself witnessing a village girl's seduction by a city youth on a moonlit night late in springtime. In the second tableau, in a parallel scene in the autumn, he depicts Maryam's death and burial. The last section relates the story of Maryam's father, recalling the vicissitudes of his life, his participation in, and sacrifices for, the Revolution, now utterly derailed. It is here that 'Eshqi voices his frustration with the course of the Revolution. 'Eshqi closes his poem by expressing what must be a sardonic desire for annual bloodbaths to cleanse the country of all traitors.

In its entirety, including the poet's vision of violent expurgations, "The Three Tableaux" must ultimately be seen as an angry young man's frustrated outburst against the political situation in Iran during the last years of Qajar rule. In the poem itself, 'Eshqi tells his readers that it was composed as a proposal to 'Ali Dashti, the editor of the journal *Shafaq-e Sorkh* (Red Dusk), who had solicited the ideals of "the thinkers of Iran" concerning the country's future.[41] In its last section, the poem makes an attempt to turn Maryam, an innocent maiden violated and abandoned by a selfish, opportunistic pleasure-seeker, into a metaphor for the Constitutional Revolution, now thought dead at the hands of self-serving, treacherous officials.[42] The poet suggests an annual bloodbath in retaliation for the treachery that has diverted that Revolution from its original path, causing its demise.

I illustrate what is of particular relevance to my purpose by examining the descriptive passage which opens the poem. I hope to demonstrate the way in which 'Eshqi presents his verisimilar, experiential approach to imagery as a departure from all past and present conventional approaches to poetic description. What follows, then, is the opening of the first tableau in Persian, together with my literal translation:

> Ava'el-e gol-e sorkh ast o enteha-ye bahar
> neshasteh-am sar-e sangi kenar-e yek divar
> javar-e darreh-ye darband o daman-e kohsar
> faza-ye shemran andak ze qorb-e maghreb tar
> hanuz bod asar-e ruz bar faraz-e evin
>
> nemudeh dar pas-e koh afatab tazeh ghorub
> savad-e shahr-e ray az dur nist payda khub
> jahan nah ruz bovad dar shomar nah shab mahsub
> shafaq ze sorkhi nimi-sh bayraq-e ashub
> sepas ze zardi nimi-sh pardeh-ye zarrin
>
> cho aftab pas-e kuhsar penhan shod
> ze sharq az pas-e ashjar mah nemayan shod
> hanuz shab nashodeh aseman cheraghan shod
> jahan ze partov-e mahtab nur baran shod
> cho now 'arus sefidab kard ru-ye zamin
>
> agar cheh qa'edatan shab siahi ast padid
> khelaf-e har shabeh emshab degar shabi-st sepid
> shoma beh harcheh keh khub ast mah migu'id

bia keh emshab mah ast o dahr rang-e omid
beh khod gerefteh hamana dar in shab-e simin

jahan sepidtar az fekrha-ye 'erfani-st
rafiq-e ruh-e man an 'eshqha-ye penhani-st
darun-e maghzam az afkar-e khosh cheraghani-st
chera keh dar shab-e mah fekr niz nurani-st
chonan keh del shab-e tarik tireh ast o hazin

neshasteh-am beh bolandi o pish-e cheshmam baz
beh har koja keh konad cheshm kar cheshmandaz
fetadeh bar sar-e man fekrha-ye dur o deraz
bar an saram keh konam su-ye aseman parvaz
faghan keh dahr beh man par nadadeh chun shahin

fekandeh nur mah az labela-ye shakheh-ye bid
beh juybar o chamanzar khalha-ye sefid
beh san-e qalb-e por az ya's o noqtehha-ye omid
khosh an keh dowr-e javani-ye man shavad tajdid
ze si 'aqab beneham pa beh sal-e bistomin

darun-e bisheh siah o sepid-e dasht o daman
tamam-e khetteh-ye tajrish sayeh vo rowshan
ze sayeh rowshan-e omram resid khater-e man
gozashtehha-ye sepid o siah ze suz o mehan
keh ruzegar gahi talkh bud o gah shirin

beh abr-pareh cho mah nur-e khish afshanad
beh san-e panbeh-ye atesh gereteh mimanad
ze man mapors keh kabkam khorus mikhanad
cho man ze hosn-e tabi'at keh qadr midanad
magar kesan-e cho man mushekaf o nazokbin

hobab-e sabz cheh rang ast shab ze nur-e cheragh
nemudeh ast haman rang mah manzar-e bagh
neshan-e arezu-ye khish in del-e por dagh
ze labela-ye derakhtan hami gereft soragh
koja-st an keh biayad dehad mara taskin.[43]

(It's the start of the rose, the end of spring.
I am seated on a rock, next to a wall
on a sloping hillside near Darband's dell.
Shemran's horizon dimmed from the dusk;
yet above Evin some traces of the day remained.

The sun has now set behind the mountain,
the city's silhouette is only half visible from afar;
in reckoning, this moment counts as neither day nor night:
the dusk resembles half a banner of revolt in redness;
the other half is yellow, like a golden drape.

As the sun disappeared behind the mountain
the moon emerged, through the trees, from the east.
Before the day turned night, the sky became festooned with lights, and
showered the earth in streams of moonlight.
Like a new bride, the earth powdered its face white.

Commonly at night blackness appears,
yet unlike all nights, this night is all white.
You call all you love "moonlike."
Come! this night is moonlike, the world
takes on a hopeful hue on so silvery a night.

The globe is whiter than mystical thoughts.
In my soul I hold many secret loves.
My mind is lighted with countless good thoughts—
yet, a moonlit night illumines the mind,
just as a dark night blackens the heart.

I'm seated at a height, the landscape before me
stretches artless as far as the eye can see.
Thoughts stroll in my head, far and wide and deep.
I would love to fly upward to the sky.
Pity, in creation I was not given the falcon's wings.

Through the willows, the moon's silver rays
have cast white specks on the knoll, the stream,
much as heavy hearts harbor hopeful spots.
Would that half-dead youth were revived in me!
Would that from thirty I went to twenty!

The thicket is dark, the plain and field white,
Tajrish is dappled in shade and in light.
I recall some shades and lights of my own:
A past all blank, blackened by pain,
when my time was now bitter now sweet.

As the moon sprinkles light upon a cloud
it comes to look like cotton fields afire.

I am overjoyed, ask not how I feel.
Who would cherish nature's lovely charm as I do,
save those as keen as I have always been?

What would a green bulb look like when it's lit?
Such has turned the grove's color in moonlight.
My heart so scorched has forever sought
signs of its desire through the branches:
where is the one whose approach will soothe me?)

In this passage I believe there is an approach to poetic description without any precedent in the history of Persian poetry. It is this very newness, I further believe, which has given rise to deeply ambivalent judgments about 'Eshqi's poetry. In general, he has been judged as talented, yet unsophisticated and undisciplined, in his own time and ever since. He has also been seen as unversed in the art of versification.[44] I hope to move toward an understanding of the expressive mechanisms which 'Eshqi utilizes and the direction in which he guides the notion of newness in Persian poetry. Certainly the passage cited here features none of the conventional thematic treatment of approaching night in the Persian lyrical tradition. There, such scenes as the setting of sun, the approach of night, and the rising of the moon are often expressed either through mythical or warlike allusions or through highly stylized codes of idealized beauty. Jonah entering the dark insides of the biblical "big fish," an army of black slaves conquering white overlords, and more particularly, a beloved spreading her long, pitch-black hair over her white body are among the most easily remembered in a plethora of images which signal day turning into night.[45] Convenient analogues to the rising of the moon include rooftop appearances by the beloved, an ideal of beauty whose radiant face outshines the celestial luminary, or whose perfectly curved eyebrow challenges the crescent moon to a sword fight. Conversely, the scene of the moon shining atop a cypress tree reminds the lover of the beloved's face and stature.[46] In such descriptions, nature becomes the handmaiden of the poet who needs to communicate the perfect and overpowering beauty of his beloved. The absoluteness of the terms of description serves to emphasize the conceptualization of each image as a single, separate entity—in nature or in the human psyche—embodying all the attributes of the concept in question, be it darkness, beauty, or love. 'Eshqi's description defies that goal and discards the means by which it is achieved. It is only natural that it should be seen as nonpoetic and that the poet should be judged wanting in classical poetic education.

In the context of the search for a new kind of poetry, 'Eshqi's disregard of conventional expressive mechanisms becomes the first marker of a difference in "poetic" description. The passage cited here cannot be comfortably equated with prose because it does after all contain formal and generic features which communicate its demand to be seen as poetry. 'Eshqi's readers, in other words, see him engaged in creating "poetic" signs where none was previously thought to exist. By bestowing unconventional significance on such natural phenomena, he begins to articulate a previously inarticulate or mute code. In his description, the dusk, the moonlight, and the dappled shade exist not so much as analogues for other images present in the onlooker's mind but primarily as objects for poetic contemplation in their own right. 'Eshqi attempts, however, to make such natural phenomena as the sunset, the approach of the night, and the rising of the moon perceptible to his readers as processes, not as accomplished events. To do that, he finds it necessary, rather self-consciously, to place himself in the midst of the scene and to recount his own personal impressions and responses. His descriptions signal that intention in the way they structure and organize the presentation of human impressions. He communicates these to the reader as processes which permeate his being gradually, from sight to the soul. The natural signs he describes lead in the end to the sign of his heart's desire, which he seeks through the tree branches. An understanding of the mechanisms at work in each stage in this process enables us ultimately to arrive at an idea of the manner in which 'Eshqi's passage affects his contemporary readers, whether or not they are consciously comprehended.

That perception would also be framed by the immediate context surrounding "The Three Tableaux." The poem is prefaced by two prose passages, both written by the poet and designed to explain his conception of modernity in Persian poetry. In the first, 'Eshqi calls his poem "the prelude to a revolution in Iran's literature" (*dibacheh-ye enqelab dar adabiyyat-e Iran*). As he sees it, the poem's "manner of thinking" (*tarz-e fekr kardan*) and "harnessing of poetic talent" (*beh kar endakhtan-e qariheh*) are entirely different from the thought habits of former or contemporary poets of the Persian language. Understood properly and emulated, 'Eshqi says, this new approach will result in "fostering poetic thoughts" (*parvaresh-e afkar-e sha'eraneh*). His assessment of the impact of the difference between his approach and the common one is unabashed: "Every speaker of Persian will feel ecstatic [*beh vajd miayad*] at reading these tableaux, and will enjoy this manner of verse composition [*tarz-e ensha'-e nazmi*]." 'Eshqi states that he has benefited from the unsuccessful experiments of others, yet reiterates the same opinion. "The Three Tableaux" constitutes, in his judgment, "the best example of the poetic revolution of this age" (*behtarin nemuneh-ye enqelab-e she'ri-ye in asr*). Trying to contain his enthusiasm, he still feels sufficiently convinced of the novelty of his approach to conclude: "If these tableaux were the product of some other talent, I would praise them even more, for never before has there been such a composition in the Persian language."[47]

The second prose preface, addressed to "Persian speakers" (*farsi zabanha*), makes the same points more concisely and more forcefully:

> I began versifying poetic thoughts in an unprecented manner [*shekl-e nowzohur*], and I have thought to myself that the literary revolution of the Persian language must be undertaken in such a way. Read my "Three Tableaux . . ." carefully. If you see shortcomings in it, forgive me, for the work has just begun. I hope that future poets will follow in the path of this manner of articulation [*tarz-e goftar*] and perfect it.[48]

Authorial enthusiasm aside, these prefatory remarks offer no theory of composition. Nor do they constitute a guide to reading the poem. That is primarily because 'Eshqi does not explain the concepts he uses. The words he uses to define the novelty of his composition communicate a high degree of subjectivity and not a little psychologizing. He speaks of a new and pleasing style (*tarz-e now va marghub*), of the use of talent in fostering poetic thoughts, and of innovations based on good taste (*ebtekar-e zowqi*). It is not easy to attach precise conceptual or critical meanings to such terms. Like all pioneers, 'Eshqi remains ultimately unsure of the efficacy of his experimentation. His words convey a certain diffidence about the "difference" between his manner of composition and that of the more conventional poets. Of these he names one, Yahya Dowlatabadi,[49] whose poetry incorporates various elemental innovations of the kind exemplified by the works of Dehkhoda and 'Aref. In short, 'Eshqi is both convinced and unsure in the same way that an explorer attempting to navigate through uncharted waters may be guided by his instinct rather than by accumulated experience. Even as he calls his composition completely unprecedented, he seems to take back what he has said. "But maybe it is not so," he ponders midway in his first preface, "maybe my mind has gone awry."[50]

Yet, we do sense a poet determined to break with the poetic practice of his tradition by introducing subjectivity both in the moment of composition and in the process of reading. The "I" of the passage seems to be addressing a "you" that consists at once of the discerning contemporary reader and the would-be future poet. By claiming a discontinuous manner of writing poetry, he seems to appeal for an equally discontinuous reading process. In order to appreciate the newness of the text, readers must approach the experience of reading free from prior conceptions of the syntactic, semantic, and grammatical operations anchored in the classical system. What ʿEshqi communicates most clearly is his desire to have his readers judge "The Three Tableaux" as a novel poem conceived and composed in a way different from what they may have read before. In short, he would like us to see his poem as one made in view of previous unsuccessful experiments. That view does condition the reading experience.

My discussion of "The Three Tableaux" is meant to make visible that very desire for severance as it manifests itself in the text of the poem. It is intended neither to offer an interpretation of the poem nor to analyze its formal and generic features. I argue that in the passage cited above ʿEshqi makes a self-conscious attempt to dislodge various poetic signs from their systemic bases and to anchor them in subjectively observed and perceived phenomena rather than relating them to the codes associated with the traditional system of poetic signification. Such departures from strict accordance with the system of classical lyrical tradition, I think, are meant to sketch the outlines of a new system of poetic codification and to illustrate how ʿEshqi envisioned a new kind of poetry beyond the achievements of Iranian poets of his generation. As the relationship between signifiers and what they signify changes from the conventional to what can be called perceptual, existential, or experiential—all terms that connote the presence of a perceiving subject—the principle on which poetic texts communicate with readers changes also. It is the cumulative effect of an abundance of these new relationships between the poet, the text, and the reader that marks a text as signaling a systemic break with current and conventional practices. Sustained through practice, barely perceptible textual innovations eventually effect alterations in poetic structures and lead to systemic transformation. Accordingly, in illustrating this process, I anchor my argument primarily in an exploration of those expressive mechanisms through which the text attempts to set itself apart from the system of textual representation which the poet perceives as existing in descriptive passages of classical Persian poetry.

To begin at the most obvious point of entry, the idea of the poem as a trilogy of "tableaux" imparts a certain visual quality to the act of reading. The word "tableau," a recent entry from French into the Persian language, distinguishes the poem not just as a contemporary composition, but as one perhaps inspired by sources outside the native poetic tradition. It further draws attention to textual entities and objects in a manner different from that in which classical Persian poetry presents its image-making resources. Whatever structural principle may lie at the heart of the poem as poem,

'Eshqi seems to be saying, comes not from the canon—generic, formal, the-matic—with which the passage can be classed, but rather from the reader gazing into the poem itself. If the poem is a tableau, then readers just might begin to view the act of reading as a process in which meaning is produced by looking at the textual object as closely and carefully as possible. They might even begin to conceive of the sociopolitical context as a frame which surrounds the work and makes it an independent object to behold for its independent beauty as well as for its meaning. The word "tableaux" thus binds the spatial and temporal horizons of the poem, acting as a mechanism to set the poem apart as a singular visual object worthy of being approached, contemplated, and absorbed as such.

The descriptive passage that opens the first tableau presents terms of time and place in such a way as to throw the passage into perceptible contrast with the presentation of these elements in the traditional system. In the first hemistich, for instance, the two concepts of "spring" and "rose," wedded together through their association in the classical lyric tradition, are separated from each other rather forcefully. "It's the start of the rose, the end of spring," means simply that the blooming of the rose begins as spring draws to a close. However, this simple statement, factual in Tehran where the poem is situated, violates the automaticity of an already established link between the two phenomena in the classical ghazal and qasida tradition. There, the arrival of spring automatically invokes the thought of the garden society in which the rose, often surrounded by a host of other flora and fauna each metonymically associated with a particular aspect or attribute of the absent beloved, stands as the emblem of the absent one. As the zephyr (*bad-e saba*) spreads his/her fragrance all over, the nightingale (*bolbol, 'andalib, hazar-dastan, hazar* [or *hezar*]), that is, the poet, begins to sing his sad song of love and longing for union.[51]

A single example will illustrate the point. When the speaker of a Hafezian ghazal mentions the arrival of the joyous spring and the blooming of the rose conspiring to weaken his pious resolve to refrain from wine, he combines these into a single linguistic unit modified by adjectival phrases.

> Bahar o gol tarab-angiz gasht o towbeh-shekan
> beh shadi-ye rokh-e gol bikh-e gham ze del barkan.[52]

> (Spring and the rose became joy-arousing and repentance-breaking.
> To the rose's happiness, pluck the root of sorrow from your heart.)

Here, the two adjectival phrases, joy-arousing (*tarab-angiz*) and repentance-breaking (*towbeh-shekan*), govern both the spring and the rose indistinguish-ably. In the rest of the ghazal, the same qualities are then generalized by inference to such other accoutrements of the garden scene as the zephyr (*saba*), the rose blossom (*ghoncheh*), the cypress (*sarv*), the hyacinth (*sonbol*), the jasmine (*saman*), and a number of other coconspirators in the collapse of the speaker's resolve. In the end, it is not one natural phenomenon, say the arrival of spring or the blooming of the rose, but the total ambience whose impact on the speaker's psyche makes it impossible for him to refrain from drinking. The arrival of the spring and the rose assumes, establishes, and reinforces the essential and inalienable unity of a series of concepts in the system of signification regardless of whether one or another may be present or absent in a single poetic utterance.

Forcing a separation of the concepts of "spring" and "rose," 'Eshqi creates a contrast between the two semantic units "the start" (*ava'el*) and "the end" (*enteha*); he thus conveys opposition to, or at least divergence from, the system that registers the whole of the spring as a single temporal unit linked with the rose's appearance. As a result, at least two sets of concepts are disengaged from each other. First, the poet speaks of spring not as a single temporal concept but as a time span possessing a beginning, an end, and presumably a middle. He then chooses one, the end of spring, as the time when the story he will tell happened. Similarly, the blooming of the rose is described as covering a time period, beginning, as the poet implies, toward the end of spring. With this appeal to the phenomenal rather than the conventional, 'Eshqi breaks the connection between the two phenomena as it has been set up in the classical usage, making it possible for both to come to signify ideas other than those they have traditionally signified. As a result of this disengagement, the initial thought—that is, that the rose blooms at the end of spring—assumes the new potential for the poet's eventual idea, communicated at the poem's close: the springtime of the Constitutional Revolution is at an end and the feast of blood, linked with "the season of the rose" through the visual image of the color red, is about to begin.

In the second hemistich the degree of specificity achieved through spatial designations signals more dramatic departures from the strategies of description evolved through the classical poetic system. The narrator describes himself as "seated on a rock, next to a wall." The names of three real locations—Darband, Shemran and Evin, all suburbs of Tehran—are added through the first stanza to help the reader visualize the exact spot where the narrator is sitting. Together with other directional or geographic terms woven into the passage, these proper nouns help the reader visualize the narrator, as he begins to relate what he has witnessed from his vantage point. Facing east, seated at a high point that overlooks the Darband Valley, which is encircled by the mountains around the northern half of the capital city, he is watching the remaining daylight over the southeasterly village of Evin disappear as darkness begins to set in on the northern village of Shemran. Farther to the south, and slightly eastward, he can barely distinguish the silhouette of the ancient city of Ray. From this vantage point he begins to describe the darkening horizon above the northern mountains and the rising moon from behind the trees in the thicket which stretches before him between Darband and Evin.

In the first two stanzas the narrator reports the darkening of the horizon before the approach of night, a process whose symbolic significance increases in degrees until it culminates as a sky half red and half yellow. These colors make the sky resemble, in his words, "half a banner of revolt / the other half . . . a golden drape." The specific color designations here function on a symbolic plane as signifiers of a specific social situation. As we shall see presently, these textual signs lead the reader back to an understanding of Iranian society as somewhere between monarchy (golden drape) and revolution (banner of revolt). Such relations between a poetic text and its sociopolitical context are noteworthy not simply as arbitrary significations imposed on the terms "yellow" and "red," but as a manner of transforming sensory perception into culturally coded content or meaning.

By the dawn of the twentieth century, an awareness of European history, particularly of the French Revolution, had changed the vocabulary of Iranian political discourse, including the designation of certain colors as expressing political tendencies.[53] As a formative element in the emergence of new symbolic associations in various intellectual discourses, the French Revolution was a unique influence, one which had left its mark on various spheres of the Persian lexicon, including the vocabulary of color. The color yellow (golden) had thus been keyed to the opulence of royalty, a system of government that twentieth-century Iran shared with prerevolutionary France. By the time 'Eshqi composed his tableaux, the color imagery of the Bolshevik revolution in neighboring Russia, with its contrast between red and white as political designations, would be added to this. Within the intellectual circles of Iran in the 1920s, the color red clearly recalled revolt against existing rulers in general, and specifically against the monarchy, whose opulence was often expressed in terms of the color gold. Iranian political discourse of the period offers ample evidence of such color associations.[54]

Naturally, classical Persian poetry has its own system of color designation. Both gold and red have been used widely, even in senses not very different from that in which 'Eshqi employs them—that is, gold signifying wealth and opulence; red, primarily blood. What is different here is the manner in which color imagery guides the reader from the signifier to the signified. To illustrate that, let us consider for a moment a most famous adage by the thirteenth-century Persian poet Saʿdi. The well-known aphorism, "*Zaban-e sorkh sar-e sabz midehad bar bad*" (The red tongue brings about the destruction of the green head.)[55] contains two phrases *zaban-e sorkh* (red tongue) and *sar-e sabz* (green head) which act as synecdochic allusions to the outspoken speaker of truth who disregards clear and present danger to his or her survival. The aphorism builds on the correlation between the natural color of the tongue, which refers to the part of the body responsible for speech, as well as to language itself, with the blood that might be spilled in zealous pursuit of truth. The adage thus serves as a general reminder of the dangers attendant on frank speech unconstrained by circumstance. By the same token, the color green is associated with natural growth and life. Its usage here recalls the life that might thus come to an end like that of a tree or shrub—that is, by beheading. The relationship between the two color designations and their meanings, while externally determined, preserves a universal applicability, leaving Saʿdi's readers free to tailor them to their purposes as they see fit.

In ʿEshqi's usage of color symbolism, the dusk is likened half to a "banner of revolt" (for its redness), half to "a golden drape" for its yellow color. Like Saʿdi's, these color designations are externally determined, transported from outside the text into it, in this case, from the period's political discourse. However, in ʿEshqi's poem the nature of the external signifiers is such that the notion of time, both in its literal sense of the sunset hour and in the metaphorical sense of postconstitution Iran, appears constructed and bounded. Saʿdi's image derives from cumulative experience gained by contemplating an unchanging entity called human nature. It thus triggers an observation that is eternally relevant and universally valid. ʿEshqi's image, derived from two definable historical processes, concretizes the terms of their discourse as a specific image aspiring to communicate the poet's specific understanding of a culturally and politically specific situation. Operating within the space that relates impressions of the French and Russian Revolutions to the social milieu of the postconstitution Qajar monarchy in Iranian society, the image of burned clouds at sunset, seen in part as a banner of revolt and in part as a golden drape, creates a specifically topical series of associations relevant to the poem's social and temporal context.

In ʿEshqi's depiction of the sunset scene, the impression of the transitoriness of the situation is corroborated by the fact that sunsets are universally perceived as moments of transition.[56] Through the use of such verbs as "is," "is not," "has just set," ʿEshqi helps to reinforce the momentary stillness of each moment as well as the sense of its contemplation as a tableau. Descriptions of the dimming horizon, the darkening space, the opaqueness of the city's silhouette, and various other temporal markers enhance the sense of transience in the scene. The combined effect creates a feeling of a calm as ephemeral as the colors of the dusk. In contrast, the rock on which the speaker sits and the wall nearby establish a set of solid images. The resulting perception of solidity in the midst of flux gives the first two stanzas a quality which moves the reader closer to comprehending the significance of the contrast on the symbolic plane: no matter what changes the passage of time may bring to the phenomenal world, the human subject is solid enough to rise up to the challenge. Esthetically, these effects register the impression that whatever the nature's show, the poet will be capable of telling it in a manner distinctly different from that which the poetic tradition has thus far offered. The juxtaposition of revolution and royalty, the impression of the transitoriness of the moment, and the symbolic value of springtime and the rose collude to foreshadow the concept of "the feast of blood" articulated at the poem's close.

As a verbal construct, "The Three Tableaux" aspires to visual effect in yet another way: in its use of words to conjure up colors. The passage cited here owes much of its visual specificity to the terminology with which 'Eshqi recounts the changes of color in nature as day turns into night. To achieve that effect, 'Eshqi would have needed words which may not have existed in the poetic diction available to him. This process reaches its high point in the last stanza where he describes how the grove looks by moonlight. The specific color remains nameless, comprehensible only through an analogous query: "What would a green bulb look like when it's lit?" asks the speaker, leaving the question unanswered. "Such," he then observes, "has turned the grove's color in moonlight." The specificity thus achieved creates the impression of a color which, concrete as it is, may nevertheless differ from reader to reader. Individual or idiosyncratic color perceptions play their part in producing the final effect, as each reader may imagine the combination of the green of the bulb with the silver light shining from within. Through such descriptions, 'Eshqi's poetry goes beyond the need of the moment to transform ordinary objects into those possessing the attributes the poet wishes to assign to them.[57] The terms of description thus come to stand in meaningful relations to the reader insofar as they are situated within a system that includes his or her perceptions. Rather than treating sense impressions as fixed linguistic entities, the poem deliberately makes them a matter of subjective perception. Over two decades later, Nima Yushij adopts this approach to image making, as we shall observe in chapter 6.

By far the most significant lexical marker of transference of signification processes from the conventional to the perceptual relates to the image of the night, developed in stanzas 3 through 5. As the concept that gives its name to the first tableau, "The Moonlight Night" (*Shab-e Mahtab*) is the central temporal image through which the poem communicates its content. Moonlight is clearly a device the poet needs as he sets out to describe the scene of the young country girl's seduction by the city youth. 'Eshqi seizes on that necessity and turns it into an occasion for highlighting a most significant systemic departure from the conventional descriptions of the night in Persian poetry. As a device casting light on the stage of the action he is about to relate, moonlight dictates an encoding of the night different from that embedded in tradition. There, night, too, is an absolute entity much like the spring. Its pitch-black color ties together a number of stylized entities, from the beloved's tresses all the way to the lover's fortune.[58] Even when the full moon of the beloved's face appears in the sky of the lover's fortune, the pitch-black tresses of the beloved are there as a point of contrast ready to testify to the long and dark night of the lover's suffering. In 'Eshqi's poem, the function of the bright, silver moonlight demands a role for the night that runs mimetically counter to this codification. 'Eshqi uses the black/white opposition as a major structuring device for his poem, initially relating it to the pure joy that fits the occasion, then contrasting that initial feeling with the gloom that descends on the poem as the speaker relates Maryam's fate. Even though the city man's self-centered pleasure-seeking drives the poem to its "black" end, the events of the joyous moment demand a "white night." If the poetic tradition cannot accommodate such a conceptualization, then the poet will go outside that tradition in search of words and images that would be sufficient to the purpose.

The textual strategy that responds to that demand is implemented in three stages, following each other in quick succession. First, the sign is emptied of its conventional associations through the use of a series of dissociative lexical elements. The most obvious example of this occurs at the beginning of the fourth stanza. "Commonly at night blackness appears," the speaker says, "yet unlike all nights, this night is all white." Then, the image thus emptied of its traditional color attribute is tied in the following line to the visual realm through a new color designation, *sepid* (white), which is later turned into a metaphor in its own right through modifiers such as *mah* (literally meaning moonlike, here used in the colloquial sense of good and beautiful) and *simin* (literally referring to the color of silver). Both usages run counter to the conventional codification of the night, the former receiving its poeticity from colloquial usage, the latter from its association with the color of the beloved's body.[59] Finally, through such descriptive lexical units as the world being *nurani* (illumined) and "whiter than mystical thoughts" (*sepid-tar az fekrha-ye ʿerfani*) the night is related to the speaker's description of a state of mental ecstasy perceived exclusively as the domain of mystical illumination by some celestial light. As a result of all this, the sign, severed from its traditional associative links, is turned into a vehicle for conveying a mental state which the narrator has prepared as the effect of the event he is about to relate. First, words and phrases like "yet" and "unlike" help to shock the reader out of the habit of receiving the passage in the customary manner of traditional descriptions. Next, other words and phrases—"you call . . ." and "come . . . ," for example—induct the reader into a new system of poetic description, one which requires willing attention, even mindful participation.

Structurally, stanzas 4 through 6 draw their visual power from a direct linkage between the specific colors and shades of a moonlit night and a joyful emotional state. Once again, ʿEshqi achieves specificity by overcoming the conventionality of poetic connections established by the practice of centuries. All nights are not black, dreary, and therefore doleful. Rather, in poetry as well as in the outside world, just as there are gloomy nights which incite despair in the human heart, there are "other" nights which bestow on the whole world the color of hope and illuminate the human soul with joy, longing, or other pleasant feelings. The movement from sense to soul is facilitated through the intermediary of words like *cheraghan,* in the sense of decorating or festooning with lights, made familiar to a society which has just been introduced to the power of electricity. In the poem, this word first refers to the sky—*aseman cheraghan shod*—and then to the poet's thoughts—*darun-e maghzam az afkar-e khosh cheraghani-st.* In a similar way, *nurbaran* (literally, a shower of light) is used first in reference to the world and then to the poet's thoughts. Finally, the whiteness of the world is related to "those secret loves" (*an ʿeshqha-ye penhani*) which are "in my soul" (*rafiq-e ruh-e man*). It is ultimately this immediate alignment of sense perceptions and mental states which allows the poet to cast such signs as the sunset, the night, and the moonlight in an experiential mold rather than a conventional one.

The sixth stanza signals the return of the narrator by repeating the verb *neshasteh-am* (I am seated), which began the second hemistich of the first stanza. Sitting on high ground, the speaker observes that the world is open before him "as far as the eye can see," that he mulls "thoughts . . . far and wide and deep" in his head, and that he wishes he could take flight like a falcon. In addition to heightening the euphoria of the happy moment, the desire to fly high and see it all and the regret at having no wings to do so remind the reader of the limitations of the human condition. That awareness in turn brings the reader back to the world of immediate experience, of the speaker's attempt to make readers see through his eyes—and his words—the event he is about to relate.

The stanzas that follow ease the speaker's passage to the possibility of receiving some sign of fulfillment of his desire to see it all. The complete meaning of this desire becomes obvious only at the very end of the whole poem where the poet reveals the notion of the feast of blood. The process, foreshadowed in the third stanza where the moon is said to shine from behind the trees, begins with a description of the white specks of moonlight shed through the branches of a willow tree on the brook and the meadow. The scene is then likened to heavy hearts harboring hopeful spots. In this description, specks of moonlight on the meadow are related to white spots of hope in the human heart. The association is reinforced in the eighth stanza where the dappled shade of the landscape brings back to the speaker's mind the dappled shades of his past life when the bittersweet coloring of his experiences filled it with yearnings and sufferings alike. It is in such an emotional state, prompted by the beauty of the moonlit night, that he seeks the signs of his desire's fulfillment through the trees he faces.

The last stanza of the passage begins with a most remarkable innovation in image-making, one to which I have already alluded in passing. Trying to describe a color for which no single expressive word is adequate, the speaker turns to the reader to ask: "What would a green bulb look like when it's lit?" He then adds: "Such has turned the grove's color in moonlight." Through this imagined dialogue, 'Eshqi challenges his readers to summon up the color in their own minds. What is remarkable about the technique as an index of innovation relates to the absence of a descriptive word. The speaker turns this condition into an occasion to free himself altogether from the need to communicate through an existing diction. The assumption is that readers can imagine for themselves the color which the speaker is seeing but for which he can find no precise word in the lexicon. If the medium has not supplied the word to serve the purpose, 'Eshqi seems to be saying, one can always appeal for poetic communication through perceptions shared between poets and readers. In fact, what is communicated through the dislodging of poetic descriptions from conventional modifiers consists, at least in part, of the opinion that fidelity to observed experience should take precedence over considerations that render expression inexact, whether they arise from individual limitations or from inherited poetic traditions.

In passages such as those I have examined here, discursive strategies are directed not necessarily toward negating or even transgressing traditional systems of poetic articulation, but rather toward freeing the concept of poetic articulation from constraints imposed by inherited associations and the resultant fixation of meaning.[60] Just as he tries to unhinge certain associations from their traditional bases, at times ʿEshqi affirms traditional signifiers. As we have already seen, Lahuti also debunks traditional poetic significations of the beloved in the Persian lyric while at the same time confirming its content. Similarly, in discarding poetic signifiers that traditionally mark the concept of fortune, Rafʿat preserves the concept, relating it instead to images of his own making. By thus disrupting the internal dynamics that govern traditional poetic expressions, these poets signal their determination to redefine traditional poetics in accordance with the dictates of the situations they see as necessary for depicting the messages they intend to convey in the specific or precise ways they wish to convey them.

In this regard, the relationship ʿEshqi establishes between the descriptive preambles to the first two tableaux and the narrative in each of the poem's three sections constitutes a particularly apt instance of the textual manifestation of that determination. Just as the bright vernal night of Maryam's seduction relates to the mood prevalent in the first section, the dreary autumnal day of her burial foreshadows the gloom that contemplating that eventuality is designed to instigate in the reader. Significantly, the third tableaux is marked by an absence of a descriptive preamble to establish the mood of the ensuing story. We learn, rather unceremoniously, that three days after the death of Maryam, the narrator chances on her father at her grave. There, he attempts to console him, and is told the story of his life. In this way, the third tableau, subtitled "Sargozasht-e Pedar-e Maryam va Ideʾal-e U" (The Story of Maryam's Father and His Ideal), places the dialogue between the narrator and Maryam's father in the context, not of a descriptive passage, but of an assessment of human nature. The interlocutors confirm that human beings are worse than animals, or, in the words of the poem, "the rotten offspring of monkeys" (*nasl-e fased-e maymun*).[61]

The strategies of reader interpellation that Lahuti, Rafʿat, and ʿEshqi use may also be examined as an instance of their desire to modify the system of classification. As an important aspect of the way in which writers envision and execute their relationship with their readers, reader interpellation can serve as a locus of the author's intention to sustain and buttress systemic tendencies or, conversely, to bring about systemic change. As is often characteristic of systemically subversive texts, the relationships these Iranian poets seek to establish with their readers cause their texts ultimately to be classed with items hitherto nonexistent in the traditional system. In the case of Lahuti's "To the Daughters of Iran," the text establishes its antisystemic thrust in content while laying a legitimate claim to a definite formal and generic status within the system. The poem is after all a qasida, and demands to be seen as such. Raf'at's "Nowruz and the Farmer" flaunts its nonnative formal status, declaring its virtual independence from the significatory processes that govern the Persian ghazal. As the same time, in its meter, it remains well within the traditional divisions of classical Persian poetry. 'Eshqi's "The Three Tableaux" presents a more complicated case. It works to disrupt the very basis on which Persian poetry distinguishes itself from prose. In that sense, as we will see, the poem presents itself as a narrative verse that appears prosaic by traditional standards. Furthermore, it tells a story which, by traditional standards of narration, appears closer to foreign texts than verse narratives in Persian.

As an example of this important set of textual relations, let me briefly examine 'Eshqi's frequent addresses to the reader. In "The Three Tableaux" this aspect of the text's operation becomes apparent first in the descriptive passage I cited above where the narrator begins to address the reader directly: "You call all you love 'moonlike.' / Come! this night is moonlike. . . ." Such apostrophes abound throughout the first tableau, increasingly featuring an observant, resourceful, at times theatrical, speaker. Even though absent from the scene, the reader is persuaded, occasionally directly, to take an interest in what occurs between the young man and the village girl. The speaker dutifully reports the details of the goings-on, dwelling, at times at length, on how the scene guides him toward his own personal recollections and affects his emotional state. Thus, after the young man first kisses the girl, then embraces her, and finally begins to make love to her, the speaker tells the reader: "By God, this has happened to me many times." And when the young man first offers wine to the reluctant country girl, the speaker tells the reader in an aside: "Confidentially, my heart was filled with desire / for a tiny drop of all that insistence. I would have obeyed immediately!"[62] Finally, when the lovers, drunk as much with passion as with wine, begin to roll over on the grass, the narrator begs the reader to excuse him from further concentrating on the scene. He asks permission instead to report the distant singing of a quail or a nearby murmur of a waterfall.

By thus accentuating his own presence and participation while at the same time maintaining the necessary discursive control over the narrative, 'Eshqi confers a kind of subjectivity on his readers which is markedly different from that characteristic of classical narratives, poetic or otherwise. In much of the narrative poetry of the Persian classical tradition subjectivity is made all but impossible as the poet posits a stable, all-knowing, and morally correct narrator. The reader is often kept under the tutelage of such a narrator in the position of near total subjugation to his all-encompassing will. Implemented primarily through the fiction of poetic authority, the latter strategy turns readers into the ultimate target of the poet's ethos by placing them in the position of disciples lending eager ears to the master-narrator. By contrast, in the interactive environment 'Eshqi creates, poet and reader are bonded in a relationship which bestows a position of near equal subjectivity on both. Rhetorically at least, the poet places himself, as well as his reader, in the position of an onlooker subject to the vicissitudes of the narrative.

What makes this posture—modernistic in conception as well as in execution—possible is the conceptualization of the speaking voice not as a master moralist but as an accidental observer of the scene, or reporter of the story, or presenter of the idea which he then takes it upon himself or herself to share with the reader. As poet, he or she then considers it a duty to report the findings accurately and realistically. The historical specificity of scenes and stories thus related constitutes the ultimate bond between the voice speaking through the text and the ear turned attentively in its direction. Whether cloaked, as in Lahuti's "To the Daughters of Iran," in terms of a general phrase like "this age of civilization," or of an allusion to an actual historical event like the rape and massacre which Raf'at reports, or of the haunting vision of a feast of blood which 'Eshqi seems to espouse, that specificity connects poet and reader through identical fears and hopes, memories and ideals. This shared ethos can easily transcend specific sociopolitical situations and enter into the realm of the esthetic.

In closing, it is important to reiterate the part that systemic innovations of the kind we have examined in this chapter played in the process of poetic modernity in Iran. In short, they mark a new stage in recasting Persian poetry distinct from all previous attempts at expanding the elements within that system of esthetic communication or enriching the system through literary borrowing. We have already seen that the very terminology poets like Raf'at and 'Eshqi employ tends to mark their work as radical and dramatic departures, even in comparison to parallel visions advocated by their contemporaries. Their repeated appeals to other poets to adopt and advance their approach attest to a degree of awareness of a line of demarcation between the old and the new in Persian poetry separate from that which poets like Dehkhoda and 'Aref saw themselves as facing. Aware of the ground covered through the innovations initiated by these men, or even those innovations envisioned or implemented by their contemporaries, the poets we have focused on here see themselves as advancing a vision of modernity more ambitious in its conception and more consequential than those of their predecessors. Each of the three texts I examined in this chapter contains a consciously

constructed revisionary attitude toward the traditional system of poetic signification and communication in the Persian language. As we have seen, each
also contains a significant potential for disrupting the cultural system of cog-
nition and classification which separates the old from the new, the native
from the foreign, and the poetic from the prosaic.

Taken together, such texts project an alternative esthetic system with its
own internal structure and principles of structuration, as well as its own
classes and categories and rules for classification. Even though they may not
yet communicate a precise idea of the new esthetic system in all its aspects,
such texts further undermine the sense of coherence underlying the existing
system by their very presence. They do so through disrupting the internal
relations which govern the workings of the previous system as a system.
Within a cultural milieu perceived as changing, they also begin to be seen as
essentially aligned with other attempts at change, such as those that work to
alter the rules governing relations between signifiers and what they signify,
or modify the relations between signification mechanisms and poetic forms,
or distinguish poetry from prose. The powerful coalescence of forces for
change begins to further undermine the existing system's claim to coherence,
order, and structure. No longer able to classify texts which express their specific conditions according to customary distinctions, readers are left with the
task not only of comprehending and absorbing such texts qua text but also
of naming them and placing them in the total esthetic culture of their time.
For this complex of reasons, literary texts which transmit specific topical
messages through innovative esthetic approaches must be seen as providing a
crucial link in the chain of events that lead to systemic change in a literary
tradition.

Chapter Six

A New Poetic Tradition

By the early 1920s when the young 'Ali Esfandiari (1895–1960) selected the penname Nima Yushij for himself, major systemic links between the practice of poetry in Iran and the tradition of lyrical expression in classical Persian poetry had been loosened. Moreover, poets and critics like Bahar, Raf'at, Lahuti, and 'Eshqi had introduced many principles of a new system of poetic expression. Perhaps most important, Iran's cultural milieu was ripe with experimentations in the composition of poetry. What Nima initiated in cooperation with the generation of modernist poets and critics coming of age in the 1940s consisted primarily of combining these expressions into an alternative system of signification and communication. Esthetically, this system exhibited formal differences with the classical system, redefined the notion of genre and renegotiated generic boundaries, and made the use of conventional expressive devices a matter of personal choice. Socially, it based its discourse on the essential identicality of social and literary structures. Nima and his followers thus formed the core of a community of poets, critics, and readers who actively took part in interpreting the principles of the new poetic system for the reading public. In a real sense, that discourse constituted the last chapter in a literary-cultural process which had originated in the subversive discourse of a group of nineteenth-century social reformers. I intend to discuss that discursive activity in this last chapter of the book.

That is not how Nima and his followers and admirers conceived and presented their own contribution to the process. They believed themselves to be forging the new system against the steady background of a millennium-old tradition. Even today a great majority of literary Iranians perceive the process of poetic modernity in that culture as beginning with Nima rather than culminating in his work.[1] The reasons, I believe, are many and varied, some residing in general cultural tendencies, others quite specific and demonstrable. For one thing, it is a natural tendency in cultures to credit single recognizable individuals with what has in fact been the cumulative work of many generations. In this particular case, associating poetic modernity with Nima's works and views stemmed in part from the fact that he had a far greater and more substantial poetic and critical output than any previous poet or critic advocating modernism. The perceived necessity of articulating the need for poetic change with reference to constant and explicit reiterations of that fact, supported by a steady and substantial poetic output, made Nima the logical spokesperson for a modernist Persian poetry. In itself, Nima's singular determination for developing a rather limited number of ideas over forty years of patient poetic craftsmanship and substantive critical observations was sufficient to affect a whole generation of poets and readers, favorably or unfavorably. Certainly, Nima's long career and voluminous writings made possible not only a sustained dialogue with followers and detractors alike, but also allowed for close supervision and guidance of the kind that he provided, very effectively in fact, to the next generation of poets and critics.

The responsive understanding Nima mustered toward the end of his life, a crucial factor in the eventual acceptance of his vision of a modern poetry for Iranian culture, was due to several factors. Chief among these was the complementary relationship between the changes effected by the poets that preceded him and those which Nima himself felt inclined to introduce, justify, and undertake. Fundamental as the efforts of poets like Dehkhoda and 'Aref or Raf'at and Lahuti were to the process of poetic modernity, they did not result in any change visible to the naked eye or immediately perceptible in other ways. Persian poetry still appeared to readers' eyes and was absorbed by audiences' ears essentially in ways that signaled continuity rather than rupture. It was indisputably Nima who created a remarkable corpus of poems which impressed their differentness upon the reader even before they were read. Furthermore, Nima himself took a special delight in being thought of as the man who singlehandedly ousted a millennium-old poetic regime. In his own writing he invariably places himself and his work in constant and total opposition to the entire tradition of Persian poetry from Rudaki to Qa'ani, and on to his own time. Indeed, throughout his career Nima speaks about his vision in writings that surround his poems as well as through his poetry in terms of a unique and radical departure that covers all aspects of the existing tradition. Finally, as we shall see presently, without the contribution of a few devoted followers and admirers, Nima's ideas would not have circulated in Iranian society quite as successfully as they did. All this has led many critics and historians of modernity in Iranian poetry to construct Nima's career as a solitary force, almost an oddity, in modernizing Persian poetry in Iran.[2]

The ideas Nima set forth, roughly from the early 1920s to his death in 1960, gave rise to diverse social responses. Through the first two decades of his poetic career, his views went almost unnoticed. Then, in the decade that followed World War II, they attracted enough attention to revive the debate on poetic modernity, dormant since the days when Bahar and Raf'at had challenged one another in their respective journals and 'Eshqi had written his poems and prefaces. A whole series of very different cultural issues, ranging from Westernization and language purification to secularization and nationalism, had virtually removed the issue of change in Persian poetry from the social agenda. The resumption of the debate on poetry in turn placed Nima at the center of the literary scene as the most controversial living literary figure. Eventually, in the last decade of his life, Nima commanded enough attention from a younger generation of poets and critics to preside over the circulation of his poetic ideas in the society and to see them gradually turn into a full-fledged literary movement. All he had to do in the last decade of his life was to bless the movement in all its diverse forms with his elderly wisdom.

It was also during this last decade, and even more so after Nima's death, that a group of poets and literary critics, with a more or less overt political agenda, perceived the potential to turn Nima's vision of a new poetry and poetics into a literary discourse in support of their own sociopolitical struggles. They began to surround his texts with their commentaries, guiding them step by step toward a sociopolitically determinate reading. The hermeneutic environment thus established gave primacy and centrality, in fact almost exclusive validity, to a political reading of poetic compositions, not only of that time but also of all ages and all poets, thus empowering modernist poets to posture as heirs to a long tradition of social protest through writing.[3] In time, the discourse solidified into the specific sociolect of the modernist voices which emerged in the 1950s and early 1960s and which sought to legitimate the tradition of *she'r-e now* with sociopolitical interpretations of literary texts.[4] Thus, a whole new interpretive culture emerged wherein poetry was read primarily with the purpose of deciphering the poet's political views, its abstractions and ambiguities attributed to a perennial case of absence of freedoms, particularly those relating to free expression of ideas through poetry. A similar drive toward topicality, relevance, and comprehensibility, it is worth remembering, had inspired the rhetoric of the nineteenth-century reformists. Now, almost a century later, their desire had begun to be actualized, fully and finally, in the affirmation with which Nima's poetry met. *She'r-e now,* as written by Nima or following his model, was interpreted and analyzed as the supreme esthetic sign for an existing sociopolitical climate governing Iranian society. My purpose in this final chapter is to demonstrate that this was the most significant cultural construct of Iran's postwar literary culture, forged and fostered by the political discourse that surrounded Nima's compositions.

Before I turn to the place of Nima in the context of his time and literary culture, let me recapitulate briefly what I have already argued for: important departures from the tradition of Persian lyrical poetry had preceded Nima's appearance on the literary scene. These had effected significant elemental and systemic changes in the existing norms and conventions of that tradition, as stereotyped by generations of Iranians exposed to European cultures and literatures. Initially, these changes were limited to certain lexical, semantic, or syntactic innovations, introduced around the turn of the century. Textually, these innovations operated as disparate entities within the overall formal and generic categories of the classical tradition. Later generations of poets began to introduce important systemic realignments, eventually subverting the signification system of the existing poetry. Meanwhile, a concomitant movement, espoused through a series of literary debates and contestations, gradually opened up Persian poetry to new and more systemic changes. At the same time, the more the literary culture opened up, the more—and the more freely—it borrowed from Western literary cultures. All this increased the capacity of the existing poetic system to accommodate new demands on poetry. Taken together, the combination of elemental innovations and systemic restructuring subjected the significatory system of the traditional practice of poetry to a profound crisis. Texts previously considered outside the limits, generic or esthetic, of poetry now began to be seen as located well within it.

Naturally, at every stage the effort to recast Persian poetry evoked a specific kind of resistance appropriate to that stage. In general, the more systemic the departure, the more vehement and vociferous the resistance. More than any specific aspect of Nima's innovations or departures, it is this underlying principle which gave a revolutionary character to Nima's modernistic compositions and which led to the most violent reactions the effort at poetic modernization had encountered hitherto. Beyond esthetic consequences, the efforts I have illustrated in previous chapters made the sociality of the discourse on poetry plainly visible. That, in the end, a poem was seen as a kind of social structure, its specific form and function somehow related to existing social conditions, emerged as a result of the constant creativity and sustained contestations of many poets and critics against the notion that inherited poetic conventions were timeless and, therefore, ought to continue regardless of changes in sociopolitical structures. For example, even though Bahar and Raf'at represent two different positions concerning the proper nature and function of a contemporary Persian poetry, they both acknowledge the interrelatedness of poetry and society. Still, they both conceptualize this relationship in terms of the influence of social structures on literary ones. In spite of their different visions, they view literature and society as separate entities with the capacity to influence one another. In fact, throughout the cultural process for which I selected the Bahar-Raf'at debate as the most illustrative instance, poems were envisioned as a category of cultural products that must somehow "reflect" the social condition. Nima's unique and decisive contribution to the process of the emergence of modernity in Persian poetry must be seen ultimately in terms of his attempts to overcome that duality. I hope to demonstrate here that Nima conceptualized poetry as itself an aspect of the social structure mediated through language. Yet, in the zeal to emphasize his part as the sole and ultimate innovator rising up against the tyranny of rhyme and meter in a millennium-old poetic tradition, Nima's efforts to demonstrate the essential oneness of the social structures and poetic products have gone virtually unnoticed.

NIMA YUSHIJ, THEORIST OF POETRY

No figure in the entire history of Persian poetry has surrounded his works with as many observations, explanations, and interpretations of various kinds as has Nima. From the very beginning of his poetic career, Nima wrote prose pieces, mostly epistolary, in an unceasing attempt to explain his poetic vision and to dispel misunderstandings about the bases for his poetic compositions. The volume of his prose writings on poetry exceeds his poetry in size and is certainly no less important in stating the principles on which his vision of poetic modernity rests. Still, no systematic study of Nima's theoretical and practical literary criticism has thus far been undertaken. His staunch supporters and determined detractors have repeatedly flaunted some of his statements without elaborating on their precise meaning or relating them to a vision of esthetic communication. His observations, almost always anchored in specific arguments and observations, have often been perceived as sweeping pronouncements of general validity unrelated to the evolution of his own poetry. It is, therefore, essential that an attempt should be made, within the context of the process of poetic change in Iranian culture, better to understand

Nima's views about the poetic system he was instrumental in bringing about. It is also crucial that we begin to assess the part Nima's critical observations played in giving shape to the reading and writing environment that surrounded his own poetry and which continues to surround Persian poetry close to forty years after his death.

It is not easy to deduce a coherent formulation from Nima's writings on poetry. Much of the difficulty stems from three peculiarities of Nima's theoretical and critical writings as we have them now. In the first place, the language of Nima's criticism, much like the language of his poetry, is grounded in various lexical, syntactical, and grammatical idiosyncrasies which at times obscure the meaning of his statements. This feature of Nima's prose is itself significant: it highlights the problem of using language to express ideas hitherto unarticulated through it. Second, perhaps because he feels himself constantly under attack, Nima weaves replies to detractors, personal reminiscences, and other materials into his writings, giving his prose a digressionary character and a jagged shape. Finally, Nima's prose writings have yet to be submitted to critical editing.[5] Still, a close analysis of the most basic concepts he deals with may enable us to form an idea of his various pronouncements concerning poetry in general as well as the relationship between his theoretical observations and his own poetic practice. Clearly, enhanced familiarity with these notions is crucial to a better understanding of the relationship between modernist Persian poetry and its social context and the social function of poetry in Iranian society of the twentieth century.

In two of his earliest letters written to 'Eshqi, the only poet he considered a modernist in an otherwise tradition-bound cultural milieu, Nima refers to two groups of people among his readers: his detractors and his imitators. He predicts that the former would blame him for having misled 'Eshqi in his innovative poetic work. "But," he adds in what he must have thought of as a compliment, "you know I can't be blamed. You yourself had an immense talent for being misled."[6] At the same time, he describes poetic modernity as an inevitable historical process and likens the opposition to it to wishing to prevent a river from following its course. With reference to his followers, while encouraging them to proceed in spite of the prevailing cultural environment, he cautions them against reducing the complex issues involved to any single aspect. Beyond the warring factions in the elite, he points to the masses of people, changeable and changing, that will eventually choose sides in the constant tension between old and new tendencies. In closing his letter, the twenty-four-year-old poet emits an air of confidence about his own life's project that, although a rarity in the culture, comes to be the hallmark of his writing:

I am quite confident of my success, and see before my eyes that, with white hair and an elderly aspect, I shall be surrounded by the informed children of this country, a people who would look with smiling faces on me and the worth of my service and work.[7]

For the moment, he concludes, he remains willing and able to receive and withstand the disapprobation of his critics, taking heart even in their derisive comments:

It is true that one should not invite reproach. However, people's reproaches and chastisements may sometimes be taken as a criterion by which one can measure the virtues of one's work. New works and rare imaginings often move people to ridicule and disgust.[8]

From the very beginning of his poetic career, then, Nima showed a keen awareness of the specific, yet changing, environment of poetic communication within his culture and of the various responses his work instigated.

From these early writings it is almost impossible to guess at the exact nature of the poetic changes he envisioned. He speaks rather playfully of a secret (*serr*) that distinguishes the old poetry from the new and of a command (*dastur*) coming to the poet from nature (*tabi'at*), emphasizing that poets "must execute the order that nature has given to us."[9] He characterizes the efforts of his predecessors in emulating the mannerisms of Western poetry as "defective in literary expression and far more defective in poetic craftsmanship [*san'at*]"[10] and depicts himself as wishing to guide the people to the truth of poetic industry (*haqiqat-e san'at*). In one essaylike letter, under the heading of "Osul-e Aqideh-ye Man" (The Principles of My View), he envisions a coming together of verse (here, in addition to the Persian word *nazm,* he uses the French word *poétique*) and prose. In the process of such a convergence, verse would come to resemble prose in "poetic images" (*khialat-e sha'eraneh*), while prose would come to resemble poetry in "coherence and simplicity" (*tamamiyyat va sadegi*). He elaborates on this statement by stressing that in defining (*ta'rif*) and describing (*towsif*) the poet's intentions, poetry ought to approximate the "manner of craftsmanship" (*tarz-e sanaye'*) characteristic of prose.[11]

Two tendencies can be gleaned from Nima's early statements, both of which are made more explicit and more pronounced as the poet gains in personal confidence and poetic stature. First, he wishes to move the Persian poetry of his time toward what he considers "natural" as opposed to the artificiality he sees in the traditional poetry and much of the contemporary practice modeled after it. Second, in his effort to achieve that, he considers change in what he calls the *san'at* of Persian poetry crucial to his plan. To my knowledge, Nima did not elaborate on the latter concept in his early writings, but the word means "industry," and its usage in the sense of poetic craft or craftsmanship is rooted in the classical conceptions of poetry, as we will see presently.

The words *tabi'at* (nature) and *san'at*—as well as their various derivatives—occur frequently in Nima's writings on poetry. In the already-cited letter to 'Eshqi, for example, immediately after his reference to the impossibility of diverting a river's course, he challenges his readers to compare his manner of describing a spring scene with the way in which Onsori, a most celebrated poet of the early classical period, treats the same theme. He refers his correspondent to a section of his long poem "*Afsaneh,*" where the coming of the spring has been described in terms almost identical to 'Eshqi's own description of the nightfall in the preamble to "The Three Tableaux." "Read that section," Nima suggests, "and you will see for yourself [the difference between] how I have described the spring . . . and how Onsori has. You will then know which direction one must take in [describing] nature."[12]

In his preface to "*Afsaneh,*" Nima also repeatedly uses the words "nature" and "natural," particularly in reference to presenting poetic dialogues, describing objects, and the manner in which the poet's intention is communicated poetically. He opposes the simplicity and naturalness of his own descriptions to the artificialities (*takallofat*) which have constrained the old poets in expressing their ideas poetically. Essentially, then, "natural" becomes an attribute that abides in Nima's own poetry, be it in the lexical and semantic departures he initiates, in the looser rhyme schemes and metrics he uses, or in the way he modifies the traditional generic and structural boundaries. Before articulating the idea of a new kind of Persian poetry in terms of a set of verifiable differences with, and departures from, the traditional use, Nima ties it to his own practice, whatever the shape it might take. Within the carefully crafted image of a young poet taking on the whole of an established poetic tradition, this simple and deliberate opposition between natural and unnatural poetry comes to the foreground first and foremost as the sum total of the difference between Nima's poetry and that, say, of Onsori, Qa'ani, or Bahar.

The second concept, *san'at,* is more complicated. At times Nima uses it interchangeably with such concepts as *tarz-e khialat* (manner of image-making), *tarz-e ada* (manner of utterance), or *tarz-e ensha'* (manner of composition).[13] Whatever its specific connotations, *san'at* relates invariably to the means and mechanisms by which poems are produced. It may have to do with the figurative structures and manners of poetic expression or with the system or systems underlying these. In either case, it shares a substantial area of its meaning with the word's traditional usage insofar as it refers to the way poetic ideas are manifested in a language that may be called poetic.[14] The emphasis in Nima's writings on the deficiency and artificiality of *sanʿat* in classical Persian poetry thus becomes the most telling index of the specific meaning he attributes to poetic craftsmanship. This quality he calls variously the "manner" or "form" of craftsmanship (*tarz-e sanʿat* or *shekl-e sanʿat*).

Further clarification of the precise sense Nima attaches to *sanʿat* comes only gradually with the appearance of his more substantive critical writings in the 1930s and beyond. Like a general idea taking shape in its author's mind, Nima's notion of craftsmanship in Persian poetry is first tied to his own practice rather than to any deliberate and detailed exposition. Instead of providing lengthy and complicated explanations, Nima constantly holds up his own compositions as illustrating his vision of poetry. When he does set forth guidelines, they are of the most general kind. In a 1929 letter to the young literary scholar Zabihollah Safa, he emphasizes that the literary revolution he has in mind must be implemented by those familiar with foreign literary traditions, with different approaches to criticism, and "particularly with craftsmanship and its philosophy [*sanʿat va falsafeh-ye an*], otherwise known as esthetics [*ʿelm al-jamal*]." He stresses once again that a literary revolution consists not in using or discarding certain words and their poetic meanings (*lafz va maʿni*), but in the forms of poetic craftsmanship (*shekl-e sanʿat*). "That," he concludes, "is what others [before him] have not thought about at all."[15]

It is in *Arzesh-e Ehsasat dar Zendegi-ye Honarpishegan* (The Value of Feelings in the Lives of Artists), first published in installments in 1939, that Nima attempts to formulate his views on poetry in general, and particularly on the relationship between esthetics and the poetic craft.[16] He opens his arguments here by rejecting the traditional notion that artists are excessively sensitive individuals subject to rushes of quick and overpowering emotions. "Artists, too," he writes, "live their ordinary lives like everyone else." He mocks the belief that poets must be placed in nature and surrounded by the beauty of nature in order to write good poetry. This, he says, is like saying that, finally upon reaching his beloved, a painter would start to paint her portrait rather than going through the motions expected of impatient lovers. In that context he states one of his famous remarks: "Before all else comes life."[17] Relating this to his own experiences, he recalls an anecdote about a visit by a friend to his retreat in Mazandaran:

> I remember well the conversation I had with one of my friends. He had come to my remote estate for a visit. We were both seated on the dry trunk

of a wild pine high on a pass. The virgin forests and lovely, enchanting prairies of Kojur were overwhelming. "What new things have you composed?" my friend asked. The answer I gave him was this: "You must first find out what pains I have been subjected to in my life. Right now, in this environment, I have forgotten my art. I wash my body in the water like the birds, dress like the savages, and live."[18]

On the basis of the implied dichotomy between nature and culture, he rejects the notion that individuals can be separated from their environment. Rather, he emphasizes the complex of connections that make up the human existence:

A human being does not exist outside the natural conditions of his corporeal structure, in the likeness of jins and fairies. When we speak of a human being, we refer to a creature who talks, walks, and eats. His senses are in place and subjected to climatic impressions. . . . That definition embraces all that one generation inherits from another, and [all that] concerns the corporeal potentials, including the internal physical functioning of the body and a variety of connections with the outside world. For all these are conditions that, if they did not exist, the individual [human being] would have no meaning. The human creature means the sum total of all the external and internal conditions of his physical existence.

Once we have envisioned an individual human being with all the features and implications [of his or her existence], it would then be easy to place him [or her] before the conditions external to his [or her] life and to measure him [or her] in every respect. Two observations will result from such an assessment. First, that human beings are a collection of all the natural conditions of their material structure; and second, that they are related and tied to groups of humans like themselves. This collectivity, in accordance with the shape of its life—which has come into existence in consequence of historical relations—possesses its specific set of tastes, talents, thoughts, and feelings each with traces of its own, or implications of those traces, for the individuals who constitute the community.[19]

Nima's lifelong emphasis on a collective context for individual human expression has its roots in such comments. Here, he searches for a notion of the conditions of artistic creativity as profoundly determined and directed by those impressions that invade poets from outside their own being and which give rise to specific emotions and thoughts. Time and again, he speaks of the impressions (*ta'assorat*), obsessions or infatuations (*majzubiyyatha*), and connections (*ertebatat*) as conditions that spur artists to creativity. "At times," he says, "an artist's tastes and feelings testify to connections between the individual artist and the outside world, connections which are not understood well because they are complex and have remained unarticulated."[20] As such, he concludes, we cannot say that the feelings communicated through artistic texts are the product of individual desires, just as they do not arise from independent and free experiences and experiments. Far from being a process whereby a free hand shapes a concentration of internal energies into a text, poetic creativity is imaginable to Nima only as a complex, subtle, and elusive set of exchanges between human beings and their social surroundings. It is expressed ultimately within the confining capacities of language, itself a supreme example of collective creativity.

Within this description of artistic creativity, Nima concludes, in another famous statement, that artists are proper and precise representatives of specific and definite historical periods. On that basis, he surveys the evolution of Persian and European literatures through the centuries from the perspective of styles of expression, form, subject matter, genres, and meter. The survey leads to an assessment of the nineteenth-century Literary Return Movement in Persian literature as "a return, motivated by helplessness ['ajz], toward various old schools," at a time when European artists "were whisking toward a brilliant future like shining arrows." Nima fortifies this observation with still another sweeping overview of the rise of modernity in European and American literary cultures. This in turn results in an evaluation of comparable efforts in Iran. He concludes that "altogether, our poetry has demonstrated little enthusiasm and less courage in breaking down the old obstacles.[21] To these obstacles he gives the general name of "classical rules" (*moqarrarat-e kelasik*).

He uses this phrase again in his discussion of the state of critical activity in Iran. The perception of adherence to or deviation from these classical rules, he says, has formed the only basis for criticism in Iranian culture:

> In practice, our criticism tends to impose the idea of deference to the old masters [*qodama*] on young talents [*javanan*]. It advises us to articulate our meanings and intentions—those of human beings living in the twentieth century of the Christian era—in accordance with the tools available to human beings who have lived in the fourth-century Hegira.[22]

Nima's ideas about the need to change the system in which the classical rules are rooted becomes most apparent here. The rules determine the "tools" with which poets are expected to express their ideas and emotions. However, an understanding of the rules governing esthetic (Nima calls it artistic) production in different ages is possible only if we realize that "human beings do not simply take their materials [*mavad*] from nature; they make modifications [*tasarrofat*] in them in accordance with their own inclinations."[23] In the end, it is these modifications which turn a poet's impressions, intentions, or ideas into textual structures. Because of the changing nature of the interaction between poets and their environments, imposing classical rules on contemporary poets is not only constraining but also futile.

In terms of the concept I have been trying to explain, Nima's notion of *san'at* may, I think, be thought of as the totality of those processes which distinguish the literary texts of a particular age not only from the nonliterary texts of the period but also from those of another age. In this sense, the poetic use of *san'at* is set in motion by the poet's desire to communicate poetically the thoughts and feelings related to the conditions of existence of which he or she is a part. Skill in conveying that desire empowers the text to affect the reader. What distinguishes the act of poetic communication predicated on the use of *san'at* from all nonpoetic communication is crystallized in the power of the poem to go beyond informing to persuading, exciting, agitating, fascinating, or otherwise bringing the reader under its spell. Traditional literary criticism in the Islamic world may have given the totality of its constituent elements such names as *sovar-e khial, tasavir-e sha'eraneh,* or *sanaye'-e badi'i.*[24] However, Nima's conception of *san'at*, I contend, may best be conceptualized as the system of the signifying mechanisms which mediate between the theme and the text. In short, *san'at* is conceptualized here as all that poets do to heighten the expressiveness and effectiveness of their works, while conveying their thoughts, feelings, and intentions poetically. If poets are seen as conditioned by their surroundings, if artistic creativity is conceived as the process of making social structures present within textual ones, and if the successful accomplishment of the creative act turns poets into representatives of their own times and cultures, it would then follow that *san'at* consists of the artistic attempt to instill in the textual entity the power to move readers from the act of reading to a perception of the time and culture that has given rise to the poem as text.

This idea, a fairly stable one throughout Nima's writings on poetry, enables us to explore the relationship between *san'at* and the ideal of naturalness in his poetry. We know that Nima thought the expressive devices of classical Persian poetry incapable of producing a poetry that would be judged modern. We also know that his search for alternative expressive devices adequate to the task had to be undertaken in such a way as to restore to Persian poetry the perception of naturalness as an ideal. The effort to combine the two pursuits constructively forms a central part of the modern poet's quest. Toward the end of *Arzesh-e Ehsasat* (The Value of Feelings), Nima expresses the view that, in the end, it is changes in social structures that bring about those sought-for transformations in the feelings and emotions that inform artistic works. Indeed, since specific feelings of all artists result from their specific connections to the social whole, which include their sense of the self as well, "when the tastes and feelings of a specific era come together, the tendency appears [in the arts] to follow in a specific direction."[25] Here Nima comes close to characterizing changes in an individual's feelings as both conditioned and constrained by social life. While acknowledging that the relationship between the poetic text and the individual psyche is as important as that between the text and the society that surrounds it, he comes very close to envisioning the former as a consequence of the latter. Indeed, a cornerstone of Nima's views in *The Value of Feelings* is the inseparability of the two spheres of individual and social existence. On that basis, as we will see presently, he expresses the belief that in each generation poets must renew the quest for the kind of *san'at* or poetic craft that is appropriate to that generation.

Nima's notion that individual poets are inseparable from their social environment and that they therefore wish to bring the poetry of their culture closer to what may appear "natural" remains a more central concern of Nima's than of any other Iranian poet before or since. On the one hand, the belief that the individual psyche is entirely imbued with social meaning leads Nima to conclude that the relationship between products of the mind and their social contexts cannot be arbitrary or mechanical. On the other, regarding language as a social structure, he emphasizes the essential identicality of social and textual structures. Consequently, he begins to espouse a view of poetry which transposes the poetic text, as linguistic phenomenon, onto a social level. As a social phenomenon located between language and what is generally referred to as "reality," poetry has the power even to turn reality into a linguistically constructed and articulated phenomenon. In thus driving against the very notion of language as a mirror, Nima goes beyond the revolutionary-versus-evolutionary discourse of poetic modernity in Iran. Instead, he sees poetic change as a social process in itself. Instead of envisioning the relationship between social structures and poetic ones in terms of the former influencing the latter, or of the latter reflecting the former, he sees society as the living soil, the environment in which the life of poetry originates. This in turn enables him, instead of opposing a poem's form to its content, to envision all esthetic forms as social phenomena. His assertion that, within the history of Persian poetry, the specific esthetic qualities of such genres as the romance and the lyric ought to be viewed as cultural phenomena which

have acquired semantic forms and functions within different social formations must be viewed in this light. In sum, Nima can be said to have arrived
at a vantage point from which the study of the social context is seen as an
integral part of understanding poetic texts.

As a work in theoretical criticism, *The Value of Feelings* is the product of
a period of transition in Iranian literary culture. As a result of almost a century of contact with Western cultures, classical Persian poetics had begun to
wane.[26] However, the old system had yet to be replaced by a set of ideas with
the potential to go beyond the connections which Bahar, Raf'at, or 'Eshqi
had envisioned between social structures and the evolution of literary forms
and techniques. As in his earlier writings, in *The Value of Feelings,* Nima
makes reference to the West only insofar as the statements of various European philosophers, poets, and critics can be used to support his own view of
poetry. While Nima continues to submit the idea of poetry in Iranian culture
to reassessments in the critical writings which follow that work, his earlier
reliance on the authority of Western poets and critics begins to be moderated.
His theoretical pronouncements are made with an assertive self-assurance
considerably more visible as his own poetry begins to command more and
more attention. In one of his many epistolary essays of the 1940s, he even
extends the central notion of the essential identicality of social and literary
structures in two different directions. On the one hand, he proposes that in
a good poem sonic and phonetic elements are also socially determined and
socially significant. On the other, he refers to the relations that obtain between poetic texts and their social context as the reason for the emergence
and eclipse of certain forms and genres under particular historical and social
circumstances. His pronouncements on popular poetic habits and conventions of reading and writing poetry, far from epitomizing the attitude of a
young rebel poet toward an entrenched tradition, come to be inspired more
and more by his desire to stir the culture out of what he sees as a perilous
hesitancy and ambivalence stemming from inertia and ossification. "Perpet-
ual change," he writes, "is the essence of life, and the arts are part of life; and
that is why the arts are concomitant with change."[27]

Nima's second major book-length work of criticism, *Harfha-ye Hamsayeh*
(The Neighbor's Words), belongs to this phase of the poet's career. Written
in the 1940s, the book portrays the poet, now far more confident, attempting
once again to formulate his thoughts on poetry as a phenomenon. It consists
of some seventy letters addressed to an imaginary younger poet. Through
them, Nima advances many of the same arguments he had set forth in *The
Value of Feelings,* and adds new ones. Having experimented with poems that
do not fit into the metric system of classical Persian poetry, he attributes

much of the alleged artificiality of classical Persian poetry to the fact that it has evolved in close association with Iranian music, a system of sonic expression organized entirely differently. He proposes it as a task for himself and his followers to liberate Persian poetry from its links with traditional Iranian music and to instill in their compositions a natural, internal music arising from the interplay between the poem's sonic and semantic systems. He insists that teaching poets to write naturally is as important as teaching readers to read naturally. "Try to write exactly as you see. . . . When you see as the old poets did, and create in violation of what exists outside, your creation appears oblivious to life and nature."[28]

Returning once again to the central theme of *san'at,* he describes classical Persian poetry's *tarz-e san'at* (manner of craftsmanship) as inherently inconsistent. He illustrates this internal inconsistency in a rather playful manner. The poet imagines the shape of his beloved's long tresses, curved at the end, as resembling that of polo sticks (*chowgan*). Next, he fancies the color of her cheeks as resembling that of the petals on judas-tree blossoms (*arghavan*). Then, in a poem addressed to the beloved, he juxtaposes the two separately conceived resemblances: "You strike the judas flower with your polo stick [*chowgan zani bar arghavan*]." This, Nima mocks, is the classical poet's manner of expressing the pleasing sight of the beloved's curved tresses resting on her rosy cheeks. In this way, contemporary traditionalist poets who follow the inherited system of signification wherein fixed analogies have been developed for various parts of the beloved's body, end up producing a phrase that is "not only unreal and unnatural, but laughably devoid of sense."[29]

Let me pause for a brief elaboration of what I think underlies Nima's criticism here. As we have seen, Nima attributes much of the artificiality of Persian poetry of former times to its system of expressive devices. What is unreal, unnatural, and nonsensical in the image he cites is neither the resemblance in color of the beloved's cheeks to the judas flower nor the resemblance in shape of her tresses to the polo stick. Rather, the unrelatedness of the two images makes their juxtaposition ridiculous. Time and again, Nima upbraids the tendency of the lyrical tradition to assimilate autonomously conceived figures of speech into a system of image-making wherein various elements do not contribute to a single overall effect. Here, as elsewhere, the fixities of separately conceived images in relation to the totality of a sense-making system constitute the object of Nima's criticism. In the process of being handed down through the poetic tradition, diverse analogies have come to be combined, juxtaposed or otherwise related to each other indiscriminately. In the work of contemporary traditionalists, they collide with one another, giving rise to a textual space wherein a number of discordant elements compete for attention. Nima's criticism seems to suggest that the task of the modern poet is to replace the collision of elements with one where individual elements collude to create easily recognizable perceptions with the potential to produce real—or realistic—emotions. Because he works toward a comprehensive notion of relevance, he advocates a systemic break with the images repeated endlessly in Persian poetry. In its place, he envisions constant, immediate contact with the multitude of visible, audible, and palpable likenesses, analogies, and allusions which surround the person of the poet.

Nima's vision of a natural poetry is thus directly linked to the desire to move away from the linguistic and esthetic fixities of the classical tradition. The system of expressive devices poets should adopt is imagined as natural essentially because of the relative fluidity of its constituent elements. In fact, in many of the letters Nima writes to younger poets toward the end of his life, he uses the concept of *san'at* as a way of empowering words to express the content of the poet's own imagination. To make metaphors and similes is, in his mature view, to give power to the poet's thoughts. This point marks the distance Nima has come, both in refining and clarifying his earlier views and in elucidating what he had previously called the secrets of his approach: a human being can be called a poet—or an artist—only to the extent that he or she seeks and finds appropriate linguistic instruments for the expression of his or her thoughts and emotions in a naturally beautiful way.[30]

The system of poetic signification Nima devised was not uniform in its degree of departure from the classical system or from the traditional practice based on it. The metric system he adopted in approximately half of his poems, mostly written in the last two decades of his life, differed little from that evolved through the classical tradition.[31] The single most important modification he made in that system was to discard the uniform number of feet which had been a feature of classical Persian poetry almost from the beginning. The exaggerated prominence this aspect of Nima's innovations has achieved stems not so much from the poet's own estimation of its importance as from the fact that it broke the most obvious barrier in the popular perception of the difference between old and new Persian poetry.

Similarly, Nima's innovations in rhyme have been overestimated as an aspect of his vision of a new poetry. As we have seen in the writings of the nineteenth-century reformists, the monotonous regularity with which rhyme was employed in the works of classical Persian poets had made this aspect of the traditional practice a favorite target.[32] As a stylistic device signaling poeticity, the use of rhyme had spilled over into Persian prose as well. The practice of rhyming prose reached its culmination with Sa'di in *Golestan*. It remained an aspect of the literary prose well into the nineteenth century, as evidenced by Qa'ani's imitation of Sa'di's style in *Parishan*.³³ Before Nima, a few Iranian poets had attempted to compose unrhymed poems in imitation of the free-verse style current in Europe. 'Eshqi had attempted to redefine the concept of rhyme in a way that would align it with the auditory function rather than a visual aspect seen through the alphabet.³⁴

However, the task of redefining the function of rhyme within a general poetic scheme had been left largely to Nima. Still, Nima's decisive contribution to the emergence of a new Persian poetry and a new discourse accompanying it resides neither in his formal innovations nor in his casting off the traditional generic poetic categories. Rather, Nima's pivotal position in the process of poetic modernity in Iran rests on a lifelong feature of his theory and practice: his insistence on the essential unity of the poetic text and its social context and the changing nature of that context. This imbued his poetry with the same sense of historicity which pervades his theoretical observations on the nature of poetry and poetic expression and on an understanding of the meaning and mission of the new Persian poetry.

Gradually, Nima's theoretical observations and poetic practice began to merge into a single discourse, where the former corroborated and clarified the latter, while the latter upheld and illustrated the former. The pervading presence of the social structure in and through the literary text eventually became the defining characteristic of modernism in Persian poetry in the minds of Nima's immediate readers, a social group willing to experiment with the ideas spread throughout Nima's writings. As we will see shortly, this group began to conceive of the act of interpretation, applied to Nima's—and Nimaic—poetry, as a process of guiding the poetic utterance toward the proper social domain in which the poem, however privately conceived, would release its true meaning. In numerous writings, Nima's followers and admirers used a single hermeneutic pattern: various poetic signifiers were assigned signifieds relevant on the sociopolitical plane. Diverse elliptical allusions were interpreted in such a way as to supply the poem with sociopolitical content. That in doing so, they were in fact giving a specific place to the new poetry within the spectrum of political ideologies present in contemporary Iranian society or psyche served their purpose very well indeed, as we will see. Nima's poems, particularly those that were perceived as corroborating his theoretical observations in *The Value of Feelings* and subsequent writings, began to be read not so much as esthetic structures but as the poetic expressions of a recognizable sociopolitical position. When the unquestionable authority of the poet himself confirmed the interpretation or when interpreters were authorities in their own right, those perceptions bestowed ultimate validity on the reading. The rather complex issue of each poem's meaning, or of the interpretive process, was settled in a relatively exclusive writing and reading environment. Out of the flux of nearly a century of determined effort at esthetic modernity, a new interpretive community was finally born in Iran around the middle of the twentieth century.

NIGHT AND DAY: A READING OF NIMA'S "FILTHY HOPE"

A remarkable early instance of the new interpretive approach occurs in a preface by a little-known critic to a little-known poem of Nima's entitled "Omid-e Palid" (Filthy Hope). First published in 1943, the poem features a desperate struggle by a dying "night" to prevent the dawning of its opposite, "day." In spite of its certain fate, "the night" refuses to give up what the poem calls in its last line "the hope of the dawn's demise" (*ommid-e zaval-e sobhgah*). This poem, I contend, may be viewed as a case study of Nima's vision of the essential identicality of social and poetic structures. But what I hope to demonstrate here is the manner in which the poem's abstract allusions were interpreted in terms of a specific and concrete social situation. Through that interpretation, as we will see, the critic attempts to guide the poem's readers toward a reading far more determinate than the text of the poem can support or sustain. When such readings are confirmed by the authority of the poet, as was the case here, the resulting perceptions help in the gradual emergence, in the society, of a reading climate wherein certain poems, possessing specific textual properties, are interpreted on the basis of specific equivocations. Textually, these equivocations may be unsupportable. Still, they do in actuality accompany poetic texts through diverse reading processes and regulate their meaning as long as the interpretive community continues to exist. What is more, the spillover effect begins to further shape future interpretations, eventually giving rise to a fairly complete semiotic environment.

First, I present passages from Nima's "Filthy Hope," followed by my literal translation of each. As the poem opens, the speaker presents the song of the roosters who herald the approach of the dawn:

> Dar nahieh-ye sahar khorusan
> inguneh be raghm-e tiregi mikhanand
> ay amad sobh-e rowshan az dar
> bogshudeh beh rang-e khun-e khod par
> sowdagarha-ye shab gorizan
> bar markab-e tiregi neshasteh
> darand ze rah-e dur mi-ayand.[35]

(In the region of the dawn, roosters
are singing thus, despite the darkness:
"Hey! bright morning has arrived through the gate,
having opened it wings, the color of its blood.
Seated on horses of darkness,
the night's traders are fleeing,
they are now coming from afar.)

The poem next depicts sparks rising from "the world's smoky head" (*kalleh-ye basteh-dud-e donya*) and "veils that block the view." As the roosters' songs strike the veils they are torn asunder, a sight which encourages the roosters to sing even louder. The roosters now proclaim the approach of the morning as if it were the herald of a new world order:

Ay amad sobh khandeh bar lab
bar bad deh-e setizeh-ye shab
az ham gosal-e fesaneh-ye howl
payvand-neh-e qatar-e ayyam
ta bar sar-e in ghobar-e jonbandeh
bonyan-e degar konad
ta dar del-e in setizeh-ju tufan
tufan-e degar konad
ay amad sobh chost o chalak
ba raqs-e latif-e ghermeziha-sh
az qolleh-ye kuhha-ye ghamnak
az gusheh-ye dashtha-ye bas dur
ay amad sobh ta keh az khak
andudeh-ye tiregi konad pak
v-aludeh-ye tiregi beshuyad
asudeh parandeh-i zanad par.[36]

(Hey! morning is approaching, smile upon its lips,
destroyer of the night's challenge,
unraveler of the myth of fear,
connector of the train of days,
to lay a new foundation
upon this revolving mass of dust,
to raise another storm
in the heart of this defiant storm.
Hey! morning is approaching, fast and fleet-footed
with the delicate dance of reddish colors

from atop sullen peaks
from the corners of far away steppes.
Hey, morning is approaching, to wipe off
the darkness accumulated on the face of the earth,
to wash clean those contaminated by the darkness,
so a bird may open its wings in peace.)

Following this proclamation, the poem returns once again to a direct observation of the daybreak and an account of the night's thoughts and feelings on its own situation. The night is sad, crying, mournful, affected by the song of the roosters as one would be by "the news of the death of loved ones" (*khabar-e marg-e 'azizan*). Bewildered, broken, afraid of the thought of imminent flights, it eventually clings on the body of the dawn, trying to prevent particles of darkness from fleeing it, hoping in this way to keep the darkness attached to the body of the day from leaving it. The night's battle against the birth of the day forms much of the poem's motive force, ending in a desperate attempt on its part to assemble a new, artificial night out of the remnants of darkness that desert the body of the morning as murky points. The poem ends with the doleful night taking stock of a situation we know to be beyond its hope:

Mibal'ad har koja bebinad
andisheh-ye mardomi beh rahi-st dorost
v-andar deleshan omid mi-afzayad
mipayad
mipayad
ta hichkeh bar rah mo'in nayad
az zir-e sereshk-e sard-e cherkash
bar rahgozaran
mandeh negaran
misanjad rowshan o siah ra
miparvarad u beh del
ommid-e zaval-e sobhgah ra.[37]

(It devours, wherever it sees,
the thoughts of the people treading the right path
as hope increases in their hearts.
It watches
and watches,
hoping no one would set out along the path.
It stands eyeing the passers-by

from beneath its cold, slimy tears.
it gages the bright and black,
in its heart it nurtures
the hope of the dawn's demise.)

The passages and translations above do not reflect accurately the immediately perceptible novelty of Nima's poem. The following is a brief outline of some of the major ways in which the poem must have registered its newness in the eyes and minds of its original readers. As a poem, "Filthy Hope" lies outside the system of formal properties associated with poetry in the classical Persian tradition. Its use of rhyme accords with Nima's notion of the rhyme as keyed to the completion of a specific idea rather than as a cap for a fixed metric quantity. Its meter, too, while adhering to the basic units in the ʿaruz system, presents that measure in varying numbers, thus giving rise to lines of unequal length and metric value. These apparent features, while relatively unimportant in terms of the argument I present throughout this book, nonetheless constituted the most easily perceptible aspects of the poem's break with the tradition. The poem's imagery defies classification in terms available to classical Persian poetry. While the struggle between night and day is not without precedence in Persian poetry, its depiction in this particular way, and in such an expanded manner, is unprecedented. I need not dwell on this point since the reading I present as part of the history of the poem's reception addresses the issue at some length. All this gave the poem the potential to be viewed as a composition bound by rules that had yet to be articulated to aid the readers in understanding its message. The interpretation presented here was one such reading.

The poem was first published in 1943 in *Nameh-ye Mardom,* a weekly newspaper belonging to the pro-Soviet Tudeh Party of Iran. It was prefaced by a prose piece by Ehsan Tabari, a young party ideologue. Following some general remarks concerning the nature of innovation in Persian poetry, Tabari turns approvingly to Nima's poetry in general, recommending it as the true poetry of the modern times. About the poem in question he writes:

As for the following piece, which is called "Filthy Hope," it is a symbolic [*sambolik*] piece, that is to say, one based on allusions [*kenayeh-i*]. Morning [*sobh*] is an allusion to the dawning of a new society [*yek ejtemaʿ-e jadid*] and of a novel order for living [*yek nezam-e hayati-ye novin*]. Night is [an allusion to] reaction [*ertejaʿ*], backwardness [ʿaqab-mandegi], ignorance [*jahl*], and corruption [*fesad*] of the present society. Night appears in the shape of a demon [*div*] hidden in stinking swamps, fearful of the dawning of the day. It hangs itself from the ropes of darkness and sucks the light of the morning, trying to prevent it from dawning. But its filthy hope is in vain, and morning will shine.[38]

In this interpretation, the poem's main personages are equated with entities which find their immediate meaning in the political discourse of post-World War II Iran. As context for the poem, Tabari's preface bestows specific meanings on entities that, in the poem's own wording, may be subject to diverse interpretations. If *Nameh-ye Mardom* were not known as a forum for a pro-Soviet political ideology and if Tabari were not known as one of the Tudeh Party's ideologues, phrases like "the new social order" and "a novel order for living" would not necessarily convey the notion of Soviet-style communism. In the poem itself, in other words, the meaning of such entities as "night" and "darkness" or "morning" and "light" function in a more abstract and more diffuse way without the interpretation offered in the preface than with it. Through the equivocations offered above, the poem's meaning is related directly to the poet's political ideology rather than to a poetic statement about an observed phenomenon—that is, the turning of night into day. In other words, Tabari initiates a reading process which focuses on one among many of the poem's potential—and theoretically equally valid—readings. What is more, he doesn't just declare it a valid reading, but the "correct" one.

That task is achieved in a two-step process of reduction. First, by equating "morning" with "the dawning of a new society," Tabari has transferred the meaning of the word from a temporal concept observable in the phenomenal world to a concept in the world of sociopolitical formations. Even so, as the opposite of the old society, the term "new society" can suggest any number of social systems to which it may be applied. It is only in light of the reader's knowledge of the social context surrounding the poem and the commentary—the journal's ideology and the critic's political affiliation, for instance—that a phrase like "the present-day society" (*ejtema'-e konuni*) comes to mean the sociopolitical order present at the time of the poem's composition in a country called Iran. By the same token, "the novel order" comes to signify Soviet-style socialism. Stated differently, the context within which the poem and the commentary appear, including the political ideology with which the commentator and the newspaper are associated, imparts a kind of temporal and ideological specificity to these phrases and to the poem in general which would otherwise be absent.

Let us speculate a moment on how the poem may have been read if it had appeared without Tabari's comments or in a context less openly aligned with a specific political ideology. Naturally, the poem would still not come to its readers unconstrained. First of all, in Iranian society in the 1940s, the tendency to express political opinion in and through poetry was an obvious part of the esthetic process.[39] Second, even a limited knowledge of Nima's previous poetic performances would allow such a reading of "Filthy Hope" in light of such poems as *"Khanevadeh-ye Sarbaz"* (The Soldier's Family), *"Qoqnis"* (The Phoenix) and *"Vai bar Man"* (Woe and Wellaway). All of these contain the potential to be read as expressions of Nima's attitude toward the existing political system in his country of his own political convictions. More specifically, his effective use of the opposition between night and day in such previous poems as *"Ay Shab"* (O Night) and *"Anduhnak Shab"* (Sorrow-Laden Night) can be cited as evidence for the validity of a political reading of "Filthy Hope."[40] Finally, the poem's basic opposition between day and night evokes memories of such poems as Dehkhoda's "Remember . . ." and the many other compositions which have since employed similar signifying strategies. In contributing to a climate of writing and reading oriented in a specific, socially defined direction, such works act as pre-texts for the kind of reading Tabari suggests for "Filthy Hope."

A more important connection in this regard operates through the various images depicted in the poem and the lexical, metaphoric, and metonymic references used in the political writings of contemporary Iranian socialists. The political discourse of the Iranian left in the 1940s disseminated certain images through newspaper editorials, political pamphlets, and party propaganda. These included certain analogies such as a socialist victory being "as inevitable as tomorrow's rising sun" or the notion that the passage of time would bring with it "the death of capitalism" and "the dawning of socialism." Iran was often depicted as part of "a global system of exploitation" trying, even on its deathbed, to prevent "the birth of a new egalitarian world order," and Iranian intellectuals were asked to "choose sides" in the struggle.[41] In collusion, such images can be seen as marking the borders of the system of decoding within which Nima's "symbolic allusions" release their meaning. Even if the newspaper and Tabari had not been identified with a particular political party then, the poem could still have been interpreted as an expression of the poet's political views. Still, Tabari's reading is striking in that it illustrates so clearly the boundaries of purposeful determinate readings.

To continue speculating a moment longer, two sets of questions can be posed at this point with regard to the actual hermeneutic activity at work here. First, what gave Tabari the idea that his equivocations were in fact correct, that Nima did indeed mean reaction, backwardness, corruption, and ignorance when he portrayed the figure of "night" and a new social order when he depicted "day"? Second, what consequences are likely to arise once

such interpretations gain currency? Tabari's claim to "correctness" rests ultimately on his perception of the total semantic, syntactical, and lexical structures present in the poem. The reading experience may confirm or undermine
observations imposed externally on a literary text by drawing the reader's
attention to those observations or diverting it away from them. A test of the
validity of Tabari's reading, in other words, necessitates a close reading of the
poem itself from inside the reading conditions described above.

To illustrate, the poem opens with a kind of transference crucial to the
poem's mechanisms of signification and communication. The initial phrase,
dar nahieh-ye sahar (in the region of the dawn), depicts the dawn (a temporal
entity) in terms of a region (a spatial entity). This conveys an impression of
the poem as a textual locus wherein concepts traffic relatively freely between
temporal and spatial dimensions. The intermingling of the two dimensions,
in other words, prepares readers for conceptualizing the opposition between
night and day as transferable to planes other than the temporal. The phrase
"region of the dawn" thus becomes an initial sign of a manner of encoding
poetic messages and constitutes the first step toward the acceptance of the
possibility that, in depicting night and day, the poet may be alluding to the
present society and its opposite. At the same time, the phrase "despite the
darkness" places the roosters' activity in an initial contrast to their surroundings. The speaker seems to be saying that, because they are situated in—or
belong to—the region of the dawn, the roosters are singing of the approach
of dawn, this despite the darkness that surrounds them. The point reveals its
full significance where roosters come collectively to be associated with the
poem's guiding voice, the poet himself.

As the content of the roosters' song is reported, "the bright morning" is
described as a bird with blood-colored wings in flight. As a poetic description,
the adverbial clause "having opened its wings, the color of its blood" contains
at least two noteworthy features, one operating on a general plane, the other
on a more specific and more significant one. First, the imagery of morning
as a bird on the eastern horizon has no established precedent in Persian
poetry.[42] Basing the analogy on the linguistic node established through the
verb "to come" (*amadan*), Nima has constructed a new poetic sign. In Persian, this verb can be applied to birds and animals as well as to morning and
night, a fact which makes it possible for the poet to formulate the approach
of morning (the lighting up of the sky, the reddened horizon) in terms of the
flight of a red-winged bird. Second, the sky of the dawn, reddened by the
rising sun's rays, is described in terms of the color of the bird's (morning's)
own blood. The bird, having extended its wings in flight, reveals a color
which is that of its blood. As an attribute of the bird's wings, the redness

comes to signify several interdependent concepts. The red/blood node constitutes the center of this multiple signification. The redness of the approaching morning may connote revolution, especially a communist revolution. The designation has already been introduced into Persian poetry through a variety of usages, most notably 'Eshqi's depiction of the banner of revolt in "The Three Tableaux," already discussed in chapter 5. The idea of red as the color of blood in turn establishes the association between revolutions and the spilling of human blood. More specifically, in Persian one way of describing sincerity, honesty, or integrity is through the term *yekrangi* (being of one color) or its adjective *yekrang* (being of, or displaying, a single color). These terms describe one whose insides and outsides are the same. In the bird described here, the sameness of outsides (wings) and insides (blood) colors imply the quality of sincerity. Thus, the attributes accrued to the nameless bird echo, in addition to sincerity, the depth of belief in a revolutionary cause and sincere devotion to it. However it may be visualized, the bird that is morning is not only a benign bird of bright appearance but also the true herald of an approaching "red" revolution.

The lines that follow this passage describe the dawn's—or morning's—antagonist. The poem, after all, is not so much about the coming of the morning as about the night's "filthy hope" of preventing that outcome. This is communicated initially through the image of "the night's traders" seated "on mounts of darkness" (*sowdagarha-ye shab . . . / bar markab-e tiregi neshasteh*), fleeing the nearing dawn. The phrase "the night's traders" is ambiguous in the way the two components inside it relate to each other (the *ezafeh* combination in Persian, usually rendered into English with the help of the possessive " 's" or the preposition "of"). "Night" may be envisioned as the commodity the "traders" trade or as the time at which they do their trading. The traders may also be thought of as belonging to or coming from the realm of the night. All these meanings may be imagined as present in the phrase, depending on the nature of the grammatical relationship between the words "traders" (*sowdagarha*) and "night" (*shab*). What the reader learns about them is that these "traders of the night" (singularized and made more specific later in the poem as "the trader of the night") would like to make the night even blacker than it is, that they wish to contaminate the night with their breaths, and that they nurture in their hearts "the hope of the dawn's demise." That is why they cling to the carcass of darkness, suck "the light of the morning" out of dawn's body, and swallow the thoughts of the people who have begun to tread along the path.

This catalogue of attributes, inclinations, and actions leaves no doubt about the evil nature and bad intentions of these creatures. The "traders of the night" are engaged in an activity that is at once filthy and futile. To buttress that impression, at the poem's close we are presented once again with an image of "the trader of the night" as it is trying to assemble an artificial night. First it "arranges many dots of darkness one next to another," then it clings to the body of the dawn "so that darkness would not leave its body," and finally it sucks fragments of light from the bright smiling day "to perpetuate this black night." Carefully crafted images of repulsive creatures engaged in impossible and unnatural acts abound in Nima's political poems. Typically, in such compositions, the poet fosters relationships among his images that intensify the poem's intrareferential and introspective aspects. The text, in such cases, marks its personages and entities internally, without any need for external validation. Taken together, the poems provide a close-knit tapestry of interrelated themes and images, each of which makes the others meaningful. The impression thus produced in the reader is one of an ongoing battle between entities which are rendered determinate and specific by interpretations such as we have seen here.

Without interpretations such as Tabari's preface contains, in other words, the monstrous creature called "the trader of the night" would not be identified with any political structure within Iran. Nor would the image of a hopeful people treading along the path leading to a red dawn mean what it does in light of his interpretation. While building on the basic opposition of night and dawn, the poem does not ask its readers to bring to the reading experience any of the conventional attributes of the actors involved. On the contrary, it demands that they relate concepts like "hope," "heart," "black," "bright," to the interplay of inferences manufactured by the text itself and bounded by the discourse that surrounds it. As "the trader of the night" reveals its own nature through line after line, the poem draws its readers into a poetic space where they experience actions and partake of the speaker's point of view through the operations of the text itself. Readers thus brought within the orbit of the poem's vision do not depend on any previously marked poetic codes and conventions for an understanding of the poem. Nima's success in severing the reader from a traditionally grounded reading in turn enables the poet to create a poetic artifact which remains self-sufficient in its internal functions.

To succeed, the strategy would have to bring about complete coordination between the poet's implications and readers' inferences. In "Filthy Hope," for instance, the concluding passage contains two kinds of "hopes" and "hearts," each lined up against the other. The first belongs to the people along the path, the second to "the trader of the night." In the people's hearts hope is said to be "increasing" (*mi-afzayad*). The conniving, calculating monster, conversely, is portrayed as squatting pensively, nurturing (*mi-parv-arad*) the "filthy hope" of dawn's demise in its heart. Obviously, the image of a people on the march implies a destination and a purpose. We know that their march will lead to the land of the dawn. Still, the growth of hope in the people's hearts is described intransitively. The motion itself seems to fill them with hope, naturally and progressively. The reverse is true in the case of the scheming monster. The kind of hope it is nurturing in its heart is neither its nor aimed at itself. Rather, it is directed at the dawn. It is indeed the loss of hope in the people's hearts that would increase the monster's hope. To the extent to which that eventuality is predicated on the unnatural outcome of the dawn failing to arrive, the poem comes to embrace the speaker's vision of the monster's hope not just as filthy, but more importantly as false. Having the phenomenal opposition between night and day in mind, readers would not need any prior notion of hope or despair handed down through traditional poetic usages. In fact, as the title suggests, hope itself can be inscribed positively or negatively.

With descriptions of this sort, the poem's strategy of signification begins to reveal itself. The reading experience in a poem like "Filthy Hope" is guided and shaped not so much by any interaction between the text and the poetic tradition, but by the way the text aligns its entities internally. While relying on resources present in the Persian language, Nima attempts, as much as possible, to steer free of fixed traditional poetic designations, basing the process of signification on those relations that obtain between the phenomenal world and the political discourses present in his society. He invents and marks his poetic signs and expressive devices, describing them deliberately in terms virtually without any previous poetic associations. Ultimately, Nima's strategy of signification allows the reading experience to be guided throughout by the moral implications of the actions that take place within the text. Here as elsewhere, Nima's strategy emphasizes the difference between his poetry and his readers' prior poetic perceptions. This difference in turn reveals a specifically historical purpose, particularly when it begins to be interpreted as a sign of poetic modernity. Rather than depending on a series of reassuring linkages with the poetic tradition, modern Persian poetry involves a conscious endeavor to construct poetic images of the poet's own making. More than any other critic in his time or since, Nima himself was aware that his claim to poetic modernity rested not on his themes and style, but on his individual, even idiosyncratic manner of encoding ideas in images.

In assessing such discursive strategies from a historical perspective, we must take note of similar experiments of previous generations. Dehkhoda's depiction of "the night" as a dark being engaged in black deeds may come to mind most readily. However, perhaps even more crucial were the kinds of reversals and departures we saw in the poetry of the generation immediately preceding Nima. Together, these breaks from the established tradition of lyrical expression in Persian poetry began to undermine the validity of conventional approaches to poetic signification. In Nima's poetry, of course, elemental and systemic innovations become the key to interpretation in a way that they are not in the works of poets like Dehkhoda or 'Eshqi. Poets like Dehkhoda and 'Eshqi employ and transform the tradition at one and the same time, affirming aspects of its relevance while violating or negating others. Building on that basis, Nima brought about a kind of poetic significance virtually independent of all extratextual poetic linkages. It is largely for this reason that his poetry has been perceived so widely as unprecedented and genuinely new, its links with previous efforts in the same direction virtually unrecognized. In his hands, the new begins to become a tradition in its own right, capable of future emulations, modifications, or negations.

To return for a moment to the impact of Tabari's interpretive act, we can speculate that the original readers of "Filthy Hope," reading first Tabari's preface and then Nima's poem (as the newspaper must have intended), came away with the impression that the poem contains a message about the inevitability of a socialist revolution in Iran and that it does indeed communicate that message in a way different from the way Persian poems have traditionally conveyed their meaning. The validity of the type of hermeneutic activity involved here, in other words, can be said to be fairly evident, even without the weight of the poet's authority. In this instance, however, by placing his seal of approval on the interpretation provided by the young party ideologue, Nima did in fact sanction further determinate readings of his political poems and perhaps of other similar texts produced by those who had begun to write poetry in his manner. In a letter to Tabari, Nima expressed his appreciation for the interpretation the latter had offered: "I cannot leave it unsaid," he observed, "how much you have earned my trust in your judgment."[43] I cannot think of a more effective confirmation than such an authorial nod to validate the relevance of an interpretation. As readers begin to form an opinion about texts that lay a claim, even through their appearance, to differentness, interpretive acts of the kind I have cited here, especially when they are blessed by the supreme authority of the text's creator, play a crucial part in the formation of a semiotic atmosphere wherein esthetic texts communicate specific relevances to specific groups of readers.

In discussing poetic change in a culture, it is crucial to chronicle the emergence of new relevances through individual hermeneutic acts. Interpretations of the kind I have examined here often give wide currency to collective

perceptions of the way poems are to be read. They also constitute the most
readily available source of knowledge about the system of signification underlying a specific corpus of texts as distinguished from all others present in a
culture, whether produced by a previous generation or by a different social
group. In the case of Iranian poetry of the 1940s and beyond, those others
consisted primarily of two groups of poems: first, contemporary poems characterized by their apparent adherence to the visible and audible characteristics
of classical poetry; second, the classical canon of Persian lyrics, including
qasidas, ghazals, roba'is, and the like. Consequently, all contemporary practice that followed the classical models, as well as much of classical Persian
poetry, was automatically viewed, at least initially, as containing meanings
other than those judged to be relevant. Interestingly, these included many
poems written by Nima himself. To this day, traditional literary criticism in
Iran tends to regard departure from classical poetic rules and conventions as
a prerequisite for striving toward relevance, a concept which it at times
equates with the expression of political ideas through poems. Through a
chain of associations, poetic modernity is thought to express itself through
devotion to specific, socially definable political positions. Nor is there anything surprising in the widespread tendency to take the words of a poet, or
observations of those considered authorities in such matters, as the final arbiter of meaning. Attribution of relevance to poetic texts is indeed a collective
social process in which poets, critics, and readers participate.

The reception process outlined above, which we may view as an attempt
at esthetic legitimation, reaches its culmination when a sufficiently wide circle
of readers is persuaded to assign similarly conceived specific meanings to a
definable group of esthetic texts. This end is achieved most commonly
through increasingly authoritative acts of interpretation which surround such
texts within a specific social context.[44] In the case of Nima's poetry, within a
decade after his death in 1960, a dauntingly large number of perceptive and
purposeful essays were written to serve that end. As the final part of this study
of poetic change, I examine two such attempts to explicate Nima's approach
to poetic modernity to Iranian readers increasingly curious about the new
esthetic phenomenon called *she'r-e now.* These are Siavosh Kasra'i's 1965 essay
entitled "Parvazi dar Hava-ye 'Morgh-e Amin'" (A Flight in the Sphere of
"The Amen Bird") and Mehdi Akhavan-Saless's chapter on Nima's "Kar-e
Shab-Pa" (The Night Watchman's Work), published in a book entitled
Bed'atha va Badaye'-e Nima (Nima's Innovations and Novelties). Understanding the social process by which a relatively limited number of Nima's
poems were promoted, not simply as a peculiar species of twentieth-century

Persian poetry but as modern Persian poetry par excellence, is thus envisioned as the final link in a study of the process of poetic change in modern Iran.

In selecting these particular interpretive essays from among a multitude of similar writings, I have three objectives in mind. First, I have selected two of the earliest and best-known commentaries written on Nima's poems by individuals with legitimate claims to Nima's poetic mantle. This will place me in a better position to argue that when attempts at esthetic legitimation are undertaken by individuals considered authoritative, they tend to be more persuasive and therefore have a better chance to enlarge the interpretive community. Second, by concentrating on a single poem each, the two essays I have chosen allow us to continue to interpret their assertions through our own concurrent examination of the texts under scrutiny. This strategy will permit me to test the commentaries against the texts they address, thus arriving at a judgment about the validity or relevance of the observations as they relate to the poems in question. Finally, I have opted for these particular essays because they offer the texts they interpret to future poets as models worthy of emulation. This will help us maintain our focus on the process of poetic change without much need for greater elaboration. As in the previous case, I offer my discussion of the essays following an examination of the poems they address.

A "MYTHICAL" BIRD: A READING OF NIMA'S "THE AMEN BIRD"

"*Morgh-e Amin*" (The Amen Bird), one of Nima's most famous poems, was written in 1952.[45] It features a bird with no known identity in Persian poetry or mythology, either as a real animal or a mythical creature. True to his habit of placing himself in his poems, often through the figure of a bird,[46] Nima may have made up the bird's name by inverting the letters of his own pen name, thus: Nima → Amin. Following a descriptive preamble consisting of five stanzas, the poem features a dialogue in the rain between the bird and the "people" (*mardom*) or the "masses" (*khalq*). Through the dialogue the people relate their plight to the bird, and the bird attempts to soothe and console them by confirming their desire for a different future. Each time the bird and the people complete an exchange expressing their common desire for a happy future different from the present, the poem features the chant of "Amen" (*Amin* in Persian). This underscores the oneness of the people's wishes and the bird's vision. In the end, the chant becomes so loud and powerful as to crack what the poem calls "the wall of the daybreak" (*divar-e sahar-gahan*). At that, the amen bird flies away, the song of a rooster is heard from afar, and night turns into day.

The poem opens with a description of the seasoned bird:

> Morgh-e amin dard-aludi-st k-avareh bemandeh
> rafteh ta an su-ye in bidad-khaneh
> bazgashteh reghbatash digar ze ranjuri nah su-ye ab o daneh.
> nowbat-e ruz-e goshayesh ra
> dar pay-e chareh bemandeh.[47]

> (The amen bird is a pained soul who has remained a vagrant.
> He has traveled to the farthest end of this house of injustice,
> has returned, no longer desiring water or grain, because of his sufferings.
> Now he awaits
> the day of opening.)

In the passages that follow, the bird is described as one who throughout his life has been privy to many stories about the people's pains and sufferings. For his part, acting as a messenger of bitter experiences, the bird has related these stories to others. At the same time, he has consoled them, and has kept hope alive by heralding sure victory in the not too distant future. The bird has thus brought people together in a bond of sympathetic awareness and hopeful anticipation of what the opening passage calls "the day of opening" (*ruz-e goshayesh*). As he continues his efforts to lessen the gravity of the people's feelings of suffering and hopelessness, the bird himself turns into a living sign of the certainty of the people's triumph as he soothes and sustains the struggle by building "hidden bridges of words" among them. Because of all these qualities, the people, who have come to trust the bird, welcome him on their rooftops and relate stories of their tribulations to this "wakeful kin" (*mahram-e hoshyar*).

The dialogues that the bird holds with the people occur at night and in the rain. Metaphorically, the sprinkling raindrops come to parallel the disparate voices which express individual desires for an end to pain and suffering, but fail to amount to collective action:

> Zir-e baran-e nava-ha'i keh miguyand:
> bad ranj-e narava-ye khalq ra payan
> (va beh ranj-e narava-ye khalq har lahzeh mi-afzayad)
> . . . .
> morgh-e amin ra zaban ba dard-e mardom migoshayad[48]

> (In the rain of voices that say,
> "may the unjust sufferings of the masses come to an end!"

—while the unjust sufferings of the masses increase by the moment—
the Amen Bird begins to speak of the people's pain.)

In such an atmosphere, the people address the bird and ask him to bring
them salvation (*rastegari*), and to show them the path to an abode of blessing
(*'afiat-gah*). The bird promises that salvation will come in due course, and
that "the dark night will turn into bright morning" (*shab-e tireh badal ba
sobh-e rowshan gasht khahad*). In response, the people relate to the bird their
fear of the enemy, whom they now call "the world-eater" (*jahan-khareh*).
They intimate the fear that this "ancient enemy of mankind" (*adami ra
doshman-e dirin*) might in the end devour the world. The bird answers simply: "May the fulfillment of his heart's desire prove impossible!" (*dar del-e u
arezu-ye u mahalash bad*). The people then express their fears: they are afraid
of the enemy's evil might and wily machinations and of the absence of order
(*saman*) and security (*imeni*) among themselves. They complain to the bird
that their tongues are tied, their ears are filled with the sound of the enemy's
war drums, and their feet are bound by his shackles. In response, the bird
announces that the end they seek is at hand, that the enemy will die, and
that shackles will no longer bind their feet. He also assures them that the
enemy's stratagems will be in vain.

The exchange continues back and forth until finally a solitary voice from
afar utters an additional *Bada!* (Thus may it be!). Another voice from nearby
seconds the wish, and soon a whole chorus of voices emerges, uttering a series
of prayers and curses punctuated by exclamations of "Thus may it be!" and
"Amen!" Concretized in a series of suggestive images, the people's curses
against the enemy and their prayers for their own success are interlaced to
produce a tapestry of collective desire for victory over the world-eater: may
destruction, like a housemate (*hamkhaneh*), settle in the enemy's abode; may
the tongues of those who could tell of the people's pains be expressive (*guya*);
may all death-preaching (*mordegi-amuz*) thoughts vanish; may all arrant fantasies (*khial-e kaj*) die away. The tapestry of exchanges ending in curses and
wishes finally comes to an end with the bird reciting all the crimes committed
by all those who have strayed from the people's path, bringing damnation on
themselves. At the end of every one of the ten items of this indictment the
people announce their approval by shouting the word *Amen*. That word,
both the name of the bird and an affirmation of the indictment, has by now
assumed double signification.

Throughout this dramatic scene, the voice of the poem's speaker has
receded to the background, his role confined to presenting the dialogue between the bird and the people. At this point, the speaker reappears to describe
the way the meeting—and the poem—ends:

Va beh variz-e tanin-e hardam amin goftan-e mardom
(chun seda-ye rudi az ja kandeh andar safheh-ye mordab angah gom)
morgh-e amin-guy
dur migardad.
az faraz-e bam
dar basit-e khetteh-ye aram mikhanad khorus az dur
mishekafad jerm-e divar-e sahargahan
v-az bar-e an sard-e dud-andud-e khamush
harcheh ba rang-e tajalli rang dar paykar mi-afzayad
mi-gorizad shab
sobh mi-ayad.[49]

(And with the weight of the reverberations of the people's constant
    chant of "Amen!"
—resembling the roar of a river that overflows momentarily before
    descending upon a swamp—
the amen bird
flies away.
Upon a distant rooftop,
in the expanse of the peaceful realm, a rooster crows.
The wall of the dawn cracks open
and over the silent, smoke-filled horizon
all things manifest their new color:
night flies,
morning comes.)

The words *bad* and *bada*—both meaning "may it be!"—are used commonly in Persian both in private prayers and on public occasions. In "The Amen Bird," these words appear at important turning points, singly or in combination with the bird's name, Amin, thus punctuating the poem in a special rhythm. As the poem begins to relate the dialogue between the bird and the people, the word *bad* is spoken by the people, while the word "amen" is spoken by the bird. This helps to define the relationship between the people's desire and the bird's vision, confirming the people's pleas and heralding its eventual fulfillment. At the poem's culmination, while the exchange of wishes and visions continues, the voices of the bird and the people are so intermingled as to be indistinguishable.

"The Amen Bird" casts opposition between the forces of night and those of day in far more dramatic patterns than that we saw in "Filthy Hope." Furthermore, the presence of the people offers an opportunity for the verbal exchanges which eventually bring about the empathic communion between the masses and the bird. At the same time, Nima's characterization of the people's enemy as a "world-eating creature" concretizes the poem's discourse more than does the image of the "trader of the night" in the earlier poem. Dramatically, too, the verbal exchange between the bird and the people moves the gathering toward a far more climactic ending. Indeed, the crumbling of the wall separating the people from "the region of the dawn" and the sound of the rooster's song become concrete manifestations of the impact of the people's incessant chant. In terms of the poem's structure, the accumulation of sound effects bestows a symphonic quality on the poem, which turns it into an engaging utterance distinct among all of Nima's compositions. Paralleling that, a steady convergence of images gives the poem its dramatic finale. For example, the articulation of the people's individual voices in terms of a scattered spattering of rain prepares the ground for the concluding image of the massive chant of "amen" depicted as a flood that breaks down the wall of the dawn. The poem suggests that individual voices which in isolation are no more than a sprinkling rain can gain the force of a great flood when uttered in unison. Nima makes this implication all the more powerful by presenting it as the outcome of the coming together of two voices, the bird's and the people's.

In an essay entitled "A Flight in the Sphere of The Amen Bird," published five years after Nima's death in 1960,[50] Siavosh Kasra'i offers an interpretation of "The Amen Bird" which takes into account several of the above features. However, as a young poet and a member of the Tudeh Party of Iran, Kasra'i is concerned primarily with an explication of the poem's ideology. As Tabari had done almost two decades before, Kasra'i proposes to relate Nima's poem to the political situation in Iran. In part because he is already involved in a social discourse influenced by efforts such as Tabari's, Kasra'i does not need to use the kind of equivocations in which Tabari had anchored his preface. By then, the presence of an oppositional, often leftist, meaning behind the abstract images of *she'r-e now* had become a matter of course.[51] Indeed, Kasra'i himself was a central figure among a new generation of poets who had begun to explain the principles of Nima's poetry to growing audiences. Intuitively perceiving Nima's compositions as "different," many Iranian readers were still uncertain about the exact nature or significance of the differences between old and new Persian poetry. Essays such as Kasra'i's were aimed at familiarizing them not only with formal and generic features of new poems but also, more centrally, with the principles underlying these. In so doing, they also offered more or less determinate and definitive readings of the texts that laid a claim to novelty.

Kasra'i, a prominent poet in his own right, combines a unique melange of poetic prose and political polemic in his essay on "The Amen Bird." The essay opens with an overview of political changes that span the poetic career of Nima Yushij. It then focuses on the poem in question, particularly on the character of its central personage, the amen bird. Kasra'i elaborates on the bird, placing him in relation to other real or mythical birds known in Persian poetry. Referring to the description of the bird portrayed as a sad, seasoned soul who has traveled to "the farthest end of this house of injustice," he observes that the bird is weary of life in "this house of injustice in which I—and you whom I know—wander about." He supplies his own physical description of the bird as well as an account of his origin, destination, and mission. The amen bird, he says, is "a thunder of wrath in the night of our land" (*azarakhsh-e khashmi dar shab-e diar-e ma*), whose wings are "as extended as the hand of unfulfilled desire" (*beh vos'at-e aghush-e hasrat*). The bird's call, he states, is as loud as "a call resembling the roar of those who have suffered injustice" (*bangi chun ghariv-e setamkeshan*).

Using Nima's descriptions as his starting point, Kasra'i amplifies them with his own view of the bird's history and characteristics:

> A wayfarer who has gone to—and returned from—the farthest end of this house of injustice in which I—and you whom I know—wander about, the amen bird is a night-rover [*shab-gozar*] who has suffered pain, yet is not after the pleasures of his own body. He seeks neither water nor grain, and wants no nest other than the people's rooftops. He has returned to initiate something new with the masses [*jema'at*]. He has come back never to depart, ready to commit himself to restoring the people to the conduct of their affairs. He is willing to raise his voice and to sing his song, the call for the victory of the right [*neda-ye piruzi-ye haqq*], in confirmation of his people. . . .
>
> It is with such signs that we envision the bird as accessible and concrete [*dast-yaftani va malmus*], whether he should be called God or angel or given the name of a star or a bird. He can spend a night under our roof or guide us from the blind alley to the highway, from the vortex to the shore. And if he bears no resemblance to the desert-roaming Elias or the nautical Enoch, he is very much like the last image of the communistic [*mardom-gera*] Nima. And like all those who are connected to the masses with a thousand cords, he tends to people's sorrows.[52]

Doubtless the potential for this presentation of the bird as a social leader is in the poem itself. At the same time, it is emphatically the critic who makes that potential so palpable through his admiring interpretation. He begins his portrayal by associating the amen bird with angels and prophets, aligned most decisively with "the people."[53] He does so initially by setting up a series of connections between the amen bird and other mythical birds known or imaginable to the poem's readers. The comparison with Simorgh, the mythical bird of the Persian epic *Shahnameh,* is clearly aimed at underscoring the difference between present-day realities and the mythical saviors of the past. Whereas the undying bird of the Persian epic is there to rescue or relieve ancient heroes, Kasra'i says, the amen bird assists masses of sufferers in all ages, from all walks of life. Thus, Kasra'i relates the essential difference between the amen bird and Simorgh to the difference between those who stand to gain from each bird's assistance:

> Heroes are few and their needs rare, while sufferers come in multitudes, and their needs are immense. Simorgh has her nest on top of Mount Qaf, too high a place for the common man to climb; the amen-saying wanderer, however, mingles with the crowd and sits in their midst. Simorgh is a recluse, safe and secure from harm. If called upon, she appears only after her feather has been set afire. The amen bird, in contrast, is scorched by sorrow, for he has been forced out without wanting to be left out.[54]

One might, given the historical context of the essay, begin to imagine a reference in the last statement to all the nationalists, leftists, and members of the Tudeh Party of Iran who had been purged from the government bureaucracies, the educational system, and the media in the aftermath of the 1953 coup d'etat. However that might be, the contrast between Simorgh and the amen bird is next expanded to include other mythical birds such as Homa and 'Anqa.[55] All of these other birds are found wanting in comparison with the amen bird, either in their connections with the masses of the people or in the nature of their mission. Unique among all these mythical creatures, the amen bird belongs to the suffering multitudes of present-day contemporary society; he knows them, speaks for them, and treads their path (*rah*). That path, incidentally, appears indistinguishable from what one may find in political pamphlets or a party platform. The path taken by the amen bird, writes Kasra'i, "resembles the path taken by humanity, a path whose dust has been studded by human sweat and blood." In light of the differences between all the mythical birds and the amen bird the condition for the bird's return to the people are spelled out in these terms:

> The amen bird is begotten of supplication, that deepest need of the toiling humanity. All that is needed to summon him is a heart gripped by sorrows and lips opened in a smile. And what sign is more expressive of the certitude of the great day of victory and the enemy's vulnerability than the amen bird

who, having withstood so many calamities, remains alive and active? He watches life, holding every minute of it under his eyes. Moreover, he knows the eternal foundation of life: he comes at night and departs at dawn, for this is the period when wakeful toilers give flight to their entreaties and supplications and when seasoned roamers of the night tread on their path.[56]

The bird, then, is in fact the child of the people's desires. Kasra'i refers to his presence in the people's imagination by relating what he terms a popular belief: "I have heard it said," he recalls, "that in expressing their sorrows and desires, people say: 'the amen-saying bird is on his way [*morgh-e amin-guy dar rah ast*]'." He speculates that in uttering these words the speaker may wish to refrain from presaging ill.[57] In this way, he establishes an ancestry and an identity for the amen bird, and recalls his many attributes, all for a nonexistent creature which Nima may well have invented playfully by inverting the letters of his own pen name.

Kasra'i next focuses on the relations between the bird and the people. Following the poem's structure, he discusses the idea of supplications and entreaties. Both in personal prayer for otherworldly salvation and in social actions aimed at reversing an undesirable situation, he explicates the communion of the bird and the people in words which can be applied to religious gatherings as well as to political rallies or demonstrations. "Supplication and imprecation," he says, are weapons of the powerless. Because they think themselves unable to fight their enemy, they turn to prayers. They know their enemy, but lack the means to overcome that enemy. The bird, however, knowing all the enemy's machinations, can communicate these to the crowd, but is unable to act alone. Together, the bird and the people bring about the enemy's downfall through their chants of *Bada!* and *Amin!* This, he concludes, is the poem's way of signaling their alliance. Kasra'i interprets the lines where the bird and the people wish the tongue of those who are connected with the pain of the masses to be expressive as an allusion to a situation where "the friends of the masses do have tongues to speak up, but their tongues are not expressive, for expressiveness results from their ability to speak up, not from forced silence." Here, too, the reduction from the poetic allusion to political commentaries concerning the absence of freedom of expression, or the presence of a regime of political surveillance and censorship in Iran, is effected in light of the communicative processes present in the poem.

Kasra'i sees the poem as depicting a gradual movement toward the unity of the bird and the people. The opening scene, he says, depicts the people and the amen bird as passive and separated from each other. In the end, the poem comes to resemble a court where the people appear as plaintiffs and the amen bird as the judge issuing verdicts and putting various adversaries on notice. "And as the bill of indictment [*kayfar-khast*] is read," he observes, "the people's cheering voice grows louder." Eventually, the rising chorus of indicting voices turns into the flood that sweeps away the oppressive wall of the night:

> Behold the song of the people, now at its height! It resembles not the sparse rain of scattered sounds we see at the poem's opening . . . , but a river overflowing its bedstream! It is a river, and like a river it has a direction in which it flows, and is continuous. And as it flows, it first destroys the house of the night [*khaneh-ye shab*] and makes darkness flee, then it tears asunder the wall of the dawn. With the birth of the day, things begin to assume their true colors; the amen-saying bird is no longer in the people's midst, but the people have come to know themselves anew.[58]

The "we" here may refer with equal validity to Kasra'i's political party and to "the people" or "the masses" the poet has imagined. While both the poet and the commentator find it necessary to use words of more general and neutral referentiality, the latter's use of such terms renders the poem's meaning far less general. Kasra'i's final warnings to "the traders of thought" (*sowdagaran-e andisheh*) and those of "shaky faith" (*imanha-ye larzan*) who prevent the fulfillment of "our" desires can be seen as not-so-subtle political rhetoric, particularly in a social context where the state is engaged in curtailing political activity by the party to which he belongs. It is worth recalling that at the very time Kasra'i was writing his essay, the Iranian government was arresting the most prominent members of the Tudeh Party of Iran, and that such pressures had resulted in massive defections from its ranks.[59]

In such trying times, Kasra'i's lingering on such images as the river that flows purposefully in a definitive direction or his professions of faith in the imminent collapse of the house of the night reflect a clearly purposeful reading of Nima's "The Amen Bird." As a report of a reading experience, his essay is unabashedly aimed at interpreting the poem as a political statement. Kasra'i combines his familiarity with Nima's poetry with his own authority as a poet to persuade the reader that his reading is in fact "correct." In so doing, he offers his own definition and description of the amen bird, the people, and the world-eater; describes the relationships among the poem's personages; and interprets the poem's ending. He thus directs the authority of the text toward his own purpose. Whereas Tabari's preface to "Filthy Hope" asks the reader to accept certain equivocations, Kasra'i's essay transposes an overt political position onto the text of Nima's poem. The semiotic atmosphere which has already begun to surround Nima's poetry makes it more or less unnecessary to propose such equivocations. He can claim simply to be reading the poem as the poem was meant to be read. More important, his approach implies that Nima himself would have expressed his intentions more explicitly had circumstances beyond his control allowed him to do so.

Collectively, interpretive pieces such as Tabari's preface and Kasra'i's essay help to shape a universe of discourse which facilitates the hermeneutic activity in a given culture at a given period. Poets, critics, and readers gradually come together in the perception of a fairly stable relationship between poetic signs and their meanings within the cultural context. While the act of writing invests in the text the potential for multiple interpretations, such interpretive acts offer readings relevant only in specific social contexts. They thus impose a more determinate and purposeful meaning on the texts they attempt to explicate. In transforming the poem's energies from an indeterminate potential level to a specific level relevant in terms of the present society, such hermeneutic endeavors erase—or at least render invisible—alternative meanings which may be tapped under a different set of circumstances. What they do accomplish is an elaboration of one aspect of the author's intention, namely that which relates to the creation of specific meanings. Bakhtin refers to this type of activity, where commentators seek to mediate between the text and its immediate audience, as "enclosure within the epoch."[60] While valuable to posterity as a record of contemporary perceptions of a literary creation, the "enclosure" takes little notice of other aspects of an author's intention, namely the desire to continue to evoke sympathetic responses beyond the immediate moment. It therefore falls short of the text's full potential, as imagined by the author, who still entertains visions of responsive understanding in future audiences:

> The author can never totally surrender both himself and his verbal work to the complete and definitive will of the present or near-by recipients . . . and so he imagines . . . a sort of higher instance of responsive understanding that can recede in various directions.[61]

In the case at hand, Kasra'i's reading of "The Amen Bird"—and Tabari's reading of "Filthy Hope"—have other implications as well. They have, through their readings, turned Nima's tentative analogies into solid equivocations. As the dawning of a day, a natural occurrence, is equated with the making of a political revolution, a social eventuality, the differences between the two outcomes become invisible, buried, for the moment at least, in the depths of the text. As a defining feature of the discourse of *she'r-e now*, the automatic link between the dawning of the day and the making of a revolution has had other consequences which I have addressed elsewhere.[62]

The manner in which traditional literary history in Iran articulates the emergence of the modernist Persian poetry in Iran has been governed by a similar process. In interpreting the complex social processes by which a "new" and "different" kind of Persian poetry had made its appearance, Iranian literary critics and scholars have all too often elevated Nima's vision as the single vision and *she'r-e now* as the only outcome of that vision. This approach has by and large paid no attention to the visions and works conceived or executed in ways other than by Nima. More important, it has discarded the possibility of multiple visions and works in a poetic tradition. It is illuminating in this regard that in his essay Kasra'i speaks of the meaning of "night," as it appears in "The Amen Bird," in terms of "the Nimaic night":

> For before him, night was only the night of the lover's separation or union, morning the dawn of visitation with the beloved. But because this night casts its shadow over most of Nima's work, it needs to be explicated independently, [a task] which we pass for the moment. Suffice it to say that at the time when "The Amen Bird" takes flight no remarkable movement can be detected in Persian poetry. Therefore, I will refrain from discussing the lifeless atmosphere of our poetry at that time.[63]

Clearly, this book reveals a very different process of poetic change in Iran, even as it relates to this single image. It is important to point out, however, that Kasra'i's depiction of Nima as a unique visionary singlehandedly determining the shape of modern Persian poetry is by no means unique or even exceptional. Indeed, a generation of critics, many of them poets themselves, have attributed to Nima the totality of the visions, efforts, and innovations accumulated through almost a century of deliberate attempts to effect change in Persian poetry. As a result, a view of the process of poetic change in the Persian tradition has emerged which takes little notice of the dynamic and dialogical nature of the process itself.

THE TOILER PAR EXCELLENCE:
A READING OF "THE NIGHT WATCHMAN'S WORK"

The piece I have saved for last embodies a more complex approach toward the interplay of tradition and innovation in Persian poetry and specifically toward Nima's innovations. It is Mehdi Akhavan-Saless's analysis of a 1946 poem by Nima entitled "Kar-e Shab-Pa" (The Night Watchman's

Work) which reveals an attitude similar to Tabari's and Kasra'i's in relation to poetic modernity in the Persian tradition, yet is far more sensitive to the dynamics of tradition and innovation. In that sense, it must be judged a considerably more sophisticated work than theirs. Akhavan is not only much more imaginative as a poet but also a more astute observer of the poetic tradition which has nurtured both Nima and him. As a contributor to the semiotic ambience I propose to demonstrate, he comes closest to recognizing the potential of *she'r-e now* to strive for relevances outside the sociopolitical contexts surrounding it.

In a lifetime of empathic engagement with Nima's poetry, Mehdi Akhavan-Saless (1928–1990) has written and published his views in various forms. They come to us primarily in the form of two books: *Bed'atha va Badaye'-e Nima* (Nima's Innovations and Novelties), first published in 1967, and *'Ata va Laqa-ye Nima Yushij* (Nima's Offerings and Aspect), published in 1983. The work we will focus on here, following a brief discussion of Akhavan's general assessment of Nima's poetry, forms a chapter in the first book, *Nima's Innovations and Novelties*.

Throughout the book, Akhavan draws a basic distinction between Nima's approach to poetic signification and that of certain classical poets—Nezami, Khaqani, and Anvari, in particular. He envisions this distinction in terms predicated on what we may call an essential cultural heterology. In their act of poetic signification, he says, classical Persian poets worked with a complex set of inherited devices. Akhavan mentions *tebaq* (concurrence), *tazad* (contrareity), and *mora'at-e nazir* (observance of [poetic] analogues) as the most common and the most frequently used examples of these devices.[64] Relating objects and the modality of their existence to one another formally or visually, these devices were used to mediate among diverse aspects of human perception or different spheres of human thought as expressed in poetry. Through the ages, a high degree of mutual dependence or automatic association developed between these signs and the concepts they signified. Consequently, mention of one concept recalled the other, an event which poets of later generations perceived as necessitating a mention of—or at least an allusion to—the second concept. In doing so, they displayed their intimate knowledge of the poetic tradition within which they were vying for immortality. In this way, concepts were linked together rather automatically and mechanistically.

The life around the poet and his poetry was of course changing all the while, even as the signs poets used to communicate their perceptions of—or responses to—it were becoming more and more ossified. Trying to make their figures of speech correspond with some formal, visual, or auditory aspect in the poetic tradition was tantamount to making them reflect some comparison, resemblance, or likeness extinct from the real world or invalid in it. When it is read today, Akhavan observes, classical Persian poetry often communicates a kind of knowledge to us that is either extraneous to the text or nonexistent in the world. Having solved the riddle of meaning in certain classical poems, "we come up at a point outside the space of true poetry."[65] We may learn something about an astronomical, chemical, or alchemical rule, but we do not experience the specific pleasure that arises from realizing the presence of a living work. For their part, readers have been conditioned through the centuries to anticipate adherence to defunct conventions. They look only for new ways in which poets may face conventions that bind them. In satisfying this anticipation, traditionalist poets of modern times signal to their readers only their awareness of the poetic heritage without adding anything of significance to it.

According to Akhavan, Nima achieves something quite different, quite remarkable in this regard. Sheer exercise of the human imagination has enabled him to question uncritical adherence to the traditional system of poetic signification. This in turn enables Nima's readers to visualize his images and realize the meanings he has produced. Nima asks his readers not to confirm his knowledge of the tradition, but to share his desire to turn the mass of phenomena around them into poetic signs. He rewards them not by satisfying their common esthetic inheritance of ancestral perceptions and responses, but by giving rise in them to the pleasure of discovering new analogues and analogies between the world and the poetic text. To put it another way, Nima invites his readers to participate in the act of creating meaning by contemplating the delight in their own observations. It is this aspect of Nima's poetry, Akhavan concludes, that distinguishes him from all classical poets, whatever their individual merits.

On that basis, Akhavan conceptualizes his own interpretations of Nima's poems as an act of exploration or an excursion, rather than one of explication:

> Unlike the massive commentaries that have been compiled on [the poetry of] Khaqani and others, our excursion into the spaces of Nima's poetry . . . consists simply of stopping every step, looking atentively at things without any assistance from the dead and defunct sciences and arts. . . . What this [activity] requires is only an eye with which to see (and sometimes to hear) and an ear with which to hear (and sometimes to see). The only important and necessary thing we have to remain mindful of is not to expect to taste familiar tastes or to face those familiar molds that cater to our customary indolence.[66]

Faced with unconventional texts, critics often ask readers to leave behind the interpretive tools they habitually carry around in their minds. Akhavan adds to this an appeal for an activist, almost transgressive reading. Instead of applying inherited expectations to the poem, he says, let us cooperate in making them. He thus disconnects the inherited relationship between encoding and decoding processes as much as that is possible, calling instead on readers to bring their own experiences, psychic or social, to an understanding of the text in question. What this promises is a discovery not just of what the poem communicates but also of the way in which it chooses to convey its message. Through an experiential encounter with the text, readers will come to see the mechanisms and strategies involved in making the poem. Much like a tour guide, the commentator would help in the process by pointing out important landmarks along the way. Akhavan describes his own part as that of a more experienced reader rather than an expert. "I shall accompany the newly arrived traveler," he says, "not as a trained guide, but as one who harbors no fear of journeying forth in alien environments."[67] The concept of a reader unafraid of novelties implies a redefinition of the reader's posture and of the reading process. Akhavan defines the quality he seeks to instill in Nima's readers as one coming from the reader's own being. Imbued with life "as it is lived in this society at the present time," his ideal reader seeks new ways of experiencing the poetic text as well as the act of reading itself. With all that, Akhavan sets out to offer a reading of "The Night Watchman's Work."

As its title suggests, the poem is about a night watchman, a temporary farm laborer in the rice fields of northern Iran, Nima's native land. Night watchmen are often hired to protect the newly planted rice paddies from being trampled by animals at night. Naturally, the watchman provides Nima with an occasion to comment on poverty and social inequality. The poem begins with the description of a calm, languid night in the countryside. All living creatures, great and small, seem to have found relief from the day's activities. All, that is, except for the widowed night watchman who has just begun his arduous work:

> Mah mitabad rud ast aram
> bar sar-e shakheh-ye owja tirang
> dom biavikhteh dar khab foru rafteh vali dar ayesh
> kar-e shab-pa nah hanuz ast tamam.[68]

> (The moon is shining, the river flows quietly.
> On the branch of an elm tree, the wild pheasant

sunk in sleep, has hung its tail. In the paddy, though,
the night watchman's work is not finished yet.)

The poem next focuses more sharply on the night watchman and his work. He has to make as much noise as he can to keep wild boars from grazing in the newly planted field, trampling it under their hooves. Charged with the task of creating fear in the animals, the weary man himself feels utterly vulnerable and fearful as he reflects on his own and his family's situation:

Midamad gah beh shakh
gah mi kubad bar tabl beh chub
v-andar an tiregi-ye vahshat-za
nah seda-ist bejoz in k-az ust
howl ghaleb hameh chizi maghlub
miravad duki in haykal-e ust
miramad sayeh-i in ast goraz
khab-aludeh beh cheshman khasteh
har dami ba khod miguyad baz
    cheh shab-e muzi o garmi o deraz
    tazeh morda-st zanam
    gorsneh mandeh do ta'i bachehha-m
    nist dar koppeh-ye ma mosht-e berenj
    bekonam ba cheh zaban-shan aram.[69]

(Now and then, he blows in his horn,
be beats his stick on the drum every now and then.
And in that fearsome darkness,
no sound but for the noise he makes,
fear reigns, all are subdued.
A pipit hops. "An animal's figure!" he thinks.
A shadow moves. "That is a wild boar!" says he.
Sleepy, his eyes drooping,
he murmurs to himself at every breath:
    "What a hot, long, sinister night!
    with my wife dead,
    my two children starving,
    and not a handful of rice in our hut,
    what can I say to quiet them?")

The progression from the noises the night watchman makes to his internal uproar has been conceived and expressed realistically. In fact, the narrative is entirely verisimilar, much as this style of presentation was still associated primarily with prose rather than poetry. The poem seeks confirmation of its status as "poetic" through the combined effects of a loosely conceived rhyme scheme, a modified metric pattern, and a series of stylistic features—classical lexical usages, syntactic inversions, and semantic peculiarities. More important, through its style, the poem highlights a quality hitherto nonexistent in canonical Persian poetry: lexical and syntactic localisms. First, the poem's flora and fauna are expressed in the local dialect of Mazandaran, Nima's native region. Thus, terms like *owja* (elm), *tirang* (wild pheasant), *ayesh* (paddy), and *shab-pa* (night watchman) provide local color for the story. The night watchman's speech further anchors him squarely in the local environment. Through the precision they bring to the poem as text, these stylistic elements produce an effect comparable to what a previous generation of Iranian poets—'Aref, Iraj, and 'Eshqi—sought by using a variety of colloquialisms in their poetic discourse.[70] Just as colloquialism did for these poets, the use of local speech in poetry, absent from contemporary perceptions of the classical poetic tradition, is viewed as an element of modernity in Persian poetry.

Nima's simultaneous affirmation of previous innovations and introduction of other innovations of his own making clearly contributes to the perception of his poem as new and different. His drive toward poetic modernity can be seen in all its aspects when we add to these the visible difference in rhyme and meter between Nima's poetry and the classical canon. Nima's poem, in other words, claims as its own all the characteristics which make a specific type of Iranian poetry written around the mid-twentieth century different from the millennium-old tradition of Persian poetry. In texts like "The Night Watchman's Work," Iranian readers perceive the immediate connection between language and experience and internalize it as a poetic effect.

What writings such as Akhavan's accomplish is to validate and consolidate that impression. They do so by requiring readers to relate what they experience in reading such poems to its internal dynamics and processes, and not to their store of knowledge about poetry. They guide readers to accept "The Night Watchman's Work" as a poem in light of comparable experiences and the interactions between the phenomenal world and human emotions. Finally, by requiring readers to take a position in relation to the shape of the poem on the page and its sound to the ear, commentators and critics like Akhavan establish the act of reading itself as an element of individual experience. That, I think, is why Akhavan's posture of a companion to the act of reading Nima's poetry is more important than it might appear at first glance. It provokes a deeper and more satisfactory understanding of Nima's poetry as a gateway toward appreciating in a new way the constant tension between tradition and innovation in modernist Persian poetry. In spite of his pose as a detached guide to understanding Nima's poetry, Akhavan's views must ultimately be understood as a plea for a more accepting attitude toward poetry in general, including his own, as the following comment illustrates:

> With a little attention, we will see that he [Nima] has supplied all that is needed for the poem's ambience, all that is to be seen and heard, all the concrete names of . . . man and beast, the broad outlines of the scene, sound and silence, and all the invisible elements, abstractions and states [of mind], like anguish and sorrow, and other instruments of the stagecraft, mostly with very simple and expressive descriptions.[71]

With that plea, Akhavan begins to demonstrate how "The Night Watchman's Work" functions as a poem. In the opening scene, he says, the moonlight is necessary to cast light on the main point of the poem's focus, the watchman himself. It allows just enough light for us to see the quietly flowing river, the sleeping pheasant, and the poem's poor protagonist. As it begins to tell the story of the watchman's life, the poem wastes not one word on a convention. In setting the stage, Akhavan believes, Nima shows "only what is essential and appropriate." Similarly, in describing the night watchman's recollection of his children in sleep, he is "more concise, more complete and more expressive than any painter may be imagined to be."[72] Nima's refusal to commit himself to conventional usages, in other words, allows him to present only those details which draw the reader toward the scenes of the night watchman's work and life. At the same time, his approach to description and narration allows him an economy of means which serves the poem's ultimate purpose well. The initial juxtaposition of nature's peace and tranquility, Akhavan believes, is designed deliberately to contrast with the night watchman's internal turmoil and commotion, further focusing the reader's attention on the story the poem tells. The internalization of the contrast, highlighted through the nature of the night watchman's work—his job requires him to produce noise—gives rise to an inaudible turmoil in the reader, generating an emotional charge that remains an informative part of the poem's discourse.

Akhavan next zeros in on the word *howl* (fear) in the opening passage. He argues that Nima might well have used several monosyllabic words with the same metric measure. The word he has selected best suits his depiction because "[the word] 'howl' is wet, mingled with the night, fog and the forest" (*howl martub ast shabnak o meh-alud o jangali ast*). This leads to a resounding affirmation of the poet's choice of the word. Says Akhavan: "Yes, 'howl' is better and more appropriate to Nima's description here."[73] What is more, Akhavan adds, Nima objectifies it with reference to the night watchman's fear-inspired fantasies. Movements of a pipit or a silhouette are as threatening to him as the approach of a boar or another wild creature. Once the poet has arrested the reader's attention by such means, he can sit back and allow the man to tell his story directly. As he does so, the poem confers individuality on him by reproducing his speech patterns. This, in Akhavan's estimation, makes the story not only precise and purposeful, but real as well. Indeed, Nima's strategy of reproducing the protagonist's own speech leads not just to a perception of specificity, but beyond that to one of authenticity:

> [The night watchman] speaks neither like a foreman or a landowner, nor like a village preacher, a headman, or the gendarme at the nearby military station. No, the space around him may be foggy, but we are not mistaken. This is he, the very night watchman from Mazandaran. He is wearing his own clothes and feels weary of his own painful existence. He knows what to say and what not to say to us; and he understands what "oughts" and "ought nots" are governing his life.[74]

Through such an affirmative rhetoric Akhavan works his way toward an admiring evaluation of Nima's work. The rhetorical devices he employs in communicating his appreciative reading are crucial to his purpose. He commences with an account of anonymous criticisms of Nima's poetry: "At times one hears it said here and there that Nima's poetry is complex and complicated [*pichideh va boghranj*]." He rejects the criticism summarily on the basis of the analogy we have seen before: experiencing modernist Persian poetry is like arriving in a new city, and newcomers must find their way around. They may feel stranded momentarily, but they will before long "discover its streets and alleyways, its thoroughfares and neighborhoods, and even its cellars with their familiar, sad, and sombre silhouettes." Imagining himself in the company of such curious but skeptical explorers, Akhavan begins to direct his observations increasingly toward modernist poetry in general. In opposition to the nameless critics who criticize the new poetic tradition, he uses the pronoun *ma* (we) to include not just Nima but the entire group of modernist poets whom he describes as following in Nima's footsteps. He closes by citing the entire poem, asking the reader to experience the poem once again in light of his commentary. "After reading these comments," he says, "a second reading of the whole poem will be of a different quality and will produce a different mood [*hal o kaifiyyat-e digar darad*]."[75]

As an example of the validating rhetoric surrounding Nima's poetry,

Akhavan's commentary accomplishes two things even before it begins to discuss Nima's poem itself. First, it urges readers to accept that these poems have their own separate criteria. They are, as Akhavan's analogies make clear, works of accomplished and elaborate structures where every form has its own specific function thoughtfully produced and tastefully presented. If they appear unfamiliar to the onlooker, it is because they are based on principles other than those to which he or she has grown accustomed. All the reader needs is a mind free of prejudice and some guidance in the process of discovery. Beyond that, by aligning the critic and the reader in a bond of camaraderie in discovering those premises and principles, it characterizes those opposed to the new poetry as sedentary individuals unaccustomed to exploration and unwilling to set foot in new environments.

After he has explicated the poem in all its major aspects, Akhavan is ready to rest his case. He sums up his argument in this loving assessment:

> "The Night Watchman's Work" is one of Nima Yushij's exemplary poems. In this poem, some of the priniciples of his approach [to poetry] have attained perfection, manifesting some of his artistic virtues. Here we see in full Nima's sad and simple human aspect, his pity for and sympathies with suffering and the sufferers; we see the mist-covered, melancholic spaces of his poetry and the power of his poetic design, his comparisons and descriptions, and his fascinating ruptures and severances; we see his singular combinations, coordinations and reversions and the refrains which, working much like grafts and insertions, prevent the story from falling apart. Here we see his rhymes, all ensconced in their proper places, and the leisurely and measured rhythm which his poem appropriates, and so on and so forth. Here we see it all: from Nima's slow, soblike murmuring and his peculiar diction to the simplicity of his expressions and the rustic purity of his mountains. All and each can be seen in this story, and so appropriate an ending to boot, one that recalls [in us] the poem's wholesome beginning.[76]

This final summation is designed to celebrate the fulfillment of the promise with which Akhavan opens his essay: that an attentive reading of "The Night Watchman's Work" would verify his claims on behalf of the poem. An inherently "modern" poem, it is esthetically pleasing and socially relevant. What is more, it is entirely accessible, only if readers free themselves from conventional modes of understanding poetry.

A NEW POETRY FOR A NEW REALITY

We may recall at this point that almost a century before Akhavan wrote his essay, a generation of Iranian intellectuals challenged the poets of their time to produce a poetry that would be relevant, effective, and comprehensible. Their desire to change the Persian poetry of their culture initiated the process of change which, I would argue, found its full fruition in the critical assessments we have examined in this chapter. My argument seems indeed to have come full circle. Through a complicated series of contestations, negotiations, and evaluations, the rhetoric of subversion that men like Akhundzadeh, Kermani, and Malkom initiated led to the resounding affirmation that Tabari, Kasra'i, and Akhavan gave to Nima's poetry. In the process, a number of poets produced a series of works each of which may be thought to contain a vision of the esthetic principles underlying the desired change. Testifying to the presence of a poetry different from the traditional practice of the culture, the commentaries I have examined in this chapter invite readers to accept the new phenomenon as the final fruit of that cultural effort. The keys they provide for this purpose are designed to enable Iranian readers of the late twentieth century to adopt a reading process that privileges the expression of social concerns. They also posit in the new phenomenon fundamental differences with the poetic practice which adheres to the conventions of the classical tradition in Persian. In time, these keys would begin to unlock the doors to a universe of poetic discourse with its own distinct premises and tendencies.

Let me elaborate on that point. To assume that particular words signify particular concepts or beliefs when used in a particular kind of poetry is tantamount to advocating a particular decoding system. Within the Iranian context, the system thus nurtured has by now become the dominant mode of thought about the relations that obtain between the "modern" poetry and its social ambience. As I bring this book to a close, I think it appropriate to place the tradition of *she'r-e now,* as it has evolved in Iran, in that context.

I have examined here some of the most important innovations which at least three generations of poets and critics have brought about in Persian poetry as it is practiced in contemporary Iran. These include significant elemental and systemic departures from the classical poetic codes and conventional modes of perceiving them. As I demonstrated in chapter 2, around the time of the constitutional movement, poets like Dehkhoda and 'Aref began to experiment with various lexical, semantic, and rhetorical innovations within the overall formal and generic categories of the classical tradition in Persian poetry. This resulted in the cohabitation of new and old poetic elements within a single poetic space. What is known in the language of traditional literary criticism as the political ghazal and patriotic qasida of the twentieth century exemplifies this trend. This practice has continued throughout the twentieth century, and is currently practiced in Iran. It has found its best expression in such prominent poets as Bahar, Iraj, Parvin, and Farrokhi-Yazdi, as well as in later generations such as Shahriar, Amiri, Avesta, Mo'allem, and others. It can also be found, in modified forms to be sure, in the works of many prominent modernist poets, from Nima, Akhavan, and Farrokhzad to Kho'i and Shafi'i'. The status of such works has remained obscure in traditional literary criticism, primarily because the system of classification it offers renders the presence of such phenomena as anachronistic, or at best problematic.[77] Nonetheless, as a category of poetic texts, they continue to expand the significatory processes of classical Persian poetry without subverting the system in which those processes are anchored. They have, I believe, considerably enhanced the capacity of the classical system under the pressures of constantly changing social and esthetic configurations. Still, separate studies are needed to assess the nature and extent of such changes.

The second type of innovation I have examined in this book has historically positioned itself against the classical system, striving to alter aspects of the traditional system to make possible the articulation of subjective or personal experiences. Poetic texts containing this type of innovation have pushed against formal and generic boundaries of the tradition as perceived through the canon of past performances. Generally speaking, they run counter to traditional norms in that they subject the existing significatory systems to a crisis. In their intuitive or deliberate refusal of the kinds of coherence or codifications upheld by the inherited tradition, these texts take part in a kind of cultural upheaval in that they work against the existing system of encoding and decoding poetic signs. Historically speaking, such texts have evoked a degree of resistance within the Iranian culture, although this may be a peculiarity of the Persian poetic tradition. Whereas texts of the first type are gradually absorbed in the texture of the tradition, those of the second type tend to be seen as rootless, overly revolutionary, potentially capable of undermining the integrity of the native tradition, or a combination of these. That, I suspect, should account, at least in part, for the fact that poets like Lahuti, Raf'at and 'Eshqi continue to be considered second-rate Persian poets.

Finally, this last chapter should serve as testimony to the claim about the perceived incompatibility of the classical system of poetic signification and communication to adapt itself to all aspects of the esthetic expression contemporary Iranians have come to view as appropriate for their culture. Even after the crowning achievements of Nima and his followers, which turned it into the dominant mode of poetic expression in present-day Iranian culture, *she'r-e now* has continued to retain much of its "revolutionary" character. That is because any attempt at moving away from its principles and premises is perceived as ultimately serving the cause of strengthening the classical system and, therefore, a reactionary move. This helps to explain why a 1960s poetic tendency known as "The New Wave" (*mowj-e now*) is still being widely brushed aside as an unimportant deviation from the Nimaic norm in Iranian poetry.[78] The polarity implied in the modernist discourse also accounts in part for the fact that many of the poets I have examined here—Dehkhoda, 'Aref, Bahar, Iraj, and Parvin, in particular—have for so long been placed within the classical tradition.

In the end, all the poets we have focused on here—and many we have not—have helped to chart the course of modernity in Persian poetry as it is practiced in contemporary Iran. They took the risk of creating what their culture might—and in many cases did—view as nonpoetry, nonsense, or both. That is, they have produced texts which their readers might have failed to recognize as poetry or failed to understand. Such risks are an inherent part of all efforts at innovation as they arrive on the cultural scene. In terms of my theoretical assumptions, such failures may be signaled by the absence of esthetic pleasure, or perceived as what Yuri Lotman calls "cultural noise."[79]

The process I have examined here is indeed the reverse. From its inception in the writings of Akhundzadeh, Kermani, and Malkom, arguments about the necessity of change in Persian poetry were considered a meaningful and important cultural concern. Following these men, countless others contributed to a social process whose end no one could have imagined, but of whose necessity they were all convinced. Throughout the twentieth century, in fact, the whole of the Iranian culture seemed to have agonized over the prospects and perils inherent in casting one of its most valuable products into a new mold. As it submitted the idea of Persian poetry to profound rethinking, it summoned to the task the entire thought process it had inherited from the past and began to borrow models and ideas as it had never done before.

When Nima began systematically to break the habitual link between poetry's appearance and sound patterns, he took the greatest risk there was. Disrupting the most apparent perceptions of poeticity was no small feat. However, his attempt to sever the idea of poetic order from the visual and auditory, constituted the final act made possible by a series of previous breaks with the esthetic tradition. My focus in this final chapter on Nima's theoretical observations must be seen ultimately as a tribute to his adoption of a timely idea. Theoretically speaking, Nima's view of language as a collective artifact located between the literary text and what is generally referred to as reality, recasts reality as a subspecies lingua. Through the manner in which he articulates the relationship between language and the content of his own poetry, Nima indeed seems to have provided answers, however tentative, to

Raf'at's questions about the proper way of communicating contemporary social concerns through poetry. We have indeed come full circle in a single culture: from the categorical charge that Persian poetry does not relate to life through a succession of attempts to make it do so, to Nima's emphatic assertion that his poetry is nothing but life. What is made absolutely clear in the process is the idea of the sociality of poetry. That the poetic text is also a kind of abstract social structure, its forms and functions somehow related to—and reflective of—the evolution of concrete social structures, emerges as the main point of agreement in the process of recasting Persian poetry. The process, begun when poetry is viewed as a category of cultural product that must somehow reflect changes on the social scene, culminates in a recognition of poetry as an aspect of the social setup mediated through language. It is there, I think, that Nima's unique and decisive contribution to the emergence of modernity in Persian poetry can best be located, and it is that contribution to which I have devoted my attention in the first part of this last chapter.

Last but not least, my focus on the validating rhetoric that began to surround Nima's poetry in the 1950s and 1960s ought to be viewed as a recognition of the fact that, within the culture, nothing is a certainty. The meanings that Iranians sought in Nima's poetry must be understood in terms of their perceptions of the relevances he discovered. Tabari, Kasra'i, and Akhavan exemplify the need to transfer the textual energies of Nima's modernist poems from their abstract and potential meanings to the specific sociopolitical statements they judged relevant to contemporary readers. Beyond the application to Nima's poetry, their interpretations provide part of the background to future efforts at forging new codes and modes of poetic communication. Perceptions thus forged become one determinant of meaning, part of the cultural processes through which valid and valuable meanings are sought—and found—in poetic texts. To deny the relevances that accrue to poems in contexts historically or culturally removed from the poet and his or her immediate audiences would be to reduce poetic texts to no more than historical documents. By exploring the processes which lead readers to regard the poetry of a former time as communicating relations hitherto unexplored, we may begin to see the emergence of new variables and relations governing the act of esthetic communication.

I have tried here to show the kinds of activities that poets, critics, and readers engage in as they attempt to oust one network of socially instituted esthetic agreements and empower another. In the course of time, as it happened in the case of *she'r-e now* in Iran, the culture may conceive new signs, new signifying relations, and new systems of signification. As the culture begins to support structures previously unmarked or marked differently, a new esthetic system may emerge. While I have had space only to show glimpses of one such process, poetic change itself must be conceptualized as ongoing, whether or not its exact contours, or even its presence, may be perceptible. Let me underline this conviction by giving the last word on the matter to Mikhail Bakhtin, the thinker to whom this study owes so much:

> Nothing conclusive has yet taken place in the world, the ultimate word of the world and about the world has not been spoken, the world is open and free, everything is still in the future and will always be in the future.[80]

Notes

1. I am referring here to classical Persian literature, a heritage shared by three modern countries: Iran, Afghanistan, and Tajikistan. See Browne, *Literary History of Persia*; Rypka, *History of Iranian Literature*; and ʿAini, *Nemunehha-ye Adabiyyat-e Tajik* (Selections from Tajik Literature).

2. The Ottoman roots of Iranian modernity are more or less well established. The Indian connection is, I think, far more extensive and elaborate than has been recognized. See Tavakoli-Targhi, "Refashioning Iran."

3. Among Iranian critics, there has been much discussion about the relative merits of the phrases *sheʿr-e now* (new poetry) versus *sheʿr-e emruz* (poetry of today). From the perspective assumed in this book the two differ only in the ideological bearings assigned to each.

4. Iranian historiography of literary modernization is replete with binaries of this kind. See Shafiʿi-Kadkani, *Advar-e Sheʿr-e Farsi az Mashrutiyyat ta Soqut-e Saltanat* (Periods of Persian Poetry); see also Langarudi, *Tarikh-e Tahlili-ye Sheʿr-e Now* (Analytical History of the Modernist Poetry).

5. Such is the case with Hafez. See Ahmad Shamlu's Introduction to Hafez, *Hafez-e Shiraz beh Ravayat-e Ahmad Shamlu* (Hafez of Shiraz according to Ahmad Shamlu), 25–58.

6. The idea of a "literary revolution" was first advanced through the literary circles of Tehran in the years following the Constitutional Revolution. See below, chapter 3. See also Arianpur, *Az Saba ta Nima* (From Saba to Nima), 2: 2–77.

7. Many chroniclers of poetic modernity in Iran do not distinguish among the poets that preceded Nima Yushij. While relating modernity almost exclusively to Nima, they nonetheless assign small but equal shares to poets before him. See Hamid Zarrinkub, *Cheshm-andaz-e Sheʿr-e Now-e Farsi* (Landscape of the Modernist Persian Poetry); see also Hosuri, *Zaban-e Farsi dar Sheʿr-e Emruz* (Persian Language in Today's Poetry).

8. Iranian readers are becoming increasingly aware of Nima's continued practice of writing traditional poetry. See Tahbaz's "Compiler's Note" in Yushij, *Majmuʿeh-ye Kamel-e Ashʿar-e Nima Yushij* (Complete Collection of Nima Yushij's Poetry), 9–11.

9. For an early and influential articulation of this, see Shamlu's poem entitled "She'ri keh Zendegi-st" (Poetry that Is Life) in his *Hava-ye Tazeh* (Fresh Air).

10. Browne, *Press and Poetry*, xv.

11. In a sweeping review of the modernist poetic tendencies in Arab, Persian, and Ottoman cultures, Browne speaks of a great "demand for patriotic poetry and for a note of greater sincerity and higher purpose in verse." Such Middle Eastern modernists as the Egyptian Shaykh 'Abdul-'Aziz Shawish and Ferid Bey, the Ottoman Zia Pasha and Kemal Bey, and the Persian Mirza Aqa Kermani, he believes, view the poetic tradition of the Islamic world in light of such modern needs. "But," Browne concludes, "this passion for the Fatherland is a new thing in Asia, or at any rate in Western and Central Asia, and it is perhaps natural and inevitable that its votaries should be impatient of the centuries of poetical talent devoted to other, and, in their eyes, less worthy objects" (ibid., xxxvi).

12. Some of the most notable modernist poets of present-day Iran can be counted among Nima's supporters: Ahmad Shamlu, Esma'il Shahrudi, Hushang Ebtehaj, and Mehdi-Akhavan-Saless.

13. The academic attitude toward the new poetry was largely hostile until well into the 1960s. For more recent examples, see Hariri, "She'r-e Naghz va She'r-e Bimaghz" (Sound Poetry and Hollow Poetry), *Vahid*; see also Adib-Borumand, *Payam-e Azadi* (Message of Freedom), 13–14; and Ra'di-Azarakhshi, "Darbareh-ye Sabkha-ye She'r-e Farsi va Nehzat-e Bazgasht" (Styles of Persian Poetry).

14. See Shafi'i-Kadkani, Periods of Persian Poetry, 10.

15. For an application of semiotic models to the problem of literary change, see Szabolcsi et al., eds., *Change in Language and Literature*; Shukman, "Dialectics of Change"; and Sebeok, et al., eds., *Recent Developments in Theory and History*.

16. The term "language of poetry" is used here to point to the way traditional literary criticism articulates change in the poetic system. In poststructuralist theory, the idea is expressed in such terms as "speech," "parole," or "utterance." See DeGeorge, ed., *Semiotic Themes*, particularly Todorov's essay, "Bakhtin's Theory of the Utterance."

17. For this part I am indebted to Shukman's essay referred to in note 15 above.

18. Todorov, *Mikhail Bakhtin: The Dialogical Principle*, 34.

19. Ibid., 66.

20. Lotman, "Primary and Secondary Communication-Modeling Systems," 95.

21. Lotman, "Dynamic Model," 206.

22. Shukman, "Dialectics of Change," 314.

23. Lotman, "Dynamic Model," 195.

24. Ibid., 194.

25. Ibid.

26. Ibid., 196.

27. Lotman, *Structure of the Artistic Text*, 291.

28. Lotman, "Dynamic Model," 197.

29. Ibid., 199.

30. Lotman, *Structure of the Artistic Text*, 297–98.

31. Ibid., 289.

32. Lotman, "Dynamic Model," 208.

33. Lotman, *Structure of the Artistic Text*, 22.

34. Todorov, *Mikhail Bakhtin: The Dialogical Principle*, 30.

35. Lotman, *Structure of the Artistic Text*, 293.

36. For a similar approach, see Zipoli, *Encoding and Decoding Neopersian Poetry.*

37. Lotman's observation is noteworthy here. He considers the lexical level "the ground on which the entire edifice of semantics is constructed in the internal structure of the artistic text" (*Structure of the Artistic Text*, 168).

NOTES TO CHAPTER ONE

1. E'temad al-Saltaneh, *Sadr al-Tavarikh* (Prime of Histories), 226–27. Following *Sadr al-Tavarikh*, Adamiyyat cites the incident in his famous work on the reformist prime minister. See Adamiyyat, *Amir-e Kabir va Iran* (Amir-e Kabir and Iran), 322. Almost all the scholars who have referred to the incident in the past forty years or so seem to have had one of these two works as their primary source.

2. *Sadr al-Tavarikh's* passage reads in part: "When Amir heard it [the qasida], he rebuked Qa'ani and reprimanded him. . . . Qa'ani . . . fell silent and apologized," (p. 277).

3. Qa'ani, *Divan-e Hakim Qa'ani-shirazi* (Divan), 81. For a discussion of this qasida, see Yusofi, *Cheshmeh-ye Rowshan* (Clear Fountain), 324–38.

4. Contrariety is a well-known device of the classical Persian qasida. Ehsan Yarshter, who translates it into English as "antithesis," includes it among a number of literary devices used to embellish the text "at the semantic level" by playing "on the associative meanings of words or metaphors and their connotations" (*Persian Literature*, 19).

5. Bastani-Parizi, "Tarhi az Chehreh-ye Amir-e Kabir dar Adab-e Farsi" (Sketch of Amir-e Kabir's Portrait in Persian Literature), 34.

6. The most astute observations of this kind can be seen in Yarshater's assessment: "In modernist poetry [of Iran], all formal canons of the traditional and imagistic conventions, as well as mystical dimensions of the traditional school are by and large abandoned, and the poets (taking their cues from the West rather than from native traditions) feel free to adapt their poems to the requirements of their individual tastes and artistic outlooks" (*Persian Literature*, 32).

7. The term was apparently coined by Mohammad-Taqi Bahar early in the twentieth century; see Golbon, ed., *Bahar va Adab-e Farsi* (Bahar and Persian Literature), particularly vol. 1: 53–54. For a succinct, recent account of the movement, see Hanaway, "Bazgast-e Adabi" (Literary Return), *Encyclopaedia Iranica* vol. 4: 58–60.

8. Ra'di-Azarakhshi, "Darbareh-ye Sabkaha-ye She'r-e Farsi va Nehsat-e Bazgasht" (Styles of Persian Poetry), 102–5.

9. For a remarkable recent study of the period in Persian literature, see Losensky, " 'Welcoming Fighani'," particularly 148–59.

10. Quoted in Hanaway (Literary Return), 58.

11. See Karimi-Hakkak, "Posht-e Rangha-ye Khazan" (Behind the Colors of Autumn), 241–44.

12. Azar Bigdeli is the best example of this initial assertion. See *Ateshkadeh,* p. 399 of unnumbered pages, quoted in Hanaway (Literary Return), 58.

13. Losensky, "Welcoming Fighani," 97–112.

14. On these devices, see ibid., 103–9; on *esteqbal,* also transliterated as *isteqbal,* see Rypka, *History of Iranian Literature,* 97; Hanaway (Literary Return), 59.

15. Lotman, *Structure of the Artistic Text,* 10.

16. Hanaway (Literary Return), 59.

17. Since the earliest encounters between European Orientalists and Persian poets and literary figures, first in India and later in Europe and in Iran itself, a view of the history of Persian poetry has emerged which emphasizes the purity and simplicity of the early periods and criticizes later complexities and subtleties which characterize the Indian School. On various European attitudes toward Persian poetry, see Karimi-Hakkak, "Shahnameh of Firdawsi."

18. See Dowlatabadi, "Qa'ani-Shirazi," 411–12.

19. Arianpur, *Az Saba ta Nima* (From Saba to Nima), 1: 93–94.

20. Arianpur praises Qa'ani's poetic craftsmanship in these words: "In Qa'ani's poetry lyricism and descriptions are often so original, so subtle and so innovative . . . as to cause the reader to forget the arts of all his predecessors" ([From Saba to Nima], 1: 97). Yusofi shows his agreement by citing in full the passage summarized above ([Clear Fountain], 324).

21. The view that Qa'ani and other poets like him were unaware of their own times is part of the modernist discourse in Iran. See Akhavan-Saless, *Bed'atha va Badaye'-e Nima Yushij* (Nima's Innovations and Novelties), 21–45; Baraheni, *Tala dar Mes* (Gold in Copper), 277–312, 634–42.

22. See Hedayat, *Majma' al-Fosaha* (Assembly of the Eloquent); Kalhor, *Mahkazan al-Ensha'* (Treasure-House of Composition), 15–28; Modarres-Tabrizi, *Rayhanat al-Adab* (Redolence of Literature), 1: 8–13.

23. Lotman, *Structure of the Artistic Text,* 97.

24. The standard book in Persian on Akhundzadeh is Adamiyyat's *Andishehha-ye Mirza Fath' ali Akhundzadeh* (Ideas of Mirza Fath'ali Akhundzadeh). For a recent biography in English, see Algar, "Akundzada," *Encyclopaedia Iranica,* vol. 1: 735–40.

25. Akhundzadeh, *Maktubat* (Correspondences), 8.

26. Ibid., 11.

27. Ibid., 33–34.

28. Ibid., 32.

29. Ibid., 34–35.

30. Akhundzadeh, *Maqalat-e Farsi* (Persian Essays), 29–30.

31. Ibid., 30.

32. Ibid., 33–34.

33. Ibid., 48–49.

34. Ibid., 42.

35. Akhundzadeh, Persian Essays, 52.

36. Ibid., 56.

37. Ibid., 57.

38. The line of thinking which blames Persian poetry for the moral degeneration

of Iranians reemerges in the twentieth century in Ahmad Kasravi. See, for example, his *"Hafez Cheh Miguyad?"* (What Does Hafez Say?), first published in 1939, and *"Farhang Chist?"* (What Is Culture?), first published in 1942.

39. Akhundzadeh, *Correspondences*, 47.

40. For a general assessment of the intellectual climate in Iran in the latter part of the nineteenth century, see Nikki R. Keddie, "Intellectuals in the Modern Middle East."

41. Bayat, "Aqa Khan Kermani." See also Bayat, "Mirza Aqa Khan Kermani." In Persian, the standard book on Kermani is Adamiyyat's, *Andishehha-ye Mirza Aqa Khan Kermani* (Ideas of Mirza Aqa Khan Kermani). For Adamiyyat's assessment of Kermani's views on poetry, see pp. 198–223. For an early eyewitness account of Kermani's life, see San'atizadeh-Kermani, *Ruzegari keh Gozasht* (The Age that Was), 34–99. In this autobiographical account, the author presents an intimate account of Kermani's life and ideas on the occasion of his first meeting with Kermani.

42. Kermani composed this work when he was in exile in the Black Sea port of Trebizond. His essay on Persian poetry has been deleted from the printed edition of *Nameh-ye Bastan* (Book of Ancient Times). It has been cited in Nazem al-Eslam Kermani's *Tarikh-e Bidari-ye Iranian* (History of the Iranians' Awakening), 1: 175–88. Browne cites a passage from this essay in the context of the movement toward literary modernity in the Middle East (*Press and Poetry*), xxxiii–xxxvi).

43. Quoted in Nazem al-Eslam Kermani (History of Iranians' Awakening), 175.

44. Ibid., 175–76. See also Arianpur (From Saba to Nima), 1: 393.

45. Browne, *Press and Poetry*, xxxvi.

46. Nazem al-Eslam Kermani (History of Iranians' Awakening), 176; also quoted in Arianpur (From Saba to Nima), 1: 393.

47. Nazem al-Eslam Kermani (History of Iranians' Awakening), 176.

48. Mirza Aqa Khan Kermani, *Nameh-ye Bastan* (Book of Ancient Times), 2–10; see also the continuation of Kermani's work by Adib-Kermani, titled *Salar-Nameh* (Book of the Great), 29–38.

49. Kermani undertook to write his historical works "Book of Ancient Times" and "Alexander's Mirror" in the belief that history is more important and more essential than literature. See his preface to *A'ineh-ye Sekandari* (Alexander's Mirror), 8–12.

50. For opposing views of Malkom's ideas, compare Nura'i, *Tahqiq dar Afkar-e Mirza Malkom Khan Nazem al-Dowleh* (Research into the Ideas of Mirza Malkom Khan) and Algar, *Mirza Malkum Khan.*

51. The text of "Sayyahi Guyad" (A Traveler Relates) appears with rather significant textual variations in different editions of Malkom's work. I have adopted the text cited in Arianpur (From Saba to Nima), 1: 320–22. For an earlier version with significant differences, see Malkom Khan, *Kolliyyat-e Malkom* (Complete Works), 1: 192–207. For a more complete translation of Malkom's text into English, see "Appendix B: A Traveler's Narrative," in Algar, *Mirza Malkum Khan*, 278–99.

52. The figure of the arithmomancer does not exist in Rabi'zadeh's edition of *Kolliyyat-e Malkom*. Presumably following Arianpur's version, Algar adds this character.

53. Arianpur (From Saba to Nima), 1: 320.

54. Ibid., 321.

55. Ibid., 321–22.

56. Ibid. See also Malkom Khan (Complete Works), 1: 200.

57. These ideals are expressed in various writings of the period: see Tavakoli-Targhi, "Refashioning Iran."

58. Arianpur (From Saba to Nima), 1: 393.

59. Lotman, "Dynamic Model," 206.

60. See Maragheh'i, *Siahatnameh-ye Ebrahim-Bayg* (Ebrahim-Bayg's Travelogue), 102–3.

61. E'temad al-Saltaneh (Prime of Histories), 227.

NOTES TO CHAPTER TWO

1. On the concept and various definitions of "the poetry of the constitutional movement," see Browne, *Press and Poetry,* particularly Part II, "Specimens of the Political and Patriotic Poetry of Modern Persia," 168–308; also, see Arianpur, *Az Saba ta Nima* (From Saba to Nima), 2: 121–72, and Shafi'i-Kadkani, *Advar-e She'r-e Farsi az Mashrutiyyat ta Soqut-e Saltanat* (Periods of Persian Poetry), 91–149.

2. The usages of *qasideh-ye vatani* (patriotic qasida) and *ghazal-e siasi* (political ghazal) occur in all major books on the Persian poetry of early twentieth-century Iran. For a new conceptualization of these texts, see Najmabadi, "Beloved and Mother."

3. Applying Bakhtin's notion of "genre" to Persian poetic forms, I distinguish between two conceptualizations of qasida and ghazal in Persian poetry. See Karimi-Hakkak, "Preservation and Presentation." On Bakhtin's theory of genre, see Morson, "Bakhtin, Genres, and Temporality."

4. On these concepts, see Yasemi, *Tarikh-e Adabiyyat-e Mo'aser* (History of Contemporary Literature); Sepanlu, *'Aref-e Qazvini, Sha'er-e Taraneh-ye Melli* ('Aref-e Qazvini, Poet of the National Song), 9–23.

5. Many constitution-era reformers continued the kind of discourse I examined in chapter 1. See, for example, "Tajdid-e Hayat-e Adabi" (Literary Revival), in *Sur-e Esrafil,* no. 27 (Wednesday Rabi' al-Avval 27, 1326/April 29, 1908), 2–4; reprinted as Dehkhoda and Shirazi, *Sur-e Esrafil,* "Dowreh-ye Kamel." See also Khalkhali, *Tazkereh-ye Sho'ara-ye Mo'aser-e Iran* (Biographies of Contemporary Poets of Iran), 1: 3–23; and Borqa'i, *Sokhanvaran-e Nami-ye Mo'aser* (Famous Contemporary Poets), 3–8.

6. The article is unsigned. It may have been written by Dehkhoda, since he was in charge of the literary aspects of *Sur-e Esrafil.*

7. Dehkhoda and Shirazi (Literary Revival), 3. In his study of *Sur-e Esrafil,* Baqer Mo'meni publishes this article as an appendix without identifying the author. He also cites three lines of the qasida which follows the essay, asserting that it "contains nothing new for us, either in style or in expression." See Mo'meni, *Sur-e Esrafil* (Esrafil's Trumpet call), 60.

8. Lotman, "Dynamic Model," 204.

9. Browne, *Press and Poetry,* xvi.

10. Lotman, *Structure of the Artistic Text,* 22. Lotman attributes the particular dynamics of literary tradition and innovation to the special nature of the material which makes literature, namely, language. He distinguishes between language as the material of literature and the material substances of other arts such as paint and stone. "Until they come into the hands of the artist," he says, these materials "are socially indifferent." "Language," he believes, "constitutes a special material characterized by its high degree of social activeness even before the hand of the artist touches it" (*Analysis of the Poetic Text,* 17).

11. For a concise treatment of these interrelated topics, see Meisami, "Iran," 45–62.

12. The *mosammat* is a stanzaic and strophic verse form, usually with a rhyme pattern that connects the stanzas through the refrain. It may be a survival from pre-Islamic times, but has come to us through the works of early Ghaznavid poets, particularly Manuchehri. In later centuries, Vahshi Bafqi stands out as a most prominent user of the form. Rypka mentions that twentieth-century Persian poets felt especially attracted to this form. See his *History of Iranian Literature,* 96.

13. Iranian assessments of Dehkhoda's "Remember . . ." as an innovative poem are mentioned by Munibur Rahman, among others. The poem, Rahman observes, "remained for a number of years the only outstanding example of experimental writing which obtained recognition from the accepted arbiters of literary taste" (*Anthology of Modern Persian Poetry,* 2: v).

14. Quoted in Dehkhoda (Divan), 3d ed., 6.

15. Yusofi, *Cheshmeh-ye Rowshan* (Clear Fountain), 462. Browne and Arianpur also praise the poem highly. See Browne, *Press and Poetry,* 200–201; and Arianpur (From Saba to Nima), 2: 96–97.

16. The visual context in which the poem's first appearance is set is significant. On page 4 of the third issue of *Sur-e Esrafil*'s second year, which was to be the last issue of the newspaper's brief life in exile, the top half of the page is adorned with the picture of Jahangir Khan Shirazi set in an ornate floral frame. The caption under the picture reads: "The martyr of the path to freedom and the most sincere defender of the motherland's rights, Mirza Jahangir Khan Shirazi, manager of the newspaper *Sur-e Esrafil* who, in the morning of Jemad al-Ula 24, 1324, was elevated to the rank of the martyrs. In the near future we will print and publish the biography and description of that noble being's services in the form of a book, thus celebrating his undying name" (Dehkhoda and Shirazi, *Sur-e Esrafil,* p. 284 of unnumbered pages).

17. In spite of the fact that in the original version of the poem, and many early printings of its text (including the version published in Browne, *Press and Poetry,* 202), the letter *gaf* in this word is marked by a *kasreh* to distinguish the word *gel* (mud) from *gol* (rose), many later scholars and editors, most notably Yusofi, have misread and misinterpreted this image. See Yusofi (Clear Fountain), 465.

18. Dehkhoda and Shirazi, *Sur-e Esrafil,* p. 285 of unnumbered pages.

19. Throughout this book, I have kept my translations deliberately literal. They are meant to serve analytical purposes, not esthetic ones. For another translation of Dehkhoda's poem, see Browne, *Press and Poetry,* 203–4.

20. Browne's translation of the Persian caption to the poem reads as follows:

"In Memory of my incomparable Friend: the offering of an unworthy brother at the shrine of that most high and holy spirit" (*Press and Poetry,* 203).

21. Dehkhoda (Divan), 2d ed., 6. Also quoted in part in Arianpur (From Saba to Nima), 2: 95. Writing these words some forty years after the date of the poem's composition, Dehkhoda's memory of the originating event may have lapsed somewhat. The poem was published not in the first but, as I have indicated, in the third and last issue of the newspaper in exile.

22. Browne, *Press and Poetry,* 203–64.

23. Yusofi (Clear Fountain), 460–67.

24. On the tradition of the elegy in classical Persian poetry, see Emami, *Marsieh-Sora'i dar Adabiyyat-e Farsi ta Payan-e Qarn-e Hashtom* (Elegiac Compositions in Persian Literature). On Farrokhi-Sistani's famous elegy on the death of Mahmud of Ghazneh, see Yusofi, (Clear Fountain), 45–61. On the elegiac mode in European poetic traditions, see Lipking, *Life of the Poet,* 138. In discussing Mallarmé, Lipking calls elegies "the heart of literary history, at once a memorial of the past and an attempt to improve upon it or put it to use." See also Scholes's discussion of W. S. Merwin's one-line elegy in *Semiotics and Interpretation,* 37–56.

25. Todorov, *Mikhail Bakhtin: The Dialogical Principle,* 30.

26. In his analysis of the function of Koranic and national mythologies in Persian poetry, Abdolhosayn Zarrinkub concludes that "such myths are a part of an ancient common heritage which bestows distinct identity on the particular images, signs, and themes of Persian poetry." See Zarrinkub, *Sayri dar She'r-e Farsi* (Excursion in Persian Poetry), 200.

27. The terminology of life and death, applied to light-giving inanimate objects such as lamps, lanterns, and candles, has deep roots in Zoroastrian cosmology and culture. See Boyce, *History of Zoroastrianism,* vol. 1: 191–93.

28. Hafez (Divan), 1: 150.

29. In classical Persian poetry, night is most frequently semanticized as a time of darkness, both of the lover separated from the beloved and of a mystical or intellectual darkness.

30. Sa'di, *Bustan-e Sa'di* (Bustan), 114.

31. Sa'di, *Golestan-e Sa'di* (Golestan), 50.

32. Many of the poems, written in obvious imitation or in response to "Remember . . . ," made use of the imagery of night and day, darkness and light. See Arianpur (From Saba to Nima), 2: 97. In later generations, too, the use of night as an allusion to political oppression and absence of freedom abounds. For an analysis of this image, see Karimi-Hakkak, "Revolutionary Posturing."

33. Hafez (Divan), 1: 516.

34. References to Joseph as the sign of fulfillment of dreams abound in Persian poetry. See Rowshan, *Tafsir-e Sureh-ye Yusof* (Interpretation of the Joseph Chapter); Sajjadi, ed., *Hadayeq al-Haqayeq dar Tafsir-e Sureh-ye Yusof* (Gardens of Truth in Interpreting the Joseph Chapter).

35. In classical Persian poetry, the contrast between *Bahar* (spring) and *Day* (the tenth month in the Iranian solar calendar corresponding to December 12–January 20 in the Gregorian calendar) is used metonymically to allude to the contrast between

the season of blossoming and that of wilting, much like the May–December binary in the English language. In Persian mystical poetry, the contrast extends to mental states and human moods as well. See Tusi, *Asas al-Eqtebas* (Foundations of Imitation), 132–45; Foruzanfar, *Sokhan va Sokhanvaran* (Words and Wordsmiths), 53–55.

36. Like Joseph's story, the story of Moses figures in the Koran and, more prominently, in Persian literature. Allusions to the exodus provide a particularly apt metaphor for the human desire to return to God. See Maybodi, *Kashf al-Asrar va 'Oddat al-Abrar* (Revealing Mysteries and Edifying the Pious), 2: 50–51.

37. I know of no precedent for the phrase *dowreh-ye tala'i* (the Golden Age) in classical Persian poetry. The phrase is not listed by the *Loghtnameh* of Dehkhoda either. This may mean that Dehkhoda himself does not conceive of it as a phrase current in the Persian language, an assumption which supports the idea of the phrase as a metaphor which originates in this usage by Dehkhoda.

38. In some modern literary works, pre-Islamic Iran is portrayed as a lost Golden Age. The idea may have its roots in Mirza Aqa Khan Kermani's *A'ineh-ye Sekandari* (Alexander's Mirror) and *Nameh-ye Bastan* (Book of Ancient Times). For an example of this idea in the journalistic writing of the constitutional era see Dehkhoda and Shirazi, *Sur-e Esrafil*, no. 18: 3–4.

39. In a footnote to his translation of this poem, Browne takes note of this specific political allusion: "Here," he says, under the word Shaddad, "Muhammad-'Ali, the ex-Shah, and his garden, the Bagh-i Shah, are meant" (*Press and Poetry*, 204).

40. Lotman and Uspensky, "Semiotic Mechanism of Culture," 211–33.

41. Lotman, "Dynamic Model," 193–210.

42. Dehkhoda acknowledges his debt to European poetry. In a note to Mo'azed al-Saltaneh, he writes: "I have finished the testimonial of the late Jahangir Khan, which I was supposed to compose as a poem. It is ready. I myself think that it is in the first rank of European poems, although a girl praised by her mom would be fit for her uncle." Quoted in Afshar, *Mobarezeh ba Mohammad-'Ali Shah* (Struggling against Mohammad-'Ali Shah), forty-four.

43. "Remember . . ." was widely imitated as an example of the "political poetry" Iranian literature needed. For a list of these imitations, see Arianpur (From Saba to Nima), 2, 97 n. 1.

44. For a biography of 'Aref, see Sepanlu, *'Aref-e Qazvini, Sha'er-e Taraneh-ye Melli* ('Aref Qazvini, Poet of the National Song). See also Shafaq's writings and comments in 'Aref Qazvini (Divan).

45. This title is given to this ghazal in various editions of the *Divan*. However, the poem may have been untitled originally. Browne, who makes reference to it, does not mention a title. In classical Persian poetry, poets did not assign titles to their poems.

46. For the account of the occasion at which the ghazal was sung, I rely on Browne (*Press and Poetry*, xvi–xvii).

47. Here is Browne's record of the event: "On the occasion of a representation given in Tihran [*sic*] a month before the heart-rending catastrophe of Tabriz [Browne clarifies this in a note that reads: 'i.e., about the end of November, 1911'] by the Literary Circle of the Democratic Party under the title of the National festival to

commemorate the victory of the supporters of the Constitution and the defeat of Muhammad ʿAli, ʿArif undertook the role of the minstrel, and, in a most charming and affecting manner, sung the poem which he had composed for this occasion, and which begins as follows." He then offers the first two lines of the poem and his translation of them (*Press and Poetry*, xvii).

48. ʿAref Qazvini, *Kolliyyat-e Divan* (Complete Divan).

49. My translation is deliberately literal. For another translation of this poem, see Irani, trans., *Poems of ʿAref.* Here is Browne's translation of the poem's opening lines: "Last night a message reached me from the old wine-seller: / Drink Wine, for a whole nation has come to its senses! / Despotism tore away from Persia a thousand veils: / A thousand thanks that the Constitution has come to replace these veils!"

50. Most modernist poets imagine the *locus classicus* of the classical Persian ghazal as the closed assembly of a select few. See Shafiʿi-Kadkani (Hazin Lahiji). See also Naderpur's essays titled "Tefli-e Sad Saleh-'i beh Nam-e Sheʿr-e Now" (A One-Hundred-Year-Old Infant Named New Poetry).

51. Browne states that the texts of ʿAref's poems were usually distributed to audiences before his performances and that they were also sold as lyrics to his songs. His note reads: "I possess a printed pamphlet of 13 pp. containing six of these poems, arranged for use of singers. It is dated the 26th of Shawwal, A.H., 1329 (Oct. 20, 1911), and is described as 'offered to the Literary Society in memory of the glorious Festival of the Victors,' that is, the constitutionalist armies which captured Tihran in July 1909" (*Press and Poetry*, xvii n. 2).

52. For examples of Hafez's ghazals beginning with the motif of a message from the *pir*, see Hafez (Divan), 1: 218, 288, 572, 736, 842, among other places.

53. In the classical Persian ghazal, at times historical or topical knowledge is denied or negated to allow the transference of poetic energy to the lyrical plane. ʿAref, however, seems here to rely on that kind of knowledge in order to communicate his message. Compare Hafez's line: "*ma qesseh-ye sekandar o dara nakhandeh-im / az ma bejoz hekayat-e mehr o vafa mapors*" (We have not read the story of Alexander and Darius / do not ask us anything except the story of love and loyalty) (Hafez [Divan], 1: 544).

54. Ibid., 1: 218.

55. For a discussion of the image of the Turk as the beautiful beloved, see Clinton, *Divan of Mannehihri*, 122–23; Meisami, *Medieval Persian Court Party*, 66–67.

56. ʿAref is known to have been an active supporter of a republican state in Iran. See Haʿeri, ʿ*Aref Qazvini, Shaʿ er-e Melli-ye Iran* (ʿAref-Qazvini, Iran's National Poet), 30–31.

57. The world as the place of exile is a favorite trope of mystical Persian poets. Rumi's introduction to *Spiritual Couplets* is the most extensive and best-known example of this. See Rumi, *Mathnawi of Jalaluʾddin Rumi*, vol. 1: 3–4. For another example see Hafez (Divan), 1: 684.

58. Hafez (Divan), 1: 680.

59. On the details of Mohammad-ʿAli Shah's taking refuge in the Russian embassy, see Browne, *Persian Revolution*, 321–23.

60. In general, the language of ʿAref's poetry has been judged wanting. In his

" 'Aref-Nameh" (Book of 'Aref), Iraj Mirza calls him a composer of song lyrics *(tasnif-saz)* rather than a poet *(sha'er)*. This view persists to this day, as evidenced in Hamid Zarrinkub, *Cheshmandaz-e She'r-e Now-e Farsi* (Landscape of the Modernist Persian Poetry), 30–31, and Yusofi, (Clear Fountain), 395–404.

61. Todorov, *Mikhail Bakhtin: Dialogical Principle*, 81.

62. A study of the rising fortunes of Hafez in modern Iran may provide important clues to the nature of the relevances Iranian modernists sought in the poetry of their own time.

63. Bakhtin's statement in this regard is of special significance: "The separation of style and language from genre is largely responsible for the fact that only individual overtones of style, or those of literary currents, are privileged objects of study, while the basic social tone is ignored. The great destinies of literary discourse, tied to the destiny of genres, are overshadowed by the petty vicissitudes of stylistic modification, themselves tied to individual artists and particular currents. For this reason, stylistics has been deprived of an authentic philosophical and sociological approach" (cited in Todorov, *Mikhail Bakhtin: Dialogical Principle*, 80.

64. This view of modernity informs many of Dehkhoda's and 'Aref's later poems. For an overview of this trend see Kubickova, "The Literary Life in the Years 1921–1941," particularly the section titled "The Main Trends in Poetry," in Rypka, *History of Iranian Literature*, 384–89.

65. On this point see Shukman, "Dialectics of Change."

66. Todorov, *Mikhail Bakhtin: Dialogical Principle*, 80.

NOTES TO CHAPTER 3

1. All historians of Persian literature stipulate great cultural and literary changes as a result of the Mongol and Tartar invasions. 'Abdolhosayn Zarrinkub regards those events as the cause of "an irreversible decline" in Persian poetry. See his *Sayri dar She'r-e Farsi* (Excursion in Persian Poetry), 69–92.

2. In Rashid Yasemi's essays titled "Enqelab-e Adabi" (Literary Revolution), published in *Daneshkadeh,* the opening sentence of the first essay typifies the quest for such relevancies. It reads: "Of all of French literature, the sixteenth century is most relevant to the present situation in our country." See *Daneshkadeh,* no. 1 (April 21, 1918): 23.

3. Contemporary literary scholarship in Iran tends to confirm this impression, too. See, for example, Shafi'i-Kadkani, *Advar-e She'r-e Farsi az Mashrutiyyat ta Soqut-e Saltanat* (Periods of Persian Poetry), particularly 36–48.

4. In 1910, Yusof E'tesam, a prominent translator of literary works from English and French, had published a journal called *Bahar* which was in many ways a model for *Daneshkadeh.* Strictly speaking, however, *Bahar* cannot be called a literary journal since it was more general and more diverse in its contents. On the journal *Bahar,* see Sadr-Hashemi, *Tarikh-e Jara'ed va Majallat-e Iran* (History of Iranian Journals and Periodicals), 2: 26–30; see also Yusofi, "Bahar."

5. The concept of a "literary revolution" paralleling the Constitutional Revolution was prevalent in the decades that followed the latter revolution. Naturally, different poets and critics envisioned it differently. For example, Iraj Mirza, while himself

an important agent of literary change, mocks the idea of a "literary revolution" in a poem of that name. See Iraj Mirza (Divan), 1963 ed., 118–25. Vera Kubickova characterizes the changes that occurred in the Persian literature of Iran in that period as a "literary renaissance" (see Rypka, *History of Iranian Literature*, 362–72). M. R. Ghanoonparvar believes the changes are fundamental enough to "warrant the description of a 'literary revolution' " (*Prophets of Doom*, 1–33, particularly 31–32 n. 30).

6. The essay series entitled "Tarikh-e Adabi" (Literary History), written by ʿAbbas Eqbal-Ashtiani, was a regular feature of *Daneshkadeh* up to the eighth issue. The essays were discontinued when their author ceased his collaboration with the journal as a result of a dispute with Bahar.

7. The series of essays entitled "Enqelab-e Adabi" (Literary Revolution) was written primarily by Rashid Yasemi, although one essay (*Daneshkadeh*, no. 4 [August 24, 1918]: 193–99) bears the name of Saʿid Nafisi, another member of the circle. They may be translations of portions of a contemporary French textbook on French literary history. The series covers sixteenth- through nineteenth-century French literature in a total of eight essays.

8. Ibid., no. 2 (May 22, 1918): 89.

9. Ibid., no. 1 (April 21, 1918): 22.

10. Lotman, *Structure of the Artistic Text*, 292.

11. Ibid., 293.

12. *Daneshkadeh* stopped publication exactly one year after its first issue had appeared. The last issue, numbers 11 and 12, is dated April 20, 1919. It carries an article by Bahar in which he declares the group's mission to mediate change in the literature of Iran accomplished. The cessation may have been related to the ill feelings arising from the dispute between Bahar and Eqbal-Ashtiani.

13. The word *maram* (doctrine, dogma, ideology) occurs repeatedly in three significant lead articles written by Bahar in three early issues of *Daneshkadeh*: "Maram-e Ma" (Our Ideology), no. 1 (April 12, 1918): 1–7; "Enteqadat dar Atraf-e Maram-e Ma" (Criticisms Concerning Our Ideology), no. 3 (June 22, 1918): 115–24; and "Taʾsir-e mohit dar Adabiyyat" (The Impact of the Environment on Literature), no. 4 (August 24, 1918): 171–78.

14. The words *tarz* (method, style), *sabk* (individual or period style or literary school), and *oslub* (manner, mode, fashion) were used ambiguously, sometimes interchangeably, at this time.

15. For an overview of the concept of imitation in classical Persian literature, see Losensky, " 'Welcoming Fighani'," 97–101.

16. *Daneshkadeh*, no. 1 (April 21, 1918): 3–4.

17. Ibid., 3.

18. Quoted in Arianpur, *Az Saba ta Nima* (From Saba to Nima), 2: 447. My efforts to gain access to *Tajaddod* have not been successful. I have relied on secondary sources for citations of Rafʿat's words.

19. Ibid., 448.

20. Ibid., 449.

21. The semantic ambiguities inherent in the words Rafʿat uses are significant. Lotman speculates that such indeterminacies serve a specific function in making

change in the "language" of literature possible. See Lotman, "The Alien Word in the Poetic Text," in his *Analysis of the Poetic Text,* 107–13.

22. *Daneshkadeh,* no. 3 (June 22, 1918): 115–16.

23. Ibid., 121.

24. Judging by the items translated from French and published in *Daneshkadeh,* Bahar's notion of the relationship between the lives of poets and the character of their social milieu may have been affected by biographical sketches of French romantic poets published in *Daneshkadeh.* Chief among these were Chateaubriand, Daudet, and Hugo. Raf'at's model of the relationship may have been inspired by his reading of a later generation of French poets, most notably Baudelaire and the French symbolists.

25. This attitude toward history forms a significant part of the discourse of Iranian modernity. See Karimi-Hakkak, "Nejad, Mazhab, Zaban" (Race, Religion, and Language).

26. *Daneshkadeh,* no. 4 (August 24, 1918): 171–78; and no. 5 (September 24, 1918): 227–35.

27. Bahar, "Alfaz va Ma'ani" (Words and Meanings), ibid., no. 10 (February 20, 1919): 509.

28. The normative distinction between *sha'er* (poet) and *nazem* (verisifer) first appears in the writings of Akhundzadeh, and gradually becomes a part of the stock-in-trade of all the participants in the literary debates of the twentieth century. It is still used widely as a tool by which Iranian poets, critics, and readers seek to confer the privileged status of "poet" on certain individuals or deny it to others.

29. *Daneshkadeh,* no. 5 (September 24, 1918): 256. In its citation of classical Persian poetry, *Daneshkadeh* divides them into *moteqaddemin* (the earliest poets of the classical tradition), *motevassetin* (later classics), and *mote'akhkherin* (those closest to the present time).

30. Ibid., 262.

31. These include lyrical fragments, dramatic scenes or anecdotes, and diverse literary episodes from different cultures and periods. See "Dastkesh, az Asar-e Shiler" (The Glove, by Schiller) in ibid., no. 4 (August 24, 1918): 203–4; a portion of one of Schiller's dramatic narratives in nos. 6 (October 24, 1918) and 7 (November 23, 1918): 320–24 and 380–84; an episode entitled "Seh Hendi" (Three Indians) by the German poet Nicholas Lenau; a portion of Dante's *Commedia* entitled "Madkhal-e Jahannam" (The Entrance to the Inferno), in no. 9 (January 21, 1919): 483–85; and a portion of an essay by Rousseau entitled "Vejdan" (Conscience) in no. 10 (February 20, 1919): 552–54.

32. Ibid., no. 1 (April 21, 1918): 23.

33. Ibid., no. 7 (November 23, 1918): 389–90.

34. Arianpur (From Saba to Nima), 2: 436 n. 1.

35. *Daneshkadeh,* no. 1 (April 21, 1918): 2.

36. In fact, the basic direction of cultural change in modern Iran may be illustrated through the changing fortune of Sa'di. Up until the middle of the nineteenth century, he was viewed not only as the master of the literary style but also as the propagator of the best code of moral conduct. He has gradually come to be seen by

and large as justifying a variety of moral behaviors in specific situations. See Dashti, *Dar Qalamrow-e Saʿdi* (In Saʿdi's Realm). For a discussion of this point, see Yusofi, *Chesmeh-ye Rowshan* (Clear Fountain), 230–46.

37. Rypka characterizes Qa'ani's *Parishan* as "a parallel to Golestan" (*History of Iranian Literature,* 330).

38. Among its fifty-four lessons, the ninth-grade Persian language textbook published by Iran's Ministry of Education in 1992 includes four lessons based on Saʿdi's writings as well as an essay by the contemporary scholar Gholam-Hosayn Yusofi entitled "Jahan-e Matlub-e Saʿdi dar Bustan" (Saʿdi's Ideal World in *Bustan*).

39. On the Political ramifications of Taleqani's article see "Sheʿr Chist va Shaʿer Kist?" (What Is Poetry and Who Is a Poet?); and Bahar's "Saʿdi Kist?" (Who Is Saʿdi?).

40. For an overview of this debate, see Arianpur (From Saba to Nima), 2: 437–45.

41. Quoted in ibid., 438–39.

42. Bahar (Who is Saʿdi?), 2.

43. Ibid., 3.

44. Ibid.

45. Quoted in Arianpur (From Saba to Nima), 2: 439.

46. Ibid., 444.

47. Ibid., 444–45.

48. Ibid., 440.

49. In a note, Arianpur gives the French words *impressions* and *sensations* as the equivalents of the Persian words *entebaʿat* and *tahassosat,* respectively. They may have been conceived and cited by Rafʿat himself. See ibid., 441 nn. 1, and 2.

50. Ibid., 442.

51. Lotman, *Structure of the Artistic Text,* 60.

52. Ibid.

53. Quoted in Hirschkop and Shepherd, eds., *Bakhtin and Cultural Theory,* 72.

54. Ibid., 92.

55. For a discussion of the idea of commitment in literature, see Ghanoon-parvar, *Prophets of Doom,* particularly 73–102.

56. For later manifestations of this idea, see Karimi-Hakkak, "Revolutionary Posturing," 507–9.

57. For a history of this movement, see Abrahamian, *Iran between Two Revolutions,* 112–15; see also Atabaki, *Azerbaijan,* 46–51.

58. These include some poems by Shams Kasma'i, the first woman to write blank verse in Persian. Shams Kasma'i is one of the earliest Iranian women to use the composition of modernist poetry as a means for personal expression. Unfortunately, little is known about her life. In a brief note, Arianpur includes the following sketch of her: "Shams knew Turkish, Persian, and Russian well, and was one of Iran's intellectual and learned women. When she came to Tabriz with her family, she did not have the veil covering her body, and was the first Iranian woman to appear unveiled in the streets and Bazaars of Tabriz. For this very reason she was subjected to great pains in those days at the hands of ignorant people. In Tabriz, her home was the

gathering place of writers and other learned men. Later, however, after she moved to Tehran, she spent her days in solitude and silence until she passed away in 1961" (Arianpur [From Saba to Nima], 2: 457).

59. For the most recent example of such biographical sketches, see Gholam-Reza Hamraz, "Taqi Raf'at, Sha'eri Setihandeh" (Taqi Raf'at, a Militant Poet), 64–68. My decade-long search for *Tajaddod* and *Azadistan* and for further information on Raf'at has had only limited success. Of the two short-lived journals which published Raf'at's works, *Tajaddod* is the better known. See Sadr-Hashemi (History of Iranian Journals and Periodicals), 1: 105–6. *Azadistan,* of which only three issues were published, is not mentioned here.

NOTES TO CHAPTER 4

1. Rypka, *History of Iranian Literature,* 342.
2. Arianpur, *Az Saba ta Nima* (From Saba to Nima), 1: 260.
3. In his and Cuypers's *Aux Sources de la Nouvelle Persane,* French scholar Christophe Balay does make reference to the possibility of treating the choice of the kinds of texts to be translated as signifying some cultural lack, a collective intellectual desire of sorts, particularly in relation to the forms in which the native tradition sees itself as deficient. He refers to early Persian translations of European, particularly French, fiction as revealing the depths of the tastes and desires of the literary culture throughout the latter half of the nineteenth century. However, translation as an instrument of systemic redefinition and realignment still remains unrecognized, as there have been no attempts to demonstrate its impact at the level of the literary text.
4. Borrowings from other literary traditions in forms other than translation play a significant part in modeling activities of a systemic kind and consequently in instituting change in the native system. For a study of some ways in which the Persian literature of the modern era has borrowed from European sources, see Mohandessi, "Hedayat and Rilke"; and Beard, *Hedayat's Blind Owl.*
5. Some of the best-known works of the twentieth-century Persian literature of Iran are marked as "based on" (*bar asas-e*), "modeled after" (*eqtebas az*), or "inspired by" (*ba elham az*) foreign, usually European, texts. Iraj Mirza's Zohreh va Manuchehr (Zohreh and Manuchehr), Parviz Natel-Khanlari's 'Oqab (The Eagle), and many of Bahar's qet'ehs (fragments), are only some of the best-known examples. Specific studies of the ways such texts relate to the works that have given rise to them is an urgent task of literary scholarship in this field.
6. At mid-century, the compiler of an anthology of European literary works translated into Persian wrote in his preface: "There are many poets and writers whose works in their own languages are considered masterpieces of eloquence. . . . However, as soon as such eloquent pieces are translated into another language, they leave behind all—or at least much—of their beauty and grace. A corpse is carried over to the other language, leaving its soul at home, very much like some sensitive flowers which, removed from their native clime, wilt away quickly and die." See Hamidi-Shirazi, comp., *Darya-ye Gowhar* (Ocean of Pearls), 2: ten.
7. At least one theorist argues that translated literature always constitutes "a

body of texts that is structured and functions as a system." See Even-Zohar, *Papers in Historical Poetics,* particularly the section entitled "The Position of Translated Literature within the Literary Polysystem," 21.

8. Ibid., 22.

9. Iranian newspapers of the early twentieth century usually devoted a separate section to verse or prose pieces translated or based on European texts, often under the heading *Adabiyyat* (Literature) or *Adabiyyat-e Jadid* (New Literature). In most cases, these consisted of passages from larger texts such as novels or plays.

10. Perhaps this was because these "minor" verse forms were not identified with specific thematic concerns as much as were forms like the ghazal or the qasida.

11. Both Mahjub and Arianpur mention Shakespeare's *Venus and Adonis* as the sole source for the Persian poem. Yet, they both recount the differences between the two texts. Compare Iraj Mirza (Divan), 1963 ed., 244–53; and Arianpur (From Saba to Nima), 2: 401–13. It is entirely possible, I think, that Iraj may have been working from a French version of the Greek myth or a French translation of Shakespeare's play.

12. Of these, La Fontaine's fables have been reproduced in verse translations far more than all the others. In 1913 Ashraf al-Din Gilani, known as Nasim-e Shomal, published a complete volume of verse fables based on the works of La Fontaine and Florian. See Namini, *Javdaneh Seyyed Ashraf al-Din Gilani (Nasim-e Shomal)* (Immortal Seyyed Ashraf al-Din Gilani), 794–840.

13. This poem was first published in *Daneshkadeh,* no. 9 (January 21, 1919): 505–6. It has been reprinted in successive editions of Bahar's *Divan* with no reference to the poem's origin. For the latest edition, see Bahar, *Divan-e Ashʿar-e Shadravan Mohammad-Taqi Bahar Malek al-Shoʿara* (Poetic Divan). For the text of the poems, see vol. 2: 1108.

14. La Fontaine, *Oeuvres Complètes,* vol. 1: *Fables, Contes et Nouvelles,* 191.

15. *Eqterah,* a word of Arabic derivation, literally means a test, and is used in this context as a test of poetic talent. Its usage must be seen as an attempt to conceptualize what is involved in terms of the creative process required for it. Of the six times this word is used in *Daneshkadeh,* four refer to Bahar's versification of a European text.

16. Literary competitions of various sorts were a frequent feature of many early twentieth-century newspapers and journals in Iran. For a particularly interesting one, see "Jayezeh: Yek ghazal-e Badiʿ" (Prize: A Novel Ghazal), *Zaban-e Azad,* no. 33 (October 21, 1917): 4.

17. *Daneshkadeh,* no. 1 (April 21, 1918): 22.

18. Ibid., no. 2 (May 22, 1918): 104–7.

19. Bahar (Poetic Divan), 1: 1108. For an example of the textbook reproduction of the poem, see Islamic Republic of Iran, Ministry of Education, *Farsi-e Chaharom-e Dabestan* (Persian for Fourth-Grade Elementary Schools), 104.

20. For an account of Bahar's early political life see Loraine, "Bahar in the Context of Persian Constitutional Revolution." See also Matini, "Bahar."

21. Bahar's use of the term *dehqan* is noteworthy. A class of landed gentry, the *dehqan*s were thought of at this time as having guarded Iranian identity in the crucial

period that followed the Arab conquest of Persia in the seventh century. Ferdowsi, the poet of *Shahnameh,* is identified with this social class.

22. In Bahar's *Divan,* the sources of his poems are occasionally identified. In this case, however, no mention is made of La Fontaine's poem or the first context in which Bahar's poem itself was published, this in spite of Bahar's own open attitude as gleaned from the pages of *Daneshkadeh.* Also, in his *Divan,* attributions are usually phrased in general terms, such as "translation of poems by an English poet" (tarjomeh-ye ash'ar-e sha'er-e englisi) or "translation from a French piece" (tarjomeh az yek qet'eh-ye faranseh). See Bahar (Poetic Divan), 2: 1087, 1107.

23. None of Bahar's biographers and commentators known to me has made a reference to the origins of the poem under study here. See Golbon, *Bahar va Adab-e Farsi* (Bahar and Persian Literature); Homa'i, "Takmil-e Sharh-e Hal-e Bahar" (Bahar's Complete Biography); and Matini, "Bahar."

24. See Shamisa, "Malek al-Sho'ara Bahar va Tarjomeh" (Bahar and Translation). This brief note purports to have "discovered" the "source" of Bahar's "Toil and Treasure" to be an Arabic poem entitled "Al-Fallahu wa Banuhu" (The Husbandman and His Sons) by the Arab poet Jerjis Hammam, published in a book of juvenile verse entitled *Madarij al-Qira'ah* (Graded Readings), possibly used as a school textbook. In fact, Hammam's is an independent translation into Arabic of La Fontaine's fable, unrelated to Bahar's poem.

25. Iraj Mirza (Divan), 1963 ed., 186–87.

26. "Yek Mosabeqeh-ye Adabi" (Literary Competition), *Iranshahr* 2, no. 4 (December 7, 1923): 226.

27. Iraj Mirza (Divan), 1963 ed., 272.

28. Iraj Mirza, *Divan-e Kamel-e Iraj Mirza* (Complete Divan), item 17, p. Y. Except for the introductory essay, this book is a facsimile reprint of the 1963 edition in note 27 above.

29. Richepin, *Choix de Poésies,* 113–14.

30. Sayyed Hadi Ha'eri lists five poems by Iraj in a section entitled "*Madar-Nameh*" (Book of the Mother) in his *Afkar va Asar-e Iraj* (Ideas and Works of Iraj Mirza), 99–103.

31. The effect of the Romantics, particularly French Romantic poets, on Iranian literature of the early twentieth century is an unstudied area of modern Persian literature. In general, contemporary Persian poetry has been recognized as "romantic in mood and contemplative in outlook." See, for example, Ehsan Yarshater's "Preface" to Karimi-Hakkak, trans., *Anthology of Modern Persian Poetry,* xiii–xiv. However, more extensive studies of the affinities, intertextualities, and possible influences have yet to be undertaken.

32. Throughout the first half of the twentieth century, French Romantic poets were translated into Persian far more widely than any other group of Western authors.

33. "Yek Mosabeqeh-ye Adabi" (Literary Competition), 226.

34. There is a more specific connection in classical Persian poetry between the consumption of alcohol and the impurity of the human heart. One well-known line in Hafez runs thus: *ruz dar kasb-e honar kush keh may khordan-e ruz / del-e chun ayeneh dar zang-e zolam endazad* (pursue the attainment of crafts during the day, for

drinking in daytime / conceals the mirrorlike heart under the dust of gloom). Hafez (Divan), 1: 308.

35. Yusofi, *Cheshmeh-ye Rowshan* (Clear Fountain), 367.

36. Iraj Mirza (Divan), 1963 ed., Yusofi (Clear Fountain), 365. In a note, Yusofi identifies two other poems as possible participants in the literary competition initiated by *Iranshahr:* a qasida entitled "Hobb-e Madar" (A Mother's Affection) by Mehdi Elahi-Qomsheh'i, and a *qet'eh* entitled "Mehr-e Madar" (A Mother's Love) by Yahya Dowlatabadi. See Yusofi (Clear Fountain), 365 n. 25.

37. Yusofi (Clear Fountain), 369.

38. For a discussion of this issue, see Karimi-Hakkak, "Parvin E'tesami, Sha'eri Now-Avar" (Parvin E'tesami). Another version of that essay has been published in English. See Karimi-Hakkak, "The Unconventional Parvin."

39. E'tesami, *Divan,* 117–18.

40. See Karimi-Kakkak (Parvin E'tesami) 268–69.

41. My use of the feminine pronoun for the spider (and the masculine pronoun for the lazy person) is arbitrary at this point. But I hope my argument will justify the usage. In Persian there is no gender distinction in pronouns.

42. E'tesami, *Divan,* 119.

43. Ibid., 118.

44. Ibid., 118–20.

45. The editor of the *Divan* of Parvin E'tesami has signaled a change in the interlocution by using a horizontal line at this point. Semantically, however, no shift in the interlocution appears.

46. Ibid., 120.

47. E'tesam al-Molk, " 'Azm va Neshat-e 'Ankabut" (Spider's Determination and Vivacity), *Bahar* 2, no. 7 (March 1922): 435. Reprinted in E'tesam al-Molk, *Bahar* (Bahar), 2: 165–66. I have not attempted to locate Brisbane's essay since Parvin did not know English and could not have read it herself.

48. E'tesam, (Bahar), vol. 2: 165–66.

49. Ibid.

50. For an analysis of Iranian women's self-image in the early decades of the twentieth century, see Milani, *Veils and Words,* 100–126.

51. The allusion to God as *dust* (friend) is very prevalent in Persian mystical poetry. See Annemarie Schimmel's two books on Islamic mysticism, *Mystical Dimensions of Islam* and *As through a Veil: Mystical Poetry in Islam.*

52. For an example of this issue, see Sa'di's dialogue between the spider and the fly, which opens thus: *"Magasi goft 'ankabuti ra . . ."* in Sa'di, *Kolliyyat-e Sa'di* (Complete Works), 831.

53. This tradition is narrated by the authoritative Ahmad ibn Hanbal. The sentence he relates to the onlookers' view of the web woven at the cave's mouth is rather explicit: *". . . fa-ra'aw 'ala babihi nasj al-'ankabut, fa-qalu law dakhala hahuna lam yakun nasj al-'ankabut 'ala babihi"* (. . . and then they saw the spider web at the mouth of the cave, and then they said that if he had entered here, there would not have been a spider web at its mouth). See Ibn Hanbal, *Al-Musnad* 1: 348. In the Koranic sura " *'ankabut*" there is another allusion to the animal's web. Here, the

emphasis falls on the lowliness of the animal and the ephemerality of its web: "*mathal alladhina ittakhadhu min duni 'llahi ka-mathali'l 'ankabuti ittakhadhat baytan wa inna awhana'l-buyuti la-baytu'l-'ankabut law kanu ya'lamun*" (and the case of those who take a god lesser than Allah resembles that of the spider who builds a home, for the home of the spider is the lowliest of all, if they only knew.) *The Qur'an*, Sura 29: 41.

54. Parvin E'tesami, *Divan*, twenty-two.
55. 'Attar, *Manteq al-Tayr*, (Language of the Birds), 141–42.
56. 'Attar, *Conference of the Birds*, 107–8.
57. Lotman, *Structure of the Artistic Text*, 72.
58. Ibid.
59. Ibid, 73.
60. Morson and Emerson, *Rethinking Bakhtin*, 22.

NOTES TO CHAPTER 5

1. This desire is most visible in the pages of Iranian newspapers and journals of the period. In addition to *Bahar* and *Daneshkadeh*, several other journals, including *Iran-e Now*, *Zaban-e Azad*, *Nowbahar*, *Gol-e Zard*, *Kaveh*, and *Farangestan*, published in Iran or abroad, took part in the debate on changes that needed to be made in the poetry of Iran.

2. For a sampling of such writings, see the following articles, all published in *Zaban-e Azad* within the space of a single month: "She'r Chist va Sha'er Kist" (What Is Poetry and Who Is a Poet?), September 11, 1917; "Nevisandegi Tejarat Ast" (Writing Is a Trade), September 20, 1917; "Sha'er ra Beshenasid" (Know the Poet), September 23, 1917; "Emtiaz-e She'r-e Irani va Ahamiyyat-e An" (The Superiority of Iranian Poetry and Its Importance), October 4, 1917; and "*She'r—Musiqi*" (Poetry/Music), October 14, 1917. One interesting instance may illustrate the types of challenges some innovators faced. On February 12, 1918, *Nowbahar* published a poem as an advertisement with the following caption from its anonymous author: "As some modernist literati have appeared in Iran who have thought the books of the classical literati nonsensical [*yaveh*], and some others have mocked them, demanding something from them as replacement, I, a disciple of the school of modernism [*yeki az shagerdan-e maktab-e tajaddod*], advertise the following composition as a sample for the style of a new literature. Yes, I advertise this poem because unfortunately none of the editors have agreed to publish my poems in the section of their newspapers devoted to poetry. So I have to publish this as advertisement, and pay the cost too."

3. Under the sarcastic title of "Taraqqi-e Zaban-e Farsi dar Yek Qarn" (Progress of the Persian Language in a Century), *Kaveh*, a Persian journal published in Berlin, placed samples of contemporary prose and poetry next to some writings of the previous century in facing columns. The implication was obvious: modernism had caused the decline of the Persian language and its literature.

4. On Lahuti's life and works, see Sesil-Banu Lahuti, *Sokhanha-ye Verd-e Zaban* (Words on Tongues); Abolqasem Lahuti, *Kolliyyat-e Abolqasem Lahuti* (Collected Poems); and Abolqasem Lahuti (Divan). Subsequent references to Divan of Lahuti are to this last-cited book.

5. Abolqasem Lahuti (Divan), 272–75.

6. For examples of the "anatomy of the beloved" imagery in Persian poetry, see Jahanbani, comp., *Golchin-e Jahanbani* (Jahanbani Anthology). This book is a partly censored reprint of an earlier edition first published in 1936.

7. For the best-known examples of this trend see Amin-Riahi, "*She'r-e Rashid Yasemi va Rastakhiz-e Adabi-ye Iran*" (Poetry of Rashid Yasemi and Iran's Literary Renaissance), five–nineteen.

8. For an exposition of Bakhtin's theory of parody, see Morson, "Parody, History and Metaparody," 63–86.

9. Compare the opening line of a famous Hafezian ghazal: which goes "*anan keh khak ra beh nazar kimia konand / aya bovad keh gusheh-ye cheshmi beh ma konanad*" (Those who turn dust into gold by their glance / would that they turn the corner of an eye toward us), Hafez (Divan), 1: 398.

10. The most significant efforts of this kind were aimed at portraying Ferdowsi as a great patriotic poet and at defining the *Shahnameh* as the supreme document of Iranian identity. See Tavakoli-Targhi, "Refashioning Iran."

11. This trope may be rooted in the words *monavvar al-fekr* (enlightened of thought) and its later equivalent, *rowshanfekr*. These were Persian loan translations for the French word *intellectuel*.

12. The image is rooted in several classical analogies, such as the proverb, "'*alem-e bi-'amal derakhti-st bi samar*" (the person of knowledge who does not practice [what he knows] is [like] a fruitless tree), or Naser Khosrow's famous line, "*derakht-e to gar bar-e danesh begirad / beh zir avari charkh-e nilufari ra*" (should your tree bear the fruit of knowledge / you may take command of the indigo dome). See Naser Khosrow (Divan), 36.

13. This paradoxical situation may account for an error in classifying Lahuti's poem. In his *Divan,* "*Beh Dokhtaran-e Iran*" "To the Daughters of Iran" was published not under the section devoted to his qasidas, but under the heading of "Qate'at-e Gunagun va Manzumehha" (Various Fragments and Verses).

14. This allusion to the name of the hostel, *Khanvaledeh—Valedeh-Khani* in Turkish—was a continuation of *Kaveh*'s articles on the decline of Persian language and literature (see note 3 above). See Arianpur, *Az Saba to Nima* (From Saba to Nima), 2: 459 n. 2.

15. *Kaveh*, 5th year (nos. 4–5), serial nos. 39–40 (May 21, 1920): 3–4; reprinted in Afshar, *Kaveh, Chap-e Jadid* (New Printing of *Kaveh*), 321–22. The lines were part of a qasida by Ahmad Khan-Malek Yazdi. According to a footnote in the original *Kaveh,* the whole poem had been published seven years earlier in a book entitled *Binesh-e Irani* (Iranian Vision). I have not been able to locate this book.

16. Raf'at's sonnets are not the first examples of Persian poems fully in accord with a recognizable European verse form. Years before him, Ja'far Khameneh'i had composed several sonnets in Persian. Arianpur quotes two of Khameneh'i's sonnets, but does not identify them as sonnets; he uses the word *qet'eh* for them. See his (From Saba to Nima), 2: 453–54.

17. *Kaveh*, 5th year (nos. 4–5), serial nos. 39–40 (May 21, 1920): 3 n 3.

18. Raf'at was not disinterested in this, for one of the poems held up to ridicule

in *Kaveh* was his. In his response, he pointed out that what the newspaper had offered as an example of "good" prose of a century earlier in fact reflected "all the ignorance, simplemindedness, unawareness of civilization governing Iran in that dark period." He also dismissed *Kaveh*'s example of the degenerate prose of modern times as "simply unrepresentative." See Arianpur (From Saba to Nima), 2: 460.

19. Ibid.

20. The classical Persian ghazal and qasida may have begun "as virtual twins since both are written in the same rhyme scheme—monorhyme by *bayt* with the opening half-*bayt* rhyming as well." See Clinton, "Court Poetry at the Beginning of the Classical Period," 88.

21. One consequence of this change is worth noting here: whereas the *Divans* of classical Persian poets—and a majority of the poets discussed in this book—are usually organized according to the verse forms they contain and the order of the rhyming letter in the Persian alphabet, the works of modernist poets of Iran are almost always organized in accordance with the date of each poem's composition.

22. Rafʿat's positions on this issue become further clarified through his correspondence with *Gol-e Zard* (Yellow Rose), a literary journal edited by Yahya Rayhan, poet and former member of *Daneshkadeh*. This journal was published from 1918 to 1922. See *Gol-e Zard* 7: 4; 8: 3; 10: 3; 11: 3; and 14: 3. In its first year, *Gol-e Zard* also published two other sonnets by Rafʿat. See *Gol-e Zard* 15: 2 and 20: 2.

23. According to Arianpur, Rafʿat published this poem alongside Sasani's composition on Nowruz in the fourth issue of *Azadistan*. See Arianpur (From Saba to Nima), 2: 461–62.

24. Ibid.

25. Cf. Fuller, *Sonnet*, 4. Rafʿat, who knew French and had lived in Istanbul and Germany, and perhaps in France as well, may have been more familiar with the French sonnet tradition than with the English.

26. Natel-Khanlari identifies this meter as *bahr* 4 in the fifth *Selseleh* of the Aruz system of metrics, known as "*mozaraʿ-e akhrab-e makfuf-e mahzuf*," and as following the pattern of "*mafʿul-o f[aʿ]elat-o mafaʿil-o faʿelon*." He observes that this meter "is seen in abundance in the Persian ghazal." See Natel-Khanlari, *Vazn-e Sheʿr-e Farsi* (Metrics of Persian Poetry), 154.

27. On the Khiabani Movement, see Kasravi, *Tarikh-e Hejdah-Saleh-ye Azarbaijan* (Eighteen-Year History of Azerbaijan), 710–25, 751–65, 865–96. Kasravi mentions several instances of atrocities committed by the Iranian army against the civilian population in the city of Urmieh around the new year festival of Nowruz. Rafʿat's allusion may be to the February 1921 uprising led by Lahuti.

28. The origins of Nowruz and its relation to the reign of the mythical King Jamshid are mentioned, among other places, in Ferdowsi, *Shahnama of Firdausi*, 1: 84 (1905–1925 edition). See also Ferdowsi, *Shahnameh*, 1: 44 (1987 edition).

29. Customarily, Iranian newspapers and journals celebrate the approach of Nowruz by publishing occasional poems composed on the theme of the change of the year and the arrival of spring.

30. *Nowruziyyeh* or *Bahariyyeh* is a kind of lyrical poem where the arrival of spring is presented as an occasion for love, drinking, and a variety of festive actions.

It has been a part of the evolution of Persian poetry since its inception in Samanid and Ghaznavid courts. See Fouchecour, *Description de la Nature dans la Poésie Lyrique Persane du XIe Siècle*. See also Clinton, "Court Poetry," 75–95; and Moayyad, "Lyric Poetry," 120–46.

31. Afshar (New Printing of *Kaveh*), 322.

32. Ibid. This poem is also by Ahmad Khan-Malek Sasani. It is a masnavi, but is listed erroneously as a qasida.

33. Quoted in Arianpur (From Saba to Nima), 2: 461.

34. Raf ʿat's contribution to the emergence of a new poetic discourse in Iran went unnoticed until the early 1970s. In recent years, his critical stance has attracted some attention. See, for example, Naficy, "Dastan-e Bipayan" (Endless Story). His innovations as a poet, however, still await scholarly examination.

35. See Rypka, *History of Iranian Literature*, 386. Vera Kubickova mentions Machalski's "detailed analysis of Ishqi's poetry," stating that Machalski "draws particular attention to those of his ['Eshqi's] poems which, on account of the novelty of their thought and form (highly ingenious variations in the strophic form of the *musammat*, new rhymes, experiments with syllabic verse, etc.), can be considered significant for the moulding of the new style."

36. Iraj Mirza, "Enqelab-e Adabi" (Literary Revolution).

37. See Mirzadeh-ʿEshqi, *Kolliyyat-e Mosavvar-e ʿEshqi* (Complete Works), particularly 43–73.

38. Bahar, "Dar Marsiyeh-ye ʿEshqi" (Elegy for ʿEshqi), 2: 1232. Cited in Mirzadeh-ʿEshqi (Complete Works), 30.

39. Some of these comments have been collected in Mirzadeh-ʿEshqi (Complete Works), 30–73.

40. Yushij, *Namehha-ye Nima Yushij* (Letters), 51; quoted in Ajudani, " ʿEshqi" (ʿEshqi).

41. Mirzadeh-ʿEshqi (Complete Works), 171–72. Also, see Yusofi, *Cheshmeh-ye Rowshan* (Clear Fountain), 370–81.

42. For a view of Maryam as a metaphor of the constitutional revolution, see Ajudani, "Tablow-e Maryam" (Maryam's Tableau).

43. Mirzadeh-ʿEshqi (Complete Works), 174–75.

44. More recently, ʿEshqi's contribution to poetic change in Iran has been recognized in general terms. At the same time, however, scholars still view him as a minor poet unfamiliar with classical Persian poetry and therefore undeserving of serious critical attention. Amin-Riahi calls ʿEshqi representative of a group of "young and illiterate poets who, using a journalistic language and a medley of unfamiliar European words, produced worthless writings." See Amin-Riahi, "Sheʿr-e Rashid Yasemi va Rastakhiz-e Adabi-ye Iran" (Poetry of Rashid Yasemi and Iran's Literary Renaissance), ten.

45. For a variety of such images, as they have been conceived and used in classical Persian poetry, see Shafiʿi-Kadhani, *Sovar-e Khial dar Sheʿr-e Farsi* (Imagery in Persian Poetry), particularly pt. 2: 377–657. For the image of the night expressed in terms of Jonah being swallowed by a great fish (or a whale), see pp. 377–78 and 447–48.

46. Ibid., 528–30, 609–10.

47. Mirzadeh-'Eshqi (Complete Works), 172.

48. Ibid., 173.

49. Yahya Dowlatabadi, an influential intellectual of early twentieth-century Iran, was primarily responsible for the modernization of education in Iran. He has left behind an important biography (see his *Hayat-e Yahya* [Life of Yahya]). Like many literate Iranians of the period, he wrote poetry as well, some designed to suggest ways of modernizing Persian poetry. His poems were published in various literary journals; a selection was published posthumously as a book. See his *Ordibehesht va Ash'ar-e Chap-Nashodeh* (Ordibehesht and Unpublished Poems).

50. Mirzadeh 'Eshqi (Complete Works), 172.

51. See, for example, Hafez's ghazal with the opening: "*Nafas-e bad-e saba moshk-feshan khahad shod / 'alam-e pir degar-bareh javan khahad shod*" (The breath of the zephyr will become musk-scattering / once again the old world will become young), Hafez, *Divan,* 1: 336.

52. Ibid., 2: 1020. Khanlari lists this among the ghazals likely to have been attributed to Hafez.

53. See Karimi-Hakkak, "Language Reform and Its Language."

54. For examples of use of color imagery in the Persian poetry of this period, see "Sorud-e Bolshevik" (Bolshevik Song) in *Daneshkadeh,* no. 2: 95–98; "Jangjuyan" (War Mongers) in *Gol-e Zard,* no. 13: 4; and "Golha-ye Banafsheh" (Pansies) in *Gol-e Zard,* no. 18: 2. Toward the end of "The Three Tableaux" 'Eshqi makes the political undertones of his poem more obvious by naming Lenin in relation to the color red. See Mirzadeh-'Eshqi (Complete Works), 191. After 'Eshqi, this color imagery finds its most expanded form in Nima's poetry.

55. 'Eshqi makes the full potential of this expression obvious when he likens Maryam's father's tongue to "a banner of blood." See Mirzadeh-'Eshqi (Complete Works), 191.

56. Compare with Lévi-Strauss's description of the sunset (*Tristes Tropiques*), 61–69.

57. In "The Three Tableaux," other words like *khun-rang* (blood-colored), *qahveh-gun* (coffeelike), and *kafur-vash* (camphorish) reflect the same tendency.

58. The night/day dichotomy is a fundamental feature of classical Persian poetry, particularly in the ghazal tradition.

59. *Simin* (silvery), *sim-bar* (silver-bodied), and *simin-saq* (silver-legged) are among the most frequent usages of the metaphor.

60. The strategy of turning natural phenomena into poetic signs by projecting them onto the human mind has been a formative part of the process of image-making in Persian poetry. In the frequently used poetic phrase *shab-e hejran* (night of separation) the equivocation of the blackness of the night with the "color" of a lover's despair illustrates this technique. See Meisami's discussion of Rumi's distinction between "analogy" and "similitude" in her *Medieval Persian Court Poetry,* 36–39. 'Eshqi makes full use of both night/day and spring/autumn binaries in the opening stanzas of the first two tableaux before transposing these into the human realm in the passage that opens the third tableau.

61. Mirzadeh-'Eshqi (Complete Works), 183. The reference to human beings as *nasl-e fased-e maymun* (the rotten offspring of monkeys) may be taken as an occasion to point out a Darwinian tendency in "The Three Tableaux." At one point in the third tableau 'Eshqi expresses regret that "the world has not appreciated Darwin's service" (ibid., 190).

62. Ibid., 177.

NOTES TO CHAPTER **6**

1. This perception began to take shape in the 1950s when a group of young Iranian poets saw in Nima a figure they could identify with in their quest to be modern. After Nima's death, they wrote a series of laudatory essays in which they celebrated Nima's life and works. Chief among these we can count Al-e Ahmad's "Pir-Mard Cheshm-e Ma Bud" (The Old Man Was Our Eyes); Akhavan-Saless's articles entitled "*Nima Mardi Bud Mardestan*" (Nima Was a Legendary Man), reprinted later in *Bed'atha va Baday'-e Nima Yushij* (Nima's Innovations and Novelties); and many of Baraheni's polemical writings in *Tala dar Mes* (Gold in Copper). In English, Munibur Rahman's 1960 essay on Nima reflects this admiring attitude (see his "Nima Yushij: Founder of the Modernist School of Persian Poetry"). More recently, a reaction is taking place in writings which attempt to foster a more balanced view of Persian poetry in the twentieth century. Nader Naderpur's essay series (A One-Hundred-Year-Old Infant Named "New Poetry") may be seen as an example of this emerging view.

2. One consequence of the modernist construction of the Nimaic canon has been a near total marginalization of some of his more traditional works. The publication of Nima's collected poems in the 1980s made it possible for a new generation of Iranians to see Nima's continued interest in experimenting with classical forms and genres.

3. Modernist poets' attempts at claiming the mantle of past Persian poets assumes various forms. Ahmad Shamlu's writings on Hafez, most notably his introduction to Hafez's Divan entitled *Hafez-e Shiraz beh Ravayat-e Ahmad Shamlu* (Hafez of Shiraz According to Ahmad Shamlu) and Mehdi Akhavan-Saless's preoccupation with Ferdowsi's *Shahnameh* are among the most obvious of such efforts.

4. The best-known representatives of this trend include Esma'il Kho'i, Mohammad-'Ali Sepanlu, and Mohammad-Reza Shafi'i-Kadkani who, as poets, typify the diverse tendencies arising from Nima and Nimaic social discourse.

5. Nima's prose writings, particularly those addressing issues of poetic modernity, were published during his lifetime in various literary journals. They were mostly published in book form after his death. Only recently have they begun to emerge as a fairly comprehensive corpus.

6. Yushij, *Namehha-ye Nima Yushij* (Letters), 28.

7. Ibid., 34.

8. Ibid., 30.

9. Ibid., 29.

10. Yushij, "Panj Maqaleh dar She'r va Nemayesh" (Five Essays on Poetry and Drama).

11. Yushij (Letters), 31–32.

12. Ibid., 28.

13. These phrases occur in various places in Nima's writings. See, for example, Yushij (Five Essays on Poetry and Drama), 103.

14. *San'at* is an old concept in Persian poetics. For a description of its various usages in the poetry, see Homa'i, *Sena'at-e Adabi* (Literary Devices). As a concept, it is usually contrasted to a quality envisioned as "poetic nature or disposition" (*tab'-e she'r*), which is thought to be superior to *san'at*. While the latter is thought attainable through schooling, the former is conceived as a God-given quality which cannot be mastered through sheer human effort.

15. Yushij (Letters), 73.

16. Yushij, *Arzesh-e Ehsasat dar Zendegi-ye Honarpishegan* (Value of Feelings), 12.

17. Ibid., 16.

18. Ibid.

19. Ibid., 28.

20. Ibid., 68–69.

21. Ibid., 40, 83.

22. Ibid., 84.

23. Ibid., 85.

24. For a detailed discussion of classical usages of these terms, see Shafi'i-Kadkani, *Sovar-e Khial dar She'r-e Farsi* (Imagery in Persian Poetry), 157–68.

25. Yushij (Value of Feelings), 91.

26. See Shafi'i-Kadkani (Imagery in Persian Poetry), 50–155. For more specific evaluations, see Zipoli, *Encoding and Decoding Neopersian Poetry*, 18–25.

27. Yushij, "Nameh beh Shin Partow" (Letter to Shin Partow), 62.

28. Yushij, *Harfha-ye Hamsayeh* (Neighbor's Words), 50.

29. Ibid., 47.

30. Yushij (Letter to Shin Partow), 60.

31. See Natel-Khanlari, *Vazn-e She'r-e Farsi* (Metrics of Persian Poetry). The standard book on the subject in English is Elwell-Sutton's *Persian Meters*.

32. The division of the *bayt,* a single poetic unit, into two hemistiches of equal metric value has made the mechanistic nature of the rhyme scheme in Persian poetry highly visible.

33. Almost from the beginning, rhyme was a constant formal feature of Persian poetry, so much so in fact that in practice it was perceived as an essential and inalienable component of poetic composition. The custom of arranging poems in divans according to the alphabetical order of the last letter in the rhyme may have made it more prominent through time.

34. Various scholars have commented on this feature of 'Eshqi's versification. In a preface to a long poem called "Nowruzi-Nameh" (Book of The New Year's Day), 'Eshqi himself justified his modifications in these words: "In this poem I did not place my neck in the chain or shackles of rhyme as the classics [*qodama*] had done. I

wanted a wider field for composition [*sokhn-sora'i*], so I rhymed the words *gonah* [meaning 'sin,' this word ends in the Persian 'h'] with qadah [meaning "goblet," this word ends in the Arabic 'h']. It is obvious that the distinction [between the two] and the perception of the balance conveyed through rhyme is a function of the ear. I have no doubt that today we hear *gonah* and *qadah* as rhyming." See Mirzadeh-'Eshqi *Kolliyyat-e Mosavvar-e 'Eshqi* (Complete Works), 261.

35. The text of this poem appears with slight variations in different places. My version is from Yushij, *Majmu'eh-ye Asar, Daftar-e Avval: She'r* (Collected Works, Book 1: Poems), 384–88.

36. Ibid., 385.

37. Ibid., 388.

38. The text of Tabari's "preface" is reprinted in Yushij (Letters), 227–29. The passage cited occurs on p. 228.

39. On the political discourse of Persian poetry in the 1950s and 1960s, see Meskub, "Negahi beh She'r-e Mote'ahhed-e Farsi dar Daheh-ye Si va Chehel" (Survey of the Committed Poetry of the 1330s and 1340s [hegira]).

40. For an English translation of some of these poems, see Karimi-Hakkak (Anthology of Modern Persian Poetry), 30–37.

41. For an insightful examination of the Marxist discourse in the Iranian press of the 1940s, see Amir-Mokri, "Redefining Iran's Constitutional Revolution," particularly 228–68.

42. In classical Persian poetry, day and night are sometimes likened to a dappled horse and expressed through the poetic phrase *ablaq-e sobh o sham* (the dappled horse of day and night). To my knowledge, Nima's articulation of morning through the image of a bird is without precedent.

43. Yushij (Letters), 135.

44. In fact, the reception process—how a poem is interpreted by others—helps to clarify the nature of the community within which poetic communication assumes its specific character. It may become a general assumption, for example, that poets have to speak in ambiguous allusions to escape censorship. For a case study of literary communication within society see Karimi-Hakkak, "Authors and Authorities," 307–38.

45. Yushij (Collected Works), 606–12.

46. Many birds in Nima's poetry draw the reader's attention to the poet himself: the rooster in "Filthy Hope," the phoenix in "Qoqnus," "Tuka" in a poem of that name, the raven in "Ghorab," and the owl in "Joghdi Pir" (An Old Owl). Nima's imaginary birds, too, are portrayed in such a way as to convey aspects of the poet's own view of his condition, mission, and challenges. They can be found in some of Nima's most famous poems, such as *morgh-e mojassameh* (statue bird), *morgh-e gham* (sorrow bird), *morgh-e shab-aviz* (night-hanging bird), and of course *morgh-e amin* (amen bird).

47. Yushij (Collected Works), 606.

48. Ibid., 607.

49. Ibid., 612.

50. Siavosh Kasra'i, "Parvazi dar Hava-ye 'Morgh-e Amin' " (Flight in the

Sphere of "The Amen Bird"). The essay appeared in *Jong-e Marjan,* an anthology of diverse literary works written in contemporary Iran which was published for an educational organization of the same name between 1972 and 1978. According to a reference in this anthology, Kasra'i's article was first published in 1965 in a literary anthology called *Jong-e Yadnameh-ye Hamshahri.* I have not been able to gain access to this work.

51. See Shafi'i-Kadkani, *Advar-e She'r-e Farsi az Mashrutiyyat ta Soqut-e Saltanat* (Periods of Persian Poetry), 87–88.

52. Kasra'i (Flight), 18.

53. Throughout this essay, Kasra'i uses a veiled terminology for politically sensitive terms. Thus, words like *jema'at* (crowd), *rah-e haqq* (the right path), and *mardom-gera* (people-oriented) convey concepts like "the masses," "leftist ideology," and "communist" or "communistic."

54. Kasra'i (Flight), 19.

55. Among the speakers of Persian, Homa and 'Anqa are two mythical birds with proverbial qualities. Homa is known as the creature who feeds only on bones, not on flesh. 'Anqa is known for its ability to be everywhere and nowhere, ready to serve the needy. See Zahra Khanlari, *Farhang-e Adabiyyat-e Farsi-ye Dari* (Dari-Persian Literary Dictionary).

56. Kasra'i (Flight), 19. At times Kasra'i's article assumes an allegorical aspect paralleling the history of the Tudeh Party of Iran. Here, the allusion may be to secret gatherings of party members under conditions of widespread government surveillance.

57. Ibid., 17. In none of the standard reference works predating Nima's poem have I found a reference to the amen bird. Thirty years after the date of Nima's poem, Ahmad Shamlu mentions the bird in *Ketab-e Kucheh* (Book of the Alley). His entry under "Morgh-e Amin" reads: "It is a mythical bird; it is said that if one should make a wish or utter a request, the wish or request will come true instantly if the amen bird should be in flight at that moment" (*Ketab-e Kucheh,* 3: 561). Shamlu does not cite prior references to the creature. His description of the bird may itself be based on his reading of Nima's poem. If so, the "myth" of the amen bird must be viewed as a recent construct rooted in Nima's poem.

58. Kasra'i (Flight), 22.

59. On the suppression of the Tudeh Party activities in the 1950s, see Abrahamian, *Iran between Two Revolutions,* 451–53.

60. Morson, "Bakhtin, Genre, and Temporality," 1088.

61. Todorov, *Mikhail Bakhtin: Dialogical Principle,* 111.

62. Karimi-Hakkak, "Revolutionary Posturing," 527–29.

63. Kasra'i (Flight), 16.

64. Akhavan-Saless, *Bed'atha va Badaye'e Nima* (Nima's Innovations and Novelties), 243–70.

65. Ibid., 272.

66. Ibid., 272–73.

67. Ibid., 271.

68. Yushij (Collected Works), 520.

69. Ibid., 520–21.

70. Traditional literary criticism attributes colloquialism in modern Persian poetry to the desire of the poets to approach popular speech. As an attempt to produce poetic effects, the phenomenon awaits further study.

71. Akhavan-Saless (Nima's Innovations and Novelties), 273.

72. Ibid., 281.

73. Akhavan explains his preference in these words: " '*Howl*' is a wet word, whereas '*khowf*' is more of a desert word, a graveyard word, more appropriate to confined and enclosed spaces, and '*tars*' [fear] is cold, whereas the night of our night watchman man is warm and wet . . . ," (ibid., 275).

74. Ibid., 276.

75. Ibid., 287.

76. Ibid.

77. In recent years two explanations have been offered for the continued presence of traditional verse forms in the canon of modernist poets. One states that the modernist poets of Iran resorted to writing ghazals and qasida as a response to reactionary tendencies of the Islamic republic of 1979. The second views it as a new Return Movement similar to that initiated in the eighteenth century. See Nuri-'Ala, "Akherin Ketab-e Akhavan-Saless va Mas'aleh-ye Bazgasht-e Adabi" (Akhavan-Saless's Last Book).

78. For the contrary view, see Moshki, *Shahd-e She'r-e Emruz* (Nectar of Today's Poetry), particularly 198–99.

79. On the concept of cultural noise, see Lotman, *Structure of the Artistic Text*, 75–77.

80. Morson, "Bakhtin, Genre, and Temporality," 1086.

Bibliography

Abrahamian, Ervand. *Iran between Two Revolutions*. Princeton: Princeton University Press, 1982.

Adamiyyat, Feraydun. *Amir-e Kabir va Iran* (Amir-e Kabir and Iran). Tehran: Kharazmi, 1969.

―――. *Andishehha-ye Mirza Aqa Khan Kermani* (The Ideas of Mirza Aqa Khan Kermani). Tehran: Tahuri, 1967.

―――. *Andishehha-ye Mirza Fath-'Ali Akhundzadeh* (The Ideas of Mirza Fath'Ali Akhundzadeh). Tehran: Amir-e Kabir, 1970.

Adib-Borumand, 'Abd al-'Ali. *Payam-e Azadi* (The Message of Freedom). Tehran: Ruzbehan, 1978.

Adib-Kermani, Ahmad. *Salar-Nameh* (Book of the Great). Lithograph ed. Shiraz: 1898.

Afshar, Iraj, ed. *Kaveh, Chap-e Jadid* (New Printing of *Kaveh*). Offset. Tehran, 1977.

―――. *Mobarezeh ba Mohammad-'Ali Shah: Asnadi az Fa'aliyyatha-ye Azadi-Khahan-e Iran dar Orupa va Estanbul* (Struggling against Mohammad-'Ali Shah: Certain Documents of the Activities of Iranian Freedom-Seekers in Europe and Istanbul). Tehran: Tus, 1980.

'Aini, Sadreddin. *Nemunehha-ye Adabiyyat-e Tajik* (Selections from Tajik Literature). Moscow, 1926.

Ajudani, Masha'allah. " 'Eshqi: Nazariyyehha va Now-Avariha" ('Eshqi: Theories and Innovations). *Avand,* no. 1 (February 1987): 34–37. (Only one issue of this Persian journal was published in London.)

―――. "Tablow-e Maryam" (Maryam's Tableau). *Ayandeh* 12, nos. 1–3 (March–May 1986): 48–56.

Akhavan-Saless, Mehdi. *'Ata va Laqa-ye Nima Yushij* (Nima's Offerings and Aspect). Tehran: Damavand, 1983.

―――. *Bed'atha va Badaye'-e Nima Yushij* (Nima's Innovations and Novelties). Tehran: Tuka, 1967.

Akhundzadeh, Fath-'Ali. *Alefba-ye Jadid va Maktubat* (The New Alphabet and the Correspondences). Edited by Hamid Mohammadzadeh. Tabriz: Ehya, 1978.

―――. *Maktubat* (Correspondences). n.p.: Mard-e Emruz Publications, 1985.

———. *Maqalat* (Essays). Edited by Baqer Mo'meni. Tehran: Ava, 1972.

———. *Maqalat-e Farsi* (Persian Essays). Tehran: Negah, 1976.

———. *Tamsilat* (Allegories). Translated by Mirza Ja'far Qarachehdaghi. London: Sampson, Low, Marston, n.d.

Al-e Ahmad, Jalal. "*Pir-Mard Cheshm-e Ma Bud*" (The Old Man Was Our Eyes). *Arash,* no. 2 (December 1961): 65–75.

Algar, Hamid. "Akundzada." In *Encyclopaedia Iranica.* Vol. 1: 735–40. London: Routledge & Kegan Paul, 1985.

———. *Mirza Malkum Khan: A Study in the History of Iranian Modernism.* Berkeley: University of California Press, 1973.

Amin-Riahi, Mohammad. "She'r-e Rashid Yasemi va Rastakhiz-e Adabi-ye Iran" (The Poetry of Rashid Yasemi and Iran's Literary Renaissance). *In* Rashid Yasemi, *Divan-e Rashid Yasemi* (The Divan of Rashid Yasemi). Edited by Mohammad Amin-Riahi, 10. Tehran: Ebn-e Sina, 1957.

Amir-Mokri, Cyrus. "Redefining Iran's Constitutional Revolution." Ph.D. diss., University of Chicago, 1992.

Anderson, Benedict. *Imagined Communities: Reflections on the Origins and Spread of Nationalism.* London: Verso, 1983.

'Aref-Qazvini, Abolqasem. *Divan-e Mirza Abolqasem 'Aref Qazvini* (The Divan of Abolqasem 'Aref-Qazvini). Edited by Sadeq Rezazadeh-Shafaq. Berlin: Gedruckt Druckerei "Machriqi," 1924.

———. *Kolliyyat-e Divan-e 'Aref-e Qazvini* (The Complete Divan of 'Aref-Qazvini). Edited by 'Abd al-Rahman Sayf-Azad. Tehran: Amir-e Kabir, 1977.

Arianpur, Yahya. *Az Saba ta Nima* (From Saba to Nima). 2 vols. Tehran: Jibi, 1971.

Atabaki, Touraj. *Azerbaijan: Ethnicity and Autonomy in Twentieth-Century Iran.* London: British Academic Press, 1993.

'Attar, Farid al-Din. *The Conference of the Birds.* Translated by Afkham Darbandi and Dick Davis. New York: Penguin Books, 1984.

———. *Manteq al-Tayr* (Language of the Birds). Edited by M. J. Mashkur. Tehran: Tehran Publishers, n.d.

Bahar, Mohammad-Taqi. *Divan-e Ash'ar-e Shadravan Mohammad-Taqi Bahar Malek al-Sho'ara* (The Poetic Divan of the Late Mohammad-Taqi Bahar, Malek al-Sho'ara). 2 vols. 5th ed. Tehran: Tus, 1989.

———. "Sa'di Kist?" (Who Is Sa'di?). *Nowbahar,* no. 323 (January 10, 1918): 1–3.

Bakhtin, Mikhail M. *The Dialogical Imagination.* Edited by Michael Holquist, translated by Caryl Emerson and Michael Holquist. Austin: University of Texas Press, 1986.

———. *Problems of Dostoyevsky's Poetics.* Translated by Caryl Emerson. Minneapolis: University of Minnesota Press, 1984.

Balay, Christophe, and Michel Cuypers. *Aux Sources de la Nouvelle Persane.* Paris: French Institute of Iranology, 1983.

Baraheni, Reza. *Tala dar Mes* (Gold in Copper). Tehran: Zaman, 1968.

Bastani-Parizi, Mohammad-Ebrahim. "Tarhi az Chehreh-ye Amir-e Kabir dar Adab-e Farsi" (A Sketch of Amir-e Kabir's Portrait in Persian Literature). In *Amir-e Kabir va Dar al-Fonun* (Amir-e Kabir and the Dar al-Fonun). Edited by

Qodratollah Rowshani-Za'feranlu. Publications of Tehran University's Central Library, no. 8. Tehran, 1975.

Bayat, Mangol. "Aqa Khan Kermani." In *Encyclopaedia Iranica.* Vol. 2: 175–77. London: Routledge & Kegan Paul, 1987.

———. "Mirza Aqa Khan Kermani: A Nineteenth Century Persian Nationalist." In *Towards a Modern Iran: Studies in Thought, Politics and Society.* Edited by Ellie Kedouri and Syvia G. Haim. London: Frank Cass, 1980.

Beard, Michael. *Hedayat's Blind Owl as a Western Novel.* Princeton: Princeton University Press, 1990.

Blanchard, Marc E. "Reception Theory and the Semiotics of Literary History." *Semiotica* 61, nos. 3–4 (1986): 307–23.

Blonsky, Marshall, ed. *On Signs.* Baltimore: Johns Hopkins University Press, 1985.

Borqa'i, Mohammad-Baqer. *Sokhanvaran-e Nami-ye Mo'aser* (Famous Contemporary Poets). Tehran: n.p., 1950.

Boyce, Mary. *A History of Zoroastrianism.* Vol. 1. Leiden: E. J. Brill, 1975.

Browne, Edward Granville. *The Literary History of Persia.* 4 vols. Cambridge and London: Cambridge University Press, 1902–1924, reprint 1969.

———. *The Persian Revolution of 1905–1909.* Cambridge: Cambridge University Press, 1910.

———. *The Press and Poetry of Modern Persia.* Cambridge: Cambridge University Press, 1914.

Clinton, Jerome W. "Court Poetry at the Beginning of the Classical Period." In *Persian Literature.* Edited by Ehsan Yarshater. New York: Bibliotheca Persica, 1988.

———. *The Divan of Manuchihri Damghani: A Critical Study.* Minneapolis: Bibliotheca Islamica, 1972.

Dashti, 'Ali. *Dar Qhalamrow-e Sa'di* (In Sa'di's Realm). Tehran: Amir-e Kabir, 1966.

———. *Naqshi az Hafez* (An Impression of Hafez). Tehran: Ebn-e Sina, 1965.

Dastghayb, 'Abdol 'Ali. *Sayeh-Rowshan-e She'r-e Mo'aser-e Farsi* (The Ups and Downs of Contemporary Persian Poetry). Tehran: Sa'eb, 1969.

DeGeorge, Richard T., ed. *Semiotic Themes.* Lawrence: University of Kansas Press, 1986.

Dehkhoda, 'Ali-Akbar. *Divan-e Dehkhoda* (The Divan of Dehkhoda). Edited by Mohammad Dabir-Siaqi. 2d ed. Tehran: Paya, 1981.

———. *Divan-e Dehkhoda* (The Divan of Dehkhoda). Edited by Mohammad Dabir-Siaqi. 3d ed. Tehran: Tirajeh, 1983.

———. *Loghatnameh* (The Word-Book). 42 vols. Tehran: University of Tehran Press, 1947–1973.

Dehkhoda, 'Ali-Akbar, and Jahangir Khan Shirazi. *Sur-e Esrafil* (Esrafil's Trumpet Call). *"Dowreh-ye Kamel"* (complete edition of the newspaper *Sur-e Esrafil*). Tehran: Nashr-e Tarikh-e Iran, 1982.

Dowlatabadi, Yahya. *Hayat-e Yahya* (The Life of Yahya). 4 vols. 2d ed. Tehran: Ebn-e Sina, 1982.

———. *Ordibehesht va Ash'ar-e Chap-Nashodeh* (Ordibehesht and Unpublished Poems). Tehran: Ferdowsi, 1982.

———. "Qa'ani-Shirazi." *Ayandeh* 1, no. 7: 409–14.

Elwell-Sutton, L. P. *The Persian Meters.* Cambridge University Press, 1976.

Emami, Nasrollah. *Marsieh-Sora'i dar Adabiyyat-e Farsi ta Payan-e Qarn-e Hashtom* (Elegiac Compositions in Persian Literature up to the End of the Eighth Century). Ahvaz: Jahad-e Daneshgahi, 1990.

Eqbal-Ashtiani, 'Abbas. *Mirza Taqi Khan Amir-e Kabir* (Mirza Taqi Khan, the Grand Amir). Tehran: Tehran University Press, 1961.

E'temad al-Saltaneh, Mohammad Hasan. *Sadr al-Tavarikh* (The Prime of Histories). Edited by Mohammad Moshiri. Tehran: Vahid, 1970.

E'tesam Al-Molk, Yusof. " 'Azm va Neshat-e 'Ankabut" (The Spider's Determination and Vivacity). *Bahar* 2, no. 7 (March 1922): 435.

———. *Bahar: Majmu'eh-ye 'Elmi, Adabi, Falsafi, Siasi, Ejtema'i, Akhlaqi* (Bahar: A Scientific, Literary, Philosophical, Political, Social and Ethical Collection). 2d ed. 2 vols. Tehran: Majles, 1942.

E'tesami, Parvin. *Divan-e Parvin E'tesami* (The Divan of Parvin E'tesami). Edited by Heshmat Moayyad. Costa Mesa, Calif.: Mazda, 1987.

———. *A Nightingale's Lament: Selections from the Poems and Fables of Parvin E'tesami.* Translated by Heshmat Moayyad and A. Margaret Madelung. Lexington, Ky.: Mazda, 1985.

Even-Zohar, Itamar. *Papers in Historical Poetics.* Tel Aviv: The Porter Institute for Poetics and Semiotics at Tel Aviv University, 1978.

———. "Polysystem Theory." *Poetics Today* 1, nos. 1–2 (1979): 287–313.

Farrokhi-Yazdi, Mohammad. *Divan-e Farrokhi-Yazdi* (The Divan of Farrokhi-Yazdi). Edited by Hosayn Makki. Tehran: Amir-e Kabir, 1978.

Ferdowsi, Abolqasem. *Shahnameh.* Edited by Djalal Khaleghi-Motlagh. 3 vols. New York: Bibliotheca Persica, 1987– .

———. *The Shahnameh of Firdausi.* Translated by A. G. Warner and E. Warner. 9 vols. London: K. Paul, Trench, Trubner, 1905–1925.

Foruzanfar, Badi' al-Zaman. *Sokhan va Sokhanvaran* (Words and Wordsmiths). Tehran: Ma'aref, n.d.

Fouchecour, Charles-Henri de. *La Description de la Nature dans la Poésie Lyrique Persane du XIe Siècle.* Paris: Institut François de Recherche en Iran, 1969.

———. *Moralia: Les Notions Morales dans la Littérature Persane du 3e au 9e/3e au 7e Siècle.* Paris: Editions Recherché sur les Civilisations, 1986.

Foulkes, A. P. *The Search for Literary Meaning: A Semiotic Approach to the Problem of Interpretation in Education.* Bern and Frankfurt: Verlag Herbert Lang, 1975.

Fuller, John. *The Sonnet.* London: Methuen & Co., 1972.

Garakani, Fazlollah. *Tohmat-e Sha'eri* (Accusation of Being a Poet). Tehran: Rowzaneh, 1977.

Ghanoonparvar, M. R. *Prophets of Doom: Literature as a Socio-Political Phenomenon in Modern Iran.* Lanham, Md.: University Press of America, 1984.

Golbon, Mohammad, ed. *Bahar va Adab-e Farsi* (Bahar and Persian Literature). 2 vols. Tehran: Jibi, 1972.

Ha'eri, Hadi. *Afkar va Asar-e Iraj* (The Ideas and Works of Iraj Mirza). Tehran: Javidan, 1987.

————. ed. *'Aref Qazvini, Shā'er-e Melli-ye Iran* ('Aref Qazvini, Iran's National Poet). Tehran: Javidan, 1985.

Hafez, Shams al-Din Mohammad. *Divan-e Hafez.* (The Divan of Hafez). Edited by Parviz Natel-Khanlari. 2 vols. Tehran: Kharazmi, 1983.

————. *Hafez-e Shiraz beh Ravayat-e Ahmad Shamlu* (Hafez of Shiraz according to Ahmad Shamlu). 2d printing. Tehran: Morvarid, 1975.

Hamidi-Shirazi, Mehdi, comp. *Darya-ye Gowhar* (Ocean of Pearls). Vol. 2. 5th ed. Tehran: Amir-e Kabir, 1970.

Hamraz, Gholam-Reza. "Taqi Raf'at, Sha'eri Setihandeh" (Taqi Raf'at, a Militant Poet). *Ketah-e Jom'eh,* no. 35 (May 14, 1980): 64–68.

Hanaway, William L. "Bazgast-e Adabi" (Literary Return). In *Encyclopaedia Iranica,* Vol. 4: 58–60. London: Routledge & Kegan Paul, 1987.

Hariri, Ali-Asghar. "*Shé'r-e Naghz va Shé'r-e Bimaghz*" (Sound Poetry and Hollow Poetry). *Vahid* 3, no. 6 (May 1966): 480–87, and no. 7 (June 1967): 581–96.

Hedayat, Reza-Qoli. *Majma' al-Fosaha* (Assembly of the Eloquent). 2 vols. Tehran: Amir-e Kabir, 1957, 1961.

Hirshkop, Ken, and David Shepherd, eds. *Bakhtin and Cultural Theory.* Manchester, England: Manchester University Press, 1989.

Homa'i, Jalal. *Sena'at-e Adabi* (Literary Devices). Tehran: 'Elmi, 1960.

————. "*Takmil-e Sharh-e Hal-e Bahar*" (Supplement to Bahar's Complete Biography). Appended to *Akhbar-e Daneshgah-e Tehran* 5, no. 9 (1954).

Hosuri, 'Ali. *Zaban-e Farsi dar Shé'r-e Emruz* (The Persian Language in Today's Poetry). Tehran: Tahuri, 1968.

Ibn Hanbal, Ahmad. *Al-Musnad.* Edited by 'Abd al-Qadir Ahmad-'Ata and Muhammad-Ahmad Ashur. Vol. 1. Al-Qahirah: Dar al-Itisam, 1970.

Iraj Mirza. *Divan-e Iraj Mirza* (The Divan of Iraj Mirza). Edited by Mohammad-Ja'far Mahjub. Tehran: Andisheh, 1963.

————. *Divan-e Kamel-e Iraj Mirza* (The Complete Divan of Iraj Mirza [with addenda, appendices, and a new introduction]). Edited by Mohammad-Ja'far Mahjub. 6th ed. Los Angeles: Ketab Corp., 1989.

————. "Enqelab-e Adabi" (A Literary Revolution). In *Divan-e Iraj Mirza* (The Divan of Iraj Mirza). Edited by Mohammad-Ja'far Mahjub, 120. Tehran: Andisheh, 1963.

Irani, Dinshah J., trans. *The Poems of 'Aref, with English Translation and an Introduction.* Bombay: Hoor, 1933. Facsimile reprint by Nashr-e Farabi, New Jersey, 1987.

Ishaque, M. *Modern Persian Poetry,* Calcutta: Mohammad Israil, 1943.

Islamic Republic of Iran. Ministry of Education. *Farsi-e Chaharom-e Dabestan* (Persian for Fourth-Grade Elementary Schools). Tehran, 1988.

Jahanbani, Mohammad-Hosayn, comp. *Golchin-e Jahanbani* (The Jahanbani Anthology). Tehran: 'Elmi, 1984. Reprint of an earlier edition published in 1936.

Kalhor, Mohammad-Reza. *Mahkazan al-Ensha'* (Treasure-House of Composition). Tehran: n.p., 1886.

Kamali, Haydar-'Ali. *Divan-e Kamali* (The Divan of Kamali). Tehran: n.p., 1951.

Karimi-Hakkak, Ahmad, trans. *An Anthology of Modern Persian Poetry.* Boulder, Colo.: Westview Press, 1978.

———. "Authors and Authorities: Censorship and Literary Communication in the Islamic Republic of Iran." In *Persian Studies in North America: Studies in Honor of Mohammad Ali Jazayery.* Edited by Mehdi Marashi, 307–38. Bethesda, Md.: Iranbooks, 1994.

———. "Language Reform Movement and Its Language." In *The Politics of Language Purism.* Edited by Bjiorn Jernudd and Michael Shapiro, 81–104. Berlin: Morton de Gruyter, 1989.

———. "Nejad, Mazhab, Zaban: Ta'ammoli dar Seh Engareh-ye Qowmiyyat dar Iran" (Race, Religion, and Language: Three Conceptualizations of Collective Identity in Iran). *Iran-Nameh* 11, no. 4 (Fall 1993): 599–620.

———. "Parvin E'tesami, Sha'eri Now-Avar" (Parvin E'tesami, an Innovative Poet). *Iranshenasi* 1, no. 2 (Summer 1989): 264–84.

———. "Posht-e Rangha-ye Khazan: Zaban-e She'r-e Farsi dar Hend" (Behind the Colors of Autumn: The Language of Persian Poetry in India." *Iran-Nameh* 8, no. 2 (Summer 1990): 225–45.

———. "Preservation and Presentation: Continuity and Creativity in the Contemporary Persian Qasida." In *Qasida: The Literary Heritage of an Arabic Poetic Form.* Edited by Stefan Sperl. Leiden: E. J. Brill, forthcoming.

———. "Revolutionary Posturing: Iranian Writers and the Iranian Revolution of 1979." *The International Journal of Middle East Studies* (IJMES) 23, no. 4 (November 1991): 507–31.

———. "The Shahnameh of Firdawsi in France and England, 1770–1860: A Study of the European Response to the Persian Epic of Kings." Ph.D. diss., Rutgers University, 1979.

———. "The Unconventional Parvin: An Analysis of Parvin E'tesami's *Jula-ye Khoda*. In *Once upon a Dewdrop: Essays on the Poetry of Parvin E'tesami.* Edited by Heshmat Moayyad, 117–40. Costa Mesa, Calif.: Mazda, 1994.

———. "A Well amid the Waste: An Introduction to the Poetry of Ahmad Shamlu." *World Literature Today* 51, no. 2 (Spring 1977): 201–6.

Kasra'i, Siavosh. "Parvazı dar Hava-ye 'Morgh-e Amin' " (A Flight in the Sphere of "The Amen Bird"). *Jong-e Marjan,* no. 6 (1977): 16–23.

Kasravi, Ahmad. *"Farhang Chist?"* (What Is Culture?). Tehran: Bahamad-e Azadegan, 1942.

———. *"Hafez Cheh Miguyad?"* (What Does Hafez Say?). Tehran: Parcham, 1939.

———. *Tarikh-e Hejdah-Saleh-ye Azarbaijan* (An Eighteen-Year History of Azerbaijan). Tehran: Amir-e Kabir, 1978.

———. *Tarikh-e Mashruteh-ye Iran* (A History of the Iranian Constitution). 2 vols. Tehran: Amir-e Kabir, 1954.

Keddie, Nikki R. "Intellectuals in the Modern Middle East: A Brief Historical Consideration." *Daedalus* 101, no. 3 (Summer 1972): 39–57.

———. *Roots of Revolution: An Interpretive History of Modern Iran.* New Haven: Yale University Press, 1981.

Kermani, Mirza Aqa Khan. *A'ineh-ye Sekandari* (Alexander's Mirror). Lithograph ed. Tehran, 1906.

———. *Nameh-ye Bastan* (Book of Ancient Times). Also known as *Salar-Nameh.* Lithograph ed. Shiraz, 1898.

Kermani, Nazem al-Eslam. *Tarikh-e Bidari-ye Iranian* (The History of the Iranians' Awakening). Edited by ʿAli-Akbar Saʿidi-Sirjani. Vol. 1. Tehran: Bonyad-e Farhang-e Iran, 1967.

Khalkhali, ʿAli-Akbar. *Tazkereh-ye Shoʿara-ye Moʿaser-e Iran* (Biographies of Contemporary Iranian Poets). Vol. 1. Tehran: n.p., 1954.

Khanlari, Zahra. *Farhang-e Adabiyyat-e Farsi-ye Dari* (The Dari-Persian Literary Dictionary). Tehran: Bonyad-e Farhang-e Iran, 1967.

La Fontaine, Jean. *Oeuvres Complètes*, Vol. 1: *Fables, Contes et Nouvelles*. Edited by Jean-Pierre Collinet. Paris: Gallimard, 1991.

Lahuti, Abolqasem. *Divan-e Abolqasem Lahuti* (The Divan of Abolqasem Lahuti). Edited by Ahmad Bashiri. 2 vols. Piedmont, Calif.: Jahan Book, 1985. Reprint of an earlier edition published in Tehran in 1959.

———. *Kolliyyat-e Abolqasem Lahuti* (Collected Poems of Abolqasem Lahuti). Edited by Behruz Moshiri. Tehran: n.p., 1978.

Lahuti, Sesil-Banu. *Sokhanha-ye Verd-e Zaban* (Words on Tongues). Dushanbe: ʿErfan, 1967.

Langarudi, Shams. *Tarikh-e Tahlili-ye Sheʿr-e Now* (An Analytical History of the Modernist Poetry). Tehran: Nashr-e Markaz, 1991.

Lévi-Strauss, Claude. *Tristes Tropiques*. Translated by John Weightman and Doreen Weightman. New York: Atheneum, 1974.

Lipking, Lawrence. *The Life of the Poet: Beginning and Ending Poetic Careers*. Chicago: University of Chicago Press, 1981.

Loraine, Michael B. "Bahar in the Context of Persian Constitutional Revolution." *Iranian Studies* 5, nos. 2–3 (Spring–Summer 1972): 79–87.

Losensky, Paul. " 'Welcoming Fighani': Imitation, Influence and Literary Change in the Persian Ghazal, 1480–1680." Ph.D. diss., University of Chicago, 1993.

Lotman, Juri [Jurij] M. *Analysis of the Poetic Text*. Edited and translated by D. Barton Johnson. Ann Arbor, Mich.: Ardis, 1976.

———. "The Dynamic Model of a Semiotic System." *Semiotica* 21, nos. 3–4 (1977): 193–210.

———. "Primary and Secondary Communication-Modeling systems." In *Soviet Semiotics: An Anthology*. Edited by Daniel P. Lucid. Baltimore: John Hopkins University Press, 1977.

———. *The Structure of the Artistic Text*. Translated from the Russian by Ronald Vroon. Michigan Slavic Contributions no. 7. Ann Arbor: Department of Slavic Languages and Literatures, 1977.

Lotman, Yuri M., and B. A. Uspensky. "On the Semiotic Mechanism of Culture." *New Literary History* 9, no. 2 (Winter 78): 211–33.

Mahjub, Mohammad-Jaʿfar, ed. *Tahqiq dar Ahval va Asar va Afkar va Ashʿar-e Iraj Mirza* (Inquiry into Iraj Mirza's Life, Works, Thoughts and Poems). Tehran: Andisheh, 1963.

Malkom Khan, Mirza. *Kolliyyat-e Malkom* (Complete Works of Malkom). Edited by Hashem Rabiʿzadeh. Vol. 1. Tehran: Tarbiyat, 1907.

———. *Majmuʿeh-ye Asar-e Malkom* (Collected Works of Malkom). Edited by Mohammad Mohit-Tabatabaʾi. Vol. 1. Tehran: ʿElmi, n.d.

Maragheh'i, Zayn al-'Abedin. *Siahatnameh-ye Ebrahim-Bayg* (Ebrahim-Bayg's Travelogue). Edited by M. 'A. Sepanlu, 102–3. Tehran: Asfar, 1985.

Matini, J. "Bahar." In *Encyclopaedia Iranica.* Vol. 3: 476–79. London: Routledge & Kegan Paul, 1988.

Maybodi, Rashid al-Din. *Kashf al-Asrar va 'Oddat al-Abrar* (Revealing Mysteries and Edifying the Pious). Edited by 'Ali-Asghar Hekmat. Vol. 2. Tehran: Entesharat-e Daneshgah-e Tehran, 1960.

Meisami, Julie. "Iran." In *Modern Literature in Near and Middle East, 1850–1970.* Edited by Robin Ostle. London: Routledge/SOAS, 1991.

———. *Medieval Persian Court Poetry.* Princeton: Princeton University Press, 1987.

Merguerian, Gayane Karen, and Afsaneh Najmabadi. "Zulaykha and Yusuf: The Best Story." Unpublished article, 1994.

Meskub, Shahrokh. "Negahi beh She'r-e Mote'ahhed-e Farsi dar Daheh-ye Si va Chehel" (A Survey of the Committed Poetry of the 1330s and 1340s [hegira]). *Iran-Nameh* 7, no. 4 (Autumn 1989): 555–83.

Milani, Farzaneh. *Veils and Words: The Emerging Voices of Iranian Women Writers.* Syracuse, N.Y.: Syracuse University Press, 1992.

Mirzadeh-'Eshqi, Mohammad-Reza. *Kolliyyat-e Mosavvar-e 'Eshqi* (The Complete Works of 'Eshqi). Edited by 'Ali-Akbar Moshir-Salimi. 8th ed. Tehran: Amir-e Kabir, 1978.

Moayyad, Heshmat. "Lyric Poetry." In *Persian Literature.* Edited by Ehsan Yarshater. New York: Bibliotheca Persica, 1988.

———, ed. *Once upon a Dewdrop: Essays on the Poetry of Parvin E'tesami.* Costa Mesa, Calif.: Mazda, 1994.

Modarres-Tabrizi, Mohammad 'Ali. *Rayhanat al-Adab* (Redolence of Literature). 3 vols. Tehran: Sa'di, 1947 (vol. 1), 'Elmi, 1948 (vol. 2), Tab-'e Ketab, 1950 (vol. 3).

Mohandessi, Manutchehr. "Hedayat and Rilke." *Comparative Literature* 23, no. 3 (Summer 1971): 209–16.

Mo'meni, Baqer. *Sur-e Esrafil* (Esrafil's Trumpet Call). Tehran: Farayen, 1978.

Morson, Gary Saul. "Bakhtin, Genre, and Temporality." *New Literary History* 22, no. 4 (Autumn 1991): 1071–92.

———. "Parody, History and Metaparody." In *Rethinking Bakhtin: Extensions and Challenges.* Edited by Gary Saul Morson and Caryl Emerson, 63–86. Evanston, Ill.: Northwestern University Press, 1989.

Morson, Gary Saul, and Caryl Emerson, eds. *Rethinking Bakhtin: Extensions and Challenges.* Evanston, Ill.: Northwestern University Press, 1989.

Moshki, Sirus. *Shahd-e She'r-e Emruz* (The Nectar of Today's Poetry). Los Angeles: Eqbal, 1990.

Naderpur, Nader. "Tefl-e Sad Saleh-'i beh Nam-e She'r-e Now" (A One-Hundred-Year-Old Infant Named New Poetry). Essay series. *Ruzegar-e Now* 11 & 12, serial nos. 124–141, (June 1992–December 1993). Paris.

Naficy, Azar. "Dastan-e Bipayan" (Endless Story). In *Iran-Nameh, Vijeh-Nameh-ye Naqd-e Adabi dar Iran* (*Iran-Nameh,* Special Issue on Literary Criticism in Iran). Edited by Ahmad Karimi-Hakkak. Vol. 12, no. 1 (Winter 1994): 169–88.

Najmabadi, Afsaneh. "Beloved and Mother: the Erotic Vatan; to Love, to Hold, and to Protect." Paper presented at an SSRC Conference on "Questions of Modernity," held in Cairo, May 28–30, 1993.

Namini, Hosayn, ed. *Javdaneh Sayyed Ashraf al-Din Gilani (Nasim-e Shomal)* (The Immortal Sayyed Ashraf al-Din Gilani, Nasim-e Shomal). Tehran: Farzan, 1984.

Naser Khosrow, Hakim. *Divan-e Hakim Naser Khosrow Qobadiana* (The Divan of Hakim Naser Khosrow Qobadiani). Edited by Hasan Taqizadeh. Tehran: Chakameh, 1982.

Nashat, Guity. *The Origins of Modern Reform in Iran, 1870–1880.* Champaign/Urbana: University of Illinois Press, 1982.

Natel-Khanlari, Parviz. *Vazn-e She'r-e Farsi* (The Metrics of Persian Poetry). Tehran:
· Entesharat-e Daneshgah-e Tehran, 1959.

Nazer. *Negareshi bar Ash'ar-e Parvin E'tesami* (A Glance at the Poetry of Parvin E'tesami). Tehran: Sorush, 1983.

Nura'i, Fereshteh. *Tahqiq dar Afkar-e Mirza Malkom Khan Nazem al-Dowleh* (A Research into the Ideas of Mirza Malkom Khan). Tehran: Jibi, 1973.

Nuri-'Ala, Esma'il. "Akherin Ketab-e Akhavan-Saless va Mas'aleh-ye Bazgasht-e Adabi" (Akhavan-Saless's Last Book and the Problem of Literary Return). *Fasl-e Ketab* 3, no. 1 (Spring 1991): 40–53.

Qa'ani, Habibollah. *Divan-e Hakim Qa'ani Shirazi* (The Divan of Qa'ani). Edited by Naser Ha'eri. Tehran: Golsha'i, 1984.

———. *Parishan* (Disheveled). Edited by Esma'il Ashraf. Shiraz: n.p., 1959.

Ra'di-Azarakhshi, Gholam-'Ali. "Darbareh-ye Sabkha-ye She'r-e Farsi va Nehzat-e Bazgasht" (On the Styles of Persian Poetry and the Return Movement). In *Namvareh-ye Doktor Mahmud Afshar* (Festschrift for Doctor Mahmud Afshar). Edited by Iraj Afshar, 73–112. Tehran: Afshar Foundation, 1985.

Rahman, Munibur. *An Anthology of Modern Persian Poetry.* 2 vols. Aligarh: Institute of Islamic Studies, Muslim University, 1963.

———. "Nima Yushij: Founder of the Modernist School of Persian Poetry." *Bulletin of the Institute of Islamic Studies,* no. 4 (1960): 28–45.

Razi, Shams al-Din Mohammad. *Al-Mo'jam fi Ma'ir al-Ash'ar al-'Ajam* (Handbook on the Standards of Persian Poetry). Edited by Mohammad Qazvini and Modarres-Razavi. Tehran: Entesharat-e Daneshgah-e Tehran, 1959.

Rezazadeh-Shafaq, Sadeq. *Tarikh-e Adabiyyat-e Iran* (A History of Iranian Literature). Tehran: Pahlavi University Press, 1973.

Richepin, Jean. *Choix de Poésies; Nouvelle Édition Revue et Augmentée. (Préface de Maurice Genevoix).* Paris: Fasquelle Éditeurs, 1964.

Rowshan, Mohammad, ed. *Tafsir-e Sureh-ye Yusof* (An Interpretation of the Joseph Chapter). Tehran: Bongah-e Tarjomeh va Nashr-e Ketab, 1977.

Rumi, Jalal al-Din. *The Mathnawi of Jalalu'ddin Rumi.* Edited, translated, and annotated by Reynold A. Nicholson. Reissued by Nasrollah Purjavadi. Tehran: Amir-e Kabir, 1984.

Rypka, Jan. *History of Iranian Literature.* Dordrecht, Holland: D. Reidel, 1968.

Saba, Fath-'Ali. *Divan-e Ash'ar* (Poetic Divan). Tehran: Eqbal, 1962.

Sa'di, Mosleh al-Din. *Bustan-e Sa'di* (The Bustan of Sa'di). Edited by Gholam-Hosayn Yusofi. Tehran: Kharazmi, 1985.

————. *Golestan-e Saʿdi* (The Golestan of Saʿdi). Edited by Gholam-Hosayn Yusofi. Tehran: Kharazmi, 1989.

————. *Kolliyyat-e Saʿdi* (The Complete Works of Saʿdi). Edited by M. ʿA. Foruqi. Tehran: Amir-e Kabir, 1984.

Sadr-Hashemi, Mohammad. *Tarikh-e Jaraʾed va Majallat-e Iran* (History of Iranian Journals and Periodicals). 2 vols. Isfahan: Kamal, 1954.

Sajjadi, Seyyed Jaʿfar, ed. *Hadayeq al-Haqayeq dar Tafsir-e Sureh-ye Yusof* (Gardens of Truth in Interpreting the Joseph Chapter). Tehran: Amir-e Kabir, 1985.

Sanʿatizadeh-Kermani, ʿAbdolhosayn. *Ruzegari keh Gozasht* (The Age that Was). Tehran: Sokhan, 1968.

Schimmel, Annemarie. *As Through a Veil: Mystical Poetry in Islam.* New York: Columbia University Press, 1982.

————. *Mystical Dimensions of Islam.* Chapel Hill: University of North Carolina Press, 1975.

Scholes, Robert. *Semiotics and Interpretation.* New Haven: Yale University Press, 1982.

Sebeok, Thomas A., ed. *Recent Developments in Theory and History: The Semiotic Web,* Berlin: Mouton de Gruyter, 1991.

Sepanlu, Mohammad ʿAli. *ʿAref-e Qazvini, Shaʿer-e Taraneh-ye Melli* (ʿAref Qazvini, Poet of the National Song). Tehran: Agah, 1986.

Shafiʿi-Kadkani, Mohammad-Reza. *Advar-e Sheʿr-e Farsi az Mashrutiyyat ta Soqut-e Saltanat* (Periods of Persian Poetry from the Constitutional Movement to the Fall of Monarchy). Tehran: Tus, 1980.

————. *Hazin-Lahiji: Zendegi va Zibatarin Ghazalha-ye U* (Hazin Lahiji: His Life and His Most Beautiful Ghazals). Mashhad: Tus, 1963.

————. *Sovar-e Khial dar Sheʿr-e Farsi* (Imagery in Persian Poetry). Tehran: Agah, 1987.

Shamisa, Sirus. "Malek al-Shoʿara Bahar va Tarjomeh" (Bahar and Translation). *Ketab-e Jomʿeh,* no. 2 (August 2, 1979): 158–59.

Shamlu, Ahmad. *Hava-ye Tazeh* (Fresh Air). Tehran: Nil, 1984.

————. *Ketab-e Kucheh* (Book of the Alley). Vol. 3. Tehran: Maziar, 1980.

Shariʿat, Mohammad-Javad. *Parvin, Setareh-ye Aseman-e Adab-e Iran* (Parvin, a Star in the Sky of Iranian Literature). n.p.: Mashʿal, 1988.

Shukman, Ann, ed. *Bakhtin School Papers.* (Russian poetics in translation). Oxford: RTP Publications, 1983.

————. "The Dialectics of Change: Culture, Codes, and the Individual." In *Semiotics and Dialectics: Ideology and the Text.* Edited by Peter V. Zima, 311–29. Amsterdam: John Benjamins, 1981.

————. *Literature and Semiotics: A Study of the Writings of Yu. M. Lotman.* Amsterdam: North-Holland Publishing, 1977.

Soroudi, Sorour. "Poet and Revolution: The Impact of Iran's Constitutional Revolution on the Social and Literary Outlook of the Poets of the Time." *Iranian Studies* 12, nos. 3–4 (Summer–Fall 1979): 239–73.

————. "Sur-e Esrafil, 1907–08: Social and Political Ideology." *Middle Eastern Studies* 24, no. 2 (1988): 230–48.

Sorush-Esfahani, Mohammad-ʿAli. *Divan-e Sorush-Esfahani* (The Divan of Sorush Esfahani). Edited by Mohammad Jaʿfar Mahjub. Tehran: Amir-e Kabir, 1960.

Szabolcsi, Miklos, and Jozef Kovacs, eds. *Change in Language and Literature.* Budapest: Akademiai Kiado, 1986.

Taleqani, ʿAli-Asghar. "Sheʿr Chist va Shaʿer Kist?" (What Is Poetry and Who Is a Poet?). *Zaban-e Azad,* no. 17 (September 11, 1917): 3–4.

Tavakoli-Targhi, Mohamad. "Refashioning Iran: Language and Culture during the Constitutional Revolution." *Iranian Studies,* 23, nos. 1–4 (1990): 77–101.

Thomas, Clive. "Bakhtin's 'Theory' of Genre." *Studies in Twentieth Century Literature* 9, no. 1 (Fall 1984): 29–40.

Todorov, Tzvetan. "Bakhtin's Theory of the Utterance." In *Semiotic Themes.* Edited by Richard T. DeGeorge. Lawrence: University of Kansas Press, 1981.

———. *Mikhail Bakhtin: The Dialogical Principle.* Translated by Wlad Godzich. Theory and History of Literature Series, vol. 13. Minneapolis: University of Minnesota Press, 1984.

Tusi, Nasir al-Din. *Asas al-Eqtebas* (Foundations of Imitation). Edited by Modarres-Razavi. Tehran: Entesharat-e Daneshgah-e Tehran, 1958.

Yarshater, Ehsan, ed. *Persian Literature.* New York: Bibliotheca Persica, 1988.

Yasemi, Rashid. *Divan-e Rashid Yasemi* (The Divan of Rashid Yasemi). Edited by Mohammad Amin-Riahi. Tehran: Ebn-e Sina, 1957.

———. *Tarikh-e Adabiyyat-e Moʿaser* (A History of Contemporary Literature). Tehran: Rowshana'i, 1937.

"Yek Mosabeqeh-ye Adabi" (A Literary Competition). *Iranshahr* 2, no. 4 (December 7, 1923): 226–29.

Yushij, Nima. *Arzesh-e Ehsasat dar Zendegi-ye Honarpishegan* (The Value of Feelings in the Lives of Artists). Tehran: Gutenberg, 1974.

———. *Harfha-ye Hamsayeh* (The Neighbor's Words). 5th ed. Tehran: Donya, 1984.

———. *Majmuʿeh-ye Asar, Daftar-e Avval: Sheʿr* (Collected Works, Book 1: Poems). Edited by Sirus Tahbaz. Tehran: Nashr-e Nasher, 1985.

———. *Majmuʿeh-ye Kamel-e Ashʿar-e Nima Yushij* (The Complete Collection of Nima Yushij's Poetry). Edited by Sirus Tahbaz. Tehran: Negah, 1991.

———. "Nameh beh Shin Partow" (Letter to Shin Partow). In *Taʿrif va Tabsareh* (Definitions and Demonstrations), 58–111. Tehran: Amir-e Kabir, 1971.

———. *Namehha-ye Nima Yushij* (Letters of Nima Yushij). Edited by Sirus Tahbaz. Tehran: Nashr-e Abi, 1985.

Yusofi, Gholam-Hosayn. "Bahar." In *Encyclopaedia Iranica.* Vol. 3: 475–76. London: Routledge & Kegan Paul, 1988.

———. *Cheshmeh-ye Rowshan: Didari ba Shaʿeran* (Clear Fountain: Visits with Poets). Tehran: ʿElmi, 1991.

Zarrinkub, Abdolhosayn. *Sayri dar Sheʿr-e Farsi* (An Excursion in Persian Poetry). Tehran: Novin, 1984.

———. *Sheʿr-e Bi-Dorugh, sheʿr-e Bi-Neqab* (Poetry without Falsehood, poetry without Masks). Tehran: Javidan, 1976.

Zarrinkub, Hamid. *Cheshmandaz-e Sheʿr-e Now-e Farsi* (The Landscape of the Modernist Persian Poetry). Tehran: Tus, 1979.

Zipoli, Riccardo. *Encoding and Decoding Neopersian Poetry.* Rome: Cultural Institute of the Islamic Republic of Iran, 1988.

Note: In addition to the books, articles and other writings listed above alphabetically, the following newspapers, periodicals and literary journals, all published at different periods and intervals between 1860 and 1950, have been consulted and/or cited. *Akhtar, Amuzegar, Ayandeh, Bahar, Chehreh-nema, Daneshkadeh, Ermaghan, Farangestan, Gol-e Zard, Habl al-Matin, Hekmat, Iran-e Now, Iranshahr, Kaveh, Mehr-e Iran, Nowbahar, Parvaresh, Qanun, Qods, Ruh al-Qodos, Sadaf, Shokufeh, Setareh-ye Iran, Shafaq-e Sorkh, Sokhan, Sur-e Esrafil, Vahid, Yadegar, Yaghma, Zaban-e Azad*

Index